Religion
in
Jammû-Kashmîr-Ladâkh

Attention Authors

'We Convert Fighters into Writers.' That's the motto of Manas Publications since more than four decades. Our message to the world is that India can win the battle not only by the bullet but also by the pen. There is no dearth of intellectuals in our country, but their knowledge is confined to them only. No sincere effort has been made by any other publisher to channelise their knowledge in national interest. That is why the talent of a large number of intellectuals remains latent. An author transforms his knowledge into a manuscript, and it is our job to spread his/her knowledge by converting it into a beautiful book. For over four decades, Manas has been motivating the intellectuals by publishing their manuscripts and would like to publish your manuscript too. So if you or your colleagues have any manuscript ready for publication or are working on it, kindly contact us with detailed synopsis and list of contents. We will transform your work into a valuable publication. If you wish, we can also suggest you the suitable subjects for writing the books related to your area of expertise. Manas is known for its publishing quality and commitments. We take utmost care in production and give wide publicity to the book as well as its author through our national and international distribution network.

Religion *in* Jammû-Kashmîr-Ladâkh

Parvéz Dewân, IAS

Manas Publications
(We Convert Fighters into Writers)
New Delhi-110002 (INDIA)

MANAS PUBLICATIONS
(Publishers for IAS, IPS, IFS, IRS, Defence, Press, Judges etc.)
4402/5-A, Ansari Road (Opp. HDFC Bank)
Darya Ganj, New Delhi-110 002 (INDIA)
Off. ✆ 011-23260783, 23265523, Res. ✆ 011-23842660
Fax: 011-23272766
E-mail: manaspublications@gmail.com
manaspublications@yahoo.com
Website: www.manaspublications.in

ISBN 978-81-7049-432-4
₹ 995/-

Designed at
Manas Publications

Printed in India at
RK Offsets, Delhi
and published by Mrs Suman Lata for
Manas Publications, 4402/5-A, Ansari Road,
(Opp. HDFC Bank), Darya Ganj,
New Delhi-110 002 (INDIA)

For the Balis of Laridora
Munshi Atma Ram, Lakshmi Devi,
Narinder, Shakti Devi, Vimla, Manohar Lal, Brahma Nand,
Krishan, Kamal, Shilpa, Shazia, Shikha

Some of the important books written by Parvéz Dewan are:

- Amazing Kashmir: *almost everything about* Travel, trekking, religion, culture, wildlife (Manas)
- Amazing Ladakh: Travel, trekking, religion, culture, wildlife *almost everything about* Leh, Kargil, Zanskar, Siachen (Manas)
- The Other Kashmîr: Almost Everything About Aksai Chin, Baltistan, Gilgit, Hunza, Mirpur, Muzaffarabad (Manas)
- People and Culture of Jammû–Kashmîr–Ladâkh (Manas)
- Natural Heritage of Jammû–Kashmîr–Ladâkh: Wildlife, Forests, Flora, Rivers and Lakes (Manas)
- A History of Jammû (PB) (Manas)
- A History of Kashmîr (PB) (Manas)
- A History of Ladâkh–Gilgit–Baltistân (PB) (Manas)
- Parvez Dewan's Jammû–Kashmîr–Ladâkh: **Jammû** (Manas)
- Parvez Dewan's Jammû–Kashmîr–Ladâkh: **Kashmîr** (Manas)
- Parvez Dewan's Jammû–Kashmîr–Ladâkh: **Ladâkh** (Manas)

- Hiñdi-Urdû: A Language Survival Kit (Lonely Planet, Australia)
- The Civil Services (20/ 20 Publications, Delhi)
- India's Western Himâlayas (co-authored; APA, Singapore)
- Hanûmân Chalîsâ (Viking-Penguin)
- The Names of Allâh (Viking-Penguin)
- The Book of Hanûmân (Viking-Penguin)
- Tibet: 50 years after (Shubhi)

Contents

Preface

Good Americans when they die go to Paris.
Oliver Wendell Holmes, *The Autocrat of the Breakfast-Table. vi.*, 1858.[1]

The rest of us have to settle for heaven. Many, notably the Mughals, thought that Kashmîr was heaven on earth. The Kashmîris themselves think of the land as being 'a replica of heaven on earth.' Lord Jesus and Moses, the Prophet, were not just good, they were two of the very best. So, it stands to reason that they would have come to Kashmir after their death.

Well, so some people claim. Personally I believe that Lord Jesus ascended bodily to heaven, therefore, he is not buried anywhere—though there is good evidence that he travelled through Kashmir and Ladakh during his 'missing years.'

Some textbooks that we studied at school (in central and south India) all spoke of the rishis (saints) going to the hills—specifically the Himalayas—to meditate. They did not give any further details.

Jammu, Kashmir and Ladakh own up all such associations. Within the state there are written accounts upon recorded hagiographies of Buddhist saints and monks, Hindu deities (from Lord Shiv-Mother Pârvati and Sri Mata Vaishno Devi ji to briefer links with other equally exalted deities) and saints, Muslim Syeds and reshis, and Sikh gurus (no less than Gurû Nânak Dev jî and Gurû Hargobiñd jî) and soldier-saints, having been born in or at least having spent time in the state.

Kashmir exemplifies the finest traditions of undivided India. As in many other parts of the sub-continent, Muslims and Hindus often claim the same saint and his/ her shrine as their own. However, the cult of Sheikh Nûr ud Dîn/ Nund Reshi must be unique in the world—for Kashmiri Pandits took it upon themselves to record and then propagate the teachings of this Muslim saint.

**

1 That's right. Oscar Wilde merely quoted Mr. Holmes, and almost forty years later at that.

I was certainly not an atheist when, at age 22, I was 'allotted' to serve Jammu & Kashmir. However, the sum total of my religiosity consisted of offering prayers once a week.

In the 1850s the great Urdu poet Mirza Ghalib almost did a Nietzsche by declaring, 'All of us know the truth about heaven/ but it is a nice thought to fool the heart with.' Since then at least the educated classes of undivided India have been quite cynical about religion. My grandfather was. My father was a once-a-week type, which habit he gave me.

However, in my very first posting in Basohli, indeed very early during that stint, I saw saints perform what can only be described as miracles. And once I was in the Valley of Saints I began to find unique peace looking at the lights of Makhdoom Saheb, and listening to haunting Islamic evensong, both at dusk. The hilltop imam-bara at Trespon, at which the journalists and photographers accompanying me saw the sun and the moon together during the day, has similar calming effect. There I conceived the Trespon tower for which I obtained the necessary funds from Delhi. It was completed in 2011.

From there it has been a delicious journey through shrines and manuscripts dating to A.D. 1370 to books like *Tazkira é Auliya é Kashmir* and shamans in Zanskar and Banni.

And what shrines! From the huge monastery complex within an even larger cave at Phugtal, to the hilltop Aish Muqaam its stairs lit up by organic torches held by devotees. From the sublime architecture of the Khanqah i Mu'alla, and the awesome antiquity of the single-log pillars at Srinagar's Jama Masjid to the peaceful environs of Jammu's Ranbireshwar temple and the coolth of the hilltop Mahamaya temple in Jammu... One can just go on counting the best, only to omit some inadvertently.

All of it has taken me back to the simpleminded submission to God that existed before Nietzsche sanctified cynicism.

No, this is not a personalised book—though one or two per cent of the time it does dwell on my personal involvement. It is instead as thorough an account of religion in the state as is possible for laymen within a single volume.

**

To adopt objective criteria we have tried to arrange chapters in the alphabetical order of the religion featured. Within chapters we have attempted to list the three geographical regions[2] and, within sections, the districts, also in the alphabetical order. We have not always succeeded because this is not possible all the time. Sometimes within sentences we have mentioned communities in the order of their share in the population of the state.

---

2 Ladakh is part of Kashmir province.

3 "A mention of the (muslim) saints of Kashmir"

Glossary

ashtamî: The eighth day

chowk: Crossroads. The point where roads meet. Also, sometimes, the village or town square.

galî, gallâ, lâ: These are, respectively, the Urdû, Dogri and Ladâkhi words for 'mountain pass.'

gurudwârâ: Sikh temple.

havan: Classical Vedic prayer before a sacred fire.

HP: Himâchal Pradésh, the state on the eastern boundaries of the Jammû and Ladâkh regions of J&K.

J&K: Jammû and Kashmîr, the name of the state that Jammû is a part of.

jâgîrdâr: A *jâgîrdâr* was a person whom the king (all right, the state) had given a *jâgîr*. In turn, a *jâgîr* was a large tract of land, normally consisting of one or more villages. The *jâgîrdâr* was much more than a headman. He collected land revenue (and, sometimes, other taxes) on behalf of the state, was responsible for law and order and maintained a number of soldiers—cavalrymen as well as foot soldiers—for the army of his state.

jeepable road: A track on which only rugged sports-utility vehicles can ply.

kol, kuhl: Water channel.

ling/ lingam: A stone shaped like a thimble, found in most Shiv temples.

LoC: Pâkistân has illegally occupied 35.15 per cent of the state of Jammû and Kashmîr. India actually administers 45.62 per cent of the state. (China is in the illegal occupation of the rest.) A 'Line of Control' separates the portion where the Indian tricolour flies from the portion illegally occupied by Pâkistân. It is not an 'international border' (IB) because neither side accepts it as that. It serves the same purpose as a border but lacks the legal status of one.

mañdir: Hiñdû temple.

masjid: Mosque.

mohallâ: A traditional urban Indian neighbourhood.

motorable road: 'Motorable' means that in theory a car (or bus) can drive on that road. In practice most 'motorable' roads are only 'jeepable.' A 'motorable stretch' (or motorable distance) is one on which you can travel in a vehicle. You don't have to walk on that stretch, except for exercise.

muñdan: Ritual shaving of the head of a male child.

nâllâh: Stream.

navmî: Ninth day.

pass(es)/ mountain passes: What is a pass? A pass, more precisely a mountain pass, is a gap between two mountain peaks. It the highest point on a segment of a mountain road. There might be more than one pass on a road, and the next pass might be higher still. There always are mountains on the right and left of a pass. These mountains are much higher than the pass. The job of a pass is to help you cross from the place behind you to the place in front, without having to climb all the way to the top of the mountain. A pass is called a *gallî* in Urdu/ Kashmîrî, a *gallâ* in Dogri and *lâ* in Ladâkhî.

POK (Pâkistân Occupied Kashmîr): These are areas of Jammû & Kashmîr that are under Pâkistân's illegal occupation.

roadhead: This is the place to which one can travel in an automobile. In Indian English, it is the point till which there is a 'motorable' road. After this place one has to walk (or ride a pony) to get to the final destination. Conversely, on the return journey, this is the point where the trek ends and the 'motorable' road begins.

sâdhu: A Hindû ascetic, who normally lives a very frugal life.

samâdhi: This is a Hindû tradition in which a saint enters (or a group of saints enter) a cave or temple or a pit in the ground. They lock themselves in there, without food or water, and let themselves die. In Kashmîr, both Hindû and Muslim saints are known to have done this. Hindus everywhere (and in Kashmîr the Muslims, too) glorify such acts as a form of martyrdom. The act is called 'performing/ obtaining/ taking *samâdhî.*' The place where they commit this act is called a '*samâdhî.*' Thus the word is both an act and a shrine.

saptamî: The seventh day

-sar: The Hindi-Sanskrit-Dogri word for 'lake'.

sarai/ serai: A rest house, as in caravan/serai.

satsañg: Congregation of devotees

TRC is an important abbreviation to remember. It stands for 'Tourist Reception Centre.' Jammû has a fairly elaborate TRC and is supposed to offer every facility needed by a tourist, including reasonably priced accommodation. Katrâ, too, has a TRC though not as elaborate.

trekker: Indian English. A trekker is someone who treks.

urs: This is something like a Catholic Saint's Day. It is a religious occasion held at shrines, and is marked by prayer. At most shrines the *urs* is held once a year, often on the death anniversary of the saint. At some shrines (notably that of Khwaja Moinuddin Chisti at Ajmer Sharief, Râjasthân) it is held twice in a year. The Islâmic calender (Hijri) is lunar. Therefore, the dates of annual events shift every year.

However, in many parts of South Asia (including Kashmîr) *urses* are observed according to solar calendars, normally the one used by the local Hindu community as well. *Urs*, incidentally, is a singular. The plural would be *urses.*

yagya: Classical Védic prayer ceremony

yâtrâ: a Hindu pilgrimage; a journey towards a sacred shrine. 'Yâtrâ' literally means 'trip' or 'journey.' There are several important Hindu shrines in the Himalayas, especially in J&K, HP and the UP hills. Devotees normally trek up to the shrine once a year on a designated day (or set of days). These yâtrâs normally take place in summer, because in winter it would be difficult to reach the concerned shrine because of the snow. In a religious context, *yâtrâ* means 'pilgrimage.

These *yâtrâs* have a fixed starting point, normally a temple at the bottom of that hill. Devotees gather there and then trek up to the shrine in a longish procession. Most yâtrâs terminate at the hilltop shrine where, often, a colourful fair is held. Yatris (pilgrims) return to their homes in the plains or foothills not in a procession but when they please.

Pilgrimages in the hills are normally connected with Lord Shiv or the Mother Goddess Durgâ (in one of her several manifestations). Lord Shiv's wife, the goddess Pârvati, is one of Durgâ Mâtâ's best-known incarnations. Yet, some of the Mâtâ's major forms (especially that of Srî Mâtâ Vaishno Dévî jî and Ragnya Dévî) are connected with the story of Srî Râm.

yâtrî: Hiñdî for 'pilgrim'; the Dogri word for 'pilgrim' is *yâtrû.*

Pronunciation

This book has used diacritical marks to double the value of three vowels: a, i and u. Therefore

'a' is as in 'c*a*thedral'
'â' is as in 'f*â*ther'
'e' is as in 'g*e*t'
'é' is as in 'caf*é*'
'i' is as in '*i*t'
'î' is as in '*e*at'
'ñ' is a brief, almost silent 'n,' much as in 'mo*n*k.'
'o' is always as in 'g*o*'
'u' is as in 'p*u*t'
'û' is as in 'f*oo*d'

'ts' is much like the 'z' in 'Mozart'. Most Hindi, Urdu and English-speaking people settle for the 'ch' sound. They thus turn 'Tséwâñg' into 'Chéwâñg,' which the people of Ladâkh find quite acceptable.

Jammû

Bhairh Devata

Kol Kañdoli

Chapter- 1

Jammû: The Temple Circuit

During the 'season' more than twenty thousand pilgrims land up at Katra everyday.

The Srî Mâtâ Vaishno Devî jî Shrine Board tries to restrict the number of pilgrims to the holy shrine to eighteen or twenty thousand a day, so that each can spend four seconds before the *pindis* (icons).

Pilgrim accomodations around the shrine of Srî Mâtâ Vaishno Devî jî

During the auspicious Navaratras, during the Christmas to New Year period, and on long weekends, there are days when as many as fifty thousand pilgrims turn up at Katra. Obviously they have to wait for three or four days before being allowed to start trekking uphill towards the holy shrine. (As few as two to five thousand people visit the holy shrine on most days in January and February. The first few days of January see record crowds, though.)

Pilgrims to the shrine of Srî Mâtâ Vaishno Devî jî always want to know what other temples and places of pilgrimage there are nearby, which they can visit and thus enrich their pilgrimage–and spend their 'waiting time' at.

Pilgrims can branch out in three directions from Katra or Jammû in their quest for other temples and pilgrimages.

Between Jammû City and Katra

When you leave Jammû city towards Katra, you will first pass through the wooded Ramnagar Rakh. The (Muslim) shrine of Panj Peer is on the right side of the road. Hindu-Sikh devotees outnumber the Muslims at the shrine.

Nagrota is the first major habitation on the highway.

Kol Kañdoli comes next. It is some twelve kilometres ahead of Jammû. You will find a temple next to the highway, and a signboard that says "First Darshan". Before the era of buses and metalled roads, pilgrims used to walk all the way from Jammû to Katra. According to tradition and custom there were six places en route where a pilgrim had to pay homage before reaching the sanctum of Srî Mâtâ Vaishno Devî jî. These six places were convenient resting points as well. Pilgrims would not only relax their tired legs, they would also find shade to sit under, water to drink and perhaps something to eat.

They would first halt at the temple at Kol Kañdoli to worship the deity there. This is how Kol Kañdoli came to be known as the 'first darshan' or the 'first homage'.

Of the six temples that traditionally served as halting places, Kol Kañdoli alone is on the present highway. (In case you get inspired enough to do the traditional route, remember that it is not a tough trek at all: merely uncomfortable because of disuse.)

The temple: The idol of Srî Mâtâ Vaishno Devî jî at this temple is natural and not made by a human. In Hinduism such idols are called

The Shrine of Srî Mâtâ Vaishno Devî jî

svayambhû or 'self-made' (i.e. an idol created by itself). It is said that if a devotee pays homage to this particular idol, all his troubles will disappear and all his wishes will be fulfilled.

The legend: Srî Mâtâ Vaishno Devî jî is believed to have had to halt for a while at Kol Kañdoli. She organised four bhañdârâs (grand mass prayers after which vegetarian food is served to everyone) here.

There is a large barrh tree in the temple's backyard. Apparently, in ancient times a swing was suspended from its thick horizontal branches. The Mother Goddess would playfully ride on this swing. She also spent twelve years in intense prayers here.

Bhairh Devata: (Approx. 16km from Jammû.) There is a '10.6km' stone where Nagrotâ cantonment ends. This is after Kañdoli. Turn right here. You can travel another 7km in a vehicle, i.e. till Batkal Pañt. After that you will have to walk for 250m. to the river. To get to the other bank you will need to travel by boat. Till around the year 2000 the boat ride was free. Now they charge a small amount. Cross over to the other side of the river. Then walk another 2km to reach the temple of Bhairh Devata. (In all we have to walk 3.2km each way.)

Every day they slaughter (balî) a goat in honour of Kâlî Mâtâ. In addition Nâg Devata is worshipped here.

At Domel a side road on the left branches off from the national highway towards Katra. Seven kilometres before Katra there is a serene pine forest. A famous temple is located just above this forest, and quite close to the road: the shrine of Deva Mayi Maa.

The temple of **Deva Mayi Maa** was the second of the six halts on the way to the shrine of Srî Mâtâ Vaishno Devî jî.

Not far from here is a place called **Chirhai Muttal**. It is twenty kilometres before Katra. There used to be a tradition in the Jammû province of placing idols near wells. Some of the best sculptures of that kind are to be found at Chirhai Muttal. There is also a cluster of ancient temples here. What is surprising is the presence of chinar trees. The chinar is associated with Kashmir. It is not normally found growing naturally in this region, and certainly not at this relatively low height.

(To get to Chirhai Muttal: A side-road on the left leads from the National Highway to Chirhai Muttal. The point at which this branch occurs is ahead of Domel. It is also possible to go directly from Katra or Deva Mayi Maa to Chirhai Muttal.)

Between Jammû/ Katra and Patni Top

The national highway continues past Domel to Patni Top. There are two famous and ancient temples, each a few miles off the highway between Udhampur and Patni Top—Krimchi and Sudh Mahadev.

Roughly 60km after Jammû city (or 40km. from Katra), a road branches off from the highway to the left to take us to **Krimchi**. The temples are six kilometres west of the highway. Their architecture reveals Greek influences. (See also section on 'Udhampur' district).

Further ahead on the same side road is a beautiful hill station in the making. It is called **Panchairi**.

Let us return to the highway. **Udhampur** town comes next (66km from Jammû.) There is an ancient Shiv temple a few metres to the right of (and below) the highway, next to the Devika river and behind what used to be the Deputy Commissioner's residence. Like all Shiv temples it has a stone idol of the Nandi bull, with one of its feet (hooves) lifted above the ground. It is believed that this foot (hoof) has been rising upwards, miraculously, millimetre by millimetre, over the years.

Some 22km. ahead of Udhampur (87km from Jammû) on the same highway, a road branches off downwards on the right. It often passes through pines (*cheerh*) and leads to Chenaini, Gauri Kund, Sudh Mahadev and Mantalai.

We all know that the Hindu God Shiv, and his consort, Parvati, used to live in the mountains. According to some this was the stretch where they first met and got married. The legend is centred around Sudh Mahadev. It is said that the Goddess Parvati used to say her prayers here.

Gauri Kund comes first. (It is slightly away from the main road.) According to the legend Parvati Devî jî, who is also known as Gauri, used to bathe in this pond before offering prayers. It was thus that the pond, or Kund, came to be called the Gauri Kund. There are ancient temples dedicated to Shiv ji and Parvati ji nearby. A narrow mountain path leads from here to Patni Top.

Sudh Mahadev itself is further down the main road. The temple there has a Shivling that is said to be at least three thousand years old.

One day when Parvati was saying Her prayers before this Shivling, a demon called Sudheet appeared before Her. On seeing the demon Parvati ji screamed loudly.

Lord Shiv was sitting on a nearby hillock, lost deep in meditation. His concentration was shattered by Parvati's scream. He hurled his mighty trident at Sudheet, the demon. It is said that the huge trident at the Sudh Mahadev temple is a fragment of the very trident that Lord Shiv had shot through Sudheet.

However, Sudheet, the demon, did not die immediately. He happened to be a devotee of Lord Shiv. As the holy trident passed through his body, he chanted Lord Shiv's name.

Shiv realised that a mistake had been made. He said to Sudheet, 'I will not let you die. I will heal your wounds.'

Sudheet replied, 'No, Lord, let me die. If I die at your hands I will achieve nirvan.' The Lord was pleased by Sudheet's reply. He decreed, 'From this moment onwards whenever people speak of me they shall first have to mention Sudheet's name before they take my name.'

Since then this place has been known as Sudh Mahadev, Sudh after Sudheet, the demon, and Mahadev after Lord Shiv.

An 'immortal' (eternal) flame, the Amar Jyoti, has been ablaze at this temple for thousands of years now. It got extinguished only once: during the disturbances of 1947.

The fair: The annual, three-day Sudh Mahâdév fair is so important that the government allows employees posted in the district a day off to attend its first day. The fair begins on Jyésth Pûrnîmâ, the full- moon day of late May.

On the first day, devotees bathe at Gauri Kuñd and pray at the Pârvati temple. On the second day they first bathe at the Bindi Sañgam (also called Budhi Sudh) and then at the Pâp Nâshni ki Bâoli. After these two baths they go to the temple of Lord Shiv to pray.

People sing all night. Groups of dancers come over from the neighbouring villages to perform. As at all such fairs, colourful country shops are set up for the occasion.

But what had Parvati been praying so hard for? To get married to Lord Shiv.

Her prayers were answered. The Lord agreed to marry her. The wedding ceremonies were conducted at nearby **Mantalai** (approx. 1615 m). Talai is the Dogri word for *talaab* or pond. And maan means "man" or the mind. Just as the Maan-sarovar is a lake (sarovar) that emerged from the mind of Lord Shiva, Mantalai is a pond that came out of his mind.

In the 1970s, archaeologists discovered shards of pottery at Mantalai. The shards were a few thousand years old. This strengthened the local people in their belief that these were fragments of the very pots in which Lord Shiva's wedding procession had feasted.

Who knows?

Incidentally, Sudh Mahâdév and, to a lesser extent, Mântalâi are important archæological sites. The Archæological Survey of India plans to conduct major excavations there in the first decade or two of the 21st century.

There is a grove of majestic deodar trees at Mantalai. Winters there are almost exactly as in the Valley of Kashmir. (See also the chapter on 'Udhampur' for more on Mantalai and Sudh Mahadev.) Mantalai is the last place of religious significance on this road. Further down that road is a small spring called the Paap Nashni ki Baoli (the pond where sins are washed away) and the beautiful Dudu-Basantgarh area.

You will have to return to Chenaini and the highway the way you came. In fact, it would be best to retrace your steps all the way to Jammû city, though it is possible to go from Udhampur to Mansar. **Patni Top** is close to the Chenaini Morh. However, like Dudu-Basantgarh, it is a secular pleasure.

Jammû city

There are few cities in the world that have temples as numerous or diverse as does Jammû. It is because of this that Jammû is known as the City of Temples.

Jammûites consider the temple of Bawe Wali Mâtâ the most powerful shrine south of Mâtâ Vaishno Devi. The other important temples are the sprawling Raghunath temple complex, the Ranbireshwar Mandir, the picturesque Mahamaya, the Peer Kho cave temple, the 15th century Panj Vakhtar and the old Raghunath temple.

(See the section on 'Jammû City' in the chapter 'The Hindu Shirines' for details.)

Other important old temples

- Hanuman temple
- Kali Janni temple
- Lakhdata Bazar temple
- Maha Saraswati temple at Pakki Dhakki
- Mahalakshmi temple
- Nav Durga temple
- Purani Mandi Chowk temple
- Shakti temple
- Shiva temple

Twentieth century temples

- Dewans' temple, Kachi Chhawni
- Dooda Dhaari temple, Shastri Nagar
- Gadadhar temple, Dhauntali
- Hari Mandir, Rehari
- ISKCON temple, Bohri
- Kareshwar Rameshwar temple, near Tawi Bridge
- Lakshmi Narayan temple, Gandhi Nagar
- Paanch/ Panj Mandir, Green Belt, Gandhi Nagar
- Parshuram temple, Parade
- Raghunath temple, Panjtirthi

- Ram Mandir, Shastri Nagar
- Ranbir Singh Samadhi and temple
- Satya Narayan temple, Parada
- Shiv temple, near Tawi Bridge
- Shiv temple, Talab Tillo
- Vishnu temple, Trikuta Nagar

Between Jammû and Samba/ Mansar

Purmañdal : This is a temple complex a few kilometres off the Jammû-Pathankot National Highway. This pilgrimage is often called Chhotâ Kâshi, or the little Varanasi/ Benares. The temples have been arranged in two neat rows, facing each other, with a mostly-dry river in between.

Underground river: The complex has been built on the banks of the sacred Devika river. Because the river is mostly underground, it is called the Gupt Gañgâ (the invisible Ganga). It is a tributary of the Devika mentioned in the Purâns (scriptures). It is believed that this river is as effective in cleansing a person of his sins (and thus offering him absolution) as the Ganga (Ganges) itself. (See also 'Uttar Behni' below.)

The presiding deities: The main temple is dedicated to Umâpati. Even the other temples—all in a row—venerate Lord Shiv. They have several *svayambhu* Shiv Lingams (lingams that were formed naturally or, as devotees would put it, miraculously).

Apparently this is the only temple in the country where Lord Shiv and Shakti have been combined to form the Shéshâkâr icon.

The other temples in the complex are dedicated to the Lords Raghunâth and Râdhâ-Krishn.

Festivals: The main festivals are on the Shivarâtri (mid-February) and Chaitr Chaudashi days. These ancient temples are associated with Shaivites from the Valley of Kashmir. The monthly Amâvas is also an important day.

Since 1998, the Purmandal-Uttarbehni Development Committee has been organising an annual *chharhi yâtrâ.* This is a tradition successfully borrowed from the Shrî Amarnâth jî pilgrimage (yatra). A holy rod/ mace (*chharhi*) is taken in procession to Jammû's Ranbiréshwar temple.

Accommodation: There are *sarais* and shelters for pilgrims at Purmandal.

The oldest dharmshâlâs are now in ruins, but are fine specimens of Dogrâ architecture. One dharmshala has a sandstone façade while the other is made of bricks. It was probably built for the 1839 visit of Mahârâjâ Ranjit Singh. Manhotra writes, 'The sanctum, built in the tîrath style, has a spire which was profusely decorated externally with floral scrolls, flowers and vase decoration. Niches with stepped pedimental roofs on all four sides were filled with decorative lozenges and figures of deities.'

The origin of the complex: It is said that several thousand years ago a villager saw a jackal drinking the milk that flowed out of a sacred image. He shot the jackal in the head and killed it. The jackal was reborn as the daughter of King Véni (or Veen) Dutt of Awantipur, Kashmîr (some time between the 6th and 8th centuries AD). The princess had a chronic headache that simply would not go away. The raja prayed to Lord Umapati to cure his daughter. When Lord Umapati cured the girl the Raja built the first of the Purmandal temples in thanksgiving.

The present complex: Mahârâjâ Gulab Singh of Jammû built the present temple complex around AD 1843. There is a trilingual inscription to this effect, in Sanskrit, Persian and Dogri. He wanted the stretch between Purmandal and Uttar Behni to be his religious capital. So he established fourteen Shiv lings between Indréshwari and Uttar Behni. Though still very imposing to look at, much of Purmandal is in ruins.

Gulab's nobles and his successor, Mahârâjâ Ranbir Singh, built the other temples.

Manhotra calls this set of temples 'a labyrinth of cross- wise verandahs mounted by small *shikhar[s,]* housing some 121 sets of 11 marble [Shiv] lingams [each].'

The main Shiv temple: There are two temples, one small and the other somewhat bigger, in this shrine. A row of steps leads from the ground level to the elevated temples. Manhotra adds, 'The [bigger] temple houses [a] *Swayambhav Shiv*, whereas the smaller one has a bronze statue in human form of Shiv, probably in his Bhairva form. The *shilas* and *shikhars* [spires] of both temples are similar in design and style. The main Shivalya is unique. It has only one shila, in the middle of which there is a pit with a metallic frame, containing water from which a tiny Shiv Ling emerges.

'The second and strange portion of the shrine is the labyrinth of 25 corridors built at cross-angles to each other and housing Lingas. Each corridor has 55 Lingas arranged in circular groups of 11, each group embedded in a round pedestal. The corridors have flat rooms with five mini-shikhars, one over each cluster of Lingas, and a door on each side. The corridors head on each other and are entered by a *mandap* in the middle. There are 1400 Lingas in all, presenting a graceful sight of corridors and mini-shikhars arranged in the *Tantric-Yantric* style, creating a somewhat mystic influence on the mind.'

Prominent visitors: Emperor Akbar is said to have visited Purmandal on his way to the shrine of Srî Mâtâ Vaishno Devî jî. Guru Nanak Dev ji, Raja Man Singh and Maharaja Ranjit Singh are among the notable historical persons who have visited Purmandal.

Uttar Behni is around 3km. from Purmandal (and 30km. north-east of Jammû). The name of this pilgrimage literally means 'the river that flows northward'. It ranks after Purmandal in the religious hierarchy of the region. The river here, too, is the Devika, which is considered almost as sacred as the Ganges. For a few kilometres it flows from south to north, being one of the very few rivers in the world to do so.

Legend: Kashyap Rishi was a famous saint in ancient times. Kashmîr is said to have been named after him. He pleased Lord Shiv with his prayers. So, Lord Shiv decided to reward the land of the Dogras. He caused River Devika to emerge at Gauri Kund (between Patni Top and Sudh Mahadev). He also ordered the holy Ganga to come out of the earth in the Purmandal area so that people who bathed in it could attain *moksh* (salvation). As a result, after going underground for a while, it emerges at Indreshwari, four kilometres north of Purmandal. After it goes past Uttar Behni it dives back into the earth.

History: Maharaja Ranbir Singh developed Uttar Behni as a seat of religion. His father, Maharaja Gulab Singh built the *Gadâdhâri* temple of Lakshmi Nârâyan in 1850 Bikrami Samvat, as an inscription there tells us. Gulab also installed 14 Shivlings between Indreshwari and Uttar Behni. He pioneered a blend of ancient and 19th century architectures. The Gadadhari temple is a good example of this style. It was the first temple built by this Dogra dynasty.

The temples: Gulab also started work on the *Abhibhaktéshwar* temple nearby. Ranbir completed it. The Shivling here is claimed to be the biggest in India. The idol of the sacred Nandi bull at this temple is supposed to be unique, too. The Vijay Ghañtâ (victory bell) outside weighs over a ton.

The Srî *Ranbirsingheshwar* temple, in the northern corner, was started by Maharaja Ranbir, but completed after his death. There are 11 shivlings in the temple. (There are countless more shivlings in the storeroom of the Srî Ati Muktéshwar temple. They had been brought here at the behest of Ranbir.)

Two of the temple spires here have been plated with gold leaf. Around them are cells for Brahmins to live in.

Ceremonies: People from Jammû province would, till the 19th century, go all the way to Srî Gayâ ji to perform the *shrâdh* of their ancestors. Uttar Behni was developed as a sacred alternative for pilgrims from Jammû and the neighbouring states.

Similarly, a bath in Devika is supposed to cleanse people of their sins as effectively as a similar dip in the Ganges. On auspicious occasions such as the Shivarâtri, Chaturthi and on the *amâvas* (new moon night) of every month devotees visit Uttar Behni to bathe in the Devika and receive absolution.

Since 1998, there has been an annual *chharhi yâtrâ* (procession with sacred rod) to the shrine. The procession commences at Jammû's Ranbireshwar temple.

There is a Sanskrit school between Uttar Behni and Purmandal. It is a successor of sorts to the Uttar Behni Vidyâpeeth that used to compete with the Kashi Vidyapeeth of Benares (Varanasi).

It is possible to go directly from Utterbehni to the national highway, without having to go back to Purmandal. From the point where the side road meets the highway, let us resume our southward journey (i.e. in the direction of Pathankot/ Delhi)

The temple of **Chi Chi Mâtâ** is right next to the national highway, between Jammû and Mansar. The temple takes its name after the little, or Chi Chi, finger of the Mother Goddess Parvati Devi's hand. It is believed that the Goddess was once so consumed by remorse that she jumped into a fire to sacrifice herself. Lord Shiv retrieved her burnt body from the fire and carried it across the skies. During this ariel journey, parts of the burnt body kept falling down to the earth.

The place in Himachal Pradesh where Parvati's eyes are said to have landed has since been called Naina Devi. The Jwalamukhi temple, also in Himachal Pradesh, marks the place where the goddess' tongue fell. Similarly, the Chi Chi Mâtâ temple of Jammû commemorates the spot where Parvati's little finger dropped.

Chi Chi Mâtâ was the younger sister of Srî Mâtâ Vaishno Devî jî. According to journalist Renu Bala, *chi chi* also happens to be the Dogri word for 'younger.' (*The Sacred Shrine of Chichi Mâtâ*, Daily Excelsior, 11th November, 2001.)

The temple: Two icons of the goddess emerged from the earth. The larger one was placed in the temple. The other four temples in the complex are dedicated to Lord Shiv, Srî Râm, Pârvati Dévi ji, Srî Lakshman, Hanumân jî and Sîtâ jî,

Leprosy: Raja Sambh is said to have been cured of leprosy at this temple. Conventional medicines had failed to cure him. So he took to bathing in the Basañtar, which flows close to the temple, every morning. After that he would fill a pitcher with the waters of the river and take them to nearby Sâmbâ. There he would wash the Shivling at the Mahéshwar temple with this water. A few days later he was cured. (According to another version, he got caught in a storm near the present temple. The waters of that rainfall cured him overnight.)

Sambh was probably an ancient king, after whom Samba town takes its name. Some say that he was the king of Dwârkâ (Gujarat).

Ceremonies: The Chi Chi Mâtâ temple is considered a particularly auspicious place to perform the *mundan* ceremony of children at. Devotees come from neighbouring states as well the rest of Jammû province for this purpose.

Festivals: There are major events at the temple on the last three days of the *navarâtrâs*. A 'satsang' takes place on the seventh day. On the eighth day (ashtami) there is a *yagya* (grand classical prayer ceremony). A fair is held on the eighth and ninth (navmi) days.

When you travel from Jammû to Samba, the prosperous temple of Chi Chi Mâtâ will be on the left, shortly before Samba. A few hundred metres ahead of the temple, there is a major side road, also on the left, that leads to the Mansar and Surinsar lakes. (Thus, on this route, you will skip Samba town and not actually enter it. However, if you do the journey in reverse, and come up the highway from, say, Pathankot, you will pass Samba just before the Chi Chi Mâtâ shrine.)

Mansar literally means 'the lake that was created in the mind', the mind being that of Lord Brahma, the Creator. Today, the lake is known mainly for its beauty. However, it enjoys an important position in Hindu mythology, especially in stories connected with the *Mahabharat.*

Several water snakes live in Lake Mansar, because of which there are many legends about Naag Devtas (snake gods) in the area. The main legend is about Arjun, the warrior, his wife, the snake goddess Alupi, and their son, Babru Vaahan. There is a Naag Devta shrine, which attracts thousands of pilgrims, on the banks of the lake. There are also temples of Umapati-Mahadev and Lord Narasimh.

The ruins of the **Babor** temple complex (see 'Udhampur') are north of Mansar on the Dha(a)r-Udhampur road.

Shrines on the Dhar-Udhampur road

Several pilgrims to the holy shrine of Srî Mâtâ Vaishno Devî jî travel in their own chartered buses or cars from the Punjab, Haryana, Delhi and beyond. Before they reach Katra they drive past Chi Chi Mâtâ, Utterbehni, Purmandal, Jammû, Kol Kañdoli and Deva Mayi Ma (in that order). However, on their return journey they travel from Katra to Chirhai-Muttal, Tikri, Krimchi, Udhampur, Sudh Mahadev, Mantalai and then back to Udhampur. From Udhampur they take the Dhar-Udhampur road instead of the national highway. They thus cover both Babor and Mansar.

From Mansar they proceed to Pathankot/ Delhi via Sukrala Mâtâ (see 'Kathua' district) and thus cover almost all the pilgrimages of Jammû. The Sukrala Mâtâ temple is 9.6km. from Billawar and about 12km. off the Dhar-Udhampur road. Billawar itself has a famous temple (also see 'Kathua'). The temple of Sukrala Mâtâ is an extremely important pilgrimage, especially for the people of neighbouring Punjab and Himachal Pradesh. (Those who follow this route skip Jammû town on their way back.)

Pilgrims who reach Jammû by air or rail, too, can cover the shrines on the Dhar-Udhampur road. They can proceed from Sukrala Mâtâ back to Jammû. Or they can go from Sukrala Mâtâ to the Pathankot or Kathua (Gobind Sar) railway stations, which are closer. They should check if their train stops at Gobind Sar. Pathankot has two railway stations. They should check which one their train will halt at.

The Katra-Reasi-Shiv Khori route

Shiv Khori is the shrine that pilgrims to the Bhawan of Srî Mâtâ Vaishno Devî jî most like to visit. There are several important shrines on this route, which is to the west of Katra.

Agar Jitto is between seven and eight kilometres west of Katra. Baba Jitto was a revolutionary who organised peasants against landlords. It is possible to trek to the shrine of Mâtâ Vaishno Devî jî from here as well. The route is longer than the one from Katra, but is an easier climb.

The shrine of **Baba Dhansar** comes next. A stream emerges from the mountain and becomes a waterfall. A natural Shiv-ling is found at the shrine. A major fair takes place here on the occasion of Shivaratri.

The **Dera Baba Banda** Bahadur gurudwara is 25 kilometres from Katra, off the main road.

Baba Banda Bairaagi is said to have been the most beloved saint-soldier of the Sikh Guru, Govind Singh ji. During his last days Baba ji came here to meditate by the banks of the Chenab river. He would say his prayers under a berry tree, near which this grand gurudwara was later built. It is famous for the paintings on its walls. Hindus and Sikhs come from all over North India to worship at this temple. Many combine it with their pilgrimage to Katra.

Reasi has a temple of Kali Mâtâ.

Shiv Khori is considered the most amazing natural wonder of entire region. (Details in 'Udhampur'.) In terms of pilgrim traffic from distant parts of India it is second only to the shrine of Mâtâ Vaishno Devî jî. Ransu, the roadhead to the cave-shrine, is 25 kilometres ahead of Reasi and 79km. from Katra. It is 127km. from Jammû, via Katra. There is a shorter, 105km., route from Jammû to Ransu, via Akhnoor. Most pilgrims use the Katra route. Some come from Katra but return to Jammû through Akhnoor, so that they can see Akhnoor (see 'Jammû district') and its pine-clad hills as well.

The Shiv Khor(h)i cave is quite wide and almost a kilometre long. A four-foot tall, natural Shivling can be seen inside. All year around drops of milk-coloured water keep falling on the ling(am). A three-day fair takes place here to celebrate Shivaratri.

Chapter- 2

Shâhdrâ Sharief

The garden of the Shâhdrâ Sharief shrine

The most important Sufi shrine of Jammu province is Shahdra Sharief. Before the shrine was constructed here (around 1804), the place was a forest called Singh Dara or Simha Dwara or Seena Dara, all meaning 'the doorstep [or house] of the lions'. Its present name means 'the doorstep [or house] of the Shah,' after the great saint. It is 34km. north of Rajouri town and roughly 180km. from Jammu.

History

Gulab Singh was a promising young officer in the army of Maharaja Ranjit Singh. He became a disciple of a Sufi saint called Syed Ghulam Ali Shah ('Baba Saheb') who had migrated from Rawalpindi to the Rajouri kingdom, which was then ruled by Raja Karamullah.

When the Raja's son, Prince Aggar Ullah Khan, was a child, Baba Saheb had predicted that Aggar Ullah's reign as king would last only as long as he was a just ruler. On the other hand, he told Gulab that one day he would become a king. Aggar Ullah turned out to be a very cruel king. Ranjit Singh attacked Aggar Ullah's kingdom and ordered his arrest. Baba Saheb is said to have given Gulab the clues that led to Aggar Ullah's arrest.

Pleased with Gulab Singh's performance, Ranjit Singh promoted him to one senior rank after another till Gulab became a commander.

In 1846, the British ceded Kashmir to Gulab in return for an indemnity of seventy-five lakh rupees and he became the Maharaja of Jammu and Kashmir. Thus both prophecies of Baba Saheb came true.

(According to another legend, certainly incorrect, Aggar Ullah was the prince and later king of Poonch. However, I have been able to find no prince or king of Poonch by this name who might have been Baba Saheb's contemporary. On the other hand, Aggar Ullah Khan was the prince of Rajouri during that period, and king between 1806 and 1820. The Lahore Army captured him in 1820. According to most sources, Baba Saheb died in 1804. Therefore, it is unlikely that he could have provided Maharaja Ranjit the said clues.)

In 1999 alone more than twenty lakh (2 million) Muslims, Hindus and Sikhs paid homage at the shrine of Baba Ghulam Ali Shah Badshah in Shahdra Sharief, in the hope that God would perform similar miracles for them, too. Going by the stories pilgrims tell of boons granted at the shrine, they are obviously not disappointed. As a result, the number of pilgrims has been growing steadily over the years. (My wireless operator, a Sub Inspector who happened to be a Sikh, had six daughters in a row before he went to Baba Saheb's durbar (court) to beg for a son. His prayer was answered and S.I. Sher Singh has been an avid devotee ever since.)

The story of the saint

Baba Saheb was a Syed of pure pedigree, being a descendant of Musa Kazim Mashhadi, who was from the line of Hazrat Ali. His ancestral village, Saidiyan Kasarvan (or Sayedan Kasran), is in the Gujjar-Khan tehsil of Rawalpindi district. He was born in 1145 AH (c. A.D. 1726). His father, Muhammad Idris Shah was an eminent *sufi* (mystic) of the Qadri order. However, Baba Saheb's *pir* (spiritual master), Imam Bari-ul-Lateef Saheb Keki, trained him in Qadri as well as Naqshbandi doctrines.

Baba Saheb was a very young boy when he performed his first miracle. The people of his village would pay his brother and him pin money. In return his brother and he would take their goats to graze. One day the goats ate up the crop of one of the farmers, who complained to Hazrat Idris Shah. When his father scolded Baba Saheb, the boy suggested that the farmer go back and check his fields. The farmer did so. He found the crop intact.

The farmer realised that the Baba was a 'born friend of God'. He told everyone about the miracle. It was then that Hazrat Abdul Qadir Geelani, who had founded the Qadri *silsila* (order), appeared before Imam Keki in a vision. He asked that Baba Saheb be sent to the 'forest of the lions' near Thanna Mandi in the Jammu hills to establish a free kitchen and propagate Islam.

So, Baba Saheb set off from Rawalpindi in search of this 'forest of lions'. His first halt was at Noorpur, where he spent two years. After that he spent five years at Bâñdî Chechiyan, two years at Bandiyan, some time at Kalaban (near Mendhar) and ten years at Senei or Sanai (near Surankote), all in the present Poonch district. Then he went to Maidana (also in the Surankote area), where he established his *takiya* (seat or house of religion) on the banks of River Poonch.

At Surankote he is said to have defeated a Shaivite yogi in a contest of spiritual powers. The people of the region were overawed by the news. Members of the Poonch royal family were among the many who sought to become the Baba's followers.

Rustam Khan, the king of Poonch (c.1760-87), misunderstood his brother (or nephew) Yahya Khan's respect for the saint. He thought that Yahya was trying to use Baba Saheb to wrest the throne from him. So Rustam got Yahya killed. (According to another legend, Rustam, too, was a disciple of the Baba. After Rustam's soldiers had sliced Yahya's head off, Baba Saheb chanted, 'Yahya, kill them!' The headless Yahya is said to have killed seven soldiers before dying formally.)

Baba Saheb was infuriated by these developments. It is said that he cried out, 'I will turn Poonch upside down.' A major earthquake began to take place. It subsided only after the people of Poonch begged Baba Saheb to be forgiven.

In any case, Baba Saheb left Poonch. He next camped at Pataudi (near Duraba) and Chamrer Galli. In 1186 AH (around 1765 or 1766) he left for his final home, the forest where Shahdra Sharief now is. Baba Saheb began to clear a part of the forest to build the free kitchen he had been instructed to. Karamullah Khan Jaral, king of Rajouri (1765-1808), sent his army to arrest the Baba for felling trees illegally. When the soldiers reached the forest they were so filled with awe for the Baba's spiritual powers that they refused to act against him.

Meanwhile, Karamullah launched an attack on neighbouring Poonch, in an attempt to conquer it. Baba Saheb got to know of this. He advised the king to consult him before proceeding to Poonch. The king ignored the saint's message.

Karamullah fell terribly ill a few days after this. None of his doctors could cure him. The king knew that he was being punished for having offended Baba Saheb. So he asked his Rajput wife, Bansi Maeli, to go the Baba's *khanqah* to apologise on his behalf. The Baba agreed to pray for the king's recovery. The king got well and went to the *khanqah* to pay homage to Baba Saheb. He got a small house constructed for the Baba and also made a grant of considerable land for the saint to set up a shrine.

In turn, Baba Saheb went to Rajouri and stayed with the king. The room in which he would meditate was later named the Tasbeeh-khana ('the room of the rosary'), obviously after Baba Saheb's rosary. The Jaral kings thereafter used this room only for meditation.

According to A.R. Kardar it was Gulab Singh, then probably a Raja, who gave Baba Saheb 'the territory around Shahdra Sahrief as a fief'. However, this would have been after 1820, and perhaps a posthumous grant. In any case, Gulab Singh certainly helped develop the shrine and exempted the estate of all taxes. (Scholar K.D. Maini says that it was Raja Karamullah who had endowed the shrine with a large estate. This seems more likely. Maini puts the area granted at 25,000 kanals—a little more than 3,300 acres.)

Baba Saheb died at Shahdra Sharief, perhaps in 1804. He got a tomb constructed for himself during his own lifetime. He appeared in the dream of a mason in Multan (West Punjab) and asked him to reach Shahdra. There are several towns called Shahdra in North India and what is now

Pakistan. The mason landed up at a Shahdra in West Punjab before being guided to the forest of lions.

Sheikh Abdullah developed the present shrine, and the landscaping around it, in 1982. Between then and 1985, he and his successor as Chief Minister, G.M. Shah, allotted Rs.3 crore (30 million) for the shrine, from the funds of the Auqaf. The Tourism department has built guest houses and other facilities, some of them when I was the department's administrative head.

Miracles associated with the shrine

Aggar Ullah Khan became the king of Rajouri around 1806. As we have noted before, Aggar Ullah was a cruel man. Baba Saheb came to Aggar Ullah's mother in a dream. He told her that Aggar Ullah would lose his throne—indeed, the Jaral dynasty would come to an end—if Aggar Ullah continued to torture his subjects. Aggar Ullah ignored the warning.

In 1808, civil unrest started in Rajouri, as predicted,. The kingdom was ripe for the plucking. Eleven years later that's precisely what happened. Maharaja Ranjit Singh of Lahore annexed Rajouri.

The shrine

The shrine is located within a low pass. The mountains surrounding it are Mannuwala Nikka in the east, Paglan-alli and Kopra in the west, and Sirhi and Jannu Chmarer Galli in the north. A small stream flows towards the shrine. The present shrine has been constructed in the Kashmiri style, with little of Multani architecture in its exterior. A Mughal-style garden, constructed in the late 20th century, has been built on the slope that leads to the shrine.

The *langar* (free kitchen) established by Baba Saheb now feeds between four and ten thousand pilgrims a day.

The evergreen tree: There is a legendary tree, called Sada Bahar (lit.: evergreen), near the shrine. It bears fruit throughout the year. Its fruit does not rot with age. It can be stored for years without refrigeration.

North Indians and Pakistanis have this fixation for male children. (Remember my friend S.I. Sher Singh?) So, couples come to the shrine and pluck two and a half leaves from this tree. They roll the leaves into ten tiny balls. The husband and wife each eat five of these balls. It is said that this, coupled with prayers at the shrine, guarantees them a baby boy.

Evergreen Tree at the Dargah Shahdra Sharif

According to a legend the Baba was once getting food cooked for his langar. One of the twigs in the stove refused to burn, because it was either green or wet. Instead it emitted foul smoke. So the Baba pulled it out of the fire and planted it in the shrine's compound. He told the twig, 'Stay here and be green for ever.'

Others say that the tree has grown from a sapling that Baba Saheb had brought with him.

Getting to the shrine

The shrine of Baba Ghulam Shah is 34 kilometres north of Rajouri town and 4km. from Thanna Mandi. The Rattan Peer peak (8,300') towers above the shrine. All around the shrine are tall mountains and forests, meadows, springs and streams.

You can go to the shrine by bus from Rajouri. Or you can hire a taxi from Jammu or Rajouri. Since the mid-1990s, the most popular mode of transport has been the Tata Sumo taxi, which accepts individual passengers as well.

This author's failed dream: Kabir Zaminzad says that the *dargah* [shrine] of 'Baba Ghulam Ali Shah is one of the biggest and most popular shrines in the entire state… Indeed, it is said to be the *dargah* with the

Green Mosque at Shahdra Sharif

highest revenue in the state.' Kardar calls it 'the most significant [shrine] in the state.' And yet the shrine draws pilgrims only from J&K and its neighbouring states.

As Tourism Secretary I decided to launch a campaign to popularise the shrine outside the state, especially in Bangladesh, the people of which country mostly belong to the same spiritual orders as Baba Saheb. I consulted the leading clerics of Shahdra Sharief and Rajouri before launching the campaign. They loved the idea. (Apparently one of them did not, but he didn't say so then, perhaps because he felt outnumbered.)

I requested Mr. Kardar's Anjuman-i-Minhaj to help me. In 1993, the Anjuman sent *qawwals* (singers of religious songs) over from Delhi to perform at the shrine: free. They proved popular enough for me to feel encouraged to go ahead with my dream of making Shahdra Sharief the capital of religious qawwalis (songs) for all of South Asia.

In 1998, I commissioned a leading Sufi poet from Delhi to write a qawwali dedicated to Baba Saheb (and another qawwali dedicated to Peer Baba Budhan Ali Shah of Jammu). Both qawwalis had the desired effect: they drew crowds and, more importantly, the media. I tried to form a sufi circuit that started from Jammu, the 'railhead,' and culminated at Shahdra Sharief. (The circuit began at Peer Baba Satwari in Jammu City, went to Balley Bagh in Akhnoor [Jammu district] and Sâîñ Miran Saheb in Poonch and ended at Shahdra Sharief.)

Once a month, for three consecutive months, I got qawwals over from Delhi, because this tradition is absent in the state. The idea was to have qawwalis once a month for eleven months, and a grand all-South Asia final on the occasion of the annual Urs: with all the publicity that this would have brought. Pilgrims at Shahdra Sharief (and devotees at Satwari in Jammu City) loved the qawwalis. Cash offerings at the two shrines multiplied each time that we held qawwalis there.

However, one prominent person at Shahdra started opposing the idea, saying that religious songs were prohibited. (In that case, are all the Sabri, Chishti and Warsi religious singers of Pakistan and India wrong? The gentleman should have clarified that his particular order frowned on such singing.)

I gave up. I was spending good money from my department's limited budget trying to popularise the shrine in North India and Bangladesh. If the shrine's well-wishers thought that the Anjuman and I were doing something that was not necessary then why did we want to thrust these scrupulously devout songs, and substantial Tourism Department funds?

Chapter-3

The Shiv Temples and Shrines of Jammû

This section attempts to list all the important places associated with Lord Shiv in Jammû. For details please see the chapters about the respective districts, as well as the chapters on 'Jammû-The Temple Circuit'.

Dodâ-Kishtwar

Subarnag temple: A three-day April fair is held at this famous temple dedicated to Lord Shiv.

Thuba is the highest point between Bhaderwah town and Chinta. It has an ancient temple of Lord Shiv.

Jammû

The **Ranbireshwar**, built by Maharaja Ranbir Singh (1857-85), is the biggest Shiv temple in north India.

The **Peer Kho** cave temple, overlooking the Tawi river, and the **Panj Vakhtar** temple, one of the oldest in the city, are the other important Shiv temples.

Kathua

The majestic and ancient **Mahabilvakeshwar** temple of **Billawar** tops the list.

Airwan, the Shiv temple**:** A 4th century temple. Two fairs are held here every year, on Shivratri (roughly mid-February) and Baisakhi (13th or 14 April).

Basohli, the Neelkanth Mahâdev temple.

Mahanal: This is a famous shrine inside a cave.

Poonch

Budha Amarnath: A major pilgrimage.

Rajouri

No major Shiv shrines.

Udhampur-Reasi

Babore/ Babour/ Babor: Ancient temple, possibly dedicated to Lord Shiv.

Krimchi.

Shiv Khori: A very major shrine.

The path to the Shiv Khori shrine

Sudh Mahâdev, Mântalâi and Gauri Kund: Connected with the courtship, wedding and lives of Lord Shiv and the goddess Pârvati.

Chapter- 4

Sikhism in Pooñch-Rajourî (and Kashmir)

According to legends, the first Sikh missionaries came to Pooñch during the era of Guru Nânak Dev ji (1469-1539), the founder of the Sikh religion. Bhâi Mân Siñgh was the first Brâhmin of the area to convert to Sikhism. He belonged to Pathohâr (now in Pâkistânî Punjãb) but migrated to the Sudh Nutti tehsîl (sub-district) of Pooñch in A.D. 1535.[i]

Gurû Arjan Dév jî (1581-1606), was the fifth Gurû of Sikhism. He sent Bhâi Madho Sodhi to Kashmîr and Pooñch. Guru Hargobiñd Siñgh jî (1595-1646 AD) was the sixth guru. His visit to the state (in A.D. 1620 or 1644) is a historical fact. He travelled through Pooñch and Rajourî.

Some people believe that the tenth guru, Gobiñd Siñgh jî (A.D. 1666-1708) and Sañt Bhâi Phérâ (or Phéru) Siñgh (1693-1768 Bikrami) had visited Kashmîr. Bhâi Phéru Siñgh certainly came to Pooñch. He was a missionary whom Guru Gobiñd Siñgh jî had sent to the state of Jammû and Kashmîr (and to what later became the North West Frontier Province) to spread the message of Sikhism.

Bhâi (or Sañt Bâbâ) Punjãb Siñgh (1672-1736) and Bhâi Rochâ Siñgh (1688-1803) were perhaps the most effective in winning converts to Sikhism. They had received *amrit* (sacred water) from Guru Gobiñd

Siñgh jî at Mâlwâ and Damdamâ Sâheb respectively. Bhâi Punjãb Siñgh took over from Bhâi Phéru Siñgh in A.D. 1711. His seat (*dérâ*) was at Chattar Kalas, which, in 1736, he passed on to Bhâi Rochâ Siñgh, whose own seat was at Râwlâkot.

Luminaries of the Nangali Sâheb gurudwârâ who helped consolidate the faith were Thâkur Sañt Bhâi Mélâ Siñgh (1783-1854), Sañt Bhâi Mannâ Siñgh (1791-1870), Sañt Bhâi Mañgal Siñgh Dutt (1844-77), Mahañt Rattan Siñgh Sûdan (1828-1889), Sañt Bhâi Autâr Siñgh (1865-92), Mahañt Rattan Siñgh Modî (1816-1901), Sañt Bhâi Maur Siñgh (1878-1919), Sañt Bhâi Mañgal Siñgh (1880-1947) and Mahañt (or Sañt Bhâi) Bachhittar Siñgh (1918-1991), Sañt Bhâi Mañjît Siñgh Mahañt Mohan Siñgh Sûdan and Bhâi Phérâ Siñgh,[ii]

Bhâi Mélâ Siñgh succeeded Bhâi Rochâ Siñgh in 1803 and later set up his seat at Sañtpurâ Nangali Sâheb, near Pooñch. During much of the saint's lifetime the Punjãb was ruled by its greatest emperor, Mahârâjâ Rañjît Siñgh, whose nominee Râjâ Gulâb Siñgh governed Jammû on his behalf. It is said that when Bhâi Mélâ died, the Mahârâjâ and the Râjâ gave his seat to Sañt Bhâi Mannâ Siñgh. The problem with this version is that while there is no doubt that Bhâi Mannâ Siñgh took over in 1854 or that Bhâi Mélâ Siñgh had died earlier that year, Mahârâjâ Rañjît Siñgh could not possibly have been around to preside over the succession because he had died in 1839.

Na(n)gali Sâheb

Na(n)gali Sâheb: (pron.: na-gâ-li or na*n*-gâ-li) This is one of the most important gurudwârâs of the state and among the oldest in the world. It has been built in the cradle of a wooded hill on the left bank of the Drung(a)li Nâllâh, some six kilometres from Pooñch town and 240km. from Jammû city. It was established in 1810 by Thâkur Sant Bhai Mela Siñgh jî who halted here 'when he was on his way to conquer Kashmir.' (The quote is from a government publication.)

Gurudwârâ Na(n)gali Sâheb

The problem with this account is that the Punjâb empire's first success in battle in Kashmir was in 1814. It was only by 1819 that Punjâb managed to control the entire Valley. Mahârâjâ Rañjît Siñgh almost certainly visited the gurudwârâ in 1814 and is said to have been overawed by what he saw. The gurudwârâ had been in existence for a while by then. I am, therefore, inclined to agree with accounts that it was built in 1803 but had nothing to do with the Sikhs' conquest of Kashmîr.

According to yet another view, this dérâ (seat of religion) was founded by Bhâi Punjãb Siñgh and Bhâi Rochâ Siñgh.[iii] In that case it would have been established well before 1803.

In any case Mahârâjâ Rañjît Siñgh granted a large agricultural estate to the gurudwârâ, so that the produce of that land would pay for its upkeep. A few years later, in 1823, he ordered that the gurudwârâ would receive the revenues of four villages.

The official website of Pooñch district says, 'During 1947 [the] original building was completely burnt by the Pâkistân supported attacking tribesmen.' Mahañt Bachitar Siñgh jî, one of the greatest Sikh religious figures of the state in the twentieth century, spearheaded the move to reconstruct the gurudwârâ. He also re-established the gurudwârâ's lañgar (community kitchen), which serves free food to everyone who visits Nangali Sâheb.

Attendances peak on Sundays partly because that is the Sikh tradition and partly because of out of town visitors. The most important annual celebration is on Baisakhi (13 or 14 April), and the day before it.

Gurudwârâ Chhatti Pâdshâhî Bañglâ Sâheb, Rajourî

Guru Hargobiñd Siñgh jî was the sixth guru of Sikhism. In the volume about 'Kashmîr' we have gone into some detail as to why Gurû Hargobiñd jî felt the urge to go to Kashmîr. Briefly, while he was in Amritsar, he got the feeling that a devotee in Kashmîr was thinking of him and trying to contact him. He knew that he had to go to Kashmîr. So he left Amritsar for Lahore, and then Pooñch-Rajourî, which were on the route to Kashmîr.

Gurudwârâ Chhatti Pâdshâhî Bañglâ Sâheb

The great guru camped at the place where the Gurudwârâ Chhati Pâdshâhî Bañglâ Sâheb of Rajouri was later built in honour of that visit. That he was headed for Kashmîr is not in doubt. The only question is whether he was travelling in the company of the Mughal Emperor Jehâñgîr, as the legend would have it.

The Gurudwârâ was expanded somewhat after 1947, under the leadership of Sardâr Thâkur Siñgh and Bhai Jagannâth. Then, in 1964, an army engineer from the Punjãb, Sardâr Târâ Siñgh, drew up the blueprint for a new gurudwârâ. He happened to be posted in Rajourî at the time. Masons and carpenters were brought over from Punjãb for the construction.

The first phase of the proposed complex has been completed and consists of a four-storey gurudwârâ, with fifteen rooms for pilgrims, and a large Dîwân Hall. The Shri Hargobiñd Sahib Jî Institute of Education was inaugurated in April 2000. An eight-room traditional school (*pâthshâlâ*) came next.

There is a fairly large gathering of Sikhs and Hiñdus every Sunday morning. The birth anniversary of Guru Hargobiñd jî Mahârâj is the main annual function.

There are seventeen Sikh families in Rajourî town and a few Sikh families in viilages Sarânoo, Bathûni, Merâ, Sâwni, Gurdhanbâlâ and Sadhyâl, Dehriâñ-Trallâ, Chityâri.

References

i Mughal, Bashir, 'Sikhism in Pooñch,', *J&K Reporter*, November 2004.

ii Siñgh, Dévînder, and Rizvi, Baqar, in Siñgh, K.S. (editor) *People of India, Volume XXV. Jammû and Kashmîr* (2004), The Anthropological Survey of India, Manohar, New Delhi, page 576 and 'Sikhism in Pooñch,' by Bashir Mughal, *J&K Reporter*, November 2004.

iii Siñgh, Dévînder, and Rizvi, Baqar, *People of India, Volume XXV*, page 577.

Chapter- 5

Sri Mâtâ Vaishno Dévî jî
The Pilgrimage

Every year around a crore (ten million) pilgrims climb up the Trikutâ mountains to visit the cave where Mâtâ (mother) Vaishno Dévî jî lives. This, thus, is the world's most popular trek and South Asia's most frequented hill destination. The trek is relatively short, just 12km. each way. The holy cave is 1700 metres above the m.s.l.

Srî Mâtâ Vaishno Dévî jî runs the economy of much of Jammû province. And this is not superstition. The money that these 87 lakh yatris (pilgrims) inject into the economy is responsible for much of the employment (and, in many cases, affluence) created in Jammû. Take away this pilgrimage and there'll be little left of Jammû tourism. In 1998 and many subsequent years, 86 per cent of all tourists in Kashmir had gone there after a pilgrimage to the Holy Bhawan. The Valley, too, has started benefiting from Her munificence. 63 lakh pilgrims visited the shrine in 2005, 87 lakh in2010 and 1.01 crore (10.1 million) in 2011.

How to get there

To the holy cave: The Holy Bhawan (lit.: mansion; i.e. shrine) of Srî Mâtâ Vaishno Dévî jî is located in a cave, 5,200' above the sea level, in the Trikutâ mountains of Jammû. To get there you first have to reach Katrâ (2,500'), the base camp. The distance between Katrâ and the

Shri Mata Vaishno Devi Ji's Bhawan along with pilgrims accomodation

Bhawan is 12 km. Cars, taxis and buses are not allowed to go beyond Katrâ. Therefore, the most popular way to travel from Katrâ to the Bhawan is on foot—your own or someone else's.

Most people tend to walk all the way from Katrâ to the Bhawan. However, some people are unable to climb up that holy mountain. They hire a pony for the climb. For a fee, porters with crude 'palanquins' carry the old and the infirm to the shrine and back.

Three paths lead from Katrâ to the Bhawan. Two of these are moderate slopes. The third is a series of steps (a very long staircase, to wit), which reduces the distance by a few kilometres, but is much steeper.

Except when it is cold, many people prefer to climb up at night, when the track is all lit up with sodium lights. Little children and teenaged girls climb up unescorted at all hours of the day and night, without fear of molestation.

The helicopter ride from just outside Katrâ to Sâñjhî Chhat, which is close to the Bhawan, is an expensive option—Rs.2,000 per head, each way (early 2005 rates). The weather and sunlight permitting there is a sortie every fifteen minutes or so.

The old and infirm can travel from Adh Kwârî to close to the Bhawan (and back) in a battery-operated car—Rs.100 per head, each way. Tickets are available at Katrâ. This alternative is not available to the able-bodied. Besides, the van operates only two or three times a day.

How does one get to Katrâ? Most people go there from Jammû. You can also go to Katrâ directly from Srînagar, Udhampur, the Mânsar Lake or Sukrâlâ Mâtâ, without going through Jammû city.

Jammû has an airport and a railway station. Every day six flights (five from Delhi and one from Chandigarh), more than a dozen trains and countless inter-state buses leave for Jammû from the rest of India. Most of the buses then proceed towards Katrâ. Trains and aeroplanes do not.

So, most pilgrims get off at Jammû and take a bus, taxi or 'Tata Sumo' for Katrâ. All three kinds of transport are available at the Jammû Railway Station. Buses start plying from the Railway Station shortly after every train pulls in. You can also get buses, taxis and Sumos at Jammû's General Bus Stand (which is in the heart of the city). At the Bus Stand there's a bus almost every fifteen minutes between 6 am and 8 pm. (Unofficially, there might be buses even at 8.30 pm. But don't take the risk.)

Fares are low and fixed. You don't need to bargain. Buses range from the ordinary to the air-conditioned.

It's a 90 minute drive from Jammû to Katrâ (48 km.). The motorable road comes to an end at Katrâ.

At Katrâ

Permits for the pilgrimage: There's just one formality to be gone through at Katrâ: you have to collect a permit. This slip allows you to trek up from Katrâ to the Bhawan. Better known as the 'yâtrâ parchî', the permit is given, absolutely *free*, to the first 18,000 to 20,000 pilgrims every day. Its only purpose is to regulate crowds.

The yatra parchi can be obtained online @Rs.50 each. Visit maavaishnodevi.org. The same site also helps you book rooms, helicopter seats, ârti, darshan, special poojâ (prayers) and any other facility (or information) that the Shrine Board might have to offer. The going rate or rent has to be paid online and major credit cards are accepted.

The Delhi office of the Shri Mâtâ Vaishno Dévî jî Shrine Board is at the World Trade Centre, Barakhamba Road (phone 30956920), behind the Intercontinental Hotel. Incidentally, the Tourism Department of the Government of Puñjâb has a quota of 2000 yatra parchis.

Yâtrâ parchis are issued between 6 am and 10 pm every day. They are available at a booth ('counter') of the Sri Mâtâ Vaishno Dévî Shrine Board, which is located conveniently at the Katrâ Bus Stand (well before the Taxi Stand). There's a special booth near the Darshani Darwâzâ—which is a kilometre ahead of the abovementioned 'counter.' It issues permits to the first 1,000 defence personnel every day. Pilgrims who arrive in groups, in chartered buses, get their permits from the Old Mulberry Nursery (also known as 'Counter number 2'; 'two' is 'do' in Hiñdî-Dogrî).

Children below age five do not need permits. Families and groups of up to nine persons can travel on a single permit, provided that details of their group (and the name of one of them) are entered on the 'parchi'.

You have to reach Bân Gañgâ, a kilometre and a half away, within six hours of receiving the parchi, or it ceases to be valid.

The trek from Katrâ to the Bhawan

Automobiles are not allowed beyond Katrâ's Darshani Darwâzâ (2,700'). From there you have to trek up to the Bhawan of Srî Mâtâ Vaishno Dévî jî. En route there are toilets at short intervals, places to drink water at, first aid centres, places to eat at and shelters from the sun and rain. There are three alternative ways of climbing up.

Route (i) The traditional, sloping path (almost 13km): After you've walked for half a kilometre on a 'slope' that's almost flat, you will reach the first important halt, a mountain stream called the Bân Gañgâ (2,800'). You are supposed to bthe here and purify yourself before climbing up. Many pilgrims do that.

The incline begins now. The next halt is 1.5 kilometres away at Charan Pâdukâ (lit.: the shoes worn by the Holy Feet), which is associated with the Mâtâ's wooden slippers and which is at 3,378'. There is a rock here with what are said to be Her holy footprints.

Six kilometres from Katrâ and at a height of 4,784' is Ad Kuñwârî or Adh Kwârî (lit.: the ancient or eternal virgin), the most important and revered halt on the way to the Bhawan. It has a temple as well as a cave that is small and narrow—just two feet wide at places. It is considered auspicious for pilgrims to pass through this cave known as the Garbh Yoni (lit.: womb) or Garbh Joon before going to the Bhawan.

The Shrine Board provides free accommodation as well as subsidised food at Ad Kuñwârî. It also has rooms @ Rs 300 per day.

Around here begins the most difficult part of the trek, because you will now rapidly climb up to the Hâthi Matthâ (lit.: the elephant's forehead) peak (6,500'; 2.5km. from Ad Kuñwârî). The ascent is almost as vertical as the peak's name suggests.

Sâñjhî Chhat, is the next important halt. The altitude of Sâñjhî Chhat has been estimated at between 7,215' and 8,300' by different authorities. The 7,215' figure is correct. It is nine and a half kilometres from the Darshani Darwâzâ and two and a half from the Bhawan. There are two helipads, a charitable hospital, inexpensive/ free accommodation and a subsidised kitchen here. There are also rooms @ Rs 300 per day. You will get a nice view of the plains below from Sanjhi Chhat.

After Sâñjhî Chhat the worst is over. You will go down a very gentle slope to the Darbâr (lit.: the royal court), where the holy Bhawan (lit.: mansion; 5,200') of Srî Mâtâ Vaishno Dévî jî is.

Most people do the whole trek in five and a half or six hours on the way up and under four hours on the way back. But that's for people pressed for time. If you want to savour the hills and enhance the spiritual experience you should do it much slower. The whole route is so well lit at night that you can trek in the evenings or at any hour of the night. And during summer, spring and autumn that's what most weekend pilgrims do.

On their way back many pilgrims take a 2.5km. detour to go to the temple of Bhairoñ jî (6,583'), as well.

Route (ii) The steps: These steps follow the traditional route (i.e. Route i above). However, they reduce the distance by a few kilometres. As a result, the climb is much steeper and more strenuous.

Route (iii) The tiled route (almost 11.5km.)*:* A third route, a tiled, sloping path, was inaugurated in the year 2000. It reduces the total distance by 0.5km. More important, it bypasses the dreaded Hâthi Matthâ climb altogether. It stays almost a kilometre below Sânjhi Chhat and does not go higher than 5,500' at any stage. As a result the slope is extremely gentle.

The old pilgrim route: Before the era of taxis and buses, pilgrims would walk (or crawl, as many still do) all the way from Jammû (or even before) to the Holy Bhavan. According to tradition and custom there were six places after Jammû where a pilgrim had to pay homage before reaching the holy sanctum of Sri Mata Vaishno Devi ji. These six places were convenient resting points as well. Pilgrims would not only relax their tired legs, they would find shade to sit in, water to drink and perhaps something to eat.

These six *darshans* (pilgrimages), in the order that they occur after Jammû, are thus: The first four perhaps are Kol Kañdoli, Dévâ Mayî Mâ, Charan Pâdukâ and Ad Kwâri. So far the order is clear. There is no unanimity on the next two darshans. Hâthi Matthâ, Sâñjhî Chhat and Bhairoñ ji are variously considered the fifth darshan. Some say that the Holy Shrine of Srî Mâtâ Vaishno Devî jî is the sixth darshan, others that there are six darshans before the Holy Shrine.

Bal Krishan Purohit, who has written several books on the subject, says that the darshans are as follows: Kol Kañdoli, Dévâ Mayî Mâ, the Bhumikâ temple of Katrâ, Charan Pâdukâ, Ad Kwâri and, finally, the holy Bhawan itself. Thus, different authorities have different lists. There is no temple at Hâthi Matthâ, so it cannot be a darshan. Similarly, Sâñjhî Chhat has relatively little sanctity. So, the tradition recorded by Purohit seems the most accurate.

Bhairoñ ji cannot come before the holy Bhawan. So, it cannot be one of the six halts. At best, it can be the seventh halt.

Where to stay

There is no dearth of accommodation, to suit every pocket, either at the Bhawan or at Katrâ.

Where in these two places? Everywhere. Every other building has rooms for rent.

At both places, and in between, there is dormitory-type accommodation, run by the Shrine Board, where you can stay free. You'll need blankets because of the cold. To get them free all you need to do is to pay a refundable deposit. The ones provided by the Shrine Board are washed regularly.

In Jammû there is a large number of hotels, ranging from the plush to the inexpensive. (The cheaper ones are all in the heart of the town, between the General Bus Stand and the Raghunâth Temple.) The Shrine Board has a very fancy property, the Vaishnavi Dhâm, right next to the Railway Station. It's a walking distance away, even with your luggage, and has plush rooms, as well as inexpensive dormitories with free bedding and blankets.

In case you need a better class of accommodation, and are willing to pay a modest amount, you can book a room at Katrâ, Ad Kunwari, the Sâñjhî Chhat, near the Bhawan or in Jammû. Bookings are accepted at the Central Office of the Shrine Board at Katrâ. These rooms have beds like elsewhere in the world.

However, all over the Himâlayas, it is the custom at pilgrimages to sleep on the floor (i.e. on a mattress, sheet or blanket laid out on the floor), and not on raised cots/ beds. It is considered disrespectful to the deity of the pilgrimage to sleep on cots.

The Shrine Board's takeover

In 1986 the then Governor of Jammû and Kashmir, Mr. Jagmohan, authored the Vaishno Dévî Shrine Act which constituted the Sri Mâtâ Vaishno Dévî Shrine Board (SMVDSB). This Board took over the management of the shrine from the Dharamath Trust, of which the son of the last Mahârâjâ of the state was the Sole Trustee.

The Governor is the head of the Board. For the first 12 years the Chief Executive Officer was Anil Goswami, a dynamic member of India's highest-ranking civil service. The two undertook a spectacular modernisation drive. This included the construction of two first-rate paths to the shrine, night-lights for the hundreds of thousands of pilgrims who preferred to climb up at night (to avoid the heat of the day), and the introduction of internationally accepted standards of cleanliness and hygiene.

As a result, by 2001 the number of pilgrims visiting the shrine had almost quadrupled to 50 lakh (5 million), an annual increase of more than 20 per cent, boosting the economy of much of Jammû province. The growth gained further momentum in the next three years. By 2004, more than sixty lakh people were doing the pilgrimage every year—an incredible annual growth of 33 per cent. Pilgrim arrivals breached the one crore mark in 2011.

Such tourism as Jammû province has is almost entirely because of this powerful shrine—which is one of the most popular in India.

The Holy Cave

The Holy Cave is 98 feet long. Even if you are not superstitious or gullible you will be able to see the perfectly shaped head and tusk of the elephant-headed deity Ganésh sculpted *naturally* into the rock face to the left of the entrance to the cave.

Anil Goswami has, in his book, "Vaishno Devi-the shrine" (pages 33 and 34), painstakingly described each of the deities represented by the rock formations inside the cave, in the order in which they occur and their precise distance (in feet) from the entrance.[1]

Briefly, these deities are the Sûrya and Chañdr dévatâs—the Sun and Moon deities respectively; Lord Hanumân; the serpent king Shésh Nâg; auspicious symbols (the *shañkh* conch, the *chakr* wheel, the *gadâ* club [weapon] and the *padm* lotus); the five Pândavs; the seven Sapt Rishîs and the teats of the holy Kâmdhénû cow.

The supreme trinity of the Lords Brahmâ, Vishnu and Mahésh come next, followed by goddess Pârvati, the pillar worshipped by Prahlâd, some mystical symbols, the claws of the Mother Goddess' tiger, the hood of the cobra-god Shésh Nâg (again), and symbols of Lord Mahésh and Gauri (Pârvati).

The other stones jutting out of the walls or ceiling of the Holy Cave represent the Lords Ganésh, Sûrya, Chañdr, Siñh Râj—the lion king, Pashupati Nâth, the hand of Srî Mâtâ Vaishno Dévî jî and an icon of the goddess Annapûrnâ.

Finally, and most prominently, are the three *piñdîs* (natural, unsculpted stone icons) which Srî Mâtâ Vaishno Dévî jî chose to be frozen into, representing the three mother goddesses that She is made of.

The fresh, cold spring water on the floor of the cave is called the Charan Gañgâ ('the Ganges of the Holy Feet'). Devotees collect it in cans to take home. This holy water flows into the bathing area below the cave. Devotees consider it auspicious to bathe in this water before entering the Holy Cave for the darshan. And this brief *darshan* (lit.: 'vision' or 'glimpse of the Mother Goddess') is what these sixty lakh people come from distant places for.

Timings—and duration of each darshan: The cave is open to devotees for twenty hours, or 72,000 seconds, a day. (The other four hours—6 am to 8 am and 6 pm to 8 pm—are for housekeeping and ârti—rituals that can not be shared with the public). On several weekends, and in the summers, the number of devotees who land up at Katrâ, the base camp, is far in excess of the 18,000 pilgrims allowed to go up to the Holy Cave (on a first come basis). Work that out for yourself. Each devotee thus has a right to a 'darshan' of just 4 seconds. Since four or five persons can be inside at a time, this works out to about sixteen to twenty seconds for every group.

1. Or see pages 54-56 of *Vaishno Dévî—Janam kathâ tathâ nau Déviyoñ kî anar kahânî* by Bâl Krishn Sharma.

The Ârti

The Ârti [formal worship] of the Mother Goddess is performed twice a day, at sunrise and sunset, for two hours each. As mentioned above, pilgrims are not allowed inside the Holy Cave for these four hours. I can at best skim over the highlights of Anil Goswami's masterly description of the ârti (pages 86 to 90 of, as well as the annexure to, his book):[2]

The priests (pujaris) first chant the 108 names of Goddess Durgâ—whose incarnation Srî Mâtâ Vaishno Dévî jî is. Their next prayer is for their own purification and good health. After worshipping the earth (Prithvi), Sûrya, Deep (the prayer lamp) and Dhoop (herbal incense) they take an oath (*pratiggyâ sañkalp*) to worship the three Mother Goddesses represented by the three *piñdîs*. (A *pratiggyâ sañkalp*, literally, is a firm resolve, a binding resolution.)

Only the priests are allowed to remove the clothes and jewellery which these three piñdîs wear—or even see the piñdîs naked. It would be sacrilegious for any other person to do so. The priests need to do so because they have to bathe the piñdîs, as well as some of the other icons embedded in the walls of the Holy Cave, as they chant the *Swasti Vâchnan* mañtr. (Only the three main piñdîs wear clothes.) The piñdîs are washed with the water of the Charan Gañgâ, then with the five *amrits* (elixirs), namely milk, curds, *ghee* (clarified butter), honey and sugar, and then again with water. They are dried with towels, as the Ganapati Pûjanam (prayer to Lord Ganésh) is recited. The priests then beg the Goddess to forgive them for their sins by reciting the Devyapradh Kshamâpan Stotram ('verses seeking forgiveness for crimes committed'), as they dress the piñdîs again.

Before putting the clothes and jewellery back on the piñdîs, the priests have to draw certain symbols (the trident, the Indian swastik(a), the sun and the moon) with sandalwood paste and write certain Sañskrit mantrs (including Om and Shri) on paper. The dressing up of the piñdîs follows an elaborate order, as does the placing of the jewellery (which includes exquisite crowns, bangles and *chhatters* [bejewelled umbrellas/ canopies normally placed atop thrones]).

During this process, tilak and sindoor (both being auspicious herbal

2. The ârti itself has been reproduced on pages 59 and 60 (with an alternate ârtî on pages 83-84) of *Vaishno Dévî—Janam kathâ tathâ nau Déviyoñ kî amar kahânî* by Bâl Krishn Sharma. However, Anil Goswâmî's book goes into greater detail than any other, because of his unique inside knowledge and access.

pastes smeared on the foreheads of exalted humans) are applied on the piñdîs. Sacred lamps and herbal incenses are lit. A curtain drawn over them covers the piñdîs and icons. The priests start singing ârtis in Hindi and Dogri, as bells and cymbals are sounded. The priests again beg the Goddess to forgive them their sins.

Then, an important priest, who invariably is a descendant of Pañdit Shridhar, distributes prasâd among the devotees who have by now entered the mouth of the holy cave. Prasâd means 'prayer offering.' In this case it is a sweet, a fruit, a dry fruit or a combination of these, sanctified by aborementioned prayers. Finally, the priests come out of the cave with a metal plate (*thâl*) on which are placed the materials used during the prayer (*puja*). These materials are entirely herbal or vegetable. Prayers are offered at the mouth of the cave. These are prayers to Lord Ganésh, to the eternal flame that burns there and to the Holy Cave. Shouts of *Jai Mâtâ Di* go up in the air. *Charanâmrit* (sacred water, which has come from the feet of the deity) is sprinkled on the devotees assembled near the cave.

The sacred flame (*jyot*) that is brought out of the holy cave is placed on a *thâli* (metal tray) and waved in front of the pilgrims. Some of them get to move their hands over the flame, as is the Hiñdu tradition.

This brings the ârti to an end. Pilgrims, who had been stopped from entering the Holy Cave for the last two hours, can now start going in again.

There are two ways of getting to witness the ârti (formal prayer). Those who pay Rs.11,000 per person are allowed to go near the holy pindis in the cave during the ârti and stay there till the ârti is over. The number of such pilgrims cannot exceed five at a time.

Another one hundred to one hundred and fifty persons participate in a collective ârti called the *atkâ darshan*. This darshan is free but a priority slip has to be obtained from Katra for the privilege.

Festivals

The popular 'seasons'

The 9-day autumn (Ashvin) navarâtrâs and the equally long Chaitr (spring) navarâtrâs are considered the most auspicious time of the year to visit the holy shrine. The number of pilgrims peaks during these two periods.

Christmas and the Christian New Year have nothing to do with the Mother Goddess. And yet the ten or eleven day period that begins with the weekend before Christmas and lasts till after the New Year is another peak period. People want to begin the (Christian) New Year on an auspicious note, at the Court of the Mother.

Summer vacations (early April to mid-July) and the Pûjâ vacations (Sept/ Oct) are the other time when pilgrims arrive in very big numbers. Ditto for long weekends.

The Durgé Saptshati Pâth

The Durgé Saptshati Pâth is the traditional, classical prayer that is recited at Katrâ (and among devotees of Durgâ Mâtâ everywhere) during the navarâtrâs. Its name means 'the 700 prayers of (the Mother Goddess) Durgâ.' This is a very elaborate set of prayers in thirteen sections. The contents of these 13 'chapters' are:

(i) How the Mother Goddess killed the demons Madhu and Kaitabh;

(ii) How the Mother Goddess vanquished the army of Mahishâsur;

(iii) How the Mother Goddess killed the demon Mahishâsur;

(iv) An invocation to the Mother Goddess as well as Her blessings;

(v) A conversation between the Mother Goddess and the demon Chand-Mund,

(vi) How the Mother Goddess killed the demons Dhumar and Lochan;

(vii) How the Mother Goddess killed Chand-Mund;

(viii) How the Mother Goddess killed the demon Raktveej;

How the Mother Goddess vanquished the army of Mahishâsur

(ix) How the Mother Goddess killed Nishumbh, king of the demons;

(x) How the Mother Goddess killed the demon Shumbh;

(xi) Another invocation to the Mother Goddess;

(xii) The teachings and instructions of Durgâ Mâtâ; and

(xiii) The Mother Goddess blesses Surat and Vaishay and promises that their former prosperity and peace will be restored.

The Mother Goddess had to kill these demons because they had tyrannised mankind and robbed the world of its peace and prosperity.

Modern festivals

M.K. Ajatshatru Siñgh, the then Tourism Minister, started The Navarâtrâ Festival at Katrâ in 1997.

The next year I introduced an All India Devotional Songs Contest during the same autumn navarâtrâs, also at Katrâ. The winner of the first prize gets a very generous cash award from the organisers (J&K Tourism and the Srî Mâtâ Vaishno Dévî jî Shrine Board). In addition, Venus Cassettes and Records gives the main winner a recording contract. In turn, mammoth audiences receive nine days of spiritual entertainment.

The judges, invariably, are some of the most powerful men of Filmistân (hitherto known as Bollywood). Even more than the cash prize, it is the judges that attract talented singers from all over India. The singers want to catch the ears of these film producers in the hope of getting a break.

Ganésh Jain, who owns Venus and is also a major film producer, and Vikas Mohan, who publishes one of Filmistân's most influential trade journals and is also a film producer, have been with us from the very beginning. So have Pahlaj Nihalani, the President of the All India Motion Pictures and Television Programme Producers Association, Gordhan Tanwani, a leading film producer and Vijay Galani, who has produced some very successful films.

This contest has therefore snowballed, exactly as I had hoped, into a major annual event. Private organisations have started adding to the prizes that the government and the Shrine Board award. Venus Records, in its generosity, sometimes produces cassettes and CDs containing songs sung by the winners of the minor prizes as well.

These prize winners become sought after singers of devotional songs and immediately hike their professional fees for live performances. Also, as I had taken pains to ensure, the contest attracts singers from all communities. The winners of the first prize so far include Ghulam Muhammad Dhansali, Paramjeet Siñgh and Reyaz Ahmed.

During the Christmas-New Year week some private parties invite leading singers from the entertainment industries of Delhi and Bombay and get them to sing popular devotional songs.

The Yâtrâ (Pilgrimage): Tips for pilgrims

Climate and clothing: Even in summer it is quite cold at Sâñjhî Chhat, the Bhawan (i.e. the shrine itself) and Bhairoñ Ghâtî. By the time you reach Sâñjhî Chhat you'll be bathed in sweat. And then suddenly a cold breeze will blow past you, through your sweat, possibly making you sneeze. You don't want that to happen. Bringing a sweat-shirt alongwill help.

It snows at these three places between December and February, sometimes in March as well. It can get very cold in October, November and April, too, especially if it rains. So, please bring warm clothes along between October and April, very warm ones during the snow months.

You can hire canvas shoes and raincoats (wellies) at Katrâ.

Taboos: The food sold (or served free) at all places between Katrâ and the Bhawan is strictly vegetarian. Liquor and meat are not sold even to local residents in this area. Smoking along the track will not be appreciated. Nor will leather belts or wallets be inside the shrine. (There is, of course, no question of taking shoes, leather or canvas, into the Holy Cave, or any other Hindu, Muslim, Buddhist or Sikh shrine in South Asia.)

Donations: How does the Shrine Board manage to provide all these facilities free? It's because it receives huge rentals from its various properties—and donations, too. Pilgrims drop money (and other valuables, including jewellery) into designated donation boxes near and inside the Holy Cave. The Shrine Board staff will give you a receipt if you need one for tax deductions.

Miracles

Countless miracles are attributed to the Mâtâ, whose devotees hail Her by calling out *Jai Mâtâ Di* (Punjâbi-Dogri for 'Glory to the Mother').

Once some mischievous youths are believed to have said 'Glory to the Father' instead. It is said that they were immediately struck by lightning.

The fact that the number of devotees has been growing by almost twenty five per cent a year (and that on an already very high base) means that prayers *are* getting answered.

Personally, I have grown up watching the Mâtâ's ardent devotees zoom from humble circumstances to extreme riches. Apart from friends of my family, the best known example is that of Gulshan Kumar, who grew from a street corner fruit juice vendor to India's biggest taxpayer and the owner of India's biggest recorded-music empire. His company carries a picture of the Mâtâ on every single CD and cassette that it manufactures, and donates a certain portion of its earnings for charitable works in and around the Holy Shrine—including a hygienic, free kitchen (Gulshan da langar) for all pilgrims.

Chapter- 6

Sri Mâtâ Vaishno Dévî jî The Story of the Deity[i]

Mahishâsur, the demon, tyrannises the deities and angels

Mahishâsur, son of Rambh, was an extremely powerful demon. He took to torturing the deities and angels. The Lords Brahmâ and Shiv led a deputation of the deities to Vaikuñth, to meet Lord Vishnû. 'Save us from Mahishâsur,' the deities begged him.

Lord Vishnû wanted to protect the deities from Mahishâsur. However, some deities had once promised that invincible demon that no man would be able to kill or harm him. As a result, it was very difficult to defeat him.

'Only a woman can kill Mahishâsur,' Lord Vishnû concluded.

The Lord said to the deities, 'Mahishâsur enjoys the protection of some deities. If you want to kill him, then all the male deities and lady deities will have to pool their resources and work together. Every deity will have to request his or her divine powers to come out and unite with the energies of the other deities. As a result, an All-Powerful Lady Deity will be born. Every single male deity and lady deity should then worship this All-Powerful Lady Deity. Every deity has a unique divine weapon, which no one else possesses. All deities should hand their weapons over to this new Lady Deity, so that she can go and kill Mahishâsur.'

The deities liked Lord Vishnû's idea and agreed to take part in the project.

A halo then emerged from Lord Vishnû's face. Within moments, haloes started arising from the faces of the Lords Brahmâ, Shiv and Iñdr as well as the other deities. The haloes coalesced and formed themselves into a beautiful lady. Such was the glow that surrounded this lady that it lit up the Three Worlds. The Lady's radiance touched Mahishâsur as well. He got into a panic when it did. This gladdened the male and lady deities. They began to worship the All-Powerful Lady Deity, who was an embodiment of their own united energies.

The deities told her about the depredations of Mahishâsur and begged of her, 'Please kill that demon.'

The All-Powerful Lady Deity then sat on a tiger, with countless divine weapons in her many hands. It was an awesome sight. When the lady and male deities saw her thus, they started bowing before her again and again. 'Protect us from Mahishâsur,' they begged her.

The Lady Deity told the other deities, 'Give up fear. Give up all your worries.'

Vaishnavi's early years

The All-Powerful Lady Deity was named Trikûtâ when she was a child. Later, after some of Lord Vishnû's powers had become a part of her, she came to be known as Vaishnavi. The faith that she propagated is called Vaishnavism (the Vaishnav religion). The word 'Vaishno' is a colloquial form of 'Vaishnav.'

Trikûtâ was a child prodigy. She quickly mastered the scriptures, the Véds, and wanted to learn even more. Soon, there were no books left for her to study. Her father advised her to meditate and seek the answers to her questions directly from the Lord. So, Trikûtâ went south, to meditate by the sea.

There, Srî Râm told Vaishnavi, 'You need to raise your spiritual level much higher still. For this I would advise you to go north to the Trikûtâ mountain and meditate.' (Some versions claim that the peak was called Trikûtâ even before the Mâtâ went there.)

'How will I find that mountain?' Vaishnavi asked.

'Go to the Mânik [or Marinak] range of mountains in the north,' Srî Râm replied. 'There you will see a hill with three peaks. It is called Trikutâ. Each of the peaks represents a Great Divine Energy (*Shakti*). Within the hill is an exquisite cave. Cold water always flows through that cave.

'The three Great *Shakti* Deities will one day live there. This will happen in the Dwâpar Age, when Srî Krishn and the Pâñdavs establish three stone *piñdîs* in the cave.

'Go to that cave and immerse yourself in prayer. You will become immortal there. Brave *lañgûr* guards will be your watchmen.

'All humanity will throng to your shrine. They will beg you to bless them and grant them boons. Be good to them. Give them your blessings. Bestow boons upon them. If you agree to live in the Trikutâ mountain, it will become a major pilgrimage. You will be enormously famous. Word about your power and glory will spread throughout the world. People will call you Vaishnav Dévî. Don't get irritated by the ceaseless crowds of people at your shrine. A bit of me lives inside every one of them.

'If you attain the desired level, then, in the Kali Yug, in my incarnation as Kalki, I will accept you as my *shakti* (power, energy).'

The Mâtâ continues \to meditate in those mountains to this day. That is why she is known as Adi Kuñwârî or Adh Kwârî, the Eternal Virgin. She has been in that holy cave since the Trétâ Age, which was more than a million years ago. But how did she get there?

The demon appears

The All-Powerful Lady Deity, who is also called Jagadambâ, the mother of the world, gathered a group of lady attendants and went over to the Shatshriñg Mountain. They chose the Shatshriñg because they knew that the demons often visited it.

True enough, some Râkshases, who had been passing by, reported to Mahishâsur, 'An extremely beautiful young lady has set up camp on the Shatshriñg Mountain.'

The deities then sent Nârad, the celestial saint, to Mahishâsur, to provoke him. 'Why don't you marry that girl?' Nârad suggested to the demon. 'I have never seen anyone as good-looking as she.'

Mahishâsur was not a very bright person. All this talk of Jagadambâ's beauty excited him. He said to his fellow Râkshases, 'Will you go to that young lady and persuade her to be my wife?'

'And what if she does not agree?' one of the Râkshases asked.

'In that case, just pick her up and bring her here,' Mahishâsur instructed his colleagues. 'Use force if necessary.'

A Râkshas emissary, accompanied by a large number of Râkshas soldiers, went to Jagadambâ Mâ and said, 'Our leader, Mahishâsur, wants to marry you.'

Jagadambâ Mâ replied, 'I can not marry your leader—or anyone else, because I have resolved to stay unmarried all my life.'

The emissary looked at the Râkshas soldiers and said, 'All right, then. I suppose we will have to convince her through other means. Charge!'

The soldiers attacked Jagadambâ Mâ.

The Mother Deity pulled out some of the weapons that the deities had given her. A fierce battle ensued in which all the demons were killed.

When Mahishâsur learnt of the death of his emissary and soldiers, his blood began to boil. He told his powerful commander in chief, 'Take a massive army and attack that lady. We have to avenge the massacre of our comrades.'

This Râkshas force did not fare any better. The battle went on for a very long time. It came to an end only when the Râkshas commander and the last Râkshas soldier were killed.

That was when Mahishâsur stepped into the battlefield. Jagadambâ Mâ killed this powerful Râkshas, too.

When the deities heard of Mahishâsur's death, they were overjoyed. They organised a grand prayer ceremony at which all of them offered prayers and thanksgiving to Jagadambâ Mâ for having delivered them from Mahishâsur.

Bhairoñ harasses Vaishnavi

A few thousand years later (but hundreds of thousands of years before today), a powerful tâñtric (tâñtr expert) called Gorakh Nâth reached the place where Jammu city now is. His disciples accompanied him, There Gorakh heard of Vaishnavi, the great female-saint. He asked his chief disciple, Bhairoñ Nâth, to go to her âshram near Bhumikâ to check out if her legendary spiritual powers were for real.

Bhairoñ was surprised to notice that Vaishnavi always carried a bow and arrows, as well as a trident (*trishul*). These weapons were associated with warriors, not saints. He also saw a fierce tiger go in and out of her âshram every day. (Anil Goswami writes that it was a lion.) The tiger would become very gentle when in the âshram, and its normal fierce self again when it left. Black-faced monkeys (*lañgûrs*), too, surrounded the lady.

Bhairoñ lusted after the saint because of her stunning physical beauty. His constant pestering made her decide to shift her âshram further up the mostly dry Trikutâ mountain. The lañgûrs who followed her were thirsty. So was Vaishnavi. So the saint shot an arrow into the ground, and a stream—now known as the Bân Gañgâ—came gushing out. (Bân means 'arrow.')

During her uphill climb, Vaishnavi rested for a while at the place now known as the Charan Pâdukâ. Half way up the hill Vaishnavi found a narrow and secluded cave, in which she decided to stay. (The cave is now called Ad Kuñwârî or Adh Kwârî.) Vaishnavi resumed her meditation and prayer in the cave, hoping that Bhairoñ would not be able to find her there. But he did. So, to escape him, with her trident Vaishnavi bored an exit at the other end of the cave. The saint fled further uphill to another, bigger cave, which is now revered by countless millions as her Darbâr (court) or Bhawan (mansion).

Bhairoñ had to kill some of the Mother's faithful monkeys in order to get to this cave. Realising that Bhairoñ was physically too strong for her to defeat, the furious Vaishnavi decided that she had had enough. That was when the saint transformed herself into Srî Mâtâ Vaishno Dévî jî.

The Deity who thus emerged had eight arms, each hand holding a weapon, and wore red clothes. She rushed out of the cave, astride a tiger, and chopped the demon's head off with her sword. The severed head flew a kilometre and landed in the little valley now known as Bhairoñ Ghati. The rest of him collapsed in front of the cave. Because of the spiritual powers that he had acquired during the course of his life, Bhairoñ could speak even without his head. He begged the Deity to be forgiven. Srî Mâtâ Vaishno Dévî jî saw that his repentance was genuine. She offered to bring him back to life.

Bhairoñ said that to be killed by the Deity Herself would guarantee him *moksh* (nirvân—freedom from the circle of life and death). So, if the Deity would grant him a favour could She make it so that in the centuries to come people did not think ill of him, because, but for this one sin, which he was sorry for, he had been a good man all his life.

The Deity granted Bhairoñ his last wish and ordained that the pilgrimage to Her shrine would be considered complete only if, on their way back, pilgrims went to the temple of Bhairoñ Nâth. She also turned Bhairoñ's head and body into stone, so that they could be preserved forever.

Tired of a worldly life, the Deity went into the cave and transformed herself, too, into stone (*pindi*) in order to 'immerse herself in (prayer) so that she could attain (Lord) Vishnû in his incarnation as Kalki in *Kalyuga*.' (Goswami)

There are three holy stones (*pindis*) inside the cave, into which the Deity has frozen Herself. These are her three original forms, viz. the Mother Deities (Mâtâ) Mahâ Kâlî, Mahâ Lakshmi and Mahâ Saraswati.

Shrîdhar discovers the shrine

Pañdit Shrîdhar, a poor farmer, discovered the cave-shrine of Srî Mâtâ Vaishno Dévî jî around the 10th century AD. He lived in a pretty village called Hañsâlî, which is a little more than a mile away from where Katrâ now is, and has the famous Bhûmikâ temple.

Shrîdhar was a devotee of Shakti. The childless Pandit was once preparing to worship the virgin goddess in her girl-child form (*kanyâ pûjan*). He beseeched the Mother Deity thus, 'Are my prayers defective or insufficient? O Mother Deity, please tell me what is wrong with the way that I pray! You know everything that happens everywhere. Why do you not accept my prayers? O Mother of the World, please forgive me all my sins and mistakes. Or else please appear before me and tell me to my face that I am not destined to have any children. And if that is my fate, will my clan come to an end with me?'

The pandit began to cry.

At the appointed hour, six little girls from the neighbourhood assembled for the ritual. They sat cross-legged in a row, on a sheet on the ground. Just then he heard the sound of ankle-bells. When he looked up, Shrîdhar saw a child whose beauty was simply divine.

Shrîdhar panicked, because he had never seen that child before. Nor did she seem to be from his village. The halo around the girl's face was like hundreds of suns put together. Her face had the innocence of a pure, guileless child. She wore red clothes and there were ankle-bells on her feet. The girl stretched her feet out and an awe-struck Shrîdhar began to wash them.

The other little girls ate their food, took their prayer offerings and left. However, the divine child stayed on even after the ceremony was over.

Before Shrîdhar could ask any questions, the girl said, 'My name is Vaishnavi. I live across the mountain.' Soon, the two became great friends.

One day the girl vanished suddenly. This got Shrîdhar extremely worried. He stopped eating food and drinking water. He kept staring blankly at the empty space before him. When night came, he went to bed, hungry and thirsty.

In his sleep Shrîdhar felt as if someone was stroking his head—as elders, teachers and deities sometimes affectionately do. When he opened his eyes he beheld Durgâ Mâtâ, sitting majestically on a tiger, wearing stunning ornaments, holding a trident in one hand and all kinds of weapons in her other seven hands.

The pañdit got up and prostrated himself before the deity. He then lit a lamp and worshipped the Divine Mother. However, Durgâ Mâtâ reprimanded him gently, 'Why have you given up all food and water? How can you offer prayers while your stomach is being gnawed by hunger? Come, let me show you my home.'

Shrîdhar began to walk behind the deity with folded hands. They started climbing a mountain. In due course they reached an invisible cave.

The floor of the cave was covered ankle-deep with the cold water of a spring. Shrîdhar crawled into the cave that, almost a thousand years after that event, is still narrow, damp, obliquely angled, uncomfortable, mildly claustrophobic and rough on the feet and hands.

The deity then told Shrîdhar about how she had chosen to live in that cave in the form of three stones. The thought that the Mother Deity was standing before him in person moved Shrîdhar to tears. He bowed his head, offered prayers and knew that he had achieved the goal of his life.

When Shrîdhar emerged from the dark cave, the blinding light of the sun hit his eyes. It was strong enough to wake him up. It was early in the morning. Shrîdhar looked out of the window of his hut and realised that those were the red rays of the rising sun. It had only been a dream, and yet Shrîdhar was extremely happy. His mind was still filled with images of the glorious places that he had seen in the dream. In particular, the picture of the Mother Deity sitting resplendent on a tiger suffused his heart. He was able to recall every moment of the dream distinctly.

The first words that Shrîdhar spoke on getting up were, 'Glory to the Mother!'

For days at an end Shrîdhar searched the mountains, looking for the cave, but without success. One moment he would think that he was on the exact route that he had seen in the dream, and the next he would begin to have doubts. But whenever he thought that he had lost the way, flashes from the dream would come back and he would be shown the next segment of the path.

Then one day, when he reached the stream now called the Pâi Nâllâh, he saw a person in red clothes standing on a ledge near a waterfall in the Trikutâ mountains. He had to climb up a steep cliff, through what then was a dense forest. With considerable effort and physical hardship he reached the ledge. Instead of finding Vaishnavi there, he discovered a narrow cave. It was exactly what he had seen in the dream.

He was disappointed at not finding Vaishnavi inside either. Shrîdhar began to cry. He prayed to Shakti, the Mother Deity, to help him find Vaishnavi. She did. The cave was filled with a divine light. Vaishnavi stood smiling before him, transformed into a Deity with four pairs of arms, riding a tiger. She told him that she, indeed, was an incarnation of Shakti.

According to other accounts, Shrîdhar found the Mother Deity inside the cave all right, but in the form of three stone *piñdîs*, which is the form in which she lives in that holy cave to this day. In this version, on finding the *piñdîs* Shrîdhar knew that he had accomplished the goal of his life. He bowed before the *piñdîs* with folded hands and offered various kinds of prayers. He also bathed the *piñdîs*.

It was then that the Mother Deity appeared in person and said to the childless Shrîdhar. 'You will have four sons. This is my boon to you. The clan that you will found will be my devotees and servants for centuries to come. Your descendants will always be happy and prosperous. Your clan will be spoken of with respect.'

Sharing the spoils

From that day Shrîdhar took to climbing up to the Holy Cave every morning before daybreak, even during the snowy winters and harsh monsoons, to worship the Mother. Word of Shrîdhar's early morning disappearances, and the consequent glow on his face, spread.

The people of that and the neighbouring villages assumed that he had discovered a treasure of the worldly kind. These people belonged to the Drorâ, Maniotrâ and Khas clans of the Thakkar caste, and the Samnotrâ clan of the Brâhmin caste.

A group of youths representing these four clans decided to waylay Shrîdhar to force him to share his wealth with them. They beat him up till he fell down bleeding. Shrîdhar begged them not to hurt him any more and offered to take them to the Holy Cave. There he showed them the *pindis* by the light of torches (*deenees*) made of the branches of pine (*cheer*) trees. The youths were impressed and paid homage to the Deity frozen in stone.

The commercial instincts that have dogged almost every Indian pilgrimage overpowered these youths immediately—and this is recorded history, not legend. They realised they had chanced upon what could be a huge money-spinner. So, they decided to tell everyone about the cave, so that people from all over would go there, worship the pindis, and leave behind some money or other offerings, as is the Hindu custom. These offerings, the youths resolved, would, by turns be shared between the four clans that they represented. Shrîdhar was left out on the ground that being a Brâhmin he should be above money and other worldly goods.

Thus, once in every four days one of these four clans would receive all the offerings made at the Holy Cave on that day. The Hindustani/ Dogri word for 'turn' is *bâri*. Since these clans milked the shrine turn by turn, they came to known as *bârîdârs*. Over the next one thousand years the members of the four clans grew considerably. Each clan sub-divided its 'turn' among its members.

By 1986, when this system was abolished by the then Governor of Jammu and Kashmîr, Mr Jagmohan, the 'turn' of an individual member of one of these clans to collect the offerings could come only once in two or three years. The offerings made on that one day could be enough to ensure that that member need not work at all for a living. Indeed, one reason why there was little sympathy for the bârîdârs when Mr Jagmohan took their goldmine away from them was because they were seen as a set of idlers, used to the good life. This was true only of some of the bârîdârs, whose families had not multiplied as fast as the others had. The majority could only manage a middle-middle class lifestyle with their share.

Reference

i Sources for the story of Srî Mâtâ Vaishno Dévî jî include:

Mâtâ Vaishnoñ Dévî: Sat yug sé aâj kî mahimâ tak (Name of author and year of publication not stated. This edition was probably printed in 2003.), Bhavânî Pustak Mahal, Katrâ Vaishno Dévî, Jammu 182301.

Nau Déviyoñ kî Amar Kahânî, edited by Om Prakâsh Shâstrî and Shañkar Dâs (year not stated; this edition was probably printed in 2003), Bhavânî Pustak Mahal, Katrâ Vaishno Dévî, Jammu 182301.

Vaishno Dévî—Janam kathâ tathâ nau Déviyoñ kî amar kahânî by Bâl Krishn Sharma, Dâs (year not stated; this edition was probably printed in 2003), Bhavânî Pustak Mahal, Katrâ Vaishno Dévî, Jammu 182301.

Vaishno Dévî-the Shrine (published by the SMVD Board, Katrâ, 300 pages, Rs.1250, 1998) by Anil Goswami. Anil is the officer who was the executive head of the SMVD Board from its inception in 1986 to 1998, making it the finest of its kind in India. The management of this holy pilgrimage is admired all over the nation and considered a model, thanks to this senior civil servant's work.

Kashmir

The path to the Cave of Sri Amarnâth ji

Lord Sri Amarnâth ji

Chapter- 7

The Sri Amarnâthji Yatra

The cave of Sri Amarnâth ji (3,962 metres/ 12,995 ft.) contains a naturally formed Shivling made of ice. The pilgrimage (yatra) to this Holy Cave started in an organised manner around 1850, during the reign of the Dogrâ Mahârâjâ Gulab Singh. This yatra is perhaps thousands of years old. However, as far as recorded history (or memory) is concerned this ice lingam (a Shaivite fertility symbol) was discovered by Adam Malik, a Muslim shepherd from Batakot, in the 17th or 18th century A.D.

In return, the Mahârâjâ decreed that a representative of the Malik family would be present at the cave shrine along with the Mahant (priest) and the Pandits of Bhavan and Ganeshporâ. As a result, till A.D. 2000, the Maliks would receive one-third of all the offerings made at the shrine. The Mahârâjâ also granted the Maliks a large *jagir* (estate) near Pahalgâm and exempted them from having to pay land revenue. The family has since migrated to the Mattan Wudder plateau near the famous Sun temple of Martand.

Before Gulab Singh, his Sikh mentor, Mahârâjâ Ranjit Singh of Lahore (Punjab), would patronise the *yatra* (circa 1817). Ranjit paid Rs. 2 to every religious person who agreed to perform the pilgrimage. In those days the holy mace (chharhi mubarak) would be stored in Amritsar, which is close to Lahore. The procession to the Holy Cave would start from Amritsar.

The Dogrâs later shifted the resting-place of the holy chharhi to the Dashnami Akhara of Srînagar. (This is on the main Maulana Âzâd Road, just before the Budshah Bridge.) During the 1990s, the holy mace was shifted to Jammû's Ranbireshwar temple for the better part of the decade. It has since returned to Srînagar.

When to perform the yatra

The most auspicious (and comfortable) time of the year to perform the *yatra* is the month preceding the *Sawan Puranmashi*, better known to the rest of India as Raksha Bandhan. This is the first full moon night of August (rarely, late July). The routes to the Holy Cave are buried under snow at least nine months a year. So, even theoretically the journey can not be done except in the remaining two or three months. Officially the *yatra* is open almost 33 days before and some 4-5 days after the said full moon night.

Example: Date of Raksha Bandhan, 2003: the 12th August. Therefore, the date of the first *darshan*: the 12th July. The first batch will leave Pahalgâm three days before the date of the first *darshan* (9 or 10 July in this case). The last batch will return two or three days after the last *darshan* (in this case on the 15th August).

The routes

There are two pilgrims' routes to the Holy Cave: the popular, relatively easy, but time consuming trek that begins near Pahalgâm, and the more difficult 'same day return' trip from Bâltal. The Chharhi Mubarak (the Holly Mace) is carried along an extended version of the Pahalgâm route.

(The figure given after the name of a place in Column 1 represents the distance, in kilometres, from the place last mentioned.)

The route of the Chharhi mubarak	The ritual name of the place is said to be	The name of the pilgrimage(s) connected with this place
Srînagar 0		
Shrahuyar/Shuhrayur 8	Shorhash	Shorhash
Pâmpore 4	Shivpuri/ Padampur	Mâd-dein/ Bhagwati Ganga

Barsu/ Barus 9	Vareesh	Rudra Ganga
Jab Bâri (-)	Yuvati	Mishtod/ Mithvanya
Awantipore 4 (from Barsu)	Bântipur	
Mahanag 2	Mihirnag	
Hariparigam 5		Haridwar Ganpati
Bahiyar Shetar 2	Balihâr	
Hastigan (-)	Hastikarn	Nâg Ashram; there's a Ganpati called Jyesth Aasharh near the Sangam
Devkyar 4 (from Bahiyar)	Devak Dhâr	Devak
Bijbehera 2	Vijay Vihâr	Hareesh Chandra; the temple nearby is of Vrish Dhvaj Maharaj
Salar [Mattan] 17	Surya Ashram	Surya Ganga; the Lambodari river and the Paschim Vâhini Ganga
Seevras (-)	Satkar	Bhadrâg Shram (Bhatoor); Hay Sheersh (Sirhâm); Ashvatar Kshetra; Sarlak (Sabar) with its holy Anant Nag pond
Khaylan village (-)	Khilyâshr	Bâl Khilya area (Kular)
Ganshibal 14 (from Salar)	Ganesh Bal/ Mahavan	
Mamal 2	Mâmaleshwar/ Mâgeshwar	
Pahalgâm 3	The Bhrigupati Kshetra	Ranji Van and, later, the Neel Ganga
Chandanwari 16	Sthânu/Sthânav Ashram (Thâninyu)	River Saraswati
Pissu Top 5		
Wâwjan/ Shesh Nag 7	Vâyu Varjan/ Sisiram Nag	
Hatiyara Talao 3		
Panjtarni 8	Panchtarangini	
Bhairo(n) Ghati pass 2		Dâmareshwar Bhairav
Garbh Yoni 16		
Amravati Nadi 2		
Holy Cave 5		

The pilgrims' Pahalgâm route

(The first figure after the name of the place gives the distance, in km., from the place last mentioned. The second figure is the altitude, in feet.)

- Pahalgâm 0/ 7,500
- Chandanwari 16/ 9,500
- Pissu Top 3/ 11,500
- Zoji Bal (Jogi Pal) 4/ 11,000
- Naga Koti 3/ 11,500
- Shesh Nag 3/ 12,500
- Wawbal (Warbal) 1/ 12,500
- Maha Gunas Top 2.6/ 14,800
- Pabi Bal (Rabibal) 1.4/ 14,000
- Posh Pathri 1/ 12,500
- Panjtarni 6.6/ 11,500
- S.S. Parhi 3.4/ 12,500
- Holy Cave 3/ 13,500
- (Pahalgâm to the Holy Cave= 48 km.)

Notes: (i) Distances mentioned for the route of the Chharhi Mubarak are as per the 'old route.' The present route is given here as the Pilgrims' Route. The two sets of figures differ somewhat from each other. The Chharhi Mubarak deviates a bit from the pilgrims' route. (ii) Vâv+jan= *Wawjan.* It literally means 'strong winds.' (iii) Stark naked sadhus would bathe in the *Amravati Nadi* stream and then jump off a cliff. They believed that if they did not die in the process, it was because God wanted them to live. But if they succeeded in dying, as they wanted to, they believed that they would attain *moksh* (salvation). The government has, because of these suicides, banned the movement of pilgrims in the direction of the Amravati Nadi. (iv) Mattan, *Jab Bâri*, Khaylan, Seevras and Hastigan were part of an even older route. (At some stage the route went through Salar instead of Mattan.) I have got these additional places on the authority of Pt. Vyas.

The Pahalgâm route

Day 1: You should leave Pahalgâm early in the morning. Or else your vehicle will get caught in the slow-moving convoy. Your car or bus will take you some 16 kilometres, to a place just short of Chandanwari (9,500'/

2,895m.). In case you wish to camp there is a rest house and a number of tents are likely to be available.

The trek begins here. You will first walk over a huge ice field and almost immediately thereafter climb one of the steepest inclines that you will encounter during the entire pilgrimage.

Your night halt will be at the stunning Shesh Nag (3,574m.), where there is a huge fresh-water lake made of icy, whitish-green waters. You can camp either at Zojipal or, slightly further ahead, at Wawjan (pron.: wâw-junn). There are pilgrim shelters and a rest house at Wawjan.

Two days before the auspicious *Sawan Puranmashi*, under an almost full moon, this author saw an incredible sight around ten in the night. A few thousand glowing animals swam from the distant end of Lake Shesh Nag towards the end closest to the pilgrims' camp. They swam in formation, swaying (dancing?) as they moved. They took at least twenty minutes to reach our end of the lake and almost equally long to return.

The officers stationed at Shesh Nag, all of them Muslim, informed us that these animals were water snakes and the glow that we saw was that of the *manis* (jewels) on their heads. Now, Shesh Nag also happens to be the name of the famous water-cobra of Hindu mythology. The Hindus believe that after a cobra has lived long enough (a hundred years), it grows a natural *mani* on its hood.

I don't know what the scientific explanation is. I am just telling you what we saw.

Does this happen throughout the year? Perhaps not. The scientific theory is that these snakes hibernate for the rest of the year. Perhaps they come out only during this, the warmest, time of the year. In any case, who knows? For even officials go there only for the 40 days of the yatra. In 1998, these sightings were reported only during the five nights before the *Puranmashi* (full moon night).

Day 2: You will climb all the way up to the Mahagunas Pass before descending to Panjtarni (12.6 km. from Shesh Nag). Most pilgrims halt there for the night. Even amateur trekkers can make it in five hours. If you start early enough, you can reach Panjtarni by lunch.

After lunch and a brief rest, if you aren't too tired, you can leave your things in your tent at Panjtarni and go over to the Holy Cave (6.4 km. ahead). You can return to Panjtarni by late evening. I always do so. (There is a camp near the Holy Cave, too, where you can spend the night. However, it is very cold and crowded.)

Between Panjtarni and the Holy Cave (3,962m.) there is an extremely steep climb called S.S.Parhi (for Sher Singh Parhi).

Day 3: You can return from Panjtarni to Pahalgâm the way you came. In that case you will return on the fourth or fifth day (depending on whether you had visited the Holy Cave on the second or third day).

Or you can climb up the S.S.Parhi once again and thereafter proceed, mostly downhill, to Bâltal, thus completing the yatra in just three days. This is what I do. (It is 48 km from Pahalgâm to the Holy Cave.)

The Bâltal route

This route is recommended only to those who are truly fit and in a hurry. For this you should drive from Srînagar (or wherever) to Sonamarg the day before the trek. Spend the night at Sonamarg or, better still, at Bâltal, where a large pilgrim camp would have been set up. Buses, cars and jeeps go all the way to Bâltal. (You have to first drive from Sonamarg on the National Highway in the direction of the dZoji La/ Ladâkh. Two roads branch off from the highway to the right. Both lead to Bâltal. The first of these is not in a good condition for vehicles, but is recommended for trekkers. After you have driven 9 km. from Sonamarg, you will come to a point called Rangâ. The second side road branches off to the right from here. The road is rough. Bâltal is 4.5 km. from Rangâ.

Baltal seen from the Zozila Pass during the Amarnath Yatra

From Bâltal it is a very steep, mostly uphill, seven to nine-hour journey to the Holy Cave. The return takes only a little less. So, if you leave Bâltal at four in the morning, allowing for an hour or two at the Holy Cave of Sri Amarnâth ji, you can be back at Bâltal by ten or eleven that night. The slope can be dangerously slippery on the way back.

Personally, I prefer taking the picturesque Pahalgâm route to the Holy Cave and the shorter Bâltal route for the return journey.

Where to stay

The choice along the route is between tents pitched by the public sector and tents of the unorganised private sector. During the *yatra*, tents and kitchens are set up by private as well as public agencies at the four important halts (Chandanwari, Shesh Nag, the holy cave itself and Bâltal). You can expect to rent a bed (and, often, blankets or sleeping bags) in a six-or eight-bed tent for a nominal fee. (1999 rates were: Rs.45 per bed at Chandanwari, Rs.60 at the Holy Cave, and prices in between at the halts en route.)

Free cooked food, too, is available at all the important halts. Charitable organisations from Haryana, the Punjab and Delhi vie with one another to serve free vegetarian meals and snacks to all pilgrims. Except that these meals are soaked in pure ghee (or vegetable oil), they taste very good. As a result, food stalls that charge for the food that they serve have been driven out of business.

How to get there: Those who are unable to climb mountains, but want to do the yatra all the same, can hire ponies. These ponies are hardly inexpensive because they have to be fed and maintained throughout the year for a 40-day *yatra*. The very old and the infirm tend to hire *palanquins* that are even more expensive. Helicopter services started in 2003.

Medical facilities

Special dispensaries are set up at the two roadheads, Pahalgâm and Bâltal. Considering the circumstances, the facilities are quite good and include X-ray machines. There are male doctors at the major halts, (Shesh Nag, Panjtarni and Chandanwari). They are available for (free) consultation and advice. They also have some (free) medicines: naturally never enough considering that more than two-thirds of the pilgrims actually consult at least one of these doctors.

Dangers

If you are even slightly unfit you should trek these mountains very carefully because a very large number of people tend to throw up at those high altitudes. There is no escaping sunburn either. As I learnt the hard way, a cap, sunglasses, full-sleeved shirts, vaseline and sunscreen lotion are a must.

Around 25,000 pilgrims tend to visit each of the five government-run medical camps along the route every year. Some of them have serious ailments. Every year one or two pilgrims (out of a total of almost 1,90,000) die during the journey, because of the strain. In years when there are snowstorms the death toll is much higher. Internationally, there are upper-age (and obesity) limits for people who want to climb such high mountains. Attempts to even suggest that the old and unfit should not perform this *yatra* have wilted under the wrath of the system. At the very least yatris should not come in rubber bathroom slippers and thin cotton clothes, as almost half of them do. It can be very cold at night: close to zero at some of the camps.

In 1928, there was a major natural disaster, perhaps unseasonal snowfall, at Aastan Marg and Hatiyara Talao (lit.: the murderous pond). Several pilgrims died. Between August 22 and 24, 1996, heavy rains and unexpected snow trapped thousands of pilgrims and their porters. As many as 173 of them died because of the cold, the stampede and by slipping off slopes. While unforeseen snowstorms can not be prevented, panic can perhaps be. In 2000, 2001 and 2002, armed terrorists killed some pilgrims.

Tips

The pilgrimage is strenuous even from the Pahalgâm side. You have to climb up to the Mahagunas pass (14.400'), which is as high as the highest peak in Europe. Therefore, the old, the infirm and the very young (under 12) are advised not to undertake the pilgrimage at all. Besides, the entire Bâltal route is meant only for the truly fit.

Don't let me scare you, though. Lots of unfit, middle-aged people do the trek from the Pahalgâm side every year. However, do get yourself examined medically.

You might like to go up to the Holy Cave by the gentler, three-day, Pahalgâm route, and come down by the shorter, steeper, seven-hour Bâltal route.

Night temperatures along the route are close to zero. So please bring adequate woollens along. Even if you skip gloves, carry woollen socks and a warm cap. If it is sunny, during the day you'll just need a T-shirt, but stick to a full-sleeved shirt to avoid sunburn.

Try to stay close to the pony that carries your supplies and luggage.

Don't walk faster than your body can take.

In 1996, one of the government servants employed along the route was killed when an explosive device (planted by terrorists) went off.

Religious lore connected with the places en route

The darshan/Holy Cave

Pt. Basantlal Vyas of Mathura, writing perhaps in the 1990s, promises that, 'Humans become like immortal Gods just by looking at [i.e. by a *darshan* of] the Amrawati. Bathe in the *amrit* [loosely: ambrosia/ nectar]-like waters [of the Amrawati 'river']. Smear ash on your body. Your body will become white because of the holy ash. Now climb the hill of Lord Amarnâth either naked or wrapped in *bhoj patra* [birch bark]. Dance as you climb and enter the Amarnâth Cave.'

Today-since at least the 1950s-only the naked sadhus do this, not the common man. However, apparently this was not always so.

A 19th century British account describes the scene thus, '[The pilgrims perform] their ablutions in the *Am[a]r Veyut* [the Amrawati], the stream which flows at the bottom; the men divest themselves of all clothing, and enter the cave either entirely naked, or with pieces of birch-bark, which do duty for fig leaves. The women content themselves for the most part with laying aside all superfluous articles of clothing, and shrouding themselves in a long sheet or blanket.' (The *Gazetteer*.)

Elsewhere, Pt. Vyas warns, 'Those who wear impure clothes or do not pray or do not donate money during the *darshan* are consigned to hell. Those who do not smear themselves with holy ash during the *darshan* become lepers in future births.' I hope he is exaggerating. Because I don't recall smearing myself with ash during any of my numerous *darshans*.

Kular/ Khaylan—the Bâl Khilya pilgrimage

In ancient times, the celibate Bâl Khilya saints decided to please God by undertaking a very difficult prayer. For thousands of years they prayed, standing on their big toes, eating nothing and controlling not only their actions but also their desires. Lord Vishnu was, indeed, pleased. He appeared before the saints, who emerged from deep prayer and bowed before the Lord. They requested Lord Vishnu to create a pilgrimage where they could obtain *siddhi* (a form of salvation; literally, 'perfection').

Lord Vishnu touched the ground with his big toe. The Bhagwati Ganga, a river, emerged from the spot that he had thus touched. This area is, therefore, known to the devout as the Narayan pilgrimage as well.

Mamal—the Mâmaleshwar pilgrimage

There once lived a devotee of Lord Shiva, a man called Mâmlak. His prayer so impressed Lord Shiva that the Lord decided to live at the place that is now called Mamal. After a while Lord Shiva decided to move on. On his way he rested for a spell at Saint Dandak's hermitage, which is above Khilnak. Some angels saw him there and came down to meet him.

Lord Shiva cried out to the angels, 'Mâ! Mâ!' (Don't [come here]! Don't [come here]!) Lord Ganpati, who lived in Pâtâl, the Hindu Hades, emerged from beneath the ground on hearing the words, 'Mâ! Mâ!' The angels, too, immersed themselves in the words 'Mâ! Mâ!' and attained salvation. That is how this place came to be called Mâmal.

Lord Shiva then appointed Lord Ganesh the guardian of the two courtyards here.

The story of River Lambodari

Once when Lord Shiva and the Goddess Parvati were still on Mount Kailash they wanted to converse undisturbed. So they asked Lord Ganesh and Nandi to guard the door and screen out all unwelcome visitors.

In those days, Tripurasur, a demon, had been terrorising the angels (devtâs). So, led by Lord Indra, the angels came to meet Lord Shiva. Lord Ganesh stopped them from going in. This offended Indr, the rain god, who started lashing at him with thunderbolts and lightning. Lord Ganesha reacted by merely growling. That was enough to paralyse one of Indra's arms.

Indr knew that he had erred. He bowed before Lord Ganesh and started chanting melodious prayers in a praise of the elephant-headed deity. Ganesh was pleased. He forgave Indr and set his arm right. Indr returned to the land of angels.

However, all that anger and growling made Lord Ganesh feel very hungry-and thirsty. So he ate a lot of fruit-and drank up the entire Ganges. This caused his belly to swell enormously. When Lord Shiva emerged from his chamber he noticed that the Ganges had dried up. He prodded Ganesh's stomach with his hand-held, double-headed drum.

This caused a river to start flowing from Lord Ganesh's stomach. The ancients knew the river variously as the Lambodari and the Lambodari Ganga. It is said that if a person bathes in this river, all his sins get cleansed.

Pahalgâm—the Bhrigupati pilgrimage

In ancient times there was a maharishi, a great saint, called Bhrigu. He went to the Parisheelan forest to pray. His prayer was so intense that after Bhrigu had been at it for a thousand years, Lord Vishnu, accompanied by other Gods, appeared before the saint.

Bhrigu was so overjoyed that he began repeating a prayer in praise of Vishnu and bowing repeatedly before the Lord. Bhrigu's devotion pleased Sri Vishnu. He clasped the saint against his chest. As they did so, a drop of sweat rolled down from their bodies and fell in the Parisheelan forest.

Pahalgâm, called the Land of Bhrigu by some, is said to have been created where that drop fell.

The Ranjanopal and the Neel Ganga

(Ranjanopal must be the woods just before Chandanwari and the Neel Ganga the river that flows there.)

Ranjanopal: Lord Ram, Sri Lakshman and Sita ji passed through these woods during their 14-year exile. When demons suddenly appeared before the Lord, he broke into a sweat. Drops of Sri Ram's sweat dropped to the ground and created holy pools here. He then killed the demons. The little hillocks of this region turned red because of the demons' blood. The parts that Sri Ram walked on became green.

The Neel Ganga: Lord Shiva's lips once touched Goddess Parvati's eyes. The kohl on her eyes blackened the Lord's lips. So he washed them with the water of the Holy Ganges. This caused the waters that he had rinsed his lips with to grow dark. It was thus that the river here came to be called 'the Blue Ganges.'

Chandanwari—the Sthânv Aashram

It is said that it was in these chandan (sandalwood)-like woods that the Goddess Parvati worshipped Lord Shiva, her future husband, through severe, self-denying prayer and meditation. At times, being all alone in these woods would scare Parvati ji. However, the Lord was so deeply lost in his own meditation that he wasn't even aware of the Goddess' prayers.

Pissu Ghati—the Peshnâkhya hill

Once the angels and the demons decided to go to the mountains for a *darshan* (glimpse) of the Divine Couple, Shiva and Parvati. Each group wanted to be the first to climb the hill. This resulted in a battle between the gentle angels and the ferocious demons. The frightened angels started praying to Lord Shiva for protection. Lord Shiva bestowed his blessings on the angels. This enabled them to grind the demons to dust. The dust piled up into a huge heap that was known to the ancients as the Peshnâkhya hill and to us as the Pissu Ghati.

The Shesh Nag

Angels from the Siddh and Gandharv clans once went on a pilgrimage to Sri Amarnâth ji. There was a demon that had, through prayer, grown enormously powerful and arrogant. He could become like the wind. So, he started scattering the angels about.

The angels, led by Indra, went to Lord Shiva for his protection. The Lord agreed that the demon was behaving wickedly. But, he told the angels, he had given the demon a boon, therefore he could not destroy him. So, could they go to Lord Vishnu instead?

They did. Lord Vishnu came over with all his weapons. He also persuaded Shesh Nâg, the lord of the serpents, to come over from *Pâtâl* (the Hindu Hades). Shesh Nag has the power to swallow the wind. Therefore, Lord Vishnu gave Shesh Nag the task of eating up the wind-like demon, then and for all times to come.

Parts of the Amarnâth Yatra route are prone to very, almost devilishly, strong winds. I have been to the Shesh Nag area four times and each time it was calm. Perhaps it always remains so. Hence the legend that the Shesh Nag had devoured the winds. Incidentally, Nâg means 'snake' as well as 'lake.' So there's a pun hidden in the name.)

Wâwjan—the Vâyu Varjan pilgrimage

After the angels had killed most of the demons, an ogre called *Prishtat* teamed up with the winds to torment the angels. (Yet another reference to the winds' torment.) Lord Shiva told the angels that if they were to build a little hermitage of stones, the stones would stop the winds. The angels did so and were able to live there peacefully—for a while.

One day the ogre decided to bother them again. Lord Indra, the Chief of the angels, killed the demon with a thunderbolt (vajra). Since then the place has been known as the *Vâyu (wind) Varjan* pilgrimage.

The Hatiyara Talab/ Talao (pond)

The few demons that survived the onslaughts of the Lords Shiva and Indra began to trouble the angels, as well as the saints who had gone there to meditate. The Goddess Parvati asked her husband to help the angels and the saints. Lord Shiva called out in anger. His voice frightened the demons, who turned themselves into fish and other water animals and sought refuge in this pond. Lord Shiva was unhappy that the pond had given protection to beings that had caused pain to saints. Therefore, he caused the pond to dry up. The demons ran away.

Pilgrims are expected to be silent when they pass this waterless pond. Hatiyara means 'murderous.'

The Panjtarni

Once when Lord Shiva was performing the Tândav dance his top knotted hair got loosened. The Ganges, which lives in that topknot, flowed down to the ground in the form of five (panj) streams. Together they are known to the devout as the Panjtarni Ganga.

The immortal Lord Amaresh and the Amravati river

While Planet Earth was being created, the angels, including Lord Indra, turned into mortals. Now even they had to die someday. This made them panic. They went to Lord Shiva and begged him to make them immortal once again.

Lord Shiva promised the frightened angels, 'I will protect you from the fear of death.' He pulled Amâ, the crescent moon, out of his top-knotted hair and squeezed it. Amrit, the nectar that makes immortal all those who drink it, began to flow out. This jet of amrit went on to become the Amarvati river. Some drops fell on the Lord's chest, dried up and then dropped to the ground. These became the ice lingam in the Holy Cave. The lingam is variously known as Lord Amaresh, Lord Amareshewar and Lord Amarnâth. Lord Shiv said, 'Whoever looks at my lingam in the (holy Amarnâth) cave will stop dreading death.' The Lord also caused Amâ, the crescent moon, to eclipse from *amâvasya* (the new moon night) to the full moon night.

'Amar' means 'immortal.' The word 'amrit' is derived from 'amar.' 'Nath' means 'Lord/ master.' The lingam at the Holy Cave is said to guard people from death and grant them salvation. Therefore, it came to be called Amarnâth. However, the same legend also says that the words 'Amarnâth,' 'Amareshwar' etc., are derived from Amâ, the crescent moon, and not Amar.

The pigeons in the Holy Cave

Lord Shiva was once engrossed in dance. Two of his disciples, who were jealous of each other, started quarrelling. Their pigeon-like cackling disturbed the Lord's concentration. He decreed that the disciples would be converted into pigeons forever. They would live in the holy Amarnâth cave and their cackling would rid pilgrims of all their troubles.

If pilgrims say 'Jai!' ('Glory!') when they see the pigeons in the Holy Cave, they become 'somewhat like Lord Shiva.' To return from the Cave without having seen the pigeons is to 'betray the pilgrimage.'

The 'Muhammad' mountain

The Amarnâth Yatra takes places today because a Kashmîrî Muslim family re-discovered the cave. God clearly willed that the place be dear to both the Hindus and the Muslims. If you stand at the Holy Cave, with your back to the cave, and look at the tall rocky mountain directly in front of it, you will notice a natural pattern in the grains of the rocks.

Just below the peak, on the right is a dark cave-like depression. A very, very thick band travels from the cave to the left, horizontally. The colour of this band is lighter than that of the rocks above and below it. It consists of several horizontal lines, parallel to each other, like lines in sheet music. It is as if some divine hand ran its fingers on this rock, first horizontally and then diagonally, within this band. And as the hand moved, the fingers left their mark behind.

When the band finishes its horizontal, leftward (eastward) travel, it comes down diagonally, i.e. rightward/ westward, for a short while. It then goes down diagonally to the left till it almost touches the ground. From there it makes another circle. It then travels up, east/leftward, at a gentle angle towards a dry nallah and then to the rocky mountain on the left. From there it comes down in a curve, leftward, towards the ground.

The band is too thick and, because of its colour, too distinct to miss: or to be wishful thinking. The parallel lines travel horizontally and then go up and down along with the band.

Seen from the Holy Cave, the band spells 'Muhammad' in Arabic. By placing this mountain on the other side of the river from the Holy Cave, with a gorge in between, God seems to have ensured that even in the distant future there will be no room for conflict. Indeed, the divine signal seems to be that this place is holy for everyone, regardless of religion.

Flora and fauna

Wildlife: Marmots are the real inhabitants of the area. It's just that this shy creature probably goes into hiding when the place is overwhelmed by thousands of pilgrims, who travel in an almost non-stop procession throughout the daylight hours. After the *yatra* is over the marmots come out in bigger numbers than perhaps anywhere else in the state. Butterflies and rare birds, too, are best seen before or after the yatra.

Marmot

In 1981, Gp. Capt. J.S. Kahlon was flying a helicopter over the stretch that leads to the dZoji La. He says that when he flew over a lake (which is not on the pilgrim route) he spotted a *Yeti* (abominable snowman). The human-like creature ran into a cave when he saw the chopper.

Herbs and flowers: If you climb up from Chandanwari, then after Mahagunas you will come to Posh Pathri ('flower-stone'). Some flowers grow there with an odour so strong that horses faint on smelling it. Therefore, the owners of horses and ponies always pull their steeds away from this patch. The more experienced horses and ponies avoid it on their own.

Jogi Bâdshâh ('the hermit-emperor') is the king of medicinal herbs as far as the Bakerwâl tribals are concerned. This is a flower that grows only on mountains that are so high and difficult to climb that 'the voice of no woman or dog can reach or be heard there, only Allah's voice.' Its extract is said to cure diabetes and 'stomach ailments' (mainly dyspepsia and acidity). It is also presented as a gift to important people, because of its rarity. The flower has five to ten spots that look like eyes. Therefore, even educated Bakerwâls consider it a 'living creature' (i.e. an animal). They believe that the flower can see people. When they cut the flower from its stem they place a tiny lump of salt on the stem at the place where the flower had been. They believe that if this is not done it will rain even on a sunny day. The flower is found in the nearby Sârbal mountain and Nîl Grâth (near Sonamarg).

Patrees (known as Pivak to the Kashmîrîs) is a bitter-tasting herb that is used in Western medicines. Pickers are paid Rs.2000 for every kilogram (2001 rates). In the market it fetches several times that. It grows throughout the Tilel-Sonamarg belt.

Chhindî/dubbâ is a fibre that dealers from Delhi and Amritsar buy from here. They pay Rs.4,000 for every quintal of the dried stuff. It is used in the manufacture of cloth and cloth-based shoes. If you climb from Sangam to the Holy Cave (from the Baltal side), then just before the final climb look at the mountain across the rivulet. The whitish patches on it are chhindis.

Other Amarnâths

The Buddha Amarnâth of Poonch (Jammû) is already quite popular. There is definitely a similar Shivling in a cave at Domel on the Raman Nalah (stream) in Tilail (Bârâmullâ). It is not as tall as its counterpart at Amarnâth, and melts faster. There is a belief that there is an ice shivling in Zâñskâr (Ladâkh), too. Someday I hope to verify this legend for myself.

Modern developments

In October 2000, Dr. Farooq Abdullah, Chief Minister of Jammû & Kashmîr, enacted a legislation to create the Sri Amarnâthji Shrine Board, on the lines of the hugely successful Sri Mata Vaishno Devi ji Shrine Board. This author had the honour of drafting the bill and being appointed the founding-Chief Executive Officer of the Board. I got the Baltal route widened substantially.

Chapter- 8

Hazratbal

Hazratbal is one of the most venerable shrines for the Muslims of Kashmîr because in it is preserved a hair from the beard of Muhammad, the Holy Prophet, respectfully called Hazrat Muhammad, peace be upon him. The Kashmîri "bal" is pronounced to rhyme with the English words "hull" and "gull" and probably means "the banks of a lake". A similarly spelt Hindi/ Urdu word (but pronounced "baal") means hair. This has led to many non-Kashmîri writers (Indian as well as foreign) to assume that Hazratbal means "the prophet's hair". A better translation of the name of this famous shrine would be "the prophet's lake".

That 'bal' does not refer to hair is certain. Equally definitely it means 'place'. However, beyond that 'bal' could mean one of many kinds of places, such as 'banks of river or lake', 'a place where there is a natural spring' or even 'rendezvous; a meeting place'. Hazrat is an Arabic word meaning "sir" or "signor". The word 'bal' is of Dravidian or Shînâ origin.

The Moo-e-Muqaddas (Holy Hair) was brought from Lahore to Kashmîr by Khwaja Noor-ud-Din of Ishber (or Ishâwar), in 1700, during the reign of Aurangzeb (some writers mistakenly say Shah Jehan). In those days the place where the Dargah (shrine) is presently located is said to have been a garden, the Sher Khân Bagh. (from *Tazkara-e-Auliya* by Hassan Khuyami, the 19th century historian.)

Hazratbal

Festive Occasions/Display of the Relic

The Moo-e-Muqaddas is exhibited (in the casket in which it has been preserved) on several important occasions every year. *The Gazetteer* notes, "Numerous boats of various sizes are (on such occasions) ranged along the stone quay on the border of the open space intervening between the lake and the sacred edifice in which the relic is preserved. Sikhs, Hindus, and Kashmîris (sic) of both sexes, and of all ranks and ages, are there for the purposes of seeing and being seen; the Muhammadans crowd around the door from which the sacred relic is exhibited, and breathe forth their aspirations, whilst they touch the glass and press their lips and forehead against it with looks of the most extreme awe and veneration.

"There is also a tree near the Hazratbal, which is said to have been brought as a cutting from Mecca.

"Five or six fairs are held at the Hazratbal in the course of the year; the principal one is on the Mairaj [better known as the Shab-e-Meraj-PD], or the day on which Muhammad rode to heaven upon the mule [horse-PD] Al Borak (the Thunderer). Another great fair, held about the 1st of August, is called the Watul Myla, or fair of the Watuls [char-people; "sweepers"-PD], because that tribe intermarry on that day. Everyone that has time comes to the lake, the poorer classes on foot, and a succession of feasting, singing, and naaching [dancing?-PD] is kept up for forty-eight hours, and the entertainments are enlivened by the performances of itinerant bards."

The Watul Mélâ is a tradition that started disappearing in the 20th century. The Holy Relic is mainly displayed on the Jummat-ul-vidâ, the Eid-e-Milâd-un-Nabî (peace be on him) and the Shab-e-Meraj. The two main Eids are great festivals for the shrine but not ones on which the Relic is displayed.

Other shrines in Kashmîr that possess relics of the Holy Prophet (pbuh), too, display relics only on these days. These shrines are Kaabamarg, Khirram Sirhama and seer (all Ânañtnâg), Pinjoora Sahib (Pulwâmâ) and Jenab sahib, Soura (Srînagar)

If you are unable to go to Hazratbal on a festive occasion, going there on a Friday noon (around 1 pm.) will be a fair substitute. Devotees come in very large numbers on Fridays. Exotic foodstuffs-especially gigantic local 'bread' eaten with a paste of sweetened grain-are sold in the nearby market.

Women are not allowed inside the sanctum. As at other Muslim shrines in Kashmîr they look into the shrine and offer prayers at various viewpoints along the walls of the shrine. All Muslim shrines in Kashmîr (and elsewhere) are called *dargâhs* or *ziyârats*. However, if a Kashmîri mentions *dargâh* without specifying which one, he means Hazratbal. Do keep that in mind when asking for directions and when you hear bus conductors calling out destinations.

A Brief History of the Holy Relic and the Shrine[i]

Imam Hussain, one of the most venerable figures of Islâm, was the son of Hazrat Fatima, who in turn was the daughter of Hazrat Muhammad, peace be on him, the prophet of Islâm. Hussain was bequeathed some relics of the Holy Prophet, mostly hair from the beard.

One of these relics, the one now in Hazratbal, was passed down the generations to his descendant, Syed Abdullah of Mecca. (All descendants of the Holy Prophet are known as Syeds.) On account of some litigation that Abdullah was involved in, he was stripped of his citizenship by his government.

So in 1634, the Syed left Mecca and emigrated to Bijapur, where he was given a largeish estate by the Indian rulers, perhaps on account of his exalted ancestry. However, shortly thereafter Aurangzeb became the Mughal emperor and forfeited this estate, evicting Abdullah's son Syed Hamid from it.

Hamid went to Delhi to get the estate restored. There he met Khwaja Noor-ud-Din, a wealthy philanthropist from Srînagar. (The Khwaja is also known as Kh. Noor-ud-Din Aishawari, the last word often being mispronounced 'Ashbarry' or 'Ishberi'. His ancestors had probably migrated from Aishâwar in Central Asia. It is incorrectly believed that he was from Ishber, a village near the Nishât Gardens.) According to one version it was the Khwaja who had travelled to the Deccan from whence he obtained the Holy Relic from the younger Syed.

The precise details of the transaction between the Syed and the Khwaja are not known. Some say that the relic was gifted to the Khwaja. Others have it that the Khwaja purchased it from the Syed. In any case it does seem certain that the Khwaja had helped Hamid in some way and had thus put him under his obligation.

One source claims that the Khwaja had paid one lakh rupees to the Syed for the Holy Relic. (According to Sir Walter Lawrence, a 19th century British historian, who was obviously going by secondary sources, it was Syed Abdullah who gave the relic to the Khwaja. This can not be correct because Abdullah had died before Aurangzeb ascended to the throne.)

The Khwaja thus became the first resident of Kashmîr to receive a relic of the Prophet of Islâm, peace be on him. In his excitement he set out for Kashmîr, via Lahore. The Syed sent his attendant Kh. Maidanish, who had been the guardian of the Holy Relic, along with Kh. Noor-ud-Din.

It was when Noor-ud-Din reached Lahore that Aurangzeb got to know that the Khwaja had obtained the Holy Relic. He sent soldiers to force Kh. Noor-ud-Din to give up the Holy Relic. The emperor then sent the relic to Ajmer to be kept in the shrine of Khwaja Moinuddin Chishti. The loss was too much for Kh. Noor-ud-Din to bear. He died of the shock.

Meanwhile, it is said, Aurangzeb had a visitation in a dream in which he was reprimanded for having obtained the Holy Relic by force. So on the ninth day of confiscating it, Aurangzeb sent for Kh. Maidanish and returned the Holy Relic. On learning of Kh. Noor-ud-Din's death, Aurangzeb arranged to get Kh. Noor-ud-Din's coffin sent to Srînagar. This was on the 10th March, 1700.

The Holy Relic and the coffin travelled to Srînagar via Shopian and reached the city's Haft Chinâr area on the 5th April, 1700.

At the time Fâzil Khân was the Mughal governor of Kashmîr. On his orders the Holy Relic was kept in the Naqshband Sahib shrine of downtown Srînagar. But the crowds that came to see the Holy Relic were so large that a more commodious home had to be found. The choice fell on the lakeside orchards (bâgh) of the Mughal noble Sher Khân. (Sadiq Khân, according to another account.)

Out of deference for the public sentiment, Sher/ Sadiq Khân donated his huge mansion, located amidst the orchard, to house the Holy Relic. And out of respect for Kh. Noor-ud-Din, the good Khwaja was buried in the compound of the Holy Relic's new shrine, which was now given the name Hazratbal.

Kh. Noor-ud-Din had no son, so his daughter Anâyat Begum, and her husband Khwaja Bullaqee Banday, became the keepers of the Holy Relic. Since the relic had to be displayed to the public on important religious occasions, Banday was given the task of doing so. However, the responsibility obviously overwhelmed Banday, who could not handle large crowds, which included religious elders and the power elite. So he asked a kindly person, Shaikh Radhoo Mohhamed Chishti to take over instead.

Radhoo was thus the first keeper of the relic. On his death it passed back to Banday, who proved equal to the task this time around.

A contemporary, Mirza Qalandar Beg, was at hand to record all these events in his book "*Hujajiti Qasirah*".

Almost a hundred years later, when Kashmîr was under the Pathans, it is said that Âzâd Khân, the governor of Kashmîr, had doubts about the genuineness of the Holy Relic, as do some Muslims outside Kashmîr. (Pristine Islâm frowns at such 'idolatry'.)

In a fit of malice, Khân broke the glass tube that contained the Holy Relic. He used a (hair) tweezer to pull the Holy Relic out. Legend has it that then a miracle took place. Not only did the holy hair not come out, its tip, which was caught in the tweezer, started getting sucked inwards into what remained of the tube.

Âzâd Khân later died a painful, miserable death.

Every mosque in cold climes has a hammâm which consists of a heated room (in Kashmîr this is done by heating stones below the floor) and warm water for the wuzoo (ablutions performed before each prayer). The original Hammâm Masjid (mosque) at Hazratbal was constructed in 1798 by Nawab Ahsanullah Khân of Dhaka (formerly Dacca), a noble of Kashmîri origin.

The 1940s: The MAT takes charge

In the 1940s, Sheikh Muhammad Abdullah, who went on to become the first Prime Minister (and later Chief Minister) of independent Jammû and Kashmîr, and his colleagues, took over the management of the shrine, through the MAT (Muslim Auqâf Trust). Since then a nominee of the MAT has normally read the Friday sermon. He happens to be a member of the Banday clan. The Sheikh was the Chief Trustee of the MAT. Dr. Farooq Abdullah, later the Chief Minister of J&K, inherited his father'sposition in the MAT.

The Sheikh was enormously popular. His followers came from all over rural Kashmîr (and Jammû and Ladâkh), and are generally known as the shér (lion) people, after his title "the lion of Kashmîr".

Those of his politico-religious rival, on the other hand, were concentrated in the "inner city" of Srînagar, and their leader manages the Jâmâ Masjid. This group was known as the bakra (buckraa; goat) "party" because of the goatee beards of some of their leaders. Relations between the two groups used to be extremely tense and if a wife's parents belonged to the other group, she would have to put up with considerable coldness from her husband and in-laws if there had been a sher-bakra clash recently. However, since the mid-1980s, relations have improved considerably, after the younger leaders of the two groups initiated an *entente.*

The Winter of 1963/ 1964: The Relic Disappears

On the 27th December, 1963, all of India was rocked when the Moo-e-Muqaddas suddenly disappeared.

A committee of the leading religious figures of Kashmîr was formed. It was called the Majlis-e-Amal-e-Husooli-e-Moo-e-Muqaddas (lit.: the action committee for the restoration of the holy hair). The then Mîrwaiz, Maulvi Muhammad Farooq, was its Chairman and Maulana Masoodi its Secretary General.

To the Kashmîri Muslim this is the most revered symbol of Islâm outside Mecca and Madina. A hundred thousand people, distraught at the loss, gathered at the Lal Chowk to seek solace in the words of Maulana Masoodi, who was to address them.

Just then it started to snow. Those who had brought umbrellas along reached for them. But one of the speakers forbade the crowd from seeking the protection of umbrellas. So the crowd listened to the Maulana for an hour and a half, unmindful of the two inches of snow that gathered on their heads and shoulders.

While the Kashmîris claim that this is one of the many miracles associated with the Holy Relic, this certainly shows the discomfort they are prepared to endure for it.

Things quietened after the Holy Relic was recovered, equally mysteriously, on the 4th January, 1964. A committee of experts vouched for the genuineness of the relic that was recovered.

The then Deputy Prime Minister of India, Lal Bahadur Shastri, and the Prime Minister of Jammû and Kashmîr, Shamsuddin, were present at the identification, along with the members of the Majlis (committee), leading saints, and the keeper of the shrine, Ghulam Muhammad Farooqui.

When the Holy Relic was brought out for identification, Shamsuddin "fainted and fell on the ground" (-Hagroo).

Syed Mirak Shah Kâhshâni was easily the most respected saint in all of Kashmîr at the time. There are several legends associated with this modern day saint and it was said that Allah would never deny him a wish. He was also said to be clairvoyant.

Syed Mirak's testimony was an important factor in accepting the relic that had been recovered as the genuine object. Farooqui's was the other critical vote in its favour. In the event there was unanimity that the relic was the original one. Among other things, there can be no doubt that the glass casket containing the Holy Relic was the same.

1967: A new building

Because of its massive following and political stature Hazratbal needed bigger premises. The J&K Muslim Auqaf Trust built the present mosque and ziyârat, as well as the Hamam Masjid, in 1967. Hazratbal has since been housed in one of the most impressive post-war mosques anywhere in the world-a modern, Indo-Islâmic (rather than Indo-Saracenic) building. It was the first shrine of importance in all of Kashmîr built in this modern, pan-Indian style. (The example has been infectious. Hardly any shrine or mosque built in Kashmîr after that has been in the traditional Iranian-Kashmîrî style.)

On the 21st February, 1992, the Madinatul Aloom, a religious school in the premises, its irreplaceable library and its mosque were set on fire. This fire also caused some damage to the Hamam Mosque.

Events of the 1990s Occupation and Siege of 1993

The fire was only one of the many traumas that Hazratbal had to go through during the 1990s. Indeed, the fortunes of Kashmîr's beloved shrine during that turbulent decade mirrored the ups and downs of Kashmîr itself. Various militant groups took control of the shrine in 1990. An inter-group scuffle took place on a stage in the shrine's premises later that year.

On Friday, the 15th October, 1993, the Holy Relic was once again the centre of a major crisis. A local policeman reported that an attempt had been made to tamper with one of the locks that secured the Holy Relic.

Government forces surrounded the shrine and laid siege in an attempt to get the armed militants inside the shrine to surrender. Some devotees also got trapped inside.

After a 32-day siege, during which life in the urban areas of Kashmîr came to a standstill as never before, on the 16th November, 1993, the militants (and the devotees) came out of the shrine and were taken into custody by the police. They left their assault rifles and explosives behind in the shrine, from where the army recovered them. The whole episode, fortunately, was bloodless.

In 1994, control of the shrine lapsed back into the militants' hands: and remained with them till the end of March 1996. Then the state police flushed the militants out after a prolonged encounter. Thirty-two people died in that incident.

However, after that the militants could not regain control of the shrine. The MAT moved back. It stayed there for the next seven years.

September 2003: The government takes over from the MAT

In September 2003 the state government assumed direct charge of Hazratbal and several other Muslim shrines thitherto controlled by the MAT.

References

i. Many parts of this section are based on Ghulam Nabi Hagroo's *History of the Holy Relic-Hazrat Bal*. The 20th century parts are based on the author's own notes and conversations with Ahmed Ali Fayyaz of the *Daily Excelsior*. G.R. Bhat has written a book on the subject in Urdu. The reference to Aishâwar are based on conversations with him.

Chapter- 9

Hindus and Hinduism in ancient Kashmir

The Mahabharat era It can safely be assumed from the available chronology that Gonanda I, the earliest known king of Kashmîr, ruled around 2,500 BC. Mediæval historian Kalhan tells us that Gonanda I assumed power twenty years before the Mahabharat war. He was on the side of the Kauravs, being a relative of Jarasand of Magadh.

The Nagas And why does Kashmîr get so cold in winter? Kalhan's *Rajatarangini* tells us that at some stage the Kashmîris stopped worshipping the Nagas and became Buddhists instead. This angered the Nagas who decreed that Kashmîr would be very cold in winter. The Nagas are a recurrent theme in the history of KashmirThey were among the earliest settlers, were Shaivites and later some of them became Buddhists. Their descendants founded the Karkota dynasty around AD 627.

Lalitaditya's all-India outreach King Lalitaditya Lalitaditya- Muktapida (AD 725- 753 or 724-761) defeated King Javita Gupt, who ruled over Gaur and Magadh (Bengal and Bihar, respectively). Karnataka, Gujarât and Mahârâshtra were the next to fall to his might. He overran the seven Konkans (which include Keralâ, Goa, parts of Maharashtra and what is still known as Konkan).

The Kashmîrîs settle in- and rule and influence- Keralâ

The migration of Saraswat Brâhmins: During the course of four unconnected field studies (in Goa and Mahârâshtra and about Karla and the Mangalore area), I noticed a tendency among the Saraswat Brâhmins to trace their ancestry to KashmîrThis is also true of the Christians of the Konkan. Many of them claim that their ancestors were Saraswats before their conversion to Christianity. Even some Maharashtrian Barhmins make this claim. These Saraswats say that their ancestors had migrated from Kashmîr around the turn of the previous millennium- perhaps with the Shankarâchârya, when he returned from Srinagar to Keralâ.

The very Kashmîri complexion and light eyes of people like Miss World Aishwarya Rai (whose community, too, claims a Kashmîrî origin) indicates that there might be something to this belief. It would be rewarding to study the family trees of such Konkanese people to trace their roots to particular villages in Kashmîr.

P.V. Mathew[i] takes this theme forward enormously by offering irrefutable evidence- and making startling (and pathbreaking) claims. For instance, he says that 'Kashmîrî culture reached Keralâ almost twelve centuries back, which also paved the way for the *formation of [the] 'Malayalam' language.*' (Emphasis mine.)

Mathew's theory: Kashmîr's links with Keralâ

Karnataka fell into Lalitaditya's lap without much effort. Not only Queen Ratta but also the people of the state welcomed the Kashmîrî conqueror 'and offered [him] hospitality.' Apparently Keralâ (then called Cherânâd) had been devastated only a few centuries before by a storm of meteors. This seems to have destroyed the cities—and also the high culture—of Keralâ. So, when Lalitaditya came calling he does not seem to have 'encountered any king [or] for that matter any cultured people,' Mathew tells us. He did meet some aboriginal people, though.

Mathew adds, 'It is this king who first gets mentioned in the legend of Keralâ as "Parasurâm", which word might be the shortened form of "Parihaspura" or "Parihasakeshwa".' [But Parasuram is also an ancient name in its own right.-PD]

This man called Parasurâm (presumably Lalitaditya) took over the entire Konkan tract between Goa (then called Gokarn) and Kanyâ Kumârî, because he had an army and the local people perhaps had none. They were too scattered in tribes to have put up a united front. Besides, as mentioned, they had no king. So, what did he do with the land? At least in Keralâ he gave it away to 64 Nambûdirî Brahmin families- 'the keepers of the temples'- whom he had brought with him from up north.

The Râjâtarañginî clearly mentions sixty-four royal gatekeepers, who represented the sixty- four main temples of Kashmîr. It adds that Lalitaditya sent them to construct a temple at Mahodayapura, on the lines of the temple at Mârtañd. Now, Mathew brilliantly reminds us, in those days Mahodayapuram was the Capital of Cherâ (Surâ) Nâd. It was later renamed Tirchendur. If further proof is needed, he adds, 'We can see to this day the statues of those sixty- four [gatekeepers] arranged in the Subrâhamani Swâmî temple at Tirchendur, in Tirunelveli districtof Tamil Nâdu.' Subrâhamani Swâmî is the same as Lord Mahodaya.

These sixty-four elected one of themselves as the ruler of Cherânâd. The second of these rulers was Pâñdî Perumal. Now the temple at Mârtañd is called the house of the Pâñdavs, or the Pâñdav Larî. Therefore, Mathew assumes that this ruler had come from Mârtañd.[1] The Perumals- and then the Kalâsékhar Varmâs- ruled Keralâ from the 8th to the 11th century AD. Mathew says that even the Varmâs had been sent from Kashmîr to rule Keralâ. He links them to Kashmîr's King Avantivarman. (That does explain things. I have always wondered how Keralâ's kings got the very North Indian surname Varma.)

Apparently in the eighth century, while some Kashmîrîs were Shaivite Hiñdûs, many followed the Manichæan religion.[2] This division was reflected absolutely in the religious composition of the sixty- four 'gatekeepers' from Kashmîr. Thirty- two of them were Shaivites and devotees of the Sun God. They settled north of the Alwaye River in Ernakulam.

Thirty-one of them were Manichæans and worshipped the Moon God. They colonised the area south of the river and their capital was Mahodayapuram. The sixty- fourth was the ruler, Cheraman Perumal, himself. He went to Mecca and probably converted to Islâm. The Kashmîrîs' inclination towards Islâm is, thus, as old as that.

Another important bit of evidence is that the currency in both 8th/ 9th Kashmîr and Cherânâd was the dinâr: as all of Kashmîr's old histories

1 There must be something to Mathew's theory. There is a place called Mârtañdam near Kanyâ Kumârî. Though it is in present-day Tamil Nadu, it is close to Kerala.

2 '[A] syncretic, dualistic religious philosophy taught by the Persian prophet Manes, combining elements of Zoroastrian, Christian, and Gnostic thought and opposed by the imperial Roman government, Neo-Platonist philosophers, and orthodox Christians.' From *The American Heritage® Dictionary of the English Language, Third Edition* © 1996 by Houghton Mifflin Company.

record. Mathew says that 'the old coins of Keralâ known as Parasûrâm Râssî is the Kashmîr [dinâr].'

Along with the good the Kashmîrîs took along social evils: the Devadâsî system, for instance, is mentioned in Kashmîr's old texts and vestiges of it are still found in Keralâ and several other Konkan regions.

Mathew's theory is extremely convincing- and exciting. However, he does stretch things a bit when he says that 'Nambûdiri Brâhmins from Keralâ [were] generally appointed as head priests in the majority of temples in Jammû region by the Dogrâ dynasty.' This particular claim does not stand to scrutiny. Neither during my considerable fieldwork in Jammû region nor during my colleague Anil Goswami's even more considerable experience with the temples of Jammû has either of us come across a single such case either at present or evidence of any during the Dogrâ era.

Secondly, he says that the Nâirs of Keralâ, too, are of Kashmîrî origin. Now, one can agree that *some* Nâirs- the masons and sculptors- almost certainly did, to build the Mahodaya temple at Tirchendur. They had perfected the art at Kashmîr's several stone temples. However, the Nâirs are hardly homogenous. They are divided horizontally into three major layers, with little inter- marriage at least with the third and least privileged layer. All of them could not have come from Kashmîr.

And then he says that Keralâ's matrilineal lineage, matriarchal society and polyandry came from Kashmîr. But was the incidence of polyandry in Kashmîr ever greater than in the rest of India, especially neighbouring Himachal Pradesh or Uttaranchal?

Shankarâchârya The great Shankarâchârya (AD 788- 820) is believed to have visited Kashmîr. Apparently he was influenced by Kashmîr's Shaivism.

There are several views about when the Adi Shankarâchârya was born. A second school believes that this was in AD 740. The Kanchi Math's records suggest that he might even have been born as early as in 509 BC.[3] Either way, he challenged the religious order that then dominated Kashmîr. Most people say that this religion was Buddhism. Mathew insists that it was Manichæa[n]ism. Again, either way, the scholar-saint succeeded in getting the people to see religion his way. Mathew says, 'He was the [one] who expounded the simple monistic theory [of Saivism] to counter the dualistic theory of Manichæ[an]ism.'

Poets, philosophers, creative men

Uncertain times sometimes unleash creativity. In the century that followed Queen Didda, Kashmîr produced several outstanding men of letters.

Shiva Nath Katju writes, 'For nearly 300 years beginning from the IX century A. D. till the commencement of XI century A.D. Kashmîr remained under the spell of the brilliant sages and savants who propounded the Kashmîr Shaivism and Trika Shastra. Their unbroken chain beginning from Shri Kantha and followed by Vasugupta, Kallata, Somananda, Utpalacharya, Lakshmana, Abhinavagupta, Khsemraja and Yogaraja raised Kashmîr Shaivism to sublime heights. After the Adi Shankarâchârya, no other sage or savant occupies such a dazzling place of honour among the Hindus than Mahamaheshwara Abhinavagupta.'

Abhinav Gupt, the Shaivite (born c. 950) was not only a charismatic preacher, he wrote extensively, mainly on philosophy. The Kashmîris, Hindus and Muslims alike, believe that he walked into a cave with twelve hundred disciples, never to emerge again. Dr. Sofi, quoting a 1935 dissertation by Dr. K.C.Pandey, places the said 'Bhairav cave' at 'about five miles from Magam, midway between Srinagar and Gulmarg'. (Not that Abhinav Gupt would have known it, but the first Christian millennium was about to come to an end. Such 'millenarian' behaviour took place towards the end of the twentieth century, too.)

Kshemendra, Kashmîrgreatest Sanskrit poet, wrote between 1037 and 1066, on subjects as diverse as music, medicine and grammar. He was born to a wealthy family near the present day Nishat Bâghof Srinagar. This enabled him to endow and maintain boarding schools in an era when scholars would come to Kashmîr from all over South (and, maybe, Central) Asia. Thirty- four of his books are still extant.

Bilhan, grammarian, poet and amateur historian, was born (around AD 1100) in Khunamush (present day Khunmuh, which you will pass just before you enter Srinagar by road from JammuPahalgâm). He travelled all over India. He went to tutor the daughter of the King of Kalyan

1 Mathew has a totally revisionist view of this great teacher- saint's origins. Most people believe that he was born in Keralâ but came to Kashmîr to study- and to bring about religious and social reforms. Mathew writes, 'Sree Sankara, the profound preacher of Monism (Saivism) *belonged to Kashmîr*. [Emphasis mine.] … There is no reason to believe that such a versatile scholar …was brought up in Keralâ. May be [he] was the father of Malayalam language- its creator.' Mathew's theory is that 'the folk language of Kashmîr- "Sharada"- [mixed with Tamil to] produce Malayalam.'

(Deccan), fell in love with her, married her, and succeeded to the Kalyan throne. As we have seen above, the people- and rulers- of Kashmîr had close political, religious and even ethnic links with the people of the Konkan, right up to Keralâ.

References

i Mathew, PV, *Lalitaditya- linking Kashmîr with Keralâ*, 'Shîrâzâ' (English), Vol. 1, no.2, July- December, 1988, Jammû & Kashmîr Academy of Art, Culture and Languages, Srînagar, Kashmîr.

Chapter- 10

Islâm in Kashmîr

The first Muslims in Kashmîr

According to a weak tradition[i] the first Muslims to come to Kashmîr were two companions (suhâbîs) of Prophet Muhammad (pbuh). This was during the lifetime of the Holy Prophet (c. A.D. 570-632), when 'Dânâ Datt' (or Dânâ Ditta) was said to have been the king of Kashmîr. The tradition goes on to add that the king was so impressed by the visitors that he began to lead a very austere life. He also took to donating a tenth of his income from agriculture to the poor and needy. (This is an Islâmic charitable practice called *ushr.*) However, the names of the companions are not known. Nor are there any historical records of their visit. Besides, none of Kashmîr's numerous traditional histories-written by Syed Ali, Hassan or Malik Haidar-mentions this tradition.

More important, no authentic history of Kashmîr refers to a king of this name during the period in question. The names of the kings of Kashmîr from roughly A.D. 560 to 634 are: Pravarasén II, Bâlâditya, Durlabh-vardan and Durlabhak. The kings from A.D. 634 to 733 were Chandr-pîr Vajrâditya, Tarapîr, Lalitâditya I and Kuvalya-pîr. None of them was called Dânâ Datt, Dânâ Ditta or anything similar. The king with the nearest sounding name was Rânâditya. Kings of this name ruled Kashmîr from A.D. 219 to 519. But that was almost a century before the companions of the Holy Prophet (pbuh) started taking the mission to distant lands.

About Hameem, on the other hand, there is evidence. He was a Syrian, and the first Muslim known to have entered Kashmîr. He migrated to Kashmîr around A.D. 712, in the entourage of Jaisiya, the defeated (Hindu) prince of neighbouring Sindh. That's right: 'neighbouring.' The kingdom of Sindh, at that stage, 'extended on the east to Kashmîr'. The then Rai of Kashmîr granted the fugitive Prince Jaisiya an estate called Shakalha. It is not certain that Shakalha was within Kashmîr Valley, though it was certainly a part of the kingdom of Kashmîr. (It was also in the eigth century-around A.D. 733—that Kashmîr first faced the possibility of an Arab invasion.)

Jaisiya was the son of Dâhir. Today, Dâhir is regarded, by Hindu and Muslim historians alike, as 'the last Hindu ruler of Sindh'. He was defeated and killed by Muhammad-bin-Qasim, 'the first Muslim conqueror of India'. However, neither Jaisiya nor Hameem saw the conflict as one between Hindus and Muslims. Nor did they see themselves as belonging to two hostile religions. We know that five hundred Arab Muslims had joined Dahir's army. Hameem was probably the son of one of those Arab soldiers.

Hameem was extremely close to Jaisiya. When Jaisiya fled from Sindh to Kashmîr, he accompanied his prince. And when Jasiya died it was Hameem, son of Sâma, who inherited the estate of Shakalha. Hameem constructed the first mosques in Kashmîr, on land gifted by the (Hindu) Rai, who 'much respected' Hameem and bestowed 'great honour and regard' on him.

Nothing is known about where Hameem's mosques might have been. The oldest known, surviving Islâmic monument in Kashmîr is Bulbul Lankar. It was built almost six hundred years later (around 1320) on the right bank of the Jehlum, just after the present Ali Kadal. It was at Bulbul Lankar that the first known Kashmîri converts to Islâm would gather. Sultan Rinchen, his brother-in-law (his Queen Kota Rani's brother) Râvan Chandr and his commander-in-chief set the trend by accepting Islâm. Ten thousand others followed, impressed by Syed Bilal @ Bulbul Shah's teachings. Historian G.M.D. Sufi writes, 'The newly converted people, of their own accord, converted temples into mosques in consequence of their change of faith.'

What happened in the almost six centuries between Hameem and Bulbul Shah?

In A.D. 751 the Arabs conquered Gilgit from the Chinese. A few years later (between 754 and 761) we hear of contacts between the king of Kashmîr, Vajraditya-Bappiyaka, and Muslim slave traders, as well as of the introduction of Islâmic practices in Kashmîr.

King Harsh (1089-1101) certainly employed 'Turushka' (Turkish?) Muslim officers in senior positions in his army. By the twelfth century, many Dard tribes had converted from Buddhism to Islâm. (Dardistân and Gilgit are both in Pâkistân-occupied Kashmîr.) Around 1277, Marco Polo mentioned that there were Muslims in Kashmîr.

There is some debate on who the ancestors of Shâh Mîr were and where they came from. (See 'A History of Kashmîr.') Ikrâm[ii] says that his real name was Shâh Mirzâ, that he was a saint from Swat (now in Pâkistân) and that he came over to Kashmîr in 1315 during the reign of King Singh Dev or Sambha Dev[1]. The generous king employed Shâh Mirzâ in his court. He was so impressed by Shâh Mirzâ's saintliness and talents that he soon promoted him to a very high rank.

The king then appointed Shâh Mirzâ's sons to senior positions in his government. One of the king's successors (presumably the other brother) made Shâh Mirzâ's sons his ambassadors plenipotentiary.

The first recorded conversions

Thus, Islâm had come to Kashmîr much before 1320, around which year Rinchen and ten thousand others converted, and Islâm was adopted as the state religion.

Syed Bilal Shah @ Syed Abdur Rahim Turkestâni, also known as Bulbul Shah and Syed Sharaf-ud-dîn, was a disciple of Shah Nematullah Wali Farsi. (Some believe that it was Shah Nematullah, and not his disciple, who converted Rinchen to Islâm.) Both belonged to the Suharwardy order of Sufism. (The Muslims of almost all of India, and Pâkistân, as well parts of Bâñglâ Désh belong to the Chishti order. In Kashmîr, however, the Qâdirî, Naqshbandi and Suharwardy orders are followed.)

Bulbul Shah was the first of a long line of Syeds who came to Kashmîr to proselytise. He came from Turkestân, via Baghdad.

The migration of the Syeds

Mîr Syed Ali Hamadâni, the apostle of Kashmîr, better known as the "Shah of Hamadân" and 'Ameer-e-Kabeer' (1314-1384) is arguably the most celebrated of these Syeds. The Shah was born in Hamadân, Iran. He travelled across the continents for twenty-one years, in the pursuit of knowledge. He met 1400 saints in the process before he returned to Hamadân. That was when Timur had unleashed a reign of terror, forcing seven hundred Syeds, led by the Shah of Hamadân, to flee to Kashmîr in 1372.

(The Syeds are descendants of Hazrat Muhammad, peace be upon him, the prophet of Islâm, through his daughter, Hazrat Fatima and son-in-law Hazrat Ali. The Kashmîri word for 'Syed' is 'Mal'. The neighbourhood in Srînagar where the Syeds settled is still known as Malaratta.)

The Shah went to Ladâkh around 1381 and was the first to establish a mosque there. He belonged to the Kubrawi branch of the Suharwardy order of Sufis. It was the Shah who brought this sect to Kashmîr. The Kubrawis dominate the religious establishment of Srînagar, indeed Kashmîr, to this day. The Shah is said to have induced thirty-seven thousand Kashmîris to convert to Islâm.

In the state there are four major shrines dedicated to the Shah: in the Khânqâh-e-Mu'alla (Srînagar), Trâl, Doru and Shey (Ladâkh). (There also are several lesser-known shrines of the Shah.) The Shah died either at Hazara (Pâkistân) or in Kafiristan. However, he was buried in Khatlan (Turkestân).

The Shah's son, Mîr Muhammad Hamadâni (1372-1450), returned to Kashmîr in 1393, accompanied by three hundred more Syeds. At the time Sinhabhatt/ Suhabhatt was the commander-in-chief of King Sikander's army, and later the prime minister.

Suhabhatt was extremely impressed by the Mîr. He converted to Islâm, taking the name Malik Saif-ud-dîn. He also gave the Mîr his daughter, later named Bibi Baria, in marriage. The Mîr, too, is buried in Khatlan.

The Syeds exchange ideas with the rishîs

By now there were more than a thousand Syeds, plus their descendants, in Kashmîr. They exchanged ideas with Kashmîr's own Muslim mystics, who were known as rishîs/ reshîs and bâbâs.

One of the greatest of these rishîs and saints was Sheikh Nûr-ud-Dîn (1377-1438; see 'Budgâm'). He is regarded by almost all Kashmîris, urban and rural, Hindu and Muslim, as the patron saint of Kashmîr. (The

Kashmîrî Pandits call him Nund Rishi and Sahajananda and accept him as one of their saints.)

The Sheikh's spiritual guide (and, some say, wet-nurse) is known to the Muslims as Lalla Arifa, to the Hindus as Lalleshwari, and accepted by both as the religious leader and guide, Lal Ded. Such was (and, to some extent, still is) the composite-culture of Kashmîr. (The chapter on 'Budgâm', in particular the section on the Sheikh, mentions the progress of the Rishi order, especially the Sheikh's disciples.)

The Suhabhatt Episode

Did coercion and violence play any role at all in the conversion of the Kashmîris to Islâm? There is unanimity among historians, Hindu, Muslim and British, that conversions were entirely voluntary. They were the result of the example of and preaching by the sufis and rishîs.

However, when it comes to the reign, and role, of King Sikander, the so-called 'But Shikan' (idol breaker), this agreement suddenly breaks down. Almost all Muslim historians agree with G.M.D. Sufi that 'the propagation of Islâm in Kashmîr received a strong impetus in the time of Sultan Sikandar' (1389-1413). Where they differ is about whether force was used.

The migration of Kashmîrî Pandits: Many Hindu and some colonial historians like Rev. Tyndale-Biscoe allege 'that the wholesale destruction of temples in Kashmîr was carried out by Sikandar'. The Kashmîrî Pandits have handed down these allegations from generation to generation. They believe that Sikander's reign of terror resulted in the mass conversion of Kashmîri Hindus.

Many of them preferred to flee Kashmîr rather than give up Hinduism. The Pandits believe that just eleven families from their community stayed on in Kashmîr during Sikander's time. They add that all the other Pandits fled the Valley in order to save their lives. They remained in other parts of India till the great Sultan Zain-ul-Abedin (1420-70) made it possible for them to return to Kashmîr.

The revisionist view: However, 20th century historians like Pandit Prem Nath Bazaz and my friend and colleague Abdul Ahad 'History', who belong to the revisionist school, either dismiss these allegations altogether or put them in the correct perspective. Since the first historian to talk about the destruction of idols and/ or temples was Jonarâj, the revisionists question his credibility. Most mediæval histories written by Kashmîri Muslims in the Persian language[2] refer to King Sikander as the

'But Shikan' (idol breaker). Jonarâj wrote in Sañskrit. It was not he who gave Sikander this Persian title. Besides, as we shall see later in this chapter, all subsequent accounts of the peaceful spread of Islâm in Kashmîr till 1459 are based on this resolutely secular historian: who was effusive in his praise of several Muslim kings. If we demolish him, then we lose all the evidence that he gives in support of the Islâmist/ secularist view. Above all, no historian, Hiñdû or Muslim, between the 15th and 19th centuries, has ever contradicted Jonarâj about this iconoclasm.

Sikander was mostly a minor: Some, like G.M.D. Sufi, point out that it was the infant Sikander's commander-in-chief and, later, Prime Minister Suhabhatt/ Malik Saif-ud-dîn, who was responsible.

Sufi says that Suhabhatt 'appears to be responsible for the destruction of a few temples… (He) set on foot a fierce persecution of the adherents of his old faith… probably, in order to show his zeal for his new religion. This sort of religious zeal is deplored by Islâm… It is on record that Mîr Muhammad Hamadâni warned Suhabhatta against such action.'

Since Sikander was a minor during almost half his reign, it does seem unfair to hold him responsible for Suhabhatt's actions.

Idols made during Sikander's era: The most stunning evidence in defence of Sikander is a discovery made by archæologist Jawahar Lal Bhan. This is a four-headed idol of Lord Brahmâ. Bhan found it in Srînagar's Ganesh Mandir. The eyes of the deity are elongated, which, Bhan writes, is 'a peculiarity of the tenth century A.D. sculptures.'

There is a two-line inscription in the Sarada (Shârdâ) script behind this stone sculpture. It says that Kastavaka, son of Rahul, the Sañgh-pati, consecrated the idol in the reign of 'Sakandara Saha' in the year 85. This was obviously the 85th year of Kashmîr's own Laukik era. It corresponds to 1409. This is when Sikander was king of Kashmîr. Therefore, too, 'Sakandara Saha' has to be King Sikander, the so-called idol breaker. (This, Bhan points out, is the first 'stone sculpture so far known in Kashmîr' which has a date on it.)

Apparently this idol was originally installed at Khrew. It was brought over to the said Ganesh Mandir in the Dogrâ period.

Bhan goes on to ask, 'Why [did] Sultan Sikandar spare the temples which were situated within the proximity of [Srînagar] city, namely, the temple of Puranadhisthana, modern Panderathan [sic], the temple of Shankarâchârya, etc., which are still intact[3]?…

'Why were Sultan Sikandar and his queen buried on the remains of an earlier temple retaining its shape, door and even sculptural panels, including Dwarapalas etc?'

Incidentally, Rahul is a Buddhist name and Sangh-pati ('the leader of a group of Buddhists') a Buddhist concept. Since at least the twentieth century some historians have tried to show that Hinduism and Buddhism were in conflict with each other. But the *Râjâtarañginî* is full of Buddhists who built Hindu temples: and vice versa. This inscription also shows that there were Buddhists-and wealthy ones at that-in Kashmîr as late as in the fifteenth century. This flies in the face of pop-history, according to which the Shankarâchârya had wiped Buddhism off the face of Kashmîr (indeed of all South Asia) in the ninth century A.D. But here, six centuries later, we have a Sangh-pati called Rahul, who venerates Lord Brahmâ as well. Obviously, pop-histories are wrong.

The correct perspective: What about the 'correct perspective'? Moderate historians concede that Sikander and/ or Suhabhatt might indeed have gone overboard. This is because contemporary historians say so, because there is no evidence to believe otherwise and because the entire Kashmîri Pandit community could not possibly have built all their customs and sects around a myth, that of their en masse migration during Sikander's reign. (See 'Kashmîrî Pandits' in 'The people of Kashmîr'.) However, as these historians point out, the Hindu kings who possibly destroyed Hiñdû temples (see below) were no better.

The Gazetteer of India: Kashmîr region (1999) epitomises the correct perspective in its observation that '... some of the temples in the valley were definitely destroyed and converted into mosques after the population of that particular locality converted to Islâm.'

Iconoclasm before Sikander

Mediæval historians like Pandit Kalhan say that some kings like Jayapida (764-795) made ninety-nine Brâhmins 'seek death in water'. As we have seen, Shankar Varman (883-902) looted and cannibalised temples. Abhimanyu II (958-972) got his capital, including the temple of Vardhan Swami, burnt.

Kalhan says that Harsh 'despoiled' every single temple of its images. 'Despoilation' included spitting, defecation and urination on these idols. It was Jonarâj, a Hindu and a Brâhmin like Kalhan, who recorded for us how Rajadev forced the 'Bhatts' (Brâhmins) to disown the fact that they were Brâhmins. Dulchu, the commander-in-chief of King Karmsen's army, plundered Kashmîr around 1319, causing harm to 'innumerable gods'.

We have no reason to doubt Jonarâj when he says that during Sikander's era Suhabhatt broke 'images' in nine specific temples (notably Mârtañd) as well as others not specified. It is also probable that all but eleven Kashmîri Pandit families did, indeed, have to flee Kashmîr because of Sikander/ Suhabhatt. The latter is more likely to have been the villain, because Sikander himself had quite a few Hindus in his inner circle, including wife Shri Shobha Mahadevi and first minister Rai Magrey.

However, it is also certain that the Bhatts of Mahârâshtra and certain Konkan Brâhmins, who say that their ancestors were Kashmîri, had migrated much before Kashmîr was ruled by Muslims-possibly during the reign of kings like Lalitâditya, Harsh and Rajadev (1213-1236).

So, did Hinduism and its temples go into a sudden decline because of rulers like Suhabhatt/ Sikander (1389-1413)? Or because a substantial section of the population had converted to Islâm? Far from it. More than a century later, Mirza Haidar Dughlat (c.1541-51) would go into raptures about the 'more than one hundred and fifty idol temples' which existed 'in and around Kashmîr' and which were 'first and foremost among the wonders of Kashmîr'. Emperor Jehangir (1605-27), too, spoke of 'lofty idol temples… still (being) in existence'.

King Zain-ul-Abedin was widely praised by contemporâry Hindu historians for his concern for the well being of the Hindus. However, conversions continued. Notable converts of his era include the Khakha and Hatmâl Rajpûts of the area.

Milestones in the history of conversion

The first recorded conversion of a Kashmîrî to Islâm was that of King Rinchen. His brother-in-law Râvan Chandr and ten thousand others joined him. This was Kashmîr's first mass-conversion. It happened in 1320, or perhaps a year before.

There are five major milestones in the history of conversions to Islâm in Kashmîr. Three of these were mainly individual missions and two were collective efforts. The group efforts were those of the Rishis and the Bulbul Shah-Rinchen-Râvan Chandr group. The three most influential individuals were the Shâh-é-Hamadân, Sheikh Nûr-ud-Dîn Rishî and Mîr Shams-ud-dîn Iraqi. (The Qâdirîs of Baghdad played an important role in

Kishtwâr.) Within Sheikh Nûr-ud-Dîn Rishî's overall mission there were half a dozen sub-milestones, as we shall see.

The next major conversions after Rinchen were those made at the behest of the Shâh-é-Hamadân, The Shah is said to have induced thirty-seven thousand Kashmîris to convert to Islâm some time between 1372 and 1381.[4]

In both cases, the saint who convinced people to convert had come from outside Kashmîr: from Central Asia (Turkestân and Irân), to wit. However, by 1400 or 1410 Islâm-and Islâmic mysticism-had struck such deep roots in Kashmîr that thenceforth native-born mystics (the Muslim rishîs) took over the mission of spreading Islâm. For some time both native-born rishîs and those from outside proselytised, the former increasingly outnumbering the latter. This continued till, say, the 1650s (the era of Syed Farid-ud-dîn Qâdirî of Baghdad came to an end around that the time). I can't think of any prominent Muslim missionary from abroad being active in Kashmîr after that. Kashmîr-born saints took over completely.

The Sheikh-ul-Âlam: Sheikh Nûr-ud-Dîn Rishî was born in Kaimoh, near Srînagar in 1377. Not only was he the first native-born mystic to cause the Kashmîrîs to convert to Islâm, to date he remains the foremost among them. In his case it is not only the number of people he converted that stands out but also their spiritual eminence.

Bhum Sadh was already a renowned Brâhmin saint, famous for the miracles that he would perform, before he became Bâmuddîn under Sheikh Nûr-ud-Dîn's influence. When Bhum Sadh's followers saw that their spiritual leader had converted, they followed suit.

Tulî Rainâ, was a prominent Hiñdû leader of that era. The important Rainâs of those days were mostly powerful feudal lords. However, Tulî Rainâ seems to have been a man of religion and high learning. The conversion of Bhum Sadh and his followers demoralised and irritated Tulî Rainâ and his group enormously. (See 'Bam Zoo' in the chapter on Ânañtnâg.) They met Sheikh Nûr-ud-Dîn to protest about his proselytisation drive. However, they wound up discussing the finer points of Islâm instead. By the end of the debate Tulî Rainâ and his 1,200 followers converted to Islâm.

A Brâhmin saint of Andarhâmâ has been mentioned elsewhere in this chapter. When he insisted on being buried the Muslim way, his followers took that as a signal that it was time for them to convert. Thus did another group conversion take place. Rupvan was one more village where Sheikh Nûr-ud-Dîn Rishî persuaded a large group to join him.

Sheikh Nûr-ud-Dîn's spiritual influence then crossed over to Kishtwâr-indeed to the royalty of that region. Zia Singh belonged to the line that ruled Kishtwar, which is in the Jammû province. He was the next among the Sheikh's prominent converts. As Zain-ud-dîn Walî he went on to acquire such enormous spiritual eminence that the large-hearted Sheikh would say 'Zainâ's devotion to God exceeds that of his tutor [i.e. the Sheikh himself].' (See 'Aish Muqâm' in the chapter on 'Ânañtnâg.')

The Sheikh's mission crossed the gender frontier as well. Because of his efforts a large number of women became Muslim saints. This seems to have been a major trend because neither before him nor after his time were there so many female saints.

The process of conversion to Islâm, through active proselytisation or because of the example of the rishîs, went on till the eighteenth century. Conversions after that were mostly the decisions of individual seekers.

Why did the people of Kashmîr convert to Islâm?

For that matter, why did King Rinchen convert to Islâm? Jonarâj, himself a Kashmîri Hindu, says that (the Buddhist) Rinchen tried to become a Shaivite Hindu but Shri Deva Swami and other ranking Hindu priests refused to accept him into their fold. Then Rinchen saw a dream in which he was advised to accept as his guide whoever he first saw the next day. This person turned out to be a Turkistani saint who identified himself as Abdur Rehman, but who is better known in Kashmîr as Bulbul Shah (d. 1327).

This is recorded history. But serious historians dismiss such events as anecdotal. They tend to look for deeper causes, and in Kashmîr there were several. The 'sword' (i.e. forcible conversion) was not one of them. Indeed, the whole process seems to have been extremely cordial and conducted in an atmosphere of seeking the truth. Today we see Hiñdûism and Islâm as distinct religions, and conversion from one to the other is seen as a huge transition. In the mediæval era that is not how the common man in Kashmîr-or the native-born Muslim rishîs-saw it.

The conversion made no real difference to the converts' religious practices: Sheikh Nûr-ud-Dîn Rishî's early example and poetry followed the path of the rishîs: living in the woods and meditating in caves for long periods. His closest aides did the same.[5] This won them great respect among the people, Hiñdû as well as Muslim. Hiñdû ascetics were extremely comfortable with the Muslim rishîs' practices, because they were so similar to their own. Therefore, for many of them it made little difference whether they remained Hiñdûs or slid over to this form of Islâm. Ishaq

Khân puts it in a scholarly manner thus, '...through the Rishis, [Islâm] allowed the main configuration of pre-existing Kashmîrî popular religion to adapt itself to the wider Islâmic framework.'

Sheikh Nûr-ud-Dîn Rishî's discussion with Tuli Rainâ, as recorded for posterity, indicates that he won converts by explaining Islâm to them through metaphors of their existing religion. Khân says that the Rishis continued to narrate the pre-Muslim 'folk beliefs about creation that persisted among the converts.'

Conversion in stages: For some Kashmîrî families, especially those of learned Brâhmins, conversion was not a sudden process. It took place very gradually, over centuries. It would begin with the copying of the verses of Kashmîrî Muslim saints who were revered by both communities. The second step would be to accept the message of Islâm without converting formally. (This kind of a thing happened all over India.) The next would be to accept some Muslim practices, again without converting.

The Brâhmin saint of Andarhâmâ mentioned by the mediæval writer Bâbâ Nasîbuddîn Ghâzi was one such person. He became a close friend of Sheikh Nûr-ud-Dîn and was receptive to the Sheikh's ideas. When he died he insisted on being buried in the Islâmic fashion, even though he remained a Hiñdû till his death.

The people followed their leader's example: The impact of Bhum Sadh's conversion was felt not just by his immediate followers but also by all Kashmîrîs who respected this Brâhmin saint. They started asking themselves, 'If Bhum Sadh, the greatest Hiñdû saint of our time, has crossed over to Islâm, should we not be doing the same?'

Tuli Rainâ was a major leader. 1,200 of his followers converted to Islâm when he did. Ladi (or Ludo) Rainâ was a powerful temporal chief in the Kishtwâr area who converted to Islâm as Latif-ud-Din. It is not clear if his own subjects followed suit. However, a number of others did, when they saw this thitherto wealthy man adopt a life of extreme self-denial and austerity.

Sozan was a saint who belonged to the community of weavers. Sheikh Nûr-ud-Dîn converted him through religious debate. Sozan, in turn, persuaded the Hiñdûs of Prân Bhavan, whom he had served selflessly, to follow his example.

Spiritual leaders were persuaded by their flock: Often a group of Kashmîrîs would convert to Islâm while respected Hiñdû saints of that community would not. The newly converted Muslims would then make every effort to persuade their spiritual heroes to join them in Islâm. This seems to have been something of a trend, because Sheikh Nûr-ud-Dîn coined a proverb about it.

Debate and dialogue: Tuli Rainâ was one of those who converted after a Muslim saint (in this case Sheikh Nûr-ud-Dîn Rishî) convinced them through debate. Ladi Rainâ was the lord of the Mârû [Mârwâh]-Warhwan area where Kashmîr borders Dodâ (Jammû). Sheikh Nûr-ud-Dîn Rishî convinced him not only about the Oneness of God but also about the futility of collecting material wealth.

And then there were the Brâhmins who were offering food and drinking water to departed souls by the bank of a river. This was another group that the Sheikh brought into the fold of Islâm through debate. He convinced them that it was better to feed the poor instead.

The disciples of Sheikh Nûr-ud-Dîn sought out Brâhmin saints, engaged them in discussions about God and succeeded in converting many of them.

Setting an example: Several people became Muslim rishîs because they admired the piety of those who had converted to Islâm. Sheikh Nûr-ud-Dîn Rishî's example, of course, won him thousands of followers. Gañgâ Bîbî converted because her husband, Lankar Mal, too, had done so. (More about Lankar later.)

Social service: Bâbâ Abdullâh is the best example. Not only did he construct a number of mosques, he also got many bridges and public baths built. This earned him the gratitude of the people, Hiñdû as well as Muslim. The people of Lari Bar village converted because of him. Hazrat Ganga Bâbâ Rishi got 360 mosques and as many culverts built. (See 'Budgâm.') Like Sheikh Nûr-ud-Din Rishi, Ganga Bâbâ got thousands of trees planted. Bâbâ Latif-ud-Din Qazi was another saint who served his fellow men selflessly. (Also see 'Budgâm.')

Seekers: Some, like Kati Pandit, came on their own. Kati had heard of Sheikh Nûr-ud-Dîn Rishî's austerities, as well as of the saint's 'sense of guilt and feeling of sin.' He thought that the Sheikh's example represented 'a new and better life.[iii] This made him seek the saint out. Kati joined the Sheikh's fold, with the name of Qutubuddîn.

The Brâhmin saint Dariyâ Rishî was another seeker. He sought out Bâbâ Shukuruddîn, himself a recent convert, who granted an interview most reluctantly, and only after repeated requests from Dariyâ. Abdul Shukur, also originally a Hiñdû Brâhmin, was a third. He was an admirer of Batamâlû Sâheb (18th century). Ishaq Khân points out that this seeker 'expressed his intention of becoming a Muslim during [Batamâlû Sâheb's] lifetime. But it was only after the death of [Batamâlû Sâheb] that he affirmed his faith in Islâm.' This shows that the Muslim rishîs were in no hurry to convert. The seeker, too, often spent several years pondering over his decision before he formally converted.

(Individual decisions to convert must have been very difficult because of pressures from members of the previous religion. That is why individual seekers spent years in internal debate. Sheikh Suleiman Kashmîrî is the best example of this. After his conversion to Islâm, he earned a name for being able to recite the Holy Qur'ân from memory. His conversion annoyed his older friends and relatives. They began to harass him. When the harassment became unbearable he went to Kolât to meet the Shâh-é-Hamadân and join his inner circle.

(Converting in a group, therefore, must have been much easier for all members of that village or caste. For that reason, decisions to convert in groups were infinitely faster.)

Absolution: At least some wealthy people, like the dissolute Lankar Mal, converted to Islâm out of a sense of guilt and to expiate for their sins. (His wife, Ganga, went on to become one of Kashmîr's most important Muslim saints.)

Miracles: Scholars (notably Ishaq Khân) tend to dismiss the role of miracles (performed by Muslim saints) in the spread of Islâm. And yet when we go through histories such as Hassan's 19th century *Tazkarâ-é-Aulîyâ-é-Kashmîr* the unmistakeable impression is that several group conversions took place when the people were overawed by some miracle performed by a Muslim saint. Not all of these miracles were benign. Many of them were painful punishments awarded to those who had done something wrong.

Bhum Sadh is one of the most prominent Kashmîrîs who converted to Islâm because of miracles. When still a Hiñdû, he got into a debate with Sheikh Nûr-ud-Dîn Rishî about the validity of monotheism. He asked the Sheikh to prove that there was only one God. The Sheikh miraculously made the idols present in the room start speaking about the Oneness of God. This miracle overwhelmed Bhum Sadh. He accepted Islâm at once.

Zia Singh of the Kishtwâr royal family, too, converted because of an elaborate series of miracles. He fell seriously ill in his early youth. Apparently his mother vowed that she would convert to Islâm if her son were cured. Sheikh Nûr-ud-Dîn Rishî is said to have healed the youth, who later acquired great spiritual fame as Zainuddîn. (See also 'Aish

Muqâm' in the chapter on 'Ânañtnâg.') Ladi Rainâ was another important disciple who had been cured by the Sheikh before his conversion.

Rural performing artistes disseminated the message: News that the Sheikh had scored over Bhum Sadh in the debate started spreading throughout rural Kashmîr. The finer points of the debate between the two were difficult for the common man to understand, leave alone recount. It is possible that the whole story about the idols talking about One God was a simplified way of saying, 'In the debate the Sheikh's monotheism prevailed over Bhum Sadh's beliefs.'

Stories of this kind were taken from village to village by rural minstrels, dancers, acrobats and wandering saints—the bhâñds, the dambâels, maets and faqîrs.

Sheikh Nûr-ud-Dîn's own songs became very popular all over Kashmîr. They, too, spread the message of Islâm.

The message was simple and accessible: In Kashmîr, especially during Sheikh Nûr-ud-Dîn's time, Islâm spoke the language of the people: Kashmîrî. Besides, as mentioned, the message was conveyed through simple songs and stories.

A people ripe for conversion: P.V. Mathew feels that 'the interference of Tañtrins in Kashmîr administration weakened Kashmîr. The people who had suffered them in the hands of Tañtrins and Damaras [both being powerful clans], were anxiously looking for a way out, when in the days of Sahadev the sûfîs of Islâm entered Kashmîr. The people fell easy prey to the new preachers and there was mass conversion to Islâm.'

Was conversion a revolt against the caste system/ 'Brâhmanic tyranny? At the all-India level my research shows that the overwhelming majority of people who converted were the skilled backward castes: leather workers, weavers, tailors, barbers, butchers and the makers of all kinds of handicrafts. The very poorest (e.g. scavengers) converted only in a few cases. The same is true of the upper castes: the Brâhmins, Râjpûts, Jâts, Baniâs and Jains. Large-scale conversions from these castes to Islâm did not take place. At the all-India level (which includes Bâñglâ Désh and Pâkistân's West Punjâb) my conclusion is that the Hiñdûs who converted to Islâm were those talents who had been stifled by the caste system. These were the elite of what we now call the scheduled castes and some castes now included in the 'other backward castes' category.

Does this hold true of Kashmîr? Or for that matter of Pâkistân's Balûchistân and North West Frontier Province? In all three cases conversions were near-total (90% or above). So, were conversions to Islâm in these three cases, too, a way of escaping the caste-system? At least in the case of Kashmîr this is not correct. In no state of undivided India did the so-called 'untouchable' population exceed twenty per cent. (Individual districts are another matter. In the Jammû and Kathuâ districts the scheduled caste population is much higher than the all-India norm, being 28% and 23% respectively. Yet these are the two districts of the State where the fewest conversions to Islâm took place.)

True, Sheikh Nûr-ud-Dîn Rishî himself belonged to a so-called 'low-caste' before his conversion to Islâm. It is also true that his poetry occasionally spoke out against what critics like Ishaq Khân call 'the weight of Brâhmanic tyranny.' His message, with its emphasis on the dignity of labour, gave great comfort to the working classes. Some Brâhmins even opposed his mission, alarmed by his success in winning converts, especially from the Hiñdû elite.

However, not only such Kashmîrî Brâhmins as had converted to Islâm but also those who remained Hiñdûs played an important role in popularising the verses of Sheikh Nûr-ud-Dîn Rishî. They started copying the poetry of the saint in the Shârdâ (Kashmîrî) script; and continued to do so till the seventeenth century. Thus, Brâhmins who opposed the Sheikh were few and far between. The majority of Kashmîr's Brâhmins (Hiñdû as well as newly-converted Muslim) supported him-and most enthusiastically.

True, upward social mobility was a powerful incentive for many underclass Hiñdûs. Shanga Bibi, the female saint, for example, had been a commercial sex-worker before her conversion-and, later, sainthood. Sozan had been a weaver and, thus, a 'low caste.' However, the Hiñdûs had accepted him as a saint well before he became a Muslim. He seemed to have had no problems with the Hiñdû religion. The Hiñdû social order, on the other hand, was a very different thing.

Most importantly, Kashmîrî Muslims were not above caste, either. Several underclass groups, especially the hânjîs, dombs, dambels and maets continued to languish at the bottom of the society even after conversion. Muslims from higher-ranking groups would not dream of marrying into these groups. But in some ways they were better off after their conversion. They could now dine at feasts with elite Muslims. Besides, at least in theory they were the equals of the Syeds. Hiñdûism did not permit that even in theory.

Therefore, it is not at all surprising that those at the very bottom of the social and economic ladder converted almost two centuries after the elite did. The first people to convert were the Brâhmins and the Kashmîrî and Ladâkhî castes corresponding to the highest Râjpûts. Rinchen Shâh was not just from the ruling caste, he was a Gyâpo (a tiny caste that consists of Ladâkhî royalty). Râvan Chandr, too, belonged to royalty. They converted in 1319 or 1320. Ikrâm emphasises that Bulbul Shâh converted the king and several nobles (*umrâ*) to Islâm.

The majority of Brâhmins either converted around the same time or a few decades later. A Hiñdû historian records that 2 ½ maunds of *janéû thread* (sacred threat) were burnt when the Shâh-é-Hamadân converted Hiñdûs to Islâm en masse in the 1370s. Only Brâhmins wear this sacred thread.

The truly underprivileged boatmen of Srînagar, on the other hand, converted only around 1500, and had Mîr Shams-ud-dîn Iraqi not come along their conversion might have taken place even later.

So, do these conversions suggest a revolt against 'the weight of Brâhmanic tyranny'?

Indeed, the events recounted in the last few pages show how the Brâhmins and the Rainâs were the first to convert. Other prominent elite converts included the priests of the temple of Uttar, and Latîfuddîn, a Rainâ chief. (Today the Rainâs are all seen as Brâhmins. However, my own researches suggest that at least some of them-if not the majority-held the same status and professions as Râjpûts elsewhere.) What we notice is a very civilised process of debate and discussion, with the Brâhmins listening to (and often seeking out) Muslim missionaries with an open mind. To explain conversions in Kashmîr as a revolt against 'the weight of Brâhmanic tyranny' is to devalue the spiritual appeal of Islâm and the persuasive powers of its missionaries.

The Spread of Shiism

Mîr Shams-ud-dîn Iraqi came to Kashmîr from Tâlish (Central Asia) in 1487. He was the next major preacher who was able to persuade 'thousands of people', particularly the Rainâs, to convert. The Mîr was either a Shia or a Noor Bakhshi

The Noor Bakhshis are a sect that tries to find common ground between the Shias and the Sunnis.The ideological ancestry of the Noor Bakhshis, and thus of the Mîr, can be traced to the Sunni Syed Ali Hamadâni. Therefore, there are problems in classifying the Noor Bakhshis, and thus the Mîr, as Shias. In fact, the Noor Bakhshis and the Shias have major differences on the issue of Muharram mourning.)

Drew wrote in his 19th century *Jammú and Kashmír Territories* that the Noor Bakhshis were 'a division of the Baltís... [In] their mode of prayer [they] follow one who stands in front, which, apparently the other Shías do not.'

So, if the Mîr was a Noor Bakhshi and not a Shia, why would he convert people to the Shia sect? On the face of it this does defy reason. Therefore, I can only guess. Prof. M Amin Andrabi used to mention a debate that took place in mediæval times about the creed of the Shâh-é-Hamadân. This controversy raged for years.

No one in the history of Kashmîr has converted more people to the Sunni sect of Islâm than did the Shâh. Then how can there be any doubt about the sect that he belonged to? But doubts there were. Many mediæval scholars insisted that the Shâh was a Shia but propagated the Sunni sect instead. This was because he noticed that the Sunni sect had already struck roots in Kashmîr. Apparently, the Shâh reasoned that it was more important to spread Islâm than any particular sect.[6]

Could it be that the Mîr had similarly decided that since the Noor Bakshîs had no base in Kashmîr the next best would be to work in the cause of Shiism. The Mîr was one of the most active Muslim missionaries in the history of Kashmîr. Some scholars feel that in the matter of converting people to Islâm he was even more pro-active than the Shâh. To the extent that he actively sought converts in Srînagar, rural Budgâm and some other parts of the Valley, this might be true. However, in terms of numbers converted, it would seem that the Shâh had an edge.

Sheikh Abdullah Qumî was a contemporary of the Mîr, and Syed Hassan was the Mîr's successor. These were the other two missionaries who helped spread Shiism in Kashmîr.

The Mîr was first buried near the Imâmbârâ of Jadibal (Srînagar). Later his tomb was shifted to Chadoora (Budgâm). Dr Sufi says that this was done 'to avoid desecration by non-Shias'.

Some prejudiced Hindu and Muslim historians of today assume that the Hindus and Muslims were enemies in the past. So do some Shia and Sunni historians about their sects. They claim that the great Sheikh Hamzâ Makhdoom (1494-1576) 'exercised a considerable check on Shiism', the spread of which (through Mîr Shams-ud-dîn Iraqi) 'alarmed the Sunnis'.

The Sheikh was a descendant of Chandravanshi Rajpûts and a mystic of the Kubrawi order.

But things were never as black and white as that: Shia vs. Sunni, us vs. them. Bâbâ Khalilullah, a leading Shia saint, was on the same side of the political fence as Makhdoom Sâheb. On the other were the Chaks, who happened to be Shias. However, the Chak sultan's daughter was married to the Sunni Baihaqi. Mughal emperor Jehangir's closest ally in Kashmîr was a Shia aristocrat called Malik Haidar Chadoora.

Proselytisation

Today Makhdoom Sâheb's mausoleum on the Hari Parbat/ Koh é mârâñ, first built in 1713, is considered one of the most powerful in all Kashmîr. In his lifetime the saint got several mosques built in Kashmîr, travelled all over the Valley to proselytise and was known for mystic practices such as holding his breath for long periods.

In Kishtwâr, Islâm was mainly propagated by Syed Farid-ud-dîn Qâdirî (born c.1592 in Baghdad), his four companions and two sons. They set into motion a process which resulted in the majority of the people of Kishtwâr converting to Islâm. The example of Syed Farid's son, Syed Asrar-ud-dîn (died in 1685 in Kishtwâr), was an important factor.

The most notable convert was Kirat Singh. He became the king of Kishtwâr in 1681. Emperor Aurangzeb renamed him Sâdat Yar Khân in 1687. His family and many of his subjects followed suit. (See also the section on 'Kishtwâr' in the chapter on 'Dodâ'.) The main temple of Kishtwâr, in the heart of the town, became a mosque-with the tomb of Farid-ud-dîn Sâheb inside it.

Islâm continued to gain converts in the state during Afghân and even Dogrâ (Hindu) rule. The Afghâns appointed several Kashmîrî Pandits to high office, in Srînagar as well as Kabul. Not one of these senior officials converted to Islâm in order to obtain, or retain, his position. However, in the villages some Pandits accepted Islâm after the example of the missionaries. Significant among these was a Kashmîri Pandit from Rajwer (and, later, Sovarah). Around 1760, he became a Muslim, with the name Sheikh Abdullah. Almost two centuries later, his eponymous descendant became the Prime Minister, and later Chief Minister, of the state.

The spread of Islâm in districts like Jammû and Kathuâ is one of the finest examples of the composite culture of our sub-continent. It is also evidence that Islâm did not need the sword, or even state patronage, to flourish. The population of these districts was, through most of history, mainly Hindu. Muslims did not ever rule either district. (One king of Jammû did go through the motions of converting to Islâm, though. His children, who ruled after him, remained Hiñdûs.) Yet, village after village in both districts has been named after relatively recent Muslim saints and landlords.

Some villages, like Sidhra, take their names from purely Islâmic concepts. The Mahârâjâ named several important residential areas in Jammû town after Muslim clans and individuals, notably his own Ustad (teacher). Every Thursday, to this day, Hindus and Sikhs vastly outnumber Muslims at the several dozen shrines of Muslim saints.

Equally significantly, some powerful Hindus, including Rajpûts, converted to Islâm even when their fellow Rajpût Hindus, the Dogrâs, were in power in the 19th and early 20th centuries.

The Rishi Movement

In Islâm, saints, priests and clergymen are expected to marry, unlike, say, Catholic and Buddhist monks or even some Hindu divines. And yet several sufi sects insist on celibacy. The (Muslim) rishîs of Kashmîr are one such sect. Khwaja Owais, who was a contemporary of Prophet Muhammad, peace be on him, founded what, in Kashmîr, came to be called the rishî order. The Khwaja lived, with his mother to whom he was devoted, in a village called Kurun in Yemen. Such was the respect the Holy Prophet had for the Khwaja that he refused to lead his army to Yemen. When asked why, the Prophet (PBUH) would say, 'The odour of God comes from Yemen.'

The Khwaja would have been an early sufi-certainly not the first or even the second, because those were Hazrat Ali and Hassan Basri respectively. It was Sheikh Nûr-ud-Dîn Wali who founded in Kashmîr the movement named after the rishîs (the Sañskrit word for Hindu hermits). He wanted the rishîs to create a society where 'peace between neighbours and people begins with peace within individuals, combining the delights of solitude with manual labour for the community'.

The Rishis were strict vegetarians. Like Hindu and Jain vegetarians they would not eat onions or garlic either. None of them drank alcohol or did drugs. They mainly lived on wild herbs, especially the lettuce-like wopul hak, which they gathered as they wandered through the woods.

The Rishi movement was at its peak in the 16th century. According to Abul Fazl, the 16th century Mughal historian, there were nearly two thousand rishîs in Kashmîr. Both Firishta and he have written that the rishîs lived on berries and the wild fruit of the mountains. The rishîs mostly stayed in caves or at least in the woods. They would not wear more than one garment, even if it were in tatters. The rishîs would also not to talk to the people unless absolutely necessary.

In most Eastern (Hindu, Muslim, Jain and Buddhist) religions it is considered pious and godly to go to extremes of austerity and self-abnegation. The rishîs would do this.

Abul Fazl added, 'The most respectable people of (Kashmîr) are the Rishis, who, though they do not suffer themselves to be fettered with traditions, are doubtless true worshippers of God. They revile not any other sect, and ask for nothing of anyone. They plant the roads with fruit trees, to furnish the traveller with refreshment. They abstain from flesh, and have no intercourse with the other sex.'

Emperor Akbar's army was defeated by Kashmîr's Chak kings the first three times that it tried to conquer Kashmîr in the 1580s. The Kashmîris believe that it were the prayers of Rishi Malu that ensured this. In fact, almost the entire Rishi sect had prayed for Akbar's defeat. (See also the section on Ânañtnâg district.)

Jehangir wrote about the rishîs in much the same vein as his father Akbar's biographer, Abul Fazl, '(The Muslim rishîs) have no religious knowledge or learning of any sort. Yet they possess simplicity and are without pretence. They abuse no one. They restrain the tongue of desire and the foot of seeking. They eat no flesh, they have no wives, and always plant fruit bearing trees in the fields, so that men may benefit from them, themselves desiring no advantage.' Jehangir, too, estimated their number at 2,000.

There have been some great sufi saints-even rishîs-in Kashmîr in the twentieth century. However, many scholars feel that there have been no genuine rishîs since the 17th century, possibly the result of Akbar's hostility towards them. (But then again various subsequent Mughal emperors had granted them lands and convents.) In the centuries that followed, such rishîs as were left were mostly 'the guardians of the tombs of some former canonised saints of their order.'

The way of the Rishis

The Rishis did not have a codified creed. However, some mediæval scholars, notably Mulla 'Ali Rainâ[iv], recorded the essential features of their path. These are:

i) The goal is to worship God.

ii) The only desire that a rishî has is to see (or come close to) God.

iii) This is to be done by means of fasts and self-denial. This includes giving up sex and other sensual pleasures. Thus, good food is ruled out. Even the quantity of food to be eaten has to be the barest minimum. This self-denial is so extreme that the rishîs do not allow themselves to talk more or sleep longer than is absolutely necessary. This cleans up the body as well as the soul.

iv) They deny themselves the company of their fellow men because this interferes with their spiritual pursuits. And when one of them finds himself in a situation in which he is not able to run away from human company, he feels guilty for days on end for having allowed himself this indulgence.

Some sûfî orders elsewhere, too, believe in self-denial. In India, Hiñdû and Jain monks sometimes go to such extremes. Among the Christians, the Trappists are the closest parallel. The Buddhist monastery at Rizong in Leh imposes almost identical austerities on its monks: including eating just one meal a day and staying away from fellow men to the extent possible.

v) Prayer is a very private affair. It is not something to do while others are watching. Nor are piety and mystical practices something to be shown off.

vi) The rishîs do not make an effort to perform miracles. However, because they are so exalted spiritually, they often wind up performing miracles during the course of their activities.

vii) They believe that only God knows what lies inside anyone's soul.

viii) If any material goods are given to a rishî, or to an order of rishîs, it is ensured that these things are immediately passed on to the poor.

ix) Within Islâm a wide variety of interpretations and practices is possible. The rishîs have their own interpretation. However, their practices do not go beyond the boundaries of Islâm.

Islâm does not lay any great store by renunciation or extremes of asceticism. Initially Sheikh Nûr-ud-Dîn Rishî spent considerable time in forests and meditating in a cave. His early poetry-and example-encouraged such austerity. However, later, under the influence of the Kubrawis, he gave up this rishî practice. His later poetry was critical of asceticism.

Kashmîri Sufism: Distinctive Features

There are four schools of sufism. These are the Chishti, Suharwardy, Qâdirî and Naqshbandi orders. All the sufis of the world belong to one or another of these orders. Kashmîr is perhaps the only exception to this rule in the entire Muslim world. Many of its rishîs owe allegiance to none of these orders.

Some visitors from Iran once clubbed the various sufi schools of the world into two categories: the Indian/ Pâkistâni way and the Middle Eastern/ Iranian way. When they came to Kashmîr they remarked that Kashmîr seemed to represent a third approach, a third way, quite different from the other two. The Iranian visitors noted that Kashmîri sufism has an Iranian base but its practices are neither Iranian nor mainland Indian. However, if anything, they are closer to Iran.

For instance, in mainland India flowers are offered at tombs. This does not happen at the Muslim shrines of Kashmîr and Iran. Most shrines in the Islâmic world are built around the tomb of an important saint. In Iran, Iraq and Kashmîr a turban (*amâma*) is placed on or perched above the head of the grave of the saint. It is not so in the rest of South Asia.

In the rest of India (including Jammû) the devotee enters through the main door and the grave (mazâr) of the saint is right in front. Thus the common man can go right up to the grave and touch it. In Iran and Kashmîr the grave is normally surrounded by a rectangular enclosure (*qubbâ*). This enclosure is normally like a room within a larger room. Its walls are normally made of elegantly carved wood. Lattice-or fret-work is deliberately used in these walls. That way the walls become fairly transparent and the devotee can see the grave(s) inside through the holes in the fretwork. The ziyarats of Jammû, e.g. Shahdra Sharief, do not have such enclosures.

Incidentally, shrines are called dargahs and mazârs in the rest of India, Pâkistân and even Afghânistân. In Kashmîr (and to a lesser extent in Jammû) they are called mostly called ziyârats, a word that is used as the verb for pilgrimage in many other Islâmic lands. The word dargah is used in Kashmîr-certainly in Srînagar city—to describe just one shrine, Hazratbal.

The only shrine in Kashmîr called mazâr that I can think of is Srînagar's Bat (rice) Mazâr. In Kashmîr the word mazâr is mostly used to describe exclusive cemeteries.

Devotees who pay homage at Kashmîri and Irani shrines are often found wailing. They call out loud (to God or to the patron saint) and read out their *munâjât* (supplications) for at least the people sitting next to them to hear. In the rest of India people pray silently.

The Muslims of almost all of India (except Jammû and Kashmîr) and Pâkistân are Chishtis. In Kashmîr and Jammû this is the only order that is not represented by even a single shrine. Even the Qâdirîs are to be found mainly in Jammû.

The third (Kashmîri) way: Most Rishis belong to none of the four silsilas of sufism. This is true of Bâbâ Réshî, Nund Rishi, Zain Shah Sâheb and many others. On the other hand, some Kashmîri mystics belong to the traditional orders. Thus Makhdoom Sâheb was a Suharwardy. Of the sufis from outside, Dastgîr Sâheb was a Qâdirî, Naqshband Sâheb, naturally, a Naqshbandi and Shâh-é-Hamadân a Kubrawi (a sub-sect of the Suharwardys).

References

i Mentioned by Muhammad Ashraf Fâzili in *Junûbî Hindustân mein Islâm ki Ibtedâ* (Urdu), Islâmic Productions, Buchhpora, Srînagar 190011. (Year not stated, but around 2002.)

ii Sheikh Muhammad Ikrâm, *Âb-é-Kausar* (1941), Farîd Book Depot, Daryaganj, New Delhi 110002.

iii Both quotes are from Khân, Ishaq, op cit below.

iv Mohammad Ishaq Khân, *Kashmîr's Transition to Islâm*; Manohar, New Delhi, third edition: 2002.

Aish Muqâm, on the way to Pahalgam

Bâbâ Réshî near Gulmarg

Chapter- 11

The Islâmic Shrines of Kashmîr

Some of the more important Muslim shrines of Kashmîr are mentioned below. Most of them have been named after the patron saint, who is often (but not always) buried inside the shrine. There are more detailed notes about almost all these shrines in the chapters on their respective districts.

Kulgam – Anantnag

Aish Muqâm, on the road to Pahalgâm

Bâbâ Dawood Ghani at Vailoo

Bâbâ Hyder Réshî in Ânañtnâg town

Bâbâ Naseer-ud-Din Ghazi at Bijbehara.

Bam Zoo, on the road to Pahalgâm

Harut and Marut on the Mattan karewa

Hazrat Noor Shâh Baghdadi at Kund

Hazrat Sheikh Syed Samnani at Kulgam

Kâbâ Marg

Khiram Sirhâmâ

Seer Hamadân, on the road to Pahalgâm

Bandipora – Baramulla

Âsâr Sharief at Khwâjâ Sâheb, Bârâmullâ

Bâbâ Jangi at Shilwat, Sonâwârî

Bâbâ Réshî near Gulmarg

Bâbâ Shakur-ud-din Sâheb at Watlab

Bâbâ Usman Ghani ziârat at Jahama, Bârâmullâ

Dastgîr Sâheb at Plan, Bandipore

Dastgîr Sâheb at Qazi Hamam, Bârâmullâ

Hazrat Mîr Syed Ali Hamadâni, Khânqâh-e-Mu'ala at Sopore

Hazrat Sultân-ul-Arifeen at Aham Sharief, Bandipore

Hazrat Sultân-ul-Arifeen at Ramporâ, Bandipore

Hazrat Sultân-ul-Arifeen at Tujar, Sopore

Hazrat Syed Ahmed-ud-Din Sâheb at Bulgam, Bârâmullâ

Hazrat Syed Sâheb at Kreeri

Imâmbârâ at Mohalla Sona Buran, Inderkote, Sonâwârî

Karim Shâh Sâheb at the Qadeem Idgâh, Bârâmullâ

Khwâjâ Hilal Naqshband Sâheb at Nsasbal, Sonâwârî

Khwâjâ Rahim Sâheb at Chewa, Sonâwârî

Sofi Satar Sâheb at Chakla, Rafiabad

Syed Ghareeb Sâheb at Gund Nowgam, Sonâwârî

Syed Hazrat Sultân at Kanisporâ

Syed Jâñbâz Wali at Khânporâ, Bârâmullâ

Syed Kirmani in Bârâmullâ

Syed Malik Bukhârî Sâheb at Nadihal, Bârâmullâ

Syed Muhammad Dâniyâl at Talarzoo, Sonâwârî

Syed Sâheb at Naid Khai, Sonâwârî

Budgâm

Alamdar-e-Kashmîr's ziârat at Hamchaporâ

Bâbâ Latif-ud-Din Qazi at Poshkar

Hazrat Ganga Bâbâ Rishi at Palaporâ (Poshkar)

Hazrat Saleh at Khân Sâheb

Hazrat Syed Zia-ud-Din Bukhârî at Kanihama

Imâmbârâ at Budgâm

Sham Ded at Poshkar

Sheikh Noor-ud-Din Rishi at Tsrâr [or Chrar]-e-Sharief

Syed Muhammad Samri at Lassaporâ

Syeds Taj-ud-Din and Alla-ud-Din at Sikandarporâ

Kupwâra

Bâbâ Abdullah Gazi in Kralporâ Guzrail

Mîr Muhammad Ibrahim at Kanthporâ, Lolâb

Parkash Akhoon in Gurhi

Zati Shâh in Muqâm near Drugmulla

Shopian – Pulwama

Mantaqi Sâheb at Awantipur

Akber Deen Sâheb at Dâdasar

Hazrat Ameer Kabeer Shâh-é-Hamadân at Drumbal

Sheikh Bairzid Shimnagi above Payer

Âsâr Sharief at Pinjoora

Jâmâ Masjid at Shopian

Shâh-é-Hamadân at Trâl

Hazrat Mîr Syed Muhammad Hamadâni at Trâl Pâîñ

Srînagar City

Âsâr Sharief, Kalashpurâ

Âlî Masjid

Aishan Sâheb

Akhoon Mulla Shâh

Bat Mazâr

Batamâloo Sâheb

Bulbul Lankar

Dastgîr Sâheb

Hasanabad mosque

Hazratbal

Jâmâ Masjid

Jenâb Sâheb, Soura

Khwâjâ Habib Ullah Attar

Madni Sâheb

Makhdoom Sâheb

Mirza Kâmil

Naqshband Sâheb

Naushehra

Patther Masjid

Rozabal

Shâh-é-Hamadân

Ganderbal

Lâl Bâb Shâh at Zakûrâ

Qamar Sâheb at Salora, Ganderbal

Shâh Sadiq Qalander at Wutta, Lâr

Wâñgat Sharief at Wâñgat, Kangan

The Jâmâ Masjid of Shopian

Rozabal - Supposedly the Tomb of Lord Jesus Christ in the heart of Srinagar

Rozabal - Some believe that these are the foot prints of Lord Jesus, imprinted on stone and kept in the tomb, Note the crucification scars

Chapter- 12

Lord Jesus Christ in Kashmîr and Ladâkh

A sign outside Rozabal (Khânyâr, downtown Srinagar) tells all visitors, in English, that the shrine inside is *not* the tomb of Lord Jesus Christ. Clearly the keepers of the shrine have no interest in attracting tourists by implying that it is-or might be. Nor does the tourist trade of Kashmîr. I am not sure why. In my case, I can not accept that the Lord was buried at Rozabal, because I believe that Jesus died on the cross, was buried, rose on the third day and ascended *bodily* to heaven.

And yet the evidence is too plentiful, too solid, to ignore. Even if we do not concede that Christ died in Srinagar, there seems to be proof of the highest grade that at least he lived in Kashmîr and Ladâkh for a while. That's why the controversy refuses to die.

I have an elaborate theory of 'retrospective visits' by divine persons and prophets to lands where their religion reached several centuries later. Thus, Mauritian Hindus now claim that the Hindu deity Lord Hanuman had flown over their charming island and had established a holy lake there. After Hindu soldiers started going to Ladâkh, legends arose that Hanuman ji had flown over Kargil as well, and that Draupadi ji had bathed near Drass. All Muslims hold the Biblical Solomon in high esteem. Therefore, the tallest hill in Srinagar town has retrospectively become the

Koh-e-Suleiman (Solomon's hill), on which his *takht* (throne) is said to have been kept.

The Islâmic position

Kashmîrî Muslims and Ladâkhi Buddhists have no similar incentive to invent stories about Lord Jesus. The Muslim establishment of Kashmîr neither supports nor is hostile to the idea of Rozabal being Lord Jesus' tomb. This could be because the Holy Quran does not accept that Jesus had died on the cross. (*'And they killed him not, nor did they cause his death on the cross,' [4:157].)*

On the other hand, Islâm does not oppose the doctrine of bodily ascension to heaven. There are two references in the Holy Quran to this, and both support bodily ascension:

Behold! Allah said:
"O Jesus! I will take thee
And raise thee to Myself..." (3: 55)
and
Nay, Allah raised [Jesus] up
Unto Himself; and Allah
Is Exalted in Power, Wise... (4: 158)

Thus, Islâm officially accepts that Lord Jesus was 'taken up'. Incidentally, even the Bible uses the expression 'taken up into heaven' (Mark 16: 19). Thus, if Christ did not die on the cross, he could have gone to Kashmîr after the crucifixion, to live *and* die there. And yet, if he ascended bodily to heaven then he could at best have lived in Kashmîr and not died there.

Therefore, researchers like Aziz Kashmîrî and Fida Hasnain (both Kashmîrîs) and Rabbi Dahan Levi (of Morocco and Paris) have dug up evidence *despite* indifference in Kashmîr and hostility elsewhere. The Christian establishment is not amused by claims about the existence of a tomb of Lord Jesus Christ. (Nor, as I said, am I. But after my first visit to Rozabal, I was overwhelmed by a presence that I can't explain.)

The Bhavishya Maha Puran

The clincher is a passage from the Sanskrit *Bhavishya Maha Puran* (lit.: the great scripture about the future), believed to have been written by Vyas in A.D. 115. Thanks to Aziz Kashmîrî I have seen the photocopy of a page from the 1910 edition of the book. My first reaction on reading the page was, 'This can't be true. This must be a forgery. Or at least the book wasn't originally written in A.D. 115. This could be a later interpolation.' However, there can be no reason why a Hindu Mahârâjâ should have ordered the printing of a tampered version of an ancient Hindu scripture. Certainly, not to prove that Lord Jesus had lived in Kashmîr when there was no advantage in doing so.

The said passage reads, 'There [while in a country in the mountains, Raja Shakewahin] saw [what appeared to be] a Raja of Sakas at Wien, who was fair and wore white clothes. ['Wien' is 18 km. from Srinagar, where the Khrew Cement Factory now is.] He asked the man who he was. His reply was that he was Yusashaphat [Yuz Aasaf], and had been born of a woman...

'[The man also said:] "O Raja, when truth had disappeared and there was no limit [to evil practices] in the malechha [infidel] country, I appeared there and through my work the guilty and the wicked suffered, and I too suffered at their hands."

'The Raja asked him what his religion was. He replied, "It is to establish love and truth and to purify one's heart and for this I am called *Isa Masih*." (Emphasis added.)

Aziz Kashmîrî (born 1919) has in his possession a photocopy of this page, taken from the *Bhavishya Maha Puran* (p. 282, ch. iii, sec. II, shloka 9-31, translated by Vidyavaridi Dr. Shiv Nath Shastri). The photocopy and more details about the information contained in this chapter appear in Aziz Kashmîrî's book *Christ in Kashmîr,* Roshni Publications, Srinagar. Its eighth edition was published in 1998.

The Sanskrit text has four incredible references. In verse 22 we are told of 'Ish Putram', the Son of God. The word 'Ish' is suspiciously close to 'Isa,' the Indo-Islâmic version of the name of Iesus Nazarenus, known in some Western countries as Jesus Christ.

Two verses later, the speaker says, 'Masiho Ahem', 'I am the messiah'. Verse 25 leaves nothing to the imagination. It begins with the name of 'Isha Maseeh', 'Jesus the Messiah'. Either we have a major forgery here, or a revelation of earth shaking dimensions. If these words were indeed written in A.D. 115, then there can be no doubt that this fair man in white clothes, this son of God, this messiah who calls himself Isha Maseeh, was Lord Jesus himself. Later in the same verse we have another reference to 'Maseeh', this time with a terminal 'h'. Verse 27 mentions 'Maseeha', the messiah, yet again.

'*Ish*' is the Hindu word for God. So that part can be a coincidence. But the concept of 'messiahs' is unknown to Hinduism. If the above mentioned page 282 of the A.D. 1910 edition is a faithful reproduction of the A.D. 115 original, then no further proof is needed.

And the amount of related evidence that's available is not funny.

Early Kashmîrî beliefs about Christ-like saints

That a non-Muslim saint or prophet or king ('Sultan') lies buried at Rozabal has always been known. The way the grave has been laid is unIslâmic. (Hazrat Yuz Aasaf's feet face West. The Holy Kâba is West of Kashmîr.) The stone used, the architecture, the impression on stone of a pair of gigantic feet and the decorative motifs in the tomb are all pre-Islâmic: Hindu, to be precise.

But Hindus are cremated, not buried in graves. So this saint-king must have been Jewish or Christian.

The *Râjâtarañginî* (written 1148-50) took the *Bhavishya Maha Puran's* account further. There is no question of an interpolation in this very popular book. Too many copies of it have always existed. Besides, it has been translated repeatedly. There are two Persian versions, one ordered by Kashmîr's own King Budshah Zain-ul-Abedin (15th century) and the other by the Mughal Emperor Akbar (16th century). There also are three English versions (19th and 20th centuries).

The *Râjâtarañginî* mentions Sandhimati Arya Raj, the 'greatest of all saints,' as having been a minister in the court of King Jayendra (61 B.C.-A.D. 24). This saint led a life of poverty, was imprisoned for a long while and 'died at the stake'. He was resurrected, after which he 'consented to the prayers of the citizens' and ruled Kashmîr for 47 years.

Executing people 'at the stake' is not part of the Indian tradition.

The story of Sandhimati sounds almost as if it were taken right out of the Old Testament. Witness:

'There was a rumour that the time would come when Sandhimati would reign... The king, alarmed at the probable consequences, threw Sandhimati into prison... and intended to execute [him].' (Book II, Page 30)

Shades of Herod and the Pharoah?

Matthew 27:37 says of the crucified Christ, 'And over his head they put the charge against him, which read, "This is the King of the Jews." '

The *Râjâtarañginî* says about Sandhimati, who had similarly died on a stake: 'But when [Sandhimati's master, Ishana] was going to perform the last ceremony [on Sandhimati], the following lines marked on his forehead by Vidhata [God] caught his eye: "Poverty so long as he lives, ten years' imprisonment, death on a pale, and then kingdom again." ' (Appendix C, page v, Volume I, *KOK*.)

'Kingdom again' could refer to 'Rex Iudaeorum' or to Jesus' kingdom in heaven, more likely the latter.

Or take these three aspects of the resurrection:

i) 'Necodemus also, who had at first come to him by night [after Jesus' crucifixion], came bringing a mixture of myrrh and aloes…' (John 19:39)

Ishan (a) could not sleep on the night of Sandhimati's crucifixion. 'At midnight… he felt the smell of burning incense…' (*KOK,* Vol. I, Appendix C, page v.)

ii) Mary Magdalene 'saw two angels in white, sitting where the body of Jesus had lain, one at the head and one at the feet…' (John 20:12)

Ishan (a) 'saw Yoginis [female yogis] coming that way with a burning light. They then got hold of [Sandhimati's] skeleton and ran away with it…' (*KOK,* Vol. I, Appendix C, page v.)

iii) After Sandhimati had risen from the dead, he went to the town. 'The citizens… at first doubted the identity of Sandhimati, but his speech dispelled their doubts.' ' (*KOK,* Vol. I, Appendix C, page vi.)

Didn't Thomas ('the Twin') have similar doubts, too?

Some historians, like Hassan (19th century), list Yuz Aasaf among the Muslim saints of Kashmîr.

Sufi, the 20th century historian, pooh-poohs the Christ in Kashmîr theory. He says that Yuz Aasaf was merely the Egyptian ambassador at the court of Budshah. Yet, far from clearing up the mystery, Dr. Sufi only adds to it. He points out that the name Yuz Aasaf, if written in the Arabic script, can be read as 'Bodhisattva'. (There is a parallel belief that the 'Maitreya' of Buddhism is the same as the 'Messiah'[and the Mahdi of the Shiites]. So, if Yuz Aasaf was the Bodhisattva, the plot only thickens.)

The origins of the belief

Christianity was late in coming to most of north India. The British rulers of India did not encourage its spread either. However, after they annexed much of North India (around 1857) at least the religion started looming on the consciousness of the average north-Indian.

The 'Christ came to/ is buried in Kashmîr' theory was first put forward in the mass media through a book entitled *Maseeh Hindustan Mein* (The Messiah in India). It was written around 1899 and published in 1908. Its author was Khalifa Noor-ud-Din of Jalalpur Jattan (district Gujrat, Punjab). He was a member of the then recently established Ahmadiyya Movement. Its founder, Hazrat Mirza Ghulam Ahmad, sent the Khalifa to Srinagar to research the hypothesis that was, till then, limited to folk beliefs and little known manuscripts. As many as 566 people in Kashmîr signed a statement to the effect that (they believed that) Rozabal was the tomb of Lord Jesus.

The book cited Islâmic sources to show that the Lord had travelled to Nasibain, and then through Iran and Afghânistan to Kashmîr. It claimed that the ten lost tribes of Israel had migrated to and settled in Kashmîr (and Afghânistan). It also quoted Buddhist texts which indicated that the Buddha had predicted that five hundred years after his death another Buddha, called *Mitya,* would arise. This name has been widely interpreted by not just the Ahmadiyyas but by countless Hindu and Buddhist scholars as being the same as 'messiah'.

Aziz Kashmîrî writes, '[The said book] also adduces authentic proof that Jesus Christ has been mentioned by the name of *Mi-Shi-Hu* in books written in Tibet during the 7th century A.D.' (The 'said book' is *A record of the Buddhist religion* by I. Tsing.)

Khwaja Nazir Ahmad, a barrister from Lahore, based in England, elaborated on the theme in the 1940s. He claimed to have evidence that Jesus visited Takshashila (Taxila, now in Pakistan), accompanied by 'Judas Thomas'. Apparently Mary (presumably Mother Mary), who was with them, died and was buried at Murree (also in Pakistan). There's a tomb at Murree, known as the *Shrine of Mai (mother) Mari*, who is supposed to have been Mother Mary. It is now being claimed that Muree itself has been named after Mother Mary. *Mari* does sound like Mary, but surely the Mother would have been called Mariam, which isn't quite the same.

(Hassnain and Levi say that the other famous Biblical Mary, Magdalene, was buried at Kashgar in Central Asia.)

The Khwaja added that Lord Jesus then reached Kashmîr where he lived and proselytised for 125 years, and where he died and was buried.

In 1953, Aziz Kashmîrî published an article citing historical records which indicated that Prophet Moses was buried in a tomb on a reddish mountain near Moab on Nebo Ball (Booth) in Bandiporâ.

In 1967, a group of top ranking Kashmîrî clerics and leading journalists, including Aziz Kashmîrî, went over to Rozabal. They recorded what the people of the neighbourhood, Khanyar, believed about the origins of the shrine. The people, to the last man, were of the view that a Prophet called Yuz Aasaf lay buried in the tomb and that he had come to Kashmîr during the reign of Raja Gopanand.

Thus, it will be seen, the theory was propounded, and has been kept alive, by the Ahmadiyya movement throughout the Indian sub-continent. In Kashmîr its main votaries are Aziz Kashmîrî, his family and their family-run newspaper, *Roshni.* At the academic level Prof Hasnain and, later, Rabbi Dahan Levi have taken it forward.

The West has always abounded in revisionist theories about the Bible. Aziz Kashmîrî informs us that one J.M. Robert wrote a book called *Antiquity Unveiled* (Oriental Publishing Co., Philadelphia, USA) in 1912. The book claims that insofar as there is a historical Jesus, it is Appollonius of Tayana.

Kashmîrî adds that W. Raymond Drake, who wrote *Spacemen in the Ancient East* in 1970, seemed inclined to accept the 'Jesus was really Appollonius of Tayana' theory. Drake was probably the first western writer to refer to the belief that Jesus had 'survived the cross and lived in Rome, then died in India'.

So, outside obscure manuscripts, the whole controversy is as recent as that.

Could Christ have come to Kashmîr?

'And We made the son of Mary and his mother as a Sign: We gave them both shelter of high ground, affording rest and security and furnished with springs.' The Holy Quran (23: 50)

Aziz Kashmîrî has used a commentary on the Holy Quran in which the words "(and due to greenery)" appear after the word 'ground' in the above verse. For Maulana Muhammad Ali and Aziz Kashmîrî the place referred to in verse 23: 50 is obvious: Kashmîr.

I have used the official translation published by 'The Custodian of the Two Holy Mosques' (i.e. the King of Saudi Arabia). This version, in a footnote, discourages any speculation about the place. It says, 'There is no need to look far for the place where the mother and child were given secure shelter. It is described in xix. 22-26... There was a fruitful palm-tree... and she and her child rested there until it was time for her to go to her people with her child.'

Kashmîr has no palm-trees (though I have seen some in neighbouring Jammû, on a high ground, with a spring nearby). Secondly, while Ali and Kashmîrî assume that the mother and child travelled to this place after 'the event of the Cross', the version that I have consulted implies that we are looking at the days immediately after the birth of Christ.

Verse 23: 50 lends itself to either interpretation and does not mention palm trees.

Kashmîrî cites the *Ibn Kathir* (vol.ii, p.246) to the effect that 'according to a saying of the Holy Prophet [peace be upon him], Jesus lived 120 years'. He then cites oral testimony saying that the people of Kashmîr believe that Yuz Aasaf, the prophet buried at Rozabal, had come to Kashmîr from the West 2000 years ago.

Regarding the tomb itself, Kashmîrî quotes from a 10th or 11th century Arabic book, Shaikh Al-Said-us-Sadiq's *Ikmal-ud-Din.* The book says, 'But before his death [Yuz Aasaf] sent for a disciple of his, Bâbâd by name, who used to serve him and was well versed in all matters.' (Apparently, Bâbâd was St. Thomas.) Yuz Aasaf then 'directed Bâbâd to raise a tomb over him (at the very place he died). He then stretched his legs towards the West and turned his head towards thc East and died. May God bless him.'

We learn that Bâbâd erected a tomb 'in the style of Israelites and kept the window in the same manner. [He] inscribed the mark of [Jesus'] feet on [a] stone'. The original walls and roof are gone. What remains, especially the engraved stone, is similar in style to Hindu temples like Martand, Shankaracharya and Awantiporâ.

That St. Thomas had come to India, where Hindu fanatics killed him in Chennai, is history. Was he the same as Bâbâd? And was Yuz Aasaf the same as Lord Jesus?

What do we know about H. Yuz Aasaf ?

Sixteenth and nineteenth century scholars accepted that Yuz Aasaf was from the West and was a 'prophet' and a king. But nowhere did they put a date as old as the beginning of the Christian era. Yuz, of course, is similar to several non-English pronunciations of the name 'Jesus'. It is one of the Persian names of Jesus, seen as 'the collector, the gatherer'. And Aasaf? It means 'a leper who had been cured by Lord Jesus and who had then rejoined the world of the healthy'.

The Muslims do not use the word 'prophet' lightly. Islâm accepts Hazrat Muhammad, peace be on him, as the 'seal of the prophets'. Almost all Muslims interpret this as meaning that while there were several prophets *before* Hazrat Muhammad, there will be none after him. Therefore, Hazrat Yuz Aasaf must obviously have come before.

The oldest extant historical record about Yuz Aasaf are the words of Syed Naseer-ud-din Baihaqi of Khanyar, a 15th century saint. He is buried next to Hazrat Yuz Aasaf. A Persian verse written by him indicates that H. Yuz Aasaf had died several centuries before and was a 'prophet' and a 'sultan'. *Vâqeyât-e-Kashmîr*, an early history of Kashmîr, says that God appointed Yuz Aasaf as the 'prophet of Kashmîr'. So Yuz went over to Kashmîr and 'invited the people to [accept] the truth.' However, a contemporâry of 'Budshah' (King Zain-ul-Abedin) says in '*Vaqâye-e-Kashmîr*' that 'Yuz Asap,' a descendant of Prophet Moses, was the Egyptian envoy at Budshah's court. Since no details have been given about 'Yuz Asap,' he needn't be the same as H. Yuz Aasaf.

The 19th century historian Hassan believes that the two are the same. He says that there used to be a slab on the wall of the temple on Solomon/ Shankaracharya hill. Its inscription talked of an Egyptian youth who came to Kashmîr and claimed to be a prophet. Hassan says that when the Sikhs ruled over Kashmîr, one of them got the writing on that slab erased.

Aziz Kashmîrî quotes Mulla Nadiri (15th century), the first historian of Kashmîr who happened to be Muslim, as saying about the same wall, 'During [Raja Gopadatta's] reign… the dome of the temple on top of the mound of Sulaiman cracked. [The Raja] deputed one of his ministers named Sulaiman, who had come from Persia, to repair it. The Hindus objected that he was… of another religion. During this time Hazrat Yuz Asaf from Baitul Muqaddas [Jerusalem] [came] to the holy Valley, proclaimed his prophethood… it was because of this prophet's instructions that Sulaiman, whom the Hindus call Sandeman, completed the repairs of the dome in the year fifty and four. [Regardless of which of the two main Hindu calendars was followed, this would be in the first century of the Christian era. Raja Gopaditya's era has been variously estimated at the

6th and 1st centuries A.D. Gopananda's reign was almost certainly between A.D. 79 and 109.] Further, on one of the stones of the flank walls encasing the stairs he inscribed, "In these times Yuz Asaf proclaimed his prophethood" and inscribed on the other stone of the stairs that he was Yusu, Prophet of Children of Israel.'

What is eerie about this text, if authentic, is that it takes us back to Sandhimati [Sandeman]. The difference is that now it is Yuz Asaf, a contemporâry of Sandhimati, who has the attributes of Christ. Personally, I am intrigued by the fact that Sandhimati-Arya Raj had a Guru called Isan (ee-sân) who had saved him from crucifixion. 'When he came to see his disciple Sandiman, the whole city marched to welcome him and no one remained in his house.' (See also the chapter of 'Srinagar City.') The name Isan resembles 'Isa,' the Indo-Islâmic variant of Jesus' name. Isan is also the name of the Hindu God Shiv(a), whose wife is called, among other things, by the very Biblical name Sarah (pron. sâ-râ).

Kashmîrî, however, delivers another clincher. He quotes Nadiri as saying, 'I have seen in a book of Hindus that this prophet [Yuz Aasaf] was really Hazrat Isa [Jesus] *Ruh Allah*...'

At least this explains why the hillock known today as the Shankaracharya hill, and in older days as the Gopadri hill or Jest (Jyesth) Laddar, is called the Throne of Solomon by Muslims. The Solomon of the hill is obviously not the Solomon of the Bible.

Some of the teachings attributed to Yuz Aasaf are identical to those of Lord Jesus. Aziz Kashmîrî says that Yuz Aasaf called his gospel the *Bushra,* which is the Arabic word for a Christian 'gospel'. Kashmîrî adds that even Yuz Aasaf would relate the parable of the seed-sower.

Since the 20th century, it has been made out that the Kashmîrîs had always believed that Jesus (and Moses) were buried in Kashmîr, that the Kashmîrîs had always thought that they had descended from the Jews, and so on. However, the encyclopædic Hassan does not mention any of this. He merely says that the Shias believed that H. Yuz Aasaf was a descendant of Imam Jâfar Sadiq. We are now told that ancient and mediaeval Kashmîrî manuscripts had specifically mentioned *Isha Maseeh* [Jesus, the Messiah]. This was never known at the popular, mass level though.

However, Hassan hastens to add that enlightened persons say that 'the light of prophethood' radiates from the grave of H. Yuz Aasaf.

I agree. Jesus or not, all evidence indicates that a prophet lies buried at Rozabal. And 'prophet' is a word that no Muslim would use loosely.

In Ladâkh, Nepal and China

I remember reading about a village in Japan, the inhabitants of which are Caucasoid, tall and, often, brown-haired. They claim to be the descendants of Lord Jesus. Their story could be totally untrue. But legends about Jesus' visits pop up in Murree and Lahore (both in Pakistan), then Kashmîr, Ladâkh, Benares, Nepal and China. Add these dots together and you get a clearly defined and credible 'Jesus-route' from Palestine to China and Japan. No one in regions that are either north or south of that route claims that Jesus passed through or settled in their country.

Around 1887, a Russian traveller called Nicholas Notovich created a stir by claiming that 'In his fourteenth year, young Issa [Jesus], the Blessed One, came to [the Ladâkh] side of the Sindh [River Indus] and settled among Aryans, in the country beloved of God.' Apparently, Jesus had 'discourses with the Sudras' which infuriated 'the white priests' who decided to kill Issa. Jesus got to know of this and fled to Nepal. (Aziz Kashmîrî, quoting from Notovitch's *Life of Saint Issa* and from *Nineteenth Century.*)

Notovitch claims to have found this information in the library of the Hemis monastery in Ladâkh. One keeps hearing about this manuscript, which is said to have disappeared from public view since 1922. According to Notovitch's Mother of All Conspiracy Theories, the Vatican got the manuscript whisked away. Hassnain and Levi write, 'In 1894, the Church [apparently the Church of England, this time] deputed a neo-convert, Ahmad Shah to Ladâkh in the disguise of a *hakim*... to refute the findings of Nicolas Notovitch... It is probable that out of the [sic] great fear of the then British Government in India, the Buddhist Lama [of Hemis] concealed the scrolls or handed over some fragments to Ahmad Shah.'

Apparently, Lord Jesus spent the 'missing years,' from age thirteen to twenty-nine in the East, mainly India. The Brâhmins of Benares knew him as '*Saint Issa*' and accepted him as their '*Buddha*'.

Fida M. Hassnain and Dahan Levi have quoted at length from Notovitch. They show how Lord Jesus studied Buddhism, Jainism and other eastern religions during his six years in Sind, Benares, Kapilavastu, Rajagiri, the Punjab, Rajputana, Orissa and other parts of India. They go on to assert that 'the holy book of [R]evelation was the Tibetan Gospel.'

Aziz Kashmîrî says that he saw at Hemis a sketch 'of a Lama who, quite unlike other Lamas, [had] a beard... [One of the Lamas at Hemis said that this was a portrait of] Yashosh, the Lama who was raised two thousand years ago... Yashosh corresponds with Ashosh [see 'Aish Muqâm' in the chapter on 'Ânañtnâg'].' Yashosh is also similar to Yashoo, one of the Indian names of Jesus.

Hassnain and Levi have photographed what they claim is an ancient Ladâkhi mural which has crucifixes drawn on it.

Kashmîrî says that Nelson Bruknaer has written in *The Second Life of Jesus Christ* that he found Buddhist manuscripts at Hemis and Samvas (near Lhasa, Tibet). These indicated that the coming of the Bagwa Bodhisattva Avalokitesvar (the white, enlightened great merciful [being] who sees everything) had been prophesied 500 years before the birth of Jesus. Apparently these manuscripts talk of this incarnation as one who 'came from a foreign land,' as one who 'was born of a Virgin,' who 'spoke in parables,' who spoke of 'Amit Abha, God the Father' and who had 'wheel-like marks on his hand and feet'.

Bruknaer is further quoted as saying that 'In Japan, [the] teachings [of this prophet regarding] the Father God (Amit Abha) [are] now called "Namu Amida Butsu".'

Kashmîrî says that, in 1922, Swami Abehananda, a disciple of Sri Ramakrishna, translated 124 verses from the Hemis manuscript into Bengali. So, though the original Hemis manuscript has not been seen since, the Bengali translation of a portion of the manuscript might still be available.

This author has little time for conspiracy theories, especially those that portray the Vatican as a sinister-and omnipresent-body determined to snuff out all dissent. However, Kashmîr had at least heard of the Christ through Islâm. Hemis is incredibly isolated from the rest of the world. So if there's even a mention of 'Issa' in an ancient, or even mediæval, manuscript found at Hemis or Samvas, it would indicate that the Lord had visited Ladâkh or at least Tibet.

Conclusion

If the manuscripts of the *Bhavishya Maha Puran* and Mullah Nadiri's *Târeekh-e-Kashmîr* have not been tampered with and if the Hemis manuscript exists, then there can be no doubt but that Lord Jesus had lived for at least a while in Kashmîr and Ladâkh.

Too many copies of the *Râjâtarañginî* exist in several languages for any interpolations to have been made in recent centuries. The

Râjâtarañginî refers unambiguously to a Christ-like seer who was crucified by a Herod-like king, and who lived in and ruled over Kashmîr, possibly in the 1st century A.D.

In any case, there's an enormous amount of circumstantial evidence, which indicates that Jesus might have come to Kashmîr.

I believe that Lord Jesus ascended bodily to heaven. Therefore, I find it difficult to accept that his tomb could exist anywhere in the world. However, scholars like Aziz Kashmîrî have made out a fairly plausible case that Hazrat Yuz Aasaf, who lies buried in Rozabal, might have been Lord Jesus Christ himself.

Moses in Kashmîr

When they die, all good Americans go to Paris. The rest of us have to settle for heaven. Many, notably the Mughals, thought that Kashmîr was heaven on earth. The Kashmîrîs themselves think of their land as being 'a replica of heaven on earth'. Moses, the Prophet, was not just good, he was one of the best. So, it stands to reason that he, too, would be buried in Kashmîr.

The precise location is near the tomb of Sank Bibi on the Booth Mountain in Bandipura. According to Aziz Kashmîrî, Bandipura, which is 34 miles from Srinagar, was called Bethpura in the past. I have not been able to confirm this, or any of the other details given in this section, from 19th century records. So, I mainly have Aziz Kashmîrî's word for all this.

Francois Bernier (1620-1688) was perhaps the first to record the existence of a belief that 'Moses died in the city of Kashmîr and that this took place within a league of it'. (Srinagar was known as Shehr-e-Kashmîr or the city of Kashmîr during the 15th and 16th centuries. It would seem that some people still used the name when M. Bernier came visiting.)

Actually, it was the handy *Bhavishya Maha Puran* that is said to have first alluded to Moses. Must get the original manuscript checked. If it has not been tampered with then its contents revolutionise what the world knows about Moses and—as we have seen Jesus. Apparently it says, 'The entire land is full of the followers of the [sic] Moses with the exception of sacred land of river Sarasouti,' (P.I.A. 5, shlok 30, quoted in *Christ in Kashmîr*, p.21.)

Judaism was not unknown in this part of Asia. One Jewish family continued to live in Kabul (Afghânistan) till 1998. There were eminent

Jews in Srinagar till the 1960s. Kashmîrî quotes the November 23, 1898, issue of the British *Civil and Military Gazette,* Lahore, as saying, 'One of [the manuscripts found in South India] is an old copy of the *Book of Moses*, written on a roll of leather… It was brought from Cashmere.'

What the Old Testament itself records about the death of Moses is as follows:

'1 And Moses went up from the plains of *Moab* unto the mountain of *Nebo*, to the top of *Pis'gah*, that is over and against Jericho. And the LORD shewed him all the land of Gilead, unto Dan. 2 And all Naph'ta-li, and the land of E'phra-im, and Ma-nas'seh, and all the land of Judah, unto the utmost sea… 5 So Moses the servant of the LORD died there in the land of Moab… 6 And he buried him in a valley in the land of Moab, over against *Beth-pe'or*: but no man knoweth of his sepulchre unto this day.' (*Deuteronomy, 34: 1, 2, 5, 6;* The Holy Bible, King James Version, published by The Gideons International, 1978. The italics are all mine.)

Elsewhere, *Deuteronomy* (4: 46) talks again of 'the valley over against Beth-pe'or' and of *Heshbon*. Numbers (27: 12) mentions 'mount *Ab'a-rim*'.

Aziz Kashmîrî claims that Bethpura is the old name of Bandipura. This seems plausible because Beth is the local name of River Jehlum. 'Pura' means 'town' in all north Indian languages. Kashmîrî cites authority that Booth, the mountain where the said tomb is located, is really called Nebu Ball. He adds that *Pisgah*, aka *Chasmagah*, is a mile away from the tomb. Moab, he says, is a pasture north-east of the tomb believed to be Moses'. As for Heshbon, it's a little village now called Hasbal. Mount Abarim is a hillock 4 miles from Moab, called *Abul* or *Ablu* by the local people.

Kashmîrî goes on to cite Nazim Sewharwi's *Nigaristan-e-Kashmîr* to the effect that the 'brothers Moses and Haroon [rested] at Haroon… The locality is famous as "Haroon" only because the prophet Haroon is [buried] there.' Srinagar has a suburb called Harwan. In Urdu '*Harwan*' is spelt exactly the same as '*Haroon*', the Muslim name for Aaron.

Far fetched? Perhaps. For this author it would be sufficient if it could be proved that Bandipura was indeed called Bethpura in the past.

My findings: I decided to cross-check the facts. Several elders of Bandipura said that their town was called Bethpura 'during the era of the Jews.' But the elders were merely going by what they had heard: more likely from the media than from their ancestors. Therefore, the evidence given by them is weak.

Revenue records have a section that mentions the *wajâh tasmiyâ* [the 'reason for naming' any person or place in a particular manner]. However, we could not find a single revenue record that confirmed this belief.

The oldest extant revenue record (which dates to AD 1890) says that the town took its name after its first inhabitants, the Bândey community [which is of a Turkish origin]. The name of the town's mediæval founder is Hasu (Hasan?) Mîr [again a Turkish name], who came here from Srînagar. No mention of Jews or Bethpeor.

Bandipura can *not* be a corruption of 'Bethpura' because both are full-fledged words, with distinct meanings. Bethpura (or Vethpura) means 'the town [near] River Jehlum.'

However, regarding the other italicised words, Mr. Aziz Kashmîrî does have a point. Almost all the places mentioned in the Bible and italicised by me above seem to be there. *Nebu Baal* (also called Ibâl and Mâwâ) is a hillock near Irun [pron. ee-run, rhymes with 'pun']. The tomb of Shank (or Sank, both rhyme with 'sunk') Bibi (also known as Dod Mouj or 'the milk mother') is in Bonthoo on a hillock called Booth. The so-called tomb of Moses, too, is in Bonthoo.

What Aziz Kashmîrî identifies with the biblical '*Moab*' is a meadow called '*Mâhâb*', which is close to '*Athwatoo*' (and beyond the Mântrey meadow).

And the mystery does not end there. A Vethpura (the name of which is often pronounced much like the Biblical Bethpeor) does exist in Kashmîr. It is a pretty village in the Lasjan area, right next to Srînagar City, on the banks of the Jehlum.

Note of caution: The quotes from Nâdiri's book are absolute clinchers about the 'Jesus in Kashmîr' theory: if they are authentic. But no one has seen a copy of this book in the last four hundred years. The only remnants that we have of Nâdiri's work are excerpts and quotations from it in Syed Ali's history, which was written in A.D. 1579.

The Jesus trail leads to Japan

Shingo, a farming village northeast of Tokyo (Japan), is not half as circumspect about its Jesus-connection. Indeed, its municipality has put up signboards that announce 'Tomb of Christ: Next Left.' The village, once known as Herai [which is said to be the local word for 'Hebrew'], realised in 1935 that it had a link with the Lord. That was when what is supposed to be Jesus' last will and testament was found in the neighbouring Ibaraki Prefecture.

Apparently the 21-year-old Jesus, known as Daitenku Taro Jurai in Shingo, went there to study the Shinto religion from a master. He spent twelve years in Japan before returning home to teach what he had learnt there (and perhaps also what Kashmîr, Ladâkh, Tibet and Benares had taught him).

When the Romans finally consented to the Christ's execution, the Lord managed to flee to Japan and the Romans crucified Daitenku Taro Jurai's younger brother Isukiri instead. This time Daitenku Taro Jurai travelled to Japan via Vladivostok and Alaska. In Shingo he married a girl called Miyuko, sired three daughters and died a natural death at the age of 106.

(My take is that Isukiri or Eesu Kiri is Japanese for Jesus Christ, and that is who died on the cross. The Bible does refer to someone who was the Lord's brother. Both brothers seem to have travelled from the Middle East to Pakistan, Kashmîr, Ladâkh, Tibet, Benares and finally Japan and perhaps it is the brother who is buried in Shingo.)

Chapter- 13

The Kashmîrî Pandits: Some important religious beliefs

Kashmîrî Shaivism

Pristine Hiñdûism: Justice Katju writes, 'The Kashmîri Brahmans are the only remnant left of the Hindus of Kashmîr...[They] have shown an amazing tenacity in sticking to their Vedic and Tañtrik heritage. Their shakha [branch] is Kath and their [scripture] veda is Krishna Yajurveda. Their *grihya sutra* which controls their rituals is Laughakshi, which certainly goes back prior to the Mahâbharata era.' Katju feels that the Kashmîrî Pandits are the only section of the Hindu community in India 'which has kept up its Vedic and Tañtrik heritage in all its purity unaffected by [the reform movements of later centuries].'

Kashmîrî Shaivism originated around the eighth or ninth century A.D. and continued to develop till the twelfth century.[1] It tried to resolve various religious and philosophical issues that older schools of Hiñdû thought had been unable to.

1 The Kashmîri Overseas Association's website (*Tantricism in Kashmîr*) by Acharya Dina Nath Shastri) says that the Shaivite philosophy emerged as early as in the 6th century. This is an interesting departure from the dates conventionally accepted, but no evidence has been given in support of this claim.

The Kashmîrî Pandits believe that Lord Shiv had earlier sent down sixty-four schools of thought (Bhairav-tañtrs). However, over the millennia these disappeared, mainly through disuse. So, Lord Shiv asked Durvasas, a saint, to rejuvenate these systems of learning. Durvasas, in turn, delegated this task to his 'spiritual sons.' They revived the systems or schools called Trîambaka, Amardaka and Shrinath. Kashmîrî Shaivism is based on Trîambaka. This is a 'monistic' philosophy, which is to say that it believes that reality is a unified whole and that all existing things can be ascribed to or described by a single concept or system. It rejects the view that mind and matter are formed by, or are reducible to, the same ultimate substance or principle of being.[i]

As part of the revival of the faith, Lord Shiv revealed seventy-seven Shiv Sûtrs to Shri Vâsûgupt in the early ninth century A.D. on the Mahâdev mountain near Srînagar. The story more or less echoes Moses' experience. The Lord visited the saint in a dream and said that the scripture had been etched on a rock. The saint found the rock and started spreading the message throughout Kashmîr.

Kashmîrî Shaivism is based on this scripture. It has also been influenced heavily by the Tâñtrik literature of the day and by the *tañtr* of the Buddhists.

Kashmîrî Shaivism is also known as Northern Shaivism, Pratyabhijna Darshan ('the philosophy of identification') and Trika-shâsan ('the Trika school'). Trika means 'three' or 'threefold.' Threes are auspicious in Hiñdûism in general and Shaivism in particular. Lord Shiv belongs to the divine trinity (Lord Brahmâ and Lord Vishnû are the other two members). He carries a trident. The 'three' of Trika also alludes to the three aspects of the Divine: shiv (divine benevolence), shaktî (power, energy) and the soul.

The Kashmîrî Pandits have, over the centuries, had a large number of important Gurûs and saints. That is because Kashmîrî Shaivism attaches enormous importance to meditation by devotees under the supervision of Gurûs. Meditation is the method through which the devotee becomes conscious of God (Shiv).

The Agams: There are many schools within Shaivism. The Agams are doctrines which are the basis of (and are common to) all these schools. They lay down that Shiv is the Supreme God. He accepts prayers and can be reached through yog(a).

The Agams broadly consist of the following doctrines: i) the five powers of Lord Shiv: creation, preservation, destruction, revelation and concealment;

ii) the three categories: pati, pashu and pasha [God, soul and bonds]; iii) the three bonds: anav, karm and mâyâ; iv) the three-fold power of Lord Shiv: ichhâ, kriyâ and gyân-shaktî; v) the thirty-six tattvs, or categories of existence, derived from the five elements of God; vi) the need for a satgurû (true master) and initiation (into religious practices); vii) the power of mañtr(a) (religious incantation); viii) the four pads: charya, kriyâ, yog(a) and gyân.[ii]

Tañtr(a)/ Tâñtrism

Lord Shiv has five mouths, Ishân, Tatpurush, Sadyojata, Vâmdev and Aghora. Each of these personifies one of his five energies, which respectively are Chit-shaktî (consciousness), Ânañd-shaktî (joy), Ichhâ-shaktî (volition), Gyân-shaktî (wisdom) and Kriyâ-shaktî (conduct). The science of Tañtr came out of the Lord's five mouths. His five energies unite with and control each other. Together they have enunciated the sixty-four schools mentioned earlier. These sixty-four Bhairav-tañtrs together make up Kashmîrî Shaivism and the Trika school.

What is Tañtr(a)? The word tañtr means 'ingredient,' 'temporal power,' 'enjoyment/ pleasure' and 'possessions.' But it also means 'determination,' 'decisive intentions,' 'the goal' and 'the solution.' These seemingly contradictory meanings reveal the essence of tañtr : that it links sex with spirituality.

Swati Chopra[iii] says that the word tañtr is a combination of the first syllables of the Sañskrit words *tanoti* and *trayati*. 'Tanoti' means 'to expand the consciousness' while 'trayati' means 'to liberate the consciousness.' She adds that tañtr is 'a science of sexuality/ ecstasy' that has been practiced not only in India and Tibet, but also in most indigenous cultures of the world.

However, in the context of Kashmîr, sexual and occult practices are played down. Justice Katju writes, '[Tañtr Shâstr] is one of the most misunderstood subjects not only in India but throughout the world. In popular thought and imagination a Tâñtrik is a person who dabbles in strange, awful and mysterious rites involving visits to cremation grounds and [the] use of wine and women. He is feared also because he is credited with powers of inflicting harm as also of bringing relief and good fortune… [The] earnest Tâñtrik practitioner avoids being caught in the mesh of sidhis and keeps his eyes fixed on his spiritual objective very often preferring anonymity.'

What is to be remembered is that the Tañtr Shâstr is (along with Kâvya, Nâtya, Vedâñt and Vyâkaran) one of the Dharm Shastrs (scriptures) of the Hindus. At least in Kashmîr it is mainstream, and is not a fringe practice as in much of the rest of India. Most scholars agree that it is based on the Véds. However, a small minority of scholars says that Tâñtrik practices are older than the Véds. At least in Kashmîr they are older than mainstream Shaivism, Buddhism and Vaishnavism.

Tañtr also aims to solve the mysteries and hidden secrets of religion.

What does Kashmîrî tañtr consist of? The various texts of Kashmîrî tañtr (mentioned in italics) deal with a whole range of issues, which are:

i) Methods of prayer and worship: Distinctive prayers for various gods and goddesses (*Dévî Rahasya*), how to pray to Tripur Sundari (*Vâmakéshwarî Mâtâ Vivarn*), incantations to appease the nine planets (*Dévî Rahasya*), directions for ceremonial prayers (*Gañdharv-Tañtr*) and prayers for Nîl Saraswati, the goddess of learning (*Brihat Nîl Tañtr*).

ii) Philosophy: The trika system of Shaivism (*Mâlini Vijay Tañtr* and *Mâlini Vijay Vartikam*), the principles of Shaivism (*Mrigéndr Tañtr*), general philosophical issues (*Vâmakéshwarî Mâtâ Vivarn*), how Shaktî is Tripur-Sundari (*Vâmakéshwarî Mâtâ Vivarn*) and various Shaivite ceremonials (*Vâmakéshwarî Mâtâ Vivarn*).

iii) Acquiring literary prowess: The *Brihat Nîl Tañtr* teaches how to become a good poet.

iv) Methods of meditation: Various types of meditation (*Gañdharv-Tañtr*), how to purify oneself before prayers, holy chants, and yogic and Shaivite postures (*Gañdharv-Tañtr*), the principles of spiritual yog(a) (*Vigyân Bhairav Tañtr*) and types of meditation (*Vigyân Bhairav Tañtr*).

v) Arcane philosophical issues: The two-volume *Nétr Tañtr* dwells on the destructive power of Lord Shiv's eye, when he is enraged.

vi) Health and medicine: Special yogic practices for the prevention and cure of all kinds of illnesses (*Gañdharv-Tañtr*) and various types of chemical and herbal medicines (*Uddamaréshwar Tañtr*),

vii) The occult: And, yes, despite what Justice Katju says, Kashmîrî tañtr deals with those other things, too: The worship of cremation-grounds (*Dévî Rahasya*), matters related to the distillation and consumption of alcohol (again *Dévî Rahasya*), meditation in truly desolate places like deserts, cremation-grounds, forests and remote mountains (*Brihat Nîl Tañtr*) and how to perform magic (*Uddamaréshwar Tañtr*).

Important religious beliefs of Kashmîrî Pandits

The guardian goddesses of the Kashmîrî Pandits: Almost every Hiñdû clan (*kul*) worships one particular god (*dévatâ*) or goddess (*dévî*). This is their kul dévatâ (lit.: clan deity; in effect, their guardian deity). The Kashmîrî Pandits' main Kul Dévîs are Ragnya, Shârikâ, Jwâlâ, and Bâlâ Tripur Sundarî.

Mother goddesses (mâtrikâs): Shumbh was a demon who was stunned by the beauty of Pârvatî, the mother goddess. He asked Pârvatî jî to marry him. She told the demon that she would only marry someone who could defeat her in battle and thus prove that he was a better warrior than she. A bloody series of battles began, in which Shumbh lost all his best warriors. So, Shumbh decided to go to the battlefield in person, at the head of a very powerful army.

The battle seemed quite unequal. On the one hand was a huge army, and on the other two mother goddesses: Pârvatî jî[2] and Kâlî Mâtâ. Actually, Kâlî Mâtâ is a deity who had emerged from Pârvatî jî's body in order to help her. Therefore, what Shumbh's army was up against was two forms of the same goddess, and not two different goddesses. The gods found this very unfair. So, the Shaktîs (divine energies) of the Lords Brahmâ, Vishnû, Shiv, Kârtikeya, Indr, Varâh and Narsingh left the bodies of these gods and went to the battlefield to help Pârvatî jî. These Shaktîs all became mother goddesses and were called Brâhmani, Vaishnavi, Maheshwari, Kaumâri, Indrânî, Varâhî and Narsingh respectively.

The Kashmîrî Pandits worship them as Matrikas in the Yañtr prayer of Shârikâ Bhagwati and in the Âvaran prayer of the Yañtrs of the goddesses Ragnya, Jwâlâ and Bâlâ.

Mahâ Vidyâs: These are ten goddesses: Kâli, Baglâ, Chinnamasta, Bhuvaneshwari, Mâtângî, Kamalâ Dhumavati, Tripur Sundari, Târâ and Bhairavî. The Tañtriks worship them and their qualities. While Tañtriks have several kinds of rituals, all of them worship Shaktî (lit.: power, as embodied by a mother goddess or Dévî).

---

2 'Can [this manifestation of the mother goddess] be our Shârikâ Bhawani?' Justice Katju speculates.

The stories are almost identical, even in their details. Therefore, the two must be the same. This manifestation of the goddess was certainly of Durgâ Mâtâ. Therefore, Durgâ Mâtâ and Shârikâ Bhawani, too, seem to be the same deity.

The Bhairavs: Now, the goddesses of Shaktî can not be worshipped in isolation. There is a Pârvatî jî for each Mahâ Vidyâ. The two have to be worshipped together. For the same reason, there is a Bhairav for each Kul-Dévî of the Kashmîrî Pandits.

The Kul Dévî	Her Bhairav
Ragnya	Bhuteshwar
Shârikâ	Vâmdev
Jwâlâ	Mahâdev
Bâlâ Tripur Sundarî	Karneshwar

'Self-created' icons: Throughout the Himâlayas (including Nepal)-and also some other parts of India-there are temples with swayambhû ('self-created;' pron. soyambhu by the Kashmîrî Pandits) icons. These are not idols made by any human but sacred rocks (shilâs) that emerged from the earth on their own-or which some god or goddess had converted himself (or herself) into. This is true of the shrines of Shârikâ ji and Jwâlâ ji as well. Their icons, too, are sacred rocks.

Vegetarianism: Hiñdûs who eat meat are almost always apologetic (and subconsciously guilty) about the fact. This is especially true of Brâhmins. Not so in Kashmîr. The Kashmîrî Pandits have for centuries eaten meat, fish and eggs. Other meat-eating Hiñdûs stay away from meat and eggs at least on religious occasions. On the contrary, the Kashmîrî Pandits eat meat and fish during the 'Heyrat Puja' (prayer) of the 'Khechir Mawas.'

Almost all meat-eating Hiñdûs in North India abstain from meat and eggs during the Navarâtrîs. Those Kashmîrî Pandits whose guardian goddesses are Shârikâ ji and Jwâlâ ji eat meat during the Navarâtrîs as well. Shrâdh (prayers for the dead on their death anniversaries) are solemn, meatless occasions in almost all parts of India. In Kashmîr meat is part of Shradh food as well.

Almost 95% of the population of the Valley of Kashmîr was Muslim in 1989, i.e. just before the Kashmîrî Pandits' mass-migration. Mainstream Islâm does not frown on eating meat. Therefore, it is assumed that the tiny Kashmîrî Pandit minority took to the Muslims' ways. Perhaps. However, we must remember that the Hiñdûs of several other Himâlayan regions (notably Nepal, Assam, Jourhian Mâtâ [near Jammû] and, till the early 20th century, Jammû proper), too, sacrifice (and then eat) animals on religious occasions, especially Dussehrâ.

However, many Pandits, especially women, are turning vegetarian, at least on auspicious days, after the example of Hindus from other parts of India. This trend began as a trickle in the mid-20th century, but gained momentum only in the 1990s.

The Kashmîrî Pandits' general 'laxness' in religious matters-and their fraternal relations with the Muslims: Several observers-Indian as well as British Raj-have commented on the general 'laxness' of the Kashmîrî Pandits in matters of religion. 'Intelligent Hiñdûs have often told me,' Walter Lawrence wrote, 'that a great laxness has crept into the Hiñdû religion [in Kashmîr] within the last ten years... People grumble at having to climb up the Takht-i-Suliman [the Shankarâchârya Hill] on the day of Sheorátrî... There are some curious facts about the Kashmîr Brahmans which deserve mention. They are said to be extremely strict about following the rules of Brahmanism when they visit India, but in their own country they do things which would horrify the orthodox Hiñdûs. They will drink water brought by a Musalmán; they will eat food cooked on a Musalmán boat; the foster-mother of Hiñdû children is usually a Musalmánî, while the foster-brother often obtains great power in a Hiñdû household. Mahârâjâ Gulab Singh did his utmost to stop the practice of drinking water brought by a Musalmán, and severely interdicted the eating of cheese. But it was all to no effect... the Hiñdûs failed to comply with [the Mahârâjâ's] edicts... [The Hiñdûs] are flesh-eaters. An interesting fact about the Hiñdûs of Kashmîr is that they worship the likeness of Her Majesty the Queen Empress [Victoria]. This prevails not only among the Pandits of the city, but also among the village Hiñdûs. It appears to be their custom to regard as divine the sovereign de facto, but in the case of the emperor Aurangzeb they made an exception, and his likeness was never worshipped...'

(Mahâ-) Shivarâtrî

This is the most important festival of the Kashmîrî Pandits-and has been so all through recorded history.[iv]

Antiquity: The *Nîlmat Purân* (6th or 7th century A.D., if not earlier) and The *Râjâtarañginî* (A.D. 1148) both mention Shivarâtrî as the quintessential festival of Kashmîrî Hiñdûs.

The festival: There are twelve Shivarâtrîs in a year. The Mahâshivarâtrî is the biggest of these. (Mahâshivarâtrî is loosely called just Shivarâtrî)

Shivarâtrî means 'the night of Shiv.' On this day Lord Shiv had come down to our world in order to redeem his devotees. Hiñdûs celebrate the occasion by fasting and praying all night long, at home and in temples. The festival signifies the merger of the *jîva* (a person's soul) with the *paramâtmâ* (lit. 'the supreme soul,' meaning God Himself).

For the Kashmîrî Pandits this is also the anniversary of Lord Shiv's wedding with Umâ (Pârvatî). The Pandits eat meat and fish to celebrate the festival, and offer meat as part of the sacred rituals. This, as we have seen, is unusual for a Hiñdû community. The Kashmîrî Pandits' justification is that the Bhairavs whom Lord Shiv had brought along in his wedding procession were no vegetarians. The Kashmîrî Pandits don't want to be seen as being lacking in hospitality, so they serve meat and fish to us modern-day Bhairavs.

Seasonal significance: The festival marks the end of winter and lasts several days. Different sects within the community celebrate it on different days. Married women give presents to their mothers-in-law, especially on the first 'Heyrath' after marriage (explained on next page). They also visit their parents, who give them gifts.

Spiritual significance: On this day the planets line up in a particular arrangement. The Hiñdûs believe that this injects an unusual amount of energy into the human body. This increases the efficacy of prayer and meditation.

Shiv is the source of everlasting happiness. On this night the devotee seeks to merge his identify with Lord Shiv. This helps him realise eternal Truth, Happiness and Beauty (satyam, shivam and sundaram).

Shiv, as Vasudev[v] points out, means 'that which is not.' All us-and everything else-came out of nothing, and will all go back to being nothing. Which means that we came out of Shiv and shall go back to Him. The Muslims, like the Sikhs, venerate God as the great teacher (Rashîd, Ustâd or Gurû). The Hiñdûs, too, see Shiv as the first and foremost teacher and guide.

When celebrated: Mahâshivarâtrî is the night between the thirteenth and fourteenth days of the Indian lunar month of Phâgun (Phâlgun). The main festival is normally in late-February or the first week of March. However, for the Kashmîrî Pandits the festivities start several days before. Indeed, they run through almost the entire Krishn Paksh ('dark fortnight') of Phâgun: and beyond. ('Dark' refers to the 'darkness' of the night because the moon is on the wane. The Kashmîrî word for the Krishn

Paksh is 'gatt pachh.') In all, the festivities and merriment last 21 days. They end on the 8th day of the 'bright fortnight' (Shukl Paksh) of Phâgun.

Hiñdûs elsewhere observe Mahâshivarâtrî on the 14th day of Phâgun. The Kashmîrî Pandits do so a day before, on the 13th. 'Chaturdash' is Hiñdî for 'fourteen.' So Mahâshivarâtrî elsewhere is also called 'Shiv Chaturdashi.' Now one can't commemorate a Chaturdashi on the 13th of a month. So, to compensate, the Kashmîrî Pandits celebrate Shiv Chaturdashi, too, but a month before: in the Krishn Paksh of Mâgh (Jan-Feb). On that occasion, they fast for three days, don't cook (or eat) meat and worship Lord Shiv.

Heyrath and local adaptations: The Kashmîrî Pandits call this festival 'Heyrath.' This name has allegedly been derived the Persian word 'hairat' ('surprise' or 'astonishment). The festival is said to have got this name during the Afghân era in the valley. (In that case the first heyrath must have been celebrated in 1820, a few months after Afghân rule came to an end and Sikh rule began.)

The Legend: All Kashmîrîs believe that snow falls in plenty on this auspicious occasion[3], which marks the end of the worst part of winter. Therefore, on Shivarâtrî the Kashmîrî Pandits sing *Sona shîn volun dâri dâre/ Mahârâza râza kumâr hai âv* ('Hark! Snowflakes made of gold are wafting down/ Prince Shiv, the bridegroom, has come [to marry goddess Pârvatî]').

In the nineteenth century an Afghân administrator called Jabbâr is said to have persuaded the Kashmîrî Pandits to celebrate the festival in Âshâd (June-July), which is the hottest month of the year, and when there's no question of snowflakes in the inhabited areas. The Kashmîrî Pandits obeyed, and shifted Shivarâtrî to July that year. Then, miraculously, as if on cue, there was snowfall on the great day. This was a matter of 'hairat' for everyone. That is how Shivarâtrî got its Persian name.

(The miracle might well have occurred. Snow is known to have fallen in the higher mountains-above 12,000'-in all months of the year. However, the only Afghân governor by that name was one Jabbâr Khân, who ruled

3 Whether this is a miracle or a natural phenomenon, which has to do with the time of the year, can be debated. That it snows on Shivarâtrî can not be. From November 2002 to almost the end of February 2003, Kashmîr went through its worst drought in recent memory. All of us in Kashmîr were petrified about how we would manage for drinking water in the summer. Then, on the 21st February, 2003, i.e. on Shivarâtrî day, we received so much snow and rain that many parts of Srînagar and Budgâm got flooded. Those snowflakes were more welcome- and useful- than flakes of gold.

Kashmîr for a few months in 1819: too short a tenure to have allowed him tie to make such a big change. The Kashmîrî Pandits' legend, however, implies that it was this interference with tradition that resulted in a huge famine. In any case, Afghân rule in Kashmîr came to an end with Jabbâr's brief stint.)

The sequence of the rituals:

The first six days of the Krishn Paksh of Phâgun ('from 'hur ukdoh' or the 1st Phâgun to 'hur shiyam' or the 6th Phâgun): i) As in all lands that receive snow, houses in Kashmîr need cleaning after the long winter. So the first thing to be done is to clean up the house thoroughly: and decorate it for the festival. Hur is a Kashmîrî word than means both 'singing' and 'whitewashing.' The rituals of the first nine days all have the word 'hur' prefixed to their names. ii) The next thing is to buy the things required for the rituals connected with this fortnight. These things include walnuts, utensils and Vâtuk sâmagri ('prayer materials to worship Vâtuk with') for the main prayer on Shivarâtrî day. Till the 1940s, the walls of Kashmîrî houses used to be smeared with a paste of clay and cow-dung. That is how houses in much of rural South Asia are still 'white-washed.'

The 7th, 8th and 9th days of Phâgun ('hur sattam,' 'hur atham' and 'hur navam,' respectively): People attend night-long, congregational prayers, preferably in the temples of Ganpatyâr, Shârikâ Dévî, Pokhribal (all three being in Srînagar) and Khîr Bhawânî.

The Eighth Day ('Hur Ashtamî' or 'hur atham'): On this day most Kashmîrî Pandits would (and, if in Kashmîr, still do) visit the shrine of Shârikâ Dévî and the temple at Pokhribal (both in Srînagar). This is the birth anniversary of goddess Shârikâ. Those who live outside Srînagar try to make the trip to Shârikâ Dévî's shrine. If they can't, they go to the most important temple in the neighbourhood.

The night of the Eighth Day: Some devotees stay up all night at Shârikâ Dévî's shrine where bands of skilled singers would, till 1989, sing devotional songs (bhajans) for the congregation. Devotees normally join in the singing.

'Why the all-night prayers?' Vasudev[vi] explains, 'On this day the planetary position and the energy especially in the northern hemisphere are such that it is easy to move our energies upwards. To facilitate this, one should keep the spine vertical, and hence the tradition of staying awake throughout the night on Mahâshivarâtrî.'

Keeping the spine vertical on such occasions is also said to help us receive wisdom though our third eye: the eye of the mind. Once we manage to open this eye we will be able to see Lord Shiv.

The Ninth Day: Married women go to their parental home and spend the night there.

The Tenth Day: These women return to their husbands' homes.

The 11th, 12th and 13th days of Phâgun: These are three consecutive auspicious days on which the Shivarâtrî prayers are performed.

The 12th Day: New clay pots, with flower garlands wound around their rims, are arranged in a ritual order in the prayer room.

The clay pots: Each pot stands for a Hiñdû deity. The two most prominent pots represent Lord Shiv and Pârvatî jî. Two other large pots symbolise Wâgur and Vâtuk Nâth. The smaller pots stand for other deities. They too are prepared for formal worship. Some pots depict the Bhairavs.

All the pots would have been baked specially for the festival. (Since the last decades of the 20th century some people have started using pots made of steel.) The pots are taken into the house, and then the prayer room (thokur kuth), with due ritual. They are put on a small, round grass-mat (âsan). The first pot taken inside is supposed to be Wâgur.

Sacred offerings of walnuts and pure water are placed in the pots, till they are filled to the brim. The walnuts thus get soaked.

The deities mentioned above: Wâgur was the priest who performed the rituals at the wedding of Lord Shiv and Pârvatî jî. He was also the go-between who took Lord Shiv's offer of marriage to Pârvatî jî.

Vâtuk has three possible meanings: i) 'An assortment of various things,' is the literal meaning. During the main prayer on the 13th day an 'assortment' of many kinds of things is used in the rituals. This could have resulted in one particular pot being called Vâtuk. ii) During his celibate days, i.e. till he got married, Lord Shiv was called Vâtuk Nâth or Vâtuk Dev. Therefore, on the eve of his wedding anniversary he is worshipped in this form. iii) Vâtuk Bhairav is Lord Shiv's gatekeeper. People worship him in order to keep him happy: because he controls access to Lord Shiv. So much so that Shivarâtrî prayers in Kashmîr are also known as 'Vâtuk Pûjâ.'

Pârvatî jî, of course, is the goddess whom Lord Shiv got married to. She is also called Umâ.

The 13th Day/ Trayodashî: This is the big day. It is called Trayodashi (literally 'the 13th'). Special prayers are offered on the occasion.

The 14th Day/ Salâm: The name of this day is taken from the Arabic/ Islâmic word for 'peace' or 'the peaceful one.' This is a day for festivity- and almsgiving. For minstrels it used to be an opportunity to perform at Hiñdû homes and earn some money.

The 15th Day/ The Dunyâ Mâvas ('the moonless night of the walnuts'): This is the day after the night when the moon is at its lowest and the night at its darkest. The worship of the holy vessels reaches its finale on the 15th day, which is known as the Dunyâ Mâvas. The pots are then taken to a river or stream. Prayers are offered and the soaked walnuts are removed from the pots. The empty pots are then immersed in the water.

The soaked walnuts are later distributed to (and eaten by) members of the family and others present. In South India prasâdam or prayer offering normally consists of fresh fruit and in North and Central India of sweets. During Shivarâtrî in Kashmîr soaked walnuts are offered. There are several theories about this. Some people see walnut kernels as symbols of the cycle of agriculture because, after all, they are seeds. This cycle gets renewed after the long winter. My theory is that they represent the seeds that the Bekdarat (angels) had strewn all over Kashmîr. (See 'A History of Kashmîr.')

The 8th Day of the Shukl Paksh of Phâgun/ Tîlâ Atham: This is the last day of the Heyrath festival. The soaked walnuts and other offerings continue to be distributed among family and friends till this day. G.N. Rainâ records that 'a lighted earthen lamp would be placed on ari (seat made of grass) and [set afloat on] the river... [Children] would [make a bonfire of old and unusable] kângrîs (fire-pots) in the evening, mostly on the river-bank. Known as *jatun tuun*, in [the Kashmîrî] language, the festivity was symbolic of the end of severe winter in Kashmîr.'

The most-revered shrines of Kashmîrî Pandits

'If the temple of Shârikâ Dévî [on Srînagar's Hari Parbat] is the High Court of the Kashmîrî Pandits, then Khîr Bhawânî is our Supreme Court,' a 19th century Kashmîrî Pandit saying.

K(s)hîr Bhawânî

This is the temple that the Kashmîrî Pandit community holds in the highest regard. It is dedicated to Ragnya Dévî. The community mostly lives outside Kashmîr now. However, every year tens of thousands of Kashmîrî Pandits go to Kashmîr on Jeshth Ashtami (May-June) and during the autumn Navarâtrîs to pray and seek Khîr Bhawânî's blessings.

The 'milk goddess': The temple is fondly called Khîr Bhawânî because of the countless devotees who have, over the centuries, offered milk and 'kheer' (rice pudding) to the sacred spring. The Pandits call it the temple of Tulmulâ. This is the local name of Goddess Ragnya (or Raginia), who is an incarnation of Durgâ Mâtâ.

Location: The Khîr Bhawânî temple, Tulmulâ, is 23 km. north of Srînagar. It is in the Ganderbal tehsil. It is possible to go directly from the Srînagar airport to the shrine (approximately 25 km). The village where the shrine is located is called Mahesharpora.

The temple: The site of the temple predates this millennium. The small temple, made of white marble, is located in the middle of a spring (or 'kund' or 'sarovar'). Walls-in an extended hexagon-have been built around the spring. A tiny footbridge over the spring leads to the temple. This is the style that typifies the Kashmîrî Pandit shrines of the nineteenth and twentieth centuries. (The Zeethyâr temple near Srînagar's Grand Palace hotel is another example). The vast courtyard around the temple is paved with dévrî, the most expensive stone in all Kashmîr.

The temple that that we see today is relatively recent. Mahârâjâ Pratap Singh built it in 1912. Mahârâjâ Hari Singh made some additions.

There are clear-water streams near the temple, and many chinâr trees in and around the complex. Sacred fish are found in large numbers in these streams, in which devotees bathe and then place offerings of flowers, rice, sugar and milk.

The Legend: Srî Ram, the Hindu god, is said to have prayed to goddess Ragnya Dévî during his 14-year exile. He told his lieutenant, Srî Hanumân, that when the exile was over, he, Srî Hanumân, should shift the Dévî's (goddess') seat from Lanka. According to a variant, Srî Ram wanted to do this in order to deny Râvan, the demon king, the goddess' protection. Therefore, this would have happened in the last year of exile. Justice Shiva Nath Katju[vii] gives a third version: 'The Dévî was worshipped by [Râvan] in Lanka and was brought from there and installed in Tulmula after the defeat of [Râvan] by Shri Ram Chandraji.'

In any case, Sri Hanumân carried out the orders. He uprooted the goddess' temple from Lanka and took it to a place called Shâdîporâ. Later, the mother goddess visited one Pandit Raghunath Gadroo in a dream. She indicated that she wanted her temple to be shifted to Tulmulâ.

The idol: Justice Katju notes, 'In the shrine in the Khîr Bhawânî, [the] Kund Dévî [goddess of the holy pond] Ragnya Bhagwati is sitting on the left of Her Bhairava, Bhuteshwara, and Her complexion is dark. Kâlî is Krishna-Varna [dark skinned] and has dark complexion. But as mentioned in the *dhyan* [prayer, meditation] of Ragnya Bhawânî Her complexion is very fair, like fresh snow.' Swami Lakshman joo Mahâraj, the greatest Kashmîrî Hiñdû saint of the 20th century, told Justice Katju that Ragnya Bhawânî was Kâlî, the dark-skinned goddess. Katju adds, 'It is generally believed that Ragnya Bhawânî is Tripur Sundari. But if She is Kâlî also then She combines in Herself the aspects of two [Mahâ Vidyâs].'

Fairs and auspicious occasions: Every year, on the occasion of the Jeshth Ashtami a major festival is held here. Kashmîrî Pandits, now scattered all over the country, make it a point to come here for the festival-as do tens of thousands of others. For most Kashmîrî Pandits this now is an occasion they re-establish contact with their long-lost friends and relatives.

The festival is so important that the government gives everyone in Kashmîr a day off to enable them to attend the fair. It is celebrated on the 8th day of the first lunar fortnight of the month of Jeth (May-June). This is said to be the date on which goddess Khîr Bhawânî or Ragnya Dévî had first revealed herself.

There is a large gathering in the evening. The atmosphere is charged with devotion. Everyone prays before the image of the goddess. Devotees pray that they should merge with the Creator, who has no form, who is present everywhere and who has always been there. In their hands the devotees hold lamps filled with (butter) ghee and incense sticks (dhûp) as they chant their prayers. They light these lamps and sticks and trace circles in the air with both, in the ritual manner. Priests chant devotional hymns. The ringing of sacred bells heightens the mood.

The other auspicious day to visit the temple is on the Shukla Paksh Ashthami of any month, when special prayers (hawans) are performed.

This is the eighth day of the first fortnight of every lunar month.

The Har Ashthami day, too, is an auspicious time to visit this temple. On these Ashthamis the Hindus fast, bathe in the stream near Khîr Bhawânî, and pray at the temple inside.

The changing colours of waters of the spring: The waters of the small reservoir that surround the temple come from a sacred spring. They change their colours from time to time. This is considered miraculous and is attributed to powers of the goddess. The colour of the water is examined on a particular auspicious day every year. It is believed that the colour indicates what the forthcoming year will bring for the people. (There is a similar tradition of examining the waters of a spring near Basohli in Jammû province.) which magically changes colour, turning into black, when warning of disaster. The water had turned black a day before the Indian Prime Minister Indira Gandhi's assassination, and before the 1965 war with Pâkistân.

Taboos: Devotees do not eat meat on the days they visit the shrine. The owners of the scores of shops and stalls set up on festive occasions are mostly Muslims. However, things offensive to vegetarians (meat, eggs, onions and garlic) are not sold.

The autumn Navarâtrî: It is considered auspicious for Kashmîrî Pandits to visit the temple of their guardian goddess on all nine days. On the last (ninth) Navratri, an *aarti* (prayer) is held at the temple after which people break their fast. On the tenth (Dussehrâ) day, Râvan's effigy was once burnt. This practice has faded away after the mass-migration of the Pandits in 1990. Devotees also visit the Shârikâ temple during these nine days. There is no dancing or music. Devotees only offer prayers to the goddess who is said descend to the earth during this period.

Link with Karla: This venerable Kashmiri shrine has had a deep link with South India since ancient times. Srî Parijnanashram Swamiji, the Adi Gurû of the Kanara Saraswats is believed to have migrated from Khîr Bhawânî to Karla more than a thousand years ago. To this day, during their annual festival, the Kanara Saraswats give the main Shiv Linga an 'abhishek' (anointment) of five litres of fresh milk. This is later used to prepare 'kheer' (pudding) for the 'prasad' (offering). This is sometimes followed by an 'abhishek' of 'teerth' (pilgrimage) which is taken all the way from 'Ksheer Bhavani' (Kashmîr) to Karla. (Note the spelling, which is the correct Sañskrit spelling and has not got simplified over the centuries). Kanarese devotees put in considerable effort to carry the materials for the anointment over thousands of miles. Incidentally, this reinforces the theory I had alluded to of the light-skinned, light-eyed Saraswats of India's west coast having gone there from Kashmîr. (All over India Lord Shiv has a blue skin. However, in Kashmîr his skin is white-that's right, white, and not pink or yellow. It is so in several parts of Karnataka, too.)

The Saraswats of Saurashtra, Mahârâshtra, Gujarât, Karnataka and Keralâ believe that their ancestors had come from Kashmîr. They worship Shârdâ Dévî. This goddess is the daughter of Lord Brahmâ himself and is also known as Saraswati, the goddess of learning and the arts. The main temple of Shârdâ Dévî is on the banks of the Kishan Ganga in what is now called 'Âzâd' Jammû and Kashmîr.

Khîr Bhawânî Asthapan: This sister shrine is in a village called Tikker. It is on the Chowkibal Road, roughly 1 km from Kupwârâ town. The annual festival is celebrated in the month of April-May.

Khîr Bhawânî in exile: Now that the Kashmîrî Pandits mostly live outside Kashmîr, a Kheer Bhawani temple is being set up in Jammû.

The Shârikâ Dévî Shrine

(This is also known as the shrine of Chakreshwari, Shârikâ Parbat, Shârikâ Bhagwati, the Pradyuman Peeth, the Shaktî-Peeth, the Shârikâ-Peeth, Shri Chakram, the Siddapeeth, Tripur Sundari, Mahâ Tripursundari and Rajrajeshwari. The shrine is located on the western slope of the Hari Parbat, It is behind and well away from Makhdoom Sâheb and Chhattî Pâdshâhî.)

Jagadambâ Shârikâ Bhagwati is one of the many forms of Mahâshaktî, the mother goddess. 'Jagadambâ' means 'the mother of the world.[4] 'It is the title of Goddess Durgâ in all her manifestations, of which Shârikâ is one. 'Bhagwati' means 'goddess' and Shârikâ is her personal name. 'Mahâshaktî' means 'the great energy' or 'the great power.' This divine energy assumes a human form in the shape of Goddess Durgâ and her various incarnations.

In Kashmîr, Shârikâ jî is also known as Hari (which, as explained above, means 'the bird' or 'the mynah.' The Kashmîrî Pandits believe that her home in Kashmîr is in Srînagar's Hari Parbat. For them she is the 'guardian-goddess' of Srînagar City. She is also their Isht-Dévî (favourite goddess).

4 That is the literal meaning. It actually means 'the mother of all creation.'

Goddess Shârikâ has eighteen arms (asht-dash-b[h]ujâ; the Kashmîrî Pandits drop the [h] sound). She thus combines in herself all nine incarnations of Lord Vishnû.

There are two possible meanings of the "Hari" in Hari Parbat. That it means Vishnû, the Hindu God, would have been a fair explanation if the word had been pronounced the central Indian way ("hurry"). However, in Kashmîr the word is pronounced "herr", which is the Kashmîrî word for the Indian mynah (a bird).

It is certain that the hill was once called Shârikâ Parbat. Shârikâ is the Sañskrit equivalent of "herr". Inside the shrine is a large stone (a shila). It represents Para Dévî, the goddess of the shrine. Some writers feel that this could be the very stone that goddess Shârikâ had dropped into the lake. That is not possible because that the entire hill is supposed to be an enlarged version of that divine stone. (See also 'A History of Kashmîr' for more about the goddess Shârikâ.)

This is the second most revered shrine of the Kashmîrî Pandits in all Kashmîr and the most important one in Srînagar. It is arguably as old as human settlement in Kashmîr. The Kashmîrî Pandits believe that by praying often enough at the shrine one can get whatever one has been praying for. Devotees go there for the more intense forms of Hindu prayer.

A Government of India document points out, 'There is no regular temple[5] at this place but the site where the goddess is believed to have revealed herself is pigmented and held in high esteem.

'For the convenience of pilgrims, steps made of chiselled stones have been built right from the foot of the hill to the site of the shrine which would otherwise involve a tiresome uphill journey of several hundred feet.'

Mystical geometric patterns: There is no regular idol either.[6] Instead, there is a holy rock (shilâ) on which a mystic pattern has been etched. This is the Shrî-chakr (or Mahâ-shrî-yañtr). It consists of a dot around which circles and triangles have been drawn. These mystic geometric

---

5 There is a smart, modern, temple-like concrete canopy there, even if it is not a 'regular' temple.

6 The 'Vitasta' website suggests that there used to be a 'centuries old idol' of an eighteen-armed here, which was 'stolen by some miscreants.' Be that as it may, the rock with the mystic patterns is the original and most important depiction of the goddess.

lines, and not an idol, personify Goddess Shârikâ. That is why she is called Chakreshwari and her shrine is sometimes called Shri Chakram. ('Chakr' literally means 'the circle.')

Opinder Ambardar[viii] writes, 'It is perhaps due to the Goddess Shrichakra that the capital city of Kashmîr is said to have derived its name of Srînagar (Shrinagra).' (Chakr, chakra and chakram are variants of the same word.) He adds, 'The Shrichakra is a symbolic representation of the cosmic union of Lord Shiva and Shaktî. The Shrichakra is the most famous `Yantra' [instrument] and Yantra is indispensable in the Tañtra [mystic] Worship. Every Goddess is represented by an individual `Yantra.' [A]mong all the Yantras, the most famous and venerated one is the `Shri-yantra'. The yantra inscribed with specific mantras represents the Divine Mother, who is the cause of creation, sustenance and dissolution of the Cosmos.'

Thus, the chakr of the shrine indicates that it is a tâñtric (occult) shrine. T.N. Moza[ix] says, 'A hymn from the famous "Rudra Yamala Tañtra" sums up the nature of Shri Chakram [which is] engraved on marble plates. When translated [it] reads, "The point, the triangle, the group of eight triangles, two groups of 10 triangles, the group of 14 triangles, the eight-petalled lotus, the 16-petalled lotus, three circles and the quadrangular ramparts all [a]round constitute in [sic] Shri Chakram of the Supreme Dévî. It is through Sâdhnâ and Bhakti that one reaches the state of Samadhi. The awakening of the Kundalini Shaktî depends on the fervent pursuit of Sâdhnâ. Through Bhakti one's Kundalini Shaktî is awakened. Abhinav Gupta has given first place to Bhakti for God realization."

Best time of the day: Devout Kashmîrî Pandits would go to the temple early in the morning, shortly after daybreak.

Prayers offered, especially at daybreak: The Kashmîrî Pandits would recite Sañskrit verses in praise of Durgâ Mâtâ, the same as in the rest of India. These include the Shârikâ Mahâtmya and Shakt Shâstr verses, which are found in pan-Indian texts but are referred specifically to this shrine.

Auspicious days of the year/ festivals: The most important days for community-prayers (and festivity) at the shrine are:

Horâ Ashtami or Hur Âthum: This is the Ashtamî (the eighth day) of the Krishn Paksh ('dark fortnight') of the month of Phâgun [Feb-March].

Then there are three consecutive auspicious days during the Shukl Paksh ('bright fortnight') of the month of Âshâd [June-July]: Har Satum (Saptamî/ the seventh day), Har Âthum (Ashtamî) and Har Navum (Navmî/ the ninth day).

Hâr Navum (Âshâd Navmî) is the birth anniversary of goddess Shârikâ. It was also on this day, a few thousand years ago, that the bird-goddess had dropped a divine stone on the demons that lived in the lake. The offering made on this occasion is called the 'taher-charvan'. This is a combination of boiled rice and the liver of lambs.

Traditionally, a Mahâchañdî Yagya (lit.: 'the grand ritual prayer for the great Mother Goddess') would be performed on the three days leading to the all-important Har Navum. The prayer would begin on the Har Satum. Its grand finale would be on the Har Navum, when a lamb called the Rajé-Kath would be ritually sacrificed. In more recent times (the second half of the 20th century), the all-night singing of devotional songs about Shârikâ jî has marked Har-Navum at the shrine.

The other auspicious days are a) *Navreh* (the New Year Day of the Kashmîrî Pandits), which occurs during the month of Mâgh (Mar-Apr); and b) the nine *Navrâtrâ* days (Nav-Durgâh),.

The 'parikramâ' (circumambulation) route: It is considered particularly devout to go around the temple (indeed, around the entire hill) during the month of Magh. This circumambulation (locally called 'prâkrum') would begin at the Ganishon (Ganesh) temple and end at the Kâthî Darwâzâ. The devotee can choose either of two routes: along the wall that encloses the old city or along the bottom of the hill. Between the Ganishon and the Darwâzâ are some important places at which either prayers are offered or the devotee at least bows respectfully. These are, in the order in which they occur:

i) the Satrésh[7] (the seven sons of Lord Brahmâ, known to the rest of India as the Saptrishis); ii) the temple of Goddess Kâli; iii) the Siddh-Peeth (a 1.25acre ground, which has what New Agers call powerful vortices); iv) the Dévî Ângan[8] (lit.: 'the backyard of Shârikâ jî'): it is near this place that the two routes mentioned below meet; v) the thâpnâ

7 'It is at this spot that the devotees used to ascertain their luck by [the] random picking-up of some rice grains scattered on the boulder ([an] even number [of grains meant that] bad [luck was on its way] and [an] odd number [prophesied] good luck,' says Ambardar.

8 Ambardar informs us, 'The holy shrine of Shrichakra with [an] adjacent open space [which, too, is] known [as the] Devi-angan is also [to be found] in Tamil Nadu [South India].'

(establishment) of the bird-goddess, Harî: even here, the goddess is signified by a rock; vi) the thâpnâ of Mahâ Lakshmî jî, the goddess of wealth; this is somewhat above the thapna of Hari; vii) the Kauls' temple, which is in front of the thâpnâ of Mahâ Lakshmî jî; this is Kashmîr's oldest Krishna temple; viii) the thâpnâ of the Lord Vâmdev, who is the Bhairav of Ragnya Dévî; ix) Ragnya Dévî's shrine at Pokhribal: it also houses a natural spring, the waters of which are considered holy;[9] x) Hanumân jî's temple.

Opinder Ambardar notes, 'Pîr Pandit Pâdshâh Resh Peer, one of the greatest saints of Kashmîr of [the] 17th Century, is said to have performed [this three-mile] circumambulation of [the] Hari-Parbat…on his knees for forty days in the wee hours of the morning.'

The physical appearance of Shârikâ Bhawânî: In some depictions of Shârikâ Bhawânî in paintings and literature, she has eighteen arms. In others she is seated on a lion and her clothes are all red. Vâmdev, who is her Bhairav, is normally shown next to her. Some ancient texts call her the 'parrot-coloured goddess.'

Shârikâ ji's temple in exile: Now that the Kashmîrî Pandits mostly live outside Kashmîr, a Shârikâ temple is being set up in Faridabad (a suburb of Delhi).

Zeethyâr

The temple of Jeshthâ/ Zeshthâ Devi is situated behind the Grand Palace Hotel, between it and the Raj Bhawan. The Kashmîrî Pandits have an interesting love-ignore relationship with it. On the one hand they regard it as one of their most important temples. They visit it at least once a year. On the other hand, many (if not all) Kashmîrî Pandits feel that visits to this serene temple bring bad luck. Therefore, many of them tend to avoid the temple. (Hiñdûs everywhere have a similar love-ignore attitude towards the epic *The Mahâbhârat.*)

Jalap, the son of the great central Indian Emperor Ashok, is said to have built the temple. He must have built an earlier structure at this spot, because the architecture of the present temple is quite undistinguished and looks very early-20th century (at best, late-19th century). The surroundings are at once grand and bare. The temple is some way up the vast Zaberwan mountain. But it is on the bare, treeless side of the mountain.

The temple is small, and set in the middle of a water tank, on the same lines as Khir Bhawânî. The family of its priests did not migrate to Jammû

9 Ambardar writes, 'A `samput yagnya' used to be performed [at this shrine] in honour of the Goddess Raghnya especially on Shuklapaksh Ashtamis and other auspicious days.'

Kheer Bhawani

in the 1990s, partly because the temple is near the 'high-security' zone. But because the devotees mostly migrated, the priests have been reconsidering their decision.

Incidentally, the hill that the Shankarâchârya temple is built on was, in ancient times, called the Jesth (or Zesth) Lidder. I suspect that it was dedicated to the same goddess as the Zeethyâr temple.

(Mahâ-) Shivarâtrî: other theories (and details)

Prof. Neerja Mattoo argues that the word *Hérat* (*hayrath*) actually means 'hérr + rât' or 'the night of the Lord [Shiv].' It is too ancient a concept. It can't be linked to the actions of some 19th century A.D. Governor.

The First Day of the dark fortnight of Shivarâtrî (i.e. of the month of Phâgun) is called *Hur ukdoh.*

The Tenth Day is called *Dyâr* (money) *dâhan.*' It is a day of gambling for stakes, much like Diwali elsewhere in India. Today the Kashmîrî Pandits do it with playing cards. Before the advent of cards they played with cowries.

The Eleventh Day is called *Gâdkâ* (fish). On this day enough fish is purchased to last a fortnight.

The Twelfth Day is the *Wâgur Bahâ.*

The Thirteenth Day is known as *Hérat Truvâh.*

On the Eighth Day of the Shukl Paksh (the bright fortnight), lamps are also lit in various parts of the house: at the main gate, in the kitchen, by the well and in the prayer room.

Regarding why soaked walnuts are given to friends on the Dunyâ Mâvas, Mrs. Neerja Mattoo's theory is that at that time of the year fresh fruits are not available.

References

i Excerpted from The American Heritage(r) Dictionary of the English Language, Third Edition (c) 1996 by Houghton Mifflin Company.

ii Adapted from the website Kashmîr Saivism/ Hinduism Today, Issue 94-03, hosted by the Kashmîri Overseas Association.

iii *Life Positive* magazine, New Delhi, September 2001. Pages 58-64.

iv The *Shivarâtrî* section is based, apart from primary sources and discussions with knowledgeable Kashmîrî Pandits, on: *'Shivarâtrî: Night of Bliss'* by Prof. ON Chungroo, *Daily Excelsior*, Jammû, the 2nd March, 2003; *'Open the third eye on Mahâshivarâtrî'* by Sadhguru Jaggi Vasudev, *The Times of India*, the 1st March 2003, MA Pandit's *Festivals of Kashmîr,* and several websites, notably '*Shivaratri -The Biggest Festival Of Kashmîrî Pandits*' by G.N. Rainâ

v Vasudev, op cit.

vi Vasudev, op cit.

vii From the website, 'Kashmîr Tantrism' by Justice Shiva Nath Katju

viii '*Vitasta*' magazine, Vol. XXXV (2001-2002): I gathered the material from the Vitasta website.

ix 'Shrines of Hamza Makhdum Sahib and Chakreshwari,' by T.N. Moza, *Kashmîr Times*, Jammû, 28 September, 1998. Moza's quotation marks are not clear and I have had to guess.

Chapter- 14

The discovery of a cave temple of Lord Shiv

The discovery: In August 2001 I received a 6- page letter in which an audacious assertion had been made. One Haji Muhammad Rafique Bocken claimed that his son in law, Ghulam Quadir, had discovered a cave temple dedicated to Lord Shiv. This was in a valley close to the Holy Cave of Shrî Amarnâth jî. The Haji and Quadir are both nomadic Bakerwals. And yet the letter had been composed on a computer and printed on a sophisticated printer. The English used was posh. Above all, the photographs appended had been taken with an advanced camera, then scanned into a computer and printed out with a high- resolution printer.

The Haji then mailed copies of the letter to a dozen top- ranking officials in Delhi and Srinagar. The whole thing looked too suspicious to be true. No wonder one of these officers noted in the margin of the letter, 'Too suspiciously sophisticated.'

Despite my own doubts I decided to check the claim out. The Haji's clan spends its summers near Chandanwari (Kashmir) and winters in Jindrah (Jammu). I asked the Tourism staff in Jammu to look for him in Jindrah and the PPO staff in Pahalgam to do so in the Chandanwari area. We finally established contact. I decided to check the story out.

The team: I led the team that went to the spot on the 4th September 2001 to verify the claim. The Haji and Ghulam Quadir guided us. Zee TV deputed Abdul Hamid, its Srinagar- based cameraman, to accompany us. With us also were Abdul Ahad Sheikh, the young numberdâr of Phirisilan, Muhammad Iqbal, who is the Haji's cousin, Md. Amin Sheikh and Md. Altaf, both residents of Phirisilan, and Md. Hafiz Sheikh, the works supervisor of the PPO (Pahalgam Projects Organisation), which is a wing of the Tourism Department.

The cave: The cave- temple is just above the treeline. It is located in a rocky portion of a meadow that is now being called Shiv Marg. It is a natural cave but slabs of rock have been placed atop its entrance. They might be man- made. There are at least three caves in the complex.

The first, and main, cave is quite shallow. The light inside is dim but more than enough to shoot crisp TV images with. It is less than twenty feet deep, around ten feet high and around fifteen feet wide. As soon as you enter you see a whitish stone idol, a bust of Lord Shiv, which is a little more than a foot high. Over the centuries it has been much eroded by the elements. There were no winds or dripping water inside the cave when we went there. And yet both seem to have been responsible for the weathering of the idols.

Despite the blurring of details on the main idol, certain things are clearly visible: Shiv ji's top-knot, the cobra (Nâg Devatâ) coiled around his neck and a hump on his other shoulder (probably a trishul/ trident). Some of the deity's facial features can still be seen.

There were more than a dozen Shiv lings near this idol. The oval tops of most of them had been sliced off quite neatly. Their tops were, thus, almost flat. As much as two- thirds of many of the Shiv lings had been eroded. You can tell this from the proportions of what is left. In one or two cases dripping water was definitely the culprit. This was obvious from the way the tops had been eroded. Only one Shiv ling in the first cave was fully intact. TV footage of this lingam does not do justice to the excellent state of preservation of this lingam, because it receives less natural light than the others. It is protected from the winds by another whitish idol, the features of which have been blurred even more.

All these idols and lingams have been carved out of a natural, raised platform, around five or six feet higher than the ground. To reach the platform one has to climb up a rock. The Shrî Amarnâth jî Shrine Board can get steps carved into this rock after expert archæologists give their go- ahead.

Could Haji Rafique have brought these idols over from elsewhere to con us all?

No way. The idols are all fixed to the rock below. Indeed, they have been carved out of that rock, which is rooted to the ground. Besides, the weathering is too genuine to fake.

When we face the first cave, then to its right (east) there's another, smaller cave. Actually it is a narrow extension of the first cave. This is next to a 'ventilator': an opening that lets in lots of light and air. The opening looks man- made. Or it could be a natural opening fortified by men with a stone shaft. One has to crawl up a rock to get to this level, which is about three feet higher than 'Cave 1'.

There is another idol here. It is covered with algæ. Therefore, it is difficult to say if the algæ created the elephant's trunk that can be seen, or a sculptor did. The top-knotted head and humps on the shoulders, on the other hand, suggest that this, too, is a bust of Lord Shiv- and not that of his son, Lord Ganesh. Next to it is a Shivling, the second best preserved one in the complex. Both are rooted to the rock below. In an alcove behind them is a loose idol, its features having been eroded beyond recognition. The idols near the ventilator have been worn out the most. They alone have algæ. This is because they are the closest to the winds, the sun and rain/ snow, because of the nearby ventilator.

I found plenty of what looked like ashes and partially burnt wood/ stone at this level. I also found the flat bone of a buffalo here. I thought it might have used to scrape things with. Haji Rafique says that a bear that had killed a buffalo would probably have left it there.

To the left of the main cave is third, dark cave. It is extremely deep, as we discovered by stabbing it with our walking sticks. We did not have the equipment to explore this slim, tall but deep cave. Who knows what lies inside: nothing, more idols or a Shiv Khori- style hall.

Water trickles through this cave. Run your hands along its ceiling and they will be filled with a whitish, lime- like paste. The Bakerwals, who are extremely analytical about all natural phenomena, say that rocks get reduced to a paste only after water has run over them for a few thousand years.

The Amrit Kund: The idols in the cave- temple had been eroded considerably. Only two lingams had their oval tops intact. Therefore, I left the cave- temple with mixed feelings. I was convinced that Haji Rafique had not conned us. But I was still wondering about how much of the cave, the idols and the lingams was man- made and how much had been shaped thus by the winds.

The Amrit Kund was the clincher.

This is a perennial spring some 250 metres from the cave- temple. It is located on the bed of a seasonal nallah. When the snows melt, their water comes hurtling down the nallah, bringing down loose stones, rocks and other debris.

The crystal- clear waters of this spring are stored for a while inside a man- made stone- trough. When we went there, the water inside it was about an inch deep and rested on a bed of sand and pebbles. However, the texture of the trough made me suspect that its bottom was made of chiselled rock, and not sand. So I got Hafiz and Amin to dig the sand out. When they had done so we found a neatly carved, man- made stone- trough. It is 7¼" high. Its front is about 19" long and its left and right sides are 16" each.

It has only three sides. Which means that it has no back at all. This could be because the back fits into the mountainside and is thus not needed. Or the back could have got eroded because of centuries of water going down that way. The water then turns left (west). As a result, the left side of the trough has got eroded considerably.

The best part is that the entire trough has been carved out of a single rock, as at, say, Nara Nag in Srinagar district (2nd century BC- AD 8th century). The lower halves of the inner surfaces of the trough have diagonal striations. This kind of stone carving is done at Pantha Chuk, near Srinagar City, to this day.

The upper halves of the three walls are about an inch and a half thick. That is rather thin for walls made of stone. It is easier for the stoneworker to leave a thick wall than a thin one. Besides, there is no advantage in creating thin walls.

These walls have clearly been eroded to their present thinness over the centuries. Originally they were at least 2½" thick each. Portions of the trough that have not been eroded as badly indicate this.

This kund (tank) has a tiny outlet in the front. This is typical of all *yonîs* on which the lingam is placed in Shiv temples. In normal *yonis* this slit is exactly in the middle. Here the slit is near the right corner of the main, front 'wall.' As I mentioned, water flows naturally to the left, and not through this slit in the front. Therefore, it is man-made and not a result of erosion. Besides, it is shaped too neatly like a 'U' to be natural.

If there is a *yonî*, the lingam can not be far behind. I am confident that the lingam of this yoni lies buried in the nallah below, under several centuries of rubble. Our group found a flat stone on which some religious figures had once been carved. Such flat stones with figures are common nears the wells and springs of Jammu. I could not make out what these figures might have been. The Haji spotted a trishul, though.

The routes: There are three possible routes to the cave- temple. All three originate on the motorable Pahalgam- Chandanwârî road, a short distance before we reach Chandanwârî. (All 'Km.- points' are counted from Pahalgam, which is 16km. from Chandanwârî. Thus 'Km.13' is three km. or less before Chandanwârî and 'Km.15' one km. or less before Chandanwârî.)

i) *From the bridge just before the shops at Chandanwârî ('Km.15'):* This route is around 5km. long. However, it is the steepest and the most difficult. Therefore it is not recommended for most yatris, though the Bakerwals use it.

ii) *From the 'camping site' just before Chandanwârî (also 'Km. 15'):* This route, too, is 4.5 or 5 km. long. It took us an hour and fifty minutes to climb up from the Chandanwari 'camping site' to the cave temple. It is a very steep route. The gradient exceeds 60° for long stretches. It is 45° at many, if not most, of the other stretches. The first stretch is grassy and treeless. It is possible to climb up this stretch on ponies. We then enter a shaded section, which is a dense kail forest. The next set of woods is a budlû- chîr forest. The gradient gets gentle at a 'saddle top' called Hapatgand. After that there is an exquisite and dense burzâ (bhoj patr) forest. The last section, where the cave- temple is located, is treeless. It is a sharply sloping meadow with three sets of rocks. The temple is in the middle set.

iii) *From Kud (or Kurh) Pathri ('km. 13'):* This is the longest route: about 6 or 7 km. It also has the gentlest gradient. It took us 65 minutes to descend from the cave temple to the main road on this route. Routes ii and iii meet at Hapatgand. Between the main road and Hapatgand we pass through a very dense kail forest. There are pine needles on the ground, which makes it slippery. All the same it is possible to travel by pony from the main (Pahalgam-Chandanwârî) road right up to the cave-temple, using this route. The uphill journey takes a little more than three hours, on pony or foot. At present there is a rough track made by some Bakerwals. Engineers present with us said that if they were to make a proper track, it would be around 12-13 km. long.

Hapatgand: 'Hapat' means 'bear.' Black and brown bears are found in this area. This is a 'saddle' on either side of which is a valley. The

Pahalgam valley is in the west. Route iii, too, is in the west. In the east are Chandanwârî, Pissu Top, Zojipal and the Shesh Nag hill. The Dodal mountain is in the south. (Warwan in Jammu province lies beyond Dodal.) Route ii is in the south. The cave- temple is a little more than a kilometre uphill, northwards, from here. Hapatgand is at a higher altitude than Pissu Top (11,500').

The altitude of the cave- temple: The temple and the kund are much higher than Pissu Top. Therefore, they would be at around 12,500'. From both you can see Dodal and the Phirisilan Top. Haji Rafique warned us that there was very little oxygen up there. However, this was not obvious.

Weather and clothing: Despite a blazing sun, it was unwise to have worn only a shirt. Even at the lower reaches of that hill, close to the main road, one feels the cold sharply as sweat evaporates.

Antiquity: This style of sculpture ceased around the 13th century AD. Its oldest specimens, on the other hand, date to the early centuries of the Christian era. Therefore, the cave- temple and the kund could be anywhere between eight and fifteen hundred years old. The ASI will be able to put a more precise date.

Old Kashmiri Pandits have always said that the holy Shrî Amarnâth jî cave was mentioned in ancient scriptures, that for a few thousand years it had got lost and then Âdâm Malik *re*discovered it. (My calculations, based on the Maliks' family tree, put Adam's discovery at between AD 1750 and 1775.) The Malik family, too, only claimed to have *re*discovered the cave. That way both the priests and the Maliks could give the cave and the Yatra an age thousands of years older than AD 1775.

The discovery of the cave- temple at Shiv Marg/ Hapatgand proves that the Amarnath Yatra and the sanctity of the Holy Shrî Amarnâth jî Cave dates to several centuries, perhaps a thousand years, before AD 1750.

Accessibility: The cave- temple is accessible nine months a year. Therefore, if thrown open to the public, it will be very good for the economy of the Phirisilan area and the Bakerwals who camp there. Already both communities are very excited about the discovery.

Was the temple part of an ancient Shrî Amarnâth jî route? There can be no doubt about this. A straight road and a 2½ km. uphill, oxygen-deprived climb leads to Âstânmarg. After that it is a descent all the way to Posh Pathri/ Kél Nârh, 3km. before Panjtarni. This takes the Bakerwals around 4 hours, other good climbers 6 hours and the general yatri 8 hours. Therefore, this ancient route is somewhat shorter than the present one.

Besides, since the cave- temple is snowless and accessible for more than nine months a year, it was clearly a base camp. A kund, even if a small one, was created at the spring. There was no real need to do so. It is quite convenient to collect water directly from the spring. The kund indicates that a large number of people used it, and not just some stray sadhus. Secondly, this is the only ancient or even mediæval temple ever found on the Shrî Amarnâth jî route. Therefore, this must have been the base camp.

Martand or Surya temple

Gauri Shanker Temple, Pattan

Chapter- 15

Shiva Shrines of Kashmîr

The following places are connected with Lord Shiva. For details see the chapters on the respective districts.

Ânañtnâg – Kulgam

- Martand (might have been a Shiva temple).
- Umuoh: Around three kilometres from Verinag.
- Verinag
- The Waheed Baba Wudar, to the west of Bijbehara.
- See also the chapter on the 'Sri Amarnathji Yâtrâ' for several more shrines connected with Lord Shiva.

Bârâmullâ – Bandipora

- Gulmarg was once called Gaurimarg (the meadow of Gauri, wife of Lord Shiva).
- Pattan: Two Shiva temples.

Budgâm

No major Shiva shrine.

Kupwârâ

No major Shiva shrine.

Pulwâmâ – Shopian

- Awantipora was possibly a Shiva shrine.
- Jawbrari
- Payer/ Pa Yech
- Kounsar Nag

Srînagar city

There are several Shiva temples in the town. The **Shankaracharya** temple is the most prominent.

Ganderbal

- Gangabal
- Meru Vardhan
- Nund Kol

Chapter- 16

The Sikh Gurûs and Kashmîr

Sikhism in Kashmîr

Kashmîr's contacts with Sikhism date to Gurû Nanak Dev ji (b. 1469) himself. This venerable founder of Sikhism visited Srînagar with two followers, Hassu, a smith, and Sihân, a calico printer.

Gurû Nânak Dev jî in Mattan

Gurû Nânak Dev jî went on his third missionary tour (udasi) in 1516. This took him to Srînagar, Mattan and Ânañtnâg. At Mattan, the great Gurû came upon Pandit Brahm Dâs. The Pandit was one of the most distinguished Sañskrit scholars of the time. However, his learning and his eminence had made him somewhat vain.

When Gurûji saw the Pandit come with a 'huge stock of books', he recited the following couplet, "One may read thousands of books, with a cart load of books to follow. One may study countless epics or fill one's cellars with volumes of learning. One may read for generations on end and spend every month of the year studying. And one may read all one's life till one's last breath. But, says Nânak, there is only one truth and that truth is His [God's] name. Everything else is the conceit of an egoistic mind[1]."

1 Mr. Ajit Singh's website has a slightly different translation of this verse.

Pandit Brahm Dâs realised that he had erred. He touched the feet of the Gurû. He became the first Kashmîrî to convert to Sikhism. A gurûdwârâ was built at Mattan, at the entrance of the eponymous Hiñdû pilgrimage in honour of Gurû Nânak. (The volume on 'Leh and Kargil' has some details of the noble Gurû's visit to that region, especially to Patther Sahib. During that leg of his mission he visited Mansarovar, Tibet, China and Ladâkh as well.)

Kashmîr's first Sikh Mission

The first Sikh mission (*manjî*) in Kashmîr was set up in Srînagar during the era of Gurû Amar Das, the third Gurû..

Subsequently, some Kashmîri converts to Sikhism came under pressure to recite their ancestral Sañskrit hymns. They complained to Gurû Arjan Dev ji (1581-1606), the fifth Gurû. He sent Madho Sodhi to Kashmîr to instruct the Sikhs, through sermons and *kîrtan* (prayer), on how to conduct their religious affairs. Sodhi was an expert in the religion.

Gurû Arjan Dev ji is said to have visited Shâdimarg in Kashmîr.

19th century records indicate that in religious matters the Sikhs of Kashmîr came under the jurisdiction of a Bhâî (brother) based in Poonch. And whenever this spiritual head died, the Râjâ of Poonch would appoint his successor. The Bhâî would visit Kashmîr every alternate year and would then, in the words of a British administrator, 'collect his dues from the Sikhs.'

Gurû Hargobind jî's tour of Kashmîr

Gurû Hargobind ji, the sixth Gurû (*chhatta pâdshah*), was the next to visit the Valley, around 1620 (or even as late as in 1644). He seems to have come by the Mughal route, i.e. Gujrât-Bhimbar and the Pîr Pañjâl Pass. He went back to the Punjâb through Bârâmullâ, Urî, Kathai, Dopatta, Khanda, and Muzaffarâbâd. The last four places are now in POK. Fine gurûdwârâs[2] have been built at most of these places in his honour. These include the Gurûdwârâ Thana Sahib in Bârâmullâ, the Gurûdwârâ Parampila in Urî and the Gurûdwârâ Nagâli Sâheb in Poonch. During that tour the Gurû also visited Wazirabad, Mirpur and Bhimbar Rehran.

According to some respected historians (British Raj, Hiñdû and Sikh alike), Gurû Hargobind jî came to Kashmîr with Emperor Jehângîr. He set up camp at Shalimar, which was close to the emperor's camp in the

Nishat garden. Some Sikh historians say that Empress Noor Jehan called on Gurû Hargobind ji at Shalimar to pay her respects.

Historian Ajit Singh[i] posts a caveat. He points out that Jehângîr, whose tour journals have been maintained meticulously, did not enter Kashmîr through the Bḥimbar-Pîr Pañjâl Pass route either in 1620 or even in 1622. Nor did he leave Kashmîr by the same route as the Gurû. Besides, Singh says that the Nishat garden had not been built till almost fifty years later. (One can't be too sure about this. An unrelated account suggests that by 1633 the Nishat had been in existence for some years. In any case, it was not a royal garden in 1633. So Ajit Singh is right to the extent that Jehângîr would not have camped at the Nishat.)

Even the Gurû is unlikely to have camped at Shalimar. What we know for sure is that he visited- and probably camped at- the site of the present Chhatti Pâdshâhî gurûdwârâ. Equally certainly, Jehângîr was lodged in the palace at Koh-é-mârâñ (Hari Parbat), which is only a few hundred metres uphill. Almost every time that she came down to the town, Noor Jehan would have gone past the Gurû's camp. Given the Gurû's enormous standing in the world of religion, it stands to reason that the empress would have called on him.

The Gurû camped in Srînagar for almost three months. Ajit Singh writes, '[The Gurû] held congregations [and] delivered discourses [in Kashmîr]. At Srînagar, Gurû Hargobind expounded the thesis that the Gurû's treasure chest is for the benevolence of the poor.'

Gurû Hargobind jî also met Kattu Shah, who had converted from Islâm to Sikhism, and had taken to evangelisation. Ajit Singh adds, '[A] large number of Kashmîris, both Hindus and Muslims, embraced Sikhism due to the devoted and committed preaching by Gurû jî. He appointed Bhai Garhia ji to preach the Sikh religion.'

He initiated the 'Chhatti Padshahi' Gurûdwaras of Srînagar and Bârâmullâ. He also reconverted to Sikhism such Hindus who had converted to Islâm in between.

Historian G.M.D. Sufi says that the Gurû, a refugee towards the end of his life, died in the Kashmîr hills in 1645. However, all the other sources that I have consulted say that Gurû Hargobind ji died on the 3rd March, 1644, at Kiratpur ('a city in the foothill of the Himâlayas').

---

2 Sikh houses of worship.

The Story of Srînagar's Gurûdwârâ Chhatti Pâdshâhî

A Kashmîrî Brâhmin called Sewa Das had converted to Sikhism. He took upon himself the duty of performing *sewa* (serving the faith and serving other people). He would organise religious functions and set up free kitchens (*langars*) during congregations.

His mother Bhâg Bharî was touched by her son's dedication and devotion. She, too, began to chant the name of the Gurû. She wanted to meet the sixth Gurû. However, she was too old and feeble to go over to the Punjâb to do so. Besides, she could barely see.

The only way out was for the Gurû to come to Kashmîr to meet her. Her son told her that the Gurû was *antarjâmî*: he could read everyone's thoughts and he knew what was going on throughout the world. So, if her devotion was steadfast and her intentions pure, the Gurû would get to know. And if she were to pray hard enough, he would come over to meet her.

Bhâg Bharî began to knit a garment for the Gurû. She would chant his name throughout the day.

Gurû Hargobind ji, the sixth Gurû, was in Amritsar at the time. He got the feeling that someone in Kashmîr was thinking of him and trying to

Gurûdwârâ Chhatti Pâdshâhî

contact him. He knew that he had to go to Kashmîr. So he left Amritsar for Lahore, which was on the route to Kashmîr.

Srînagar was a walled city during the Gurû's time. Bhâg Bharî lived just outside the wall, near the Kâthî Darwâzâ. When the Gurû reached Srînagar he went straight to her house. 'Give me the garment that you have been knitting for me,' he told her. 'I don't want to wear any other clothes now.'

This indicated to the almost-blind Bhâg Bharî that it was the Gurû himself who was talking to her. She fell at his feet. She compared his visit with those of the great deities and saints of India. She told him that Srî Râm had gone to the deep woods to meet Shabri, a poor Bhîl woman, to accept half-eaten berries from her. Then as Srî Krishn he went to the house of Bhagat Biddu to eat the banana peels that the devotee gave him. As Gurû Nanak he went to Ahmedabad to eat the humble bread that Bhai Lallo had to offer. 'Now,' she told the sixth Gurû, 'you have come to me. I am truly blessed.'

The Gurû drew water from the earth and gave it to Bhâg Bharî to wash her eyes with. She did so and suddenly she was able to see. Word of this miracle spread like wildfire. People began to say, 'Look, the Gurû has come all the way from Amritsar just to bless this old woman. Besides, he has cured her poor eyesight.'

Bhâg Bharî had a very advanced spirituality. She knew that she was going to die. So she sat in a yogic *aasan* (posture) till her soul left her body. Sewa Das requested Gurû Hargobind ji to light Bhâg Bharî'spyre. The Gurû did so. He then served food to the *sangat* (congregation) and left for Bârâmullâ and Urî. After that he left Kashmîr and went to Panjâ Sahib, Gujrât (a town in West Punjâb) and then Hafzabad.

A well has since been constructed around the spring from which the Gurû had drawn the holy water. The Chhatti Padshahi Gurûdwara of Srînagar has been built on the site where Bhâg Bharî's house used to be.

Kashmîrî Pandits petition Gurû Tegh Bahadur jî

In 1675, some Kashmîrî Pandits from Mattan went to Ânandpur Sâhib to meet Tegh Bahadur ji, the ninth Gurû of Sikhism. They apprised him of the various problems that they were facing. Their account stirred him as well as his son, young Sahibzada Gobind Rai. The brave prince said that if need be his father and he would lay down their lives in the course of getting the Kashmîrî Pandits' problems solved. And that is what Gurû

Tegh Bahadur did. He went to Delhi and, on November 11, 1675, was martyred while fighting for causes that included issues concerning the Kashmîrî Pandits.

The migration of some Sikhs- to and from Kashmîr

The first Sikhs of Kashmîr, as we have seen, were local converts. These were mostly Kashmîrî Pandits who had converted to Sikhism: but some, like Kattu Shah, had been Muslims before their conversion. The next to convert were Punjâbî Mohyâl Brâhmins, who had been living for several generations in what is now Bâramullâ district. After Mahârâjâ Ranjit Singh took over the government of the Valley in 1819, some of this community- mostly of the Bâlî sub-caste- took to Sikhism.

In addition to local converts, some Sikhs migrated to the state from outside. Sukh Jiwan, a Punjâbî Hiñdû, was the governor of Kashmîr from 1753 to 1762, appointed by the Kabul-based Afghân government. He brought a number of Sikhs with him. The Sikhs of Hamal have descended from this group. The Sikhs of Trâl (Pulwâmâ), too, believe that their ancestors migrated to Kashmîr during the Afghân era (1752-1819).

During the same period some Kashmîrî Sikhs and Pandits, notably from the Dachanpara area of Kashmîr, migrated in the reverse direction—from the state to Kabul.

When Mahârâjâ Ranjit Singh's forces conquered the Valley, another small group of Sikhs migrated to Kashmîr. However, despite these conversions and migrations, the number of Sikhs in the state has always been very small. The last census conducted in the state as a whole-before Pâkistân and China annexed parts of it- was in 1941. In that year 1.64% of the population of the state was Sikh. Of this the majority lived in Jammû province

References

i. Ajit Singh is a retired Deputy Conservator of Forests; he has posted his history on a website called 'Guru Hargobind Sahib's Journey to Kashmîr.'

Chapter- 17

Wângât Sharif /Bâbâ Nagri of the Lâr region

The shrine In the 21st century devotees have taken to calling it 'Bâbâ Nagri' (the little town of the saint called Bâbâ). They now say that it is located in Wâñgat, which is the name of the village. However, in the past they would call it the Durbâr Lâr Sharief or 'the holy [sharief] court [durbâr] of Lâr,' Lâr being the broad region around the shrine.

It is because of its former name that the family of the hereditary keepers of the shrine uses the title Lârvi as its surname. Lârvi means 'of Lâr.'

Followers of the shrine live not only in India and the so-called 'Azad' Jammu & Kashmir, they are found in substantial numbers in Pakistan's Punjab and Khyber Pakhtunkhwa provinces. Within India they span Jammu & Kashmir, Himachal Pradesh, Uttarakhand and the Dinâ Nagar area of Indian Punjab. Some devotees live in Arab countries and Europe.

In 2004 a reported[i] two lakh (two hundred thousand) followers turned up at the Wagah border of India and Pakistan to receive the shrine's sajjâdâ nasheen Mian Basheer.

The origin of the dynasty Bâbâ ji Sâhib was a follower of Hazrat Pîr Nizam-ud-Din Kayâni of the famous and powerful shrine called Durbâr Kaiyân Sharief, which is in what is now called the Neelum district of Pakistan Occupied Kashmir.

In the 1880s Pîr Nizam-ud-Din sent his young disciple to the Valley of Kashmir to propagate the mystic creed of their Naqshbandi order. Bâbâ ji Sâhib spent a few days wandering through this strange new valley till he came to the river bank where Wangat now is. It was a deserted forest at the time and Bâbâ ji Sâhib did not like it one bit.

So he unrolled his prayer mat, spread it on the ground, offered prayers, folded the sheet and went back to his mentor. 'There is no point in going to the Valley,' the Punjabi-Gojri speaking youth told his Pir. 'The people there do not understand a word of what we say. [They speak Kashmiri.] The place that you asked me to go to is a totally uninhabited forest. Besides, the sheet that I offered my namaz on has developed strange marks which just don't go away.'

The marks—a number of straight little lines joined like in a maze—made the sheet look like a cadastral map. Pîr Nizam-ud-Din looked at them and smiled. He said, 'These lines are the map of the village that you are going to establish there. Choose the plot where you would like your tomb to be and the one where the shrine will be.

Miâñ Nizam-ud-Din Lârvi In April 1892 a son was born to Hazrat Bâbâ ji Sâhib Lârvi at Wangat, which was to be the dynasty's home (and religious seat). The boy was named Abdul Latief. Two and a half years later Bâbâ ji Sâhib took the boy over to Kaiyân Sharief for the Pîr's blessings.

The Pîr prophesied that Abdul Latief would go on to become a great spiritual master, a champion of the downtrodden and would be respected by people of other creeds. Bâbâ ji renamed his son 'Miâñ Nizam-ud-Din,' after his spiritual guide, the great saint of Kaiyân Sharief. ('Miâñ' means 'mister.') After he completed his Haj pilgrimage in 1964-65, Miâñ Nizam-ud-Din's followers started calling him Hâji Bâbâ, the title by which people refer to him to this day.

Early training Miâñ Nizam-ud-Din was tutored at home by a regular teacher as well as a Maulvi, because there was no school in Wangat or nearby. Because his father, Bâbâ ji Sâhib, was a ranking religious leader of his scattered community he would reach out to his flock by visiting them in their camps in the mountains. Little Nizam-ud-Din would often go along with him. In the process not only did he learn how to ride and hunt, he got to know about the hardships that his people faced and the issues that bothered them.

In 1926, Baba Ji Sahib decreed that Nizam-ud-Din, then 34, would be his last khalîfâ (deputy). As the sajjâdâ nasheeñ (keeper) of Durbâr Lâr

Sharief the young mystic kept alive the teachings and traditions of Hazrat Pîr Nizam-ud-Din Kayâni as well as Bâbâ ji Sâhib Lârvi through discourses to the pilgrims that came every week or at least for the annual urs. He ensured that that there were [free] community kitchens and free accommodation for these pilgrims.

As a poet Because his father was a well known sufi poet, Nizam-ud-Din learnt the basics of mystic poetry at home. However, his own career as a poet was shaped to an even greater extent by Sâîñ Qâdar Bakhsh, who was a disciple of his father and a sufi poet from Poonch (which is in Jammu and a very considerable distance away). When Nizam-ud-Din was in his late-twenties and early thirties, Qâdar helped him refine his poetic style.

Nizam-ud-Din's mystic (sufi) poetry in Punjabi and Gojri struck such a chord with people who spoke these sister languages in the state that it started a whole movement. The trend began in 1935 when the state, indeed all of India, was in the grip of idealistic political fervour, and continued till India achieved independence (and princely states were abolished) in 1947. Following his example—and supported by him—a large number of sufi poets emerged in these two languages. (*Ishar-e-Nizami* [the verses of Nizami], a volume of the selected works of Haji Baba, was published posthumously in 1985.)

The popularity of Haji Baba's Punjabi poetry reached the great north Indian poet Hafeez Jalandhary, who took to visiting Wangat regularly after 1939 to meet Hz. Nizam-ud-Din and hear verses from the *Shâh Nâmâ é Islam*

A temporal leader of the community Most of his followers lived in remote areas. So Hz. Nizam-ud-Din took to travelling through the mountains to where the people were, conveying the message of Islam and delivering sermons. These people of the remote mountains were either illiterate or at least not comfortable with urban languages like Urdu. Therefore, he spoke to them in their own mother tongue.

In 1931 a large number of leaders and representatives of the Gujjar and Jat communities met at Poonch. In Jammu &Kashmir the Gujjars are entirely Muslim but Jats are both Muslim and Hindu. However, at the all-India level the majority of Gujjars are Hindu and this conference represented people of both faiths. Haji Baba was elected chairman. The next year, in 1932, Haji Baba founded the Gujjar Jat Conference at Parori Gujjaran, Rajouri. For the next fifteen years—till the state replaced monarchy with democracy in 1947—he was the head of this political party.

It was thus in 1932 that his mission took a social turn and he started representing his followers' grievance against landlords and moneylenders—and autocracy in general.[ii] Besides, his flock was mostly illiterate. Though they were quite well off in the sense that the notional market value of their livestock would place them in the comfortable middle-class, they were economically backward.

These were exactly the same years when Sheikh Mohammed Abdullah was emerging as the most popular leader of Kashmir ever. His own quest for the spiritual often brought him to Darbar Lar Sharief. The two young leaders became friends despite being in two different political parties. (The Sheikh was the head of the National Conference.) Hz. Nizam-ud-Din was a special guest at Sheikh saheb's wedding to a lady whose mother was from Nizam-ud-Din's community. Besides, in 1937 Haji Baba attended an annual convention of the Sheikh's party at Poonch as a special invitee.[iii]

The Sheikh also took the then towering leader of India's freedom struggle, Pt. Jawahar Lal Nehru, to Darbar Lar Sharief to seek 'the blessings of the Shrine.' [iv] This also brought the future Prime Minister of India close to Haji Baba.[1]

The Gujjar Jat Conference held major conventions in 1939 at Jammu and in 1944 at Rajouri. It contested elections to the state legislative assembly (Praja Sabha) in 1937 and won seats.

In 1947 some members of the Conference felt that it should have only Gujjars as members. Haji Baba found this thinking too narrow and left the organisation. From then he started distancing himself from politics.

His followers persuaded him to join what was the most popular political party of the time in the state—the National Conference. He won elections to the Praja Sabha in 1947 and to the renamed Legislative Assembly as an NC candidate in 1952, 1957 and 1962.[2]

A return to full-time spiritual work By 1965, when he was 73 and now a Hâjî, Miâñ Nizam-ud-Din realised 'that the politics of that time'[v] were not

1 Sheikh Sahib was arrested in 1953. That year as well as in 1957 when Pt Nehru visited Kashmir, Haji Baba leaned on the Prime Minister to release Sheikh Sahib from jail, which he did the next month.

2 Such is the goodwill that his family enjoys that, to this day, his son Mian Basheer and grandson Mian Altaf have won every election that they have contested from Kangan, typically receiving around 90% of all votes cast.

in keeping with his own principles. He withdrew from public life altogether and turned himself exclusively towards the spiritual life. He followed and promoted the practices of the Naqshbandi order (silsilâ) of sufi mystics.

In August 1972, as if he had a premonition, Haji Baba decreed that his eldest son, Mian Bashir Ahmed, a spiritualist in his own right, would be the sajjâdâ nasheen of the shrine. Three months later, in November, Haji Baba left his followers forever.

Hazrat Miâñ Bashir Ahmed Lârvi was born in 1923. When he was still in his thirties, tales gained currency of his spiritual prowess and his capacity to solve the temporal problems of his followers. Five decades later he would recall the faces and names of people whom he had helped in the 1950s.

Miâñ Saheb's role during the Pakistani aggressions of 1965 (when one of his followers told the Indian army about the whereabouts of the Pakistani infiltrators) and 1971 (when he shored up the army's supply lines) are a glorious part of India's history.[3] In 1989 Pakistan introduced a reign of terror in the state. Violence raged with extreme intensity till 1996 and at a lower level for more than a decade after that. During all this while there was not a single militant or act of militancy in the areas and communities of which Miâñ Saheb is the spiritual head.

I was the Principal Secretary to the Governor from 1994 to 1998—and theoretically one of the highest risk targets among civil servants. And yet at the peak of militancy I would go to Wangat Sharief and tour those hills for hours without a single bodyguard or bulletproof vehicle. That is the kind of moral hold the dynasty has on its followers.

And such was the following that Miâñ Saheb gathered in Pakistan and Pakistan occupied Kashmir that in the 1980s when he went to Kaiyan Sharief, where the roots of his order lie, so many thousand disciples gathered around him that 'Pakistani officials, in [view] of his political influence [on the] Indian side of Jammu and Kashmir considered [the gathering] a security risk and the Pakistani army was deployed. He was not allowed to go to the mausoleum.'[vi] Miâñ Saheb was crushed when he was told that he could not offer prayers at the grave of the spiritual mentor of his dynasty, Pir Nizam ud Din, for which purpose he had travelled a few thousand miles. With sadness he announced, 'Since politics stand between me and my spiritual master buried in this shrine I bid farewell to politics altogether.'

---

3 For further details see Parvez Dewan's *Jammu* (Manas, 2007), page 179,

Miâñ Saheb represented India at the United Nations and spoke on behalf of the people of Kashmir, nailing the falsehoods that had been spread about the situation there. That he had been elected four times to the Jammu & Kashmir Legislative Assembly, each time by a record margin, lent greater credibility to his assertions.

In 2008 a grateful nation gave Miâñ Saheb India's third highest civilian award, the Padma Bhushan.

References

i http://en.wikipedia.org/wiki/Mian_Bashir_Ahmed

ii Mani, K.D., Hazrat Mian Nizam-ud-Din Larvi Wangat, Kashmir: A great Spiritual saint of 20th century, *Kashmir Insight*, March 2011.

iii Mani, K.D., Hazrat Mian Nizam-ud-Din Larvi Wangat, Kashmir: A great Spiritual saint of 20th century, *Kashmir Insight*, March 2011.

iv Mani, K.D., Hazrat Mian Nizam-ud-Din Larvi Wangat, Kashmir: A great Spiritual saint of 20th century, *Kashmir Insight*, March 2011.

v Mani, K.D., Hazrat Mian Nizam-ud-Din Larvi Wangat, Kashmir: A great Spiritual saint of 20th century, *Kashmir Insight*, March 2011.

vi http://en.wikipedia.org/wiki/Mian_Bashir_Ahmed

Ladakh

Bodhi-Sattva Maitreya

Pre- Tibetan Buddhist rock engravings - Shey, Ladakh

Chapter- 18

Buddhism in Ladakh

It is possible that 'Aryan' Dards originally inhabited all of Ladakh. For the first few hundred years they followed Bon Chos (the Bon religion).[1] Interestingly, in all the nations and regions where lamaist Buddhism is found today, in every one of them people practised the Bon religion in ancient times. This is as true of Ladakh in the west as of Arunachal in the east, of the Indian Himalayas in the south and Mongolia in the north, and of Tibet and all other regions in between,

Several rocks with Bon Chos engravings have been discovered near Khaltse and in Kargil district. The ibex looms large in these carvings.

According to the Dards-were-the-first theory, the Dards were later squeezed in from the east by a Mongoloid people from Tibet.

The animist Buddhism of the Buddhist Dards is distinct from that of other Ladakhi Buddhists. It still bears the imprint of the pre-Buddhist Bon religion. In their Bono Na festival, held once in three years, features not found in other Ladakhi Buddhism can be seen .

1 I chanced upon a clipping of an article titled 'Rin-chen-bzan-po—Tibetan envoy of Buddhism' by Lalit Gupta. The clipping had no details of date or even name of the newspaper. I suspect it was from The Indian Express Newsline and was published between November 1998 and February 1999. The mention of Manan is too important for art historians to ignore.

Alternative theory: Reeve Heber (1923), for one, feels that Tibetan nomads were the first to come to Ladakh. They were shepherds and followed the old Bon Chos (religion), the demon worship of which was later absorbed by Lâmâism. Because they were nomads, they did not found towns or villages. Thus, though they came first, they were the last settlers.

The Mon people of north India were the next. They probably came here to propagate Buddhism and are best known for the castles they constructed. They also developed the ancient irrigation system. In this theory the Dards were the third group of settlers. Francke surmises that there were marriages between the Tibetan nomads and Dard agriculturists. A mixed race was the result.

Buddhism reaches Ladakh and Tibet: separately

It is difficult to accept that Buddhism was 'unknown' in Tibet in AD 727. Only a few decades before King Srong-tsan Gam-po, who unified Tibet, had accepted it as the state religion. Chinese historian Hui Ch'ao might have been more accurate, though, when he wrote that 'there (were) no monasteries at all' in Tibet.

Even by the ninth century Buddhism was not the dominant religion in Tibet. The ancient Bon religion was still quite popular. Its believers were in political conflict—at times bloody—with the Buddhists.

What Hui Ch'ao's account indicates is that Buddhism had reached Ladakh several centuries before Indian saints took it to Tibet. (The taking of Buddhism to Tibet is known as the 'first spreading' of Buddhism in Tibet. In AD 747 the northern Indian Buddhist monk and scholar Padma Sambhav went to Tibet. There he set up the first order of *lâmâs,* or monks. It was after this that Buddhism spread rapidly in Tibet.)

We also have (unrelated) evidence that in ancient times Kashmir used to be a flourishing centre of Buddhism. We further know that the eleventh or twelfth century murals on the walls of the Alchi monastery are the creations of Kashmiri painters. (These murals alone in all of Ladakh are purely Indian, with no Tibetan influence.)

Pre- Tibetan Buddhist rock engravings can be seen near Drâss and in Zâñskâr. At Mulbek, next to the highway, and in Kartse Khar are sculptures of the Bodhi-Sattva Maitreya (c.eighth century). These carvings are in much higher relief than those of the post- Tibetan period.

Thus there is no doubt that the Ladakhis became Buddhists much before the Tibetans did. So when did Buddhism reach Ladakh? Possibly in the first century after Christ, and certainly by the second. Equally certainly it came through Kashmir, even though a millennium later Tibetan Buddhism would overwhelm the indigenous variety.

Tibet revives Buddhism with Indian assistance

Lang Dar Ma (also spelt Glan Dharma), a descendant of King Srong-tsan Gam-po, was the king of Tibet in the first half of the ninth century. He replaced Buddhism with Bon as the state religion and strained to exterminate Buddhism from his kingdom. Lang Dar Ma (or even Lang Tarma) died around A.D. 892.

Conflict between followers of the two faiths ensued and a monk murdered the king. In 842 the Tibetan monarchy disintegrated and Tibet itself started breaking into autonomous provinces. Almost a century later, Skitde Nemagon (975- 990), a descendant of the assassinated king, migrated from Tibet to a region that borders Ladakh on the east. This region probably was Guge, which he started ruling independently. Evidently he did not subscribe to his forebear's anti- Buddhist views. Some ranking Tibetan nobles accompanied him.

Nemagon, Atîsa etc.: the second spreading

Buddhism had suffered a setback in Tibet proper. So, Skitde Nemagon and his grandson Yesh-es Od initiated its revival by sending young scholars like Rinchen (b)Zâñgpo and Atisa to centres of Buddhism in India, especially in Kashmir. This phase is known as the 'second spreading' of Buddhism in Tibet.

Lhotsawa Rinchen

Rinchen (born c. AD 985, in the Guge area) is known as *lhotsawa,* or the translator. He either founded or inspired the foundation of the monasteries at Tabo (Himachal) and Nyarma (near Thiksey, Ladakh), as well as perhaps half a dozen other gompas in present day Ladakh, Himachal and Western Tibet. These gompas include those at Alchi, Guge and Purang. (According to other old records, it was King Yesh-es Od who got Nyarma, not tomention the Shey Tsuglagkhañg [university], built.)

Rinchen went on to become the biggest propagator of Indian culture in Tibet. He translated *sûtr* and *tañtr* literature from Sanskrit into the Tibetan language. He also took Kashmiri artists, architects and craftsmen over to Tibet.

According to one account even Atisa, then a scholar at the Vikramshila University (in Central India), went to Tibet at Rinchen's invitation. Kashmiri artists gave to West Tibetan monasteries brilliant frescoes, as well as stucco and wooden sculpture. Monasteries in Tibet, Ladakh and Himachal which reveal Kashmiri workmanship include Alchi, Tsaparang, Tholing and Tabo.

Lalit Gupta, a journalist, writes[i] 'The murals of Manan temples are the only surviving frescoes of the Kashmiri idiom known today.' (Not true. The ones at Alchi, too, have survived. Besides, Mr. Gupta has not indicated where Manan is. All the same, this is important information. It must be the Manan of Himachal Pradesh, because there is no such place of any significance in Ladakh.)

Atisa founded, in Tibet, the mystical Vajrâyan school of Mahâyân Buddhism. Steeped in tañtr, this form gained mass acceptance in Tibet.

Tibetan Buddhism replaces the Kashmiri variety

When did Tibet begin to replace Kashmir and central India as the source of Ladakh's Buddhism? Perhaps around the beginning of the thirteenth century. It had certainly taken over by the reign of the Ladakhi king Lhâ-chen Ngo Rub (c.1300- 1325). The reason was obvious: by then Buddhism had disappeared from the Indian plains and was receding from Kashmir.

Some argue that Tibetan Buddhism had reached Ladakh by the eighth or ninth century AD. However, there is no archæological evidence to back this claim. B.R. Mani writes that 'Widespread traces of cultural impacts of Tibetan Buddhism and art forms of the tenth and eleventh centuries AD have been found throughout Ladakh.' On the other hand, the Alchi monastery was built sometime between the 10th and 12th centuries AD. This shows that Kashmiri Buddhism was still the dominant form till then.

By Ngo Rub's time institutional links had been forged between the monasteries of Ladakh and those of central Tibet. Tibetan Buddhist texts—many of which had been got copied in gold during this and the immediately preceding era—were brought to Ladakh. Ngo Rub got the huge Tibetan Encyclopædia as well as a book of secret chants and spells copied.

More significantly, the Ladakhis started sending young monks to central Tibet for advanced monastic training. This system continued till the 1950s, when the Chinese drove Tibet's top religious leadership out. (To this day many Ladakhi lâmâs aspire to be trained in Tibet—especially if their monastery has fraternal links with a Tibetan monastery renowned for scholarship. A few actually make it, despite the difficulties involved.)

After the 15th century, all new *gompas* in Ladakh were founded as representatives of one or the other Tibetan monastic order.

Around the 14th century Ladakh's spiritual connection with Kashmir took a new turn—one that could not have been anticipated by the events that had gone before. Ngo Rub's descendant[2] Rinchen went over to Kashmir, of which he became the king. He converted to Islam and became the first Muslim king of Kashmir. The wheel had thus turned full circle: thitherto Kashmir had been exporting its Buddhism to Ladakh, rooting out the region's pre-Buddhist religion. Now a Ladakhi ruler established Muslim political rule in Kashmir, aiding the Turkestani saint Bulbul Shah, who took Islam to the masses. This process would, over the centuries, result in almost 95% of the population of Kashmir accepting Islam.

References

i Much later the Dards of Dâ- Hânu, which is in the lower Indus region of Ladakh,converted to Buddhism, while the majority accepted Islam.

2 European scholars, writing in early 20th century, assumed that Rinchen was Ngo Rub's son. However, Janet Rizvi convincingly argues that Rinchen was probably his great- great- grandson instead.

14m high Maitreya Buddha at the Basgo Monastery

Chapter- 19

Gompâ: The important monastries of Ladâkh

A gompâ is a Buddhist monastery. Buddhist nunneries are called chomo gompâs. 'Chomo' means 'nun' and 'lâmâ' means 'monk.'

There are gompas in Leh as well as Kargil. Within Kargil they are either on the National Highway between Leh and Kargil, or in Zâñskâr,

Leh district

(All distances are from Leh town. Please allow for an error of up to +2 km. because it all depends on where you are counting from.)

Alchi: 70km. from Leh. 5km. from Saspol village.

It is generally believed that the great scholar Lotsâvâ Rinchen (b)Zâñgpo (born AD 985) founded the monastery. However, he did not introduce a monastic community here. Instead he nominated four families as the caretakers of the Chos Khor. This made a take-over by another monastery inevitable. Since the 15th century the management of the Likir monastery has been looking after Alchi as well.

This 11th century gompa is arguably the oldest extant monastery in all Ladâkh—perhaps even the region's oldest extant building of any kind.

Basgo: 39-42km. from Leh. There are three shrines at Basgo, all dedicated to the Maitreya. King Senggé Namgyâl got most of them

Basgo Monastery

constructed. They belong to the red hat sect. Snellgrove and Skorupski write that 'this is probably the only temple in Ladâkh to have survived with some of its murals intact from the 16th century.'

The Maitreya Buddha: The management of the Maitreya temples at Basgo claims that these temples are 'a world heritage site' and one of the '100 most endangered' sites in the world. Actually UNESCO has included the 75-foot, copper-coated Maitreya (future) Buddha in the latter category. It sits atop a cliff, 300 metres above the village. King Senggé Namgyâl got it constructed to honour the memory of his father, King Jamyang Namgyâl.

Chemray: 45km. (11,800'). The great King Senggé Namgyâl died in 1645. This monastery was built as part of the funeral rites, to confer merit on the dead king.

Gongo Kargyat: There are eight places in Nubra where naturally formed Buddhist Arhats are found. Gongo Kargyat is the collective name of these eight places.

Deskit: Lama Shesrab Zangpo of Stod founded this monastery when Dragspâ Bum Lde (1400-40) was the king of Ladâkh.

Thiksey Monastery

Hemis: 49km. Hemis was probably built in 1630 at the behest of King Senggé Namgyâl. It is the best known—and thus the wealthiest—gompa in Ladâkh. Its fame owes to the fact that it is the headquarters of the red-hat Drukpa sect and, for that reason, Ladâkh's biggest gompa.

Lâmâ Yûrû: (2,957m.) 127km. west of Leh. Lâmâ Yûrû is the oldest monastery still in use. It possibly became a Buddhist gompa in the 10th century AD, apparently at the behest of Lama Mahâsiddh Nâropâ.

Leh: See 'Namgyâl...' below.

Likir: 61km. to the west. The earliest that the frescoes of Likir can be dated to is the 11th century. Lama Duwang Chosje established a monastery at this spot around AD 1065.

Matho: 27km. southeast. Lama Tungpâ Dorjay built the gompa in the early 16th century. It was named Thupstan-Sharling Choskor. The then king granted the monastery a large estate in the surrounding villages.

Mangyu(r): It is believed that Lotsâvâ Rinchen Zâñgpo, the great translator, built three monasteries in the 11th century, including Mangyu. Alchi and Sumdah are the other two.

Namgyâl Tsemo Monastery, Leh : This used to one of the royal monasteries of Ladâkh. It is located in the palace complex. King Dragspâ Bum Lde built it around AD 1430.

Namgyâl Tsemo Monastery

Phyâng. 17km. to the west. The Zagâñg Snon Krâshish Chhos Rizong monastery: Around fifty monks live in this monastery, which was built in the 15th or 16th century.

Rizong: 74km. west of Leh. Rizong is the most inaccessible monastery in all Ladâkh. In its strict adherence to principles, and in its seclusion, Rizong is unique in all Ladâkh.

Sankar: 3km. This is said to be the only monastery built on flat land, in the 'plains', so to speak. (But so are Mangyu and even Alchi.) Sankar is the seat of the Yellow Hat sect and, thus, linked to Spituk.

Spituk: 9km. to the southwest. The present Spituk gompa was built in the 15th century.

Stak(h)na: 26km. from Leh or a few kilometres upstream from Thiksey. This is one of the older monasteries in Ladâkh. The Drukpa monastery itself was built around 1580 by Chosje Jamyang Palkhar, a saint.

Stok: 17km. to the south-east/ a one-hour drive from Leh. In the 1830s the Dogrâs annexed Ladâkh to the kingdom of Jammu and Kashmîr. The Ladâkhi royal family then shifted to Stok and the palace at Stok was probably built then. The Gurphuk monastery is at a short distance from the palace. It is a branch of the Spituk monastery.

Sumdo: (Roughly 65km. southwest of Leh town.) There are three temples in the complex.

Taktak: 46km. east of Leh; a few kilometres from Chemray; right above village Sâkti. This monastery is the only one in Ladâkh that belongs to Nying ma pa, the oldest Tibetan sect of monks.

Thiksey: 20km. to the south. Sherab Zâñgpo built a monastery at Stakmo. His nephew, Paldan Sherab, shifted it to Thiksey. The gompâ is said to date to the 11th century, maybe the 12th.

Nyarmâ: Close to Thiksey are the ruins of Nyarma, a monastery and seminary founded by the great 10th century scholar Rinchen (b)Zâñgpo.

Urgyan Rizong: This is a 'meditational retreat' in a little valley.

Kargil district

On or near the Leh-Kargil Highway

Mulbek(h) (3,230m.) is 45km. before and east of Kargil. It is 190km. from Leh.

Right next to the road there is a nine metre deep relief idol of the Maitreya Buddha, carved out of a rock. This is the future Buddha.

Wâkhâ (Rgyâl) has a nunnery called the Jangchup Chosling monastery, very close to the highway.

Jangchup Chosling monastery

Shargol(e) is another ten kilometres ahead of Mulbek, or 35km. before Kargil. Its small but old Ge Lugs pâ Buddhist monastery has few but interesting frescoes.

There is a tiny Buddhist nunnery nearby.

Phokar (also Fokar) is 4km. ahead of the Shargol monastery. A tall hill rises from the Phokar plain. You will have to climb it to get to the Phokar Rizong/ Urgyan Dzong.

In Suru Valley

Rangdum (3,657 metres; 130km. from Kargil town, 65km. from Pânikhar, on the road to Zâñskâr.) Around forty monks live in this 18th century gompa.

In Zâñskâr sub-division

Sani: (8km. from Padam.) Emperor Kanishka (aka Kanika) had got 108 chortens constructed in the first century. One of these 'Kanika chortens' is in Sani. Two 9th or 10th century stone slabs flank the entrance to the main hall.

Padam (240km. from Kargil town) has a monastery, but it is not one of the ranking gompas of Ladâkh. There are gompas in Pipiting and Stagrimo, both near Padam.

Karshâ (4-6km. from Padam): Around 150 monks live here, not in the gompa itself, but in houses scattered all over the town. Phagspâ Sherab (Zâñskâr Lotsâvâ) founded the gompa, perhaps in the eleventh century.

Stongdey: (20km. north of Padam on the way to Zangla.) The highlight of the Marpaling monastery is its gon khong (temple of guardian deities). Marpa, the saint, founded it.

Phugtâl/ Phuktâl is a stunning monastic village built inside a huge cave. Csoma Körös, the 18th century Hungarian mystic-scholar, wrote the *Zâñskâr Chronicles* here.

Zongkhul: The Zongkhul gompa is said to have been founded by Mahâsiddh Nâropâ. This legendary 10th century monk from Kashmîr had taught at the universities of Vikramshila and Nalanda.

Chapter- 20

The Buddhist Festivals of Leh and Zâñskâr

During Ladâkh's long winter it is not possible to work in the fields in most parts of the region. Therefore, summer is the time to work and winter the time to play. It is no coincidence that most of Ladâkh's numerous festivals take place in winter.

Almost all the festivals mentioned below are spread over two days, except Lamayuru's Kangish and the Nakrang of Gia. Buddha Purnima, Dosmochey, Losar, Galdan Namchot and Gustor are the names of festivals. The entry 'Monasteries, festivals at', too, is a general entry. In all other cases, the headword, in boldface, is the name of the monastery (gompa) or place where the fair is held.

Bardan gompa: There is a two- day festival in May.

Buddha Purnima: This is the anniversary of Lord Buddha, and is celebrated all over the Buddhist world with prayer. It is observed on the full moon night that falls between the second half of May and the first half of June. Ladakh no longer has a special local or traditional variant. Buddha Purnima has been celebrated in its present (central Indian) fōrm only since around 1985, and has since been observed according to the Hindu calendars. Before that the date of this festival was determined according to the Tibetan calendar and the festival had a more Himalâyan flavour.

On this day three important events in the life of Lord Buddha took place: his birth, his death and his enlightenment.

Chamday/ Chemray gompa fair: The gompâ is almost 40 km. from Leh town. This is normally a two- day festival (called the Angchok) in November. Its *chham* is related to Padma Sambhav, the seventh century

AD Indian saint who founded Tibetan Buddhism and is also known variously as Guru Rimpoche and Lopon Padma Jungnas.

Deskit: This gompa, also spelt Deskit, is in the Nubra . This two- day festival is held in February (on the 28th and 29th days of the 12th Tibetan month). Nubra is cut off even from the rest of Ladakh at that time of the year. Therefore, this is really a local festival. See also 'Dosmochey' below. There is an additional festival on the 4th day of the 6th Tibetan month (in 2001 this was on the 24th and 25th July.) It is normally a day of prayer. In 2001 we celebrated it as The Great Festival of Buddha (Baudh Mahotsav), with dances as well. Who knows, this trend might endure.

This day commemorates five events in the life of Lord Buddha:

i)Prince Siddharth left his kingdom and became an ascetic on this day.

ii)His son, Rahul, was born on this day.

iii)After his enlightenment, Lod Buddha preached his first sermon on this day. The venue was Sârnâth (near Benares) and the subject was the Four Noble Truths.

iv)Lord Buddha's mother, Mahamaya Devi, conceived Bodhisattv Gautam in her womb on this day.

v)In the seventh year of his enlightenment, Lord Buddha started preaching the Tavatinas Heaven. This, too, took place on the same auspcious day.

Dosmochey: (Also spelt Dosmoch(e) and Dosmachay.) This festival is celebrated near the Palace in Leh town and at the Likir and Deskit monasteries. There is a procession of monks, led by Black Hat dancers. They get out of the town/ village and burn 'offerings' for protection against evil spirits and the ravages of nature. There are eleven kinds of 'offerings', including the *Do* ('thread crosses'), which is prepared by experts in tañtr and astrology by monks from the Takthok, which is the only Nyingmapa establishment in Ladakh. The Do is supposed to trap in its threads evil spirits and demons.

The Hemis festival attracts the most tourists partly because it is in the summers. The Dosmochey- a two- day, February festival- is perhaps the most popular with the local people. Traditionally the gya(l)po (king) of Leh would perform the prayers. In the present republican age the local people have taken over the arrangements.

Galdan Namchot is the Ladakhi Buddhist equivalent of Diwali. This two- day festival celebrates the birth anniversary of Tsongkhapa, the founder of the Ge Lugs Pâ sect, and his attainment of Buddhahood. This 14th century Tibetan saint founded the Ge Lugs Pa order.

Lamps are lit in monasteries, public buildings and private houses all over Leh and Zâñskâr. People cook the *thukpa*, serve it to friends, and eat it themselves. (Thukpâ is a thick soup, with pieces of meat and vegetables.)

Gia Nakrang: This is a one- day festival, held at Gia, in February.

Gustor: This is a two- day festival of the monasteries of the reformist Ge Lugs Pâ sect. The name means 'the sacrifice of the twenty ninth day'.

The lead dancer of the Black Hats, the *jha nak*, breaks up a sacrificial cake, the *storma*, at the end of the *argham* ('the killing') ceremony. This signifies the killing of all evil. Also in the chapter on the 'History of Leh' we had read about the ninth century AD assassination by a Buddhist monk of King Lang dar ma. This is acted out during the ceremony. The masks of the dancers depict the various deities of Buddhism in particular and the yellow hat sect in particular. Sometimes, an effigy of the forces of evil is burnt.

Hemis gompa: The Tse-chu festival. (Also spelt Tshe- shu) *Major tourist attraction:* Most Ladakhi festivals take place in the winters, when there's plenty of time on the farmers' hands. The Hemis Festival, on the other hand, is celebrated the height of the tourist season: late June/ early July. On the 10th and 11th days of the 5th month of the Bodhi calendar, to be precise.

Partly because of its timing, the Tse-chu attracts more tourists than any other. It is held at the Hemis monastery.

M.A. Pandit says, 'Many days before the Hemis fair, (one) of the members of every Buddhist family (asks) the family: "Whose turn is it this year to visit (the) Hemis fair?" It is one of the musts in Ladakh to visit Hemis gompa in one's life.' Traditionally, people would come over from neighbouring villages to buy and sell handicrafts.

Origin: The festival celebrates the birth anniversary of Guru Padma Sambhav. The Guru was multi- faceted. He was a scholar and a teacher. He founded the very first order of *lamas* (monks) and he laid down religious principles. He was also a powerful tañtr- expert. And yet at Hemis he is revered for a very different side of his personality.

Here he is Guru Tagpo, an angry warrior who destroys evil. It is believed that once, long ago, demons had started terrorising the people.

The Guru fought with the demons in order to protect the people. He succeeded in defeating them.

The Tse-chu (better known as the Hemis festival) was started in the 18th century. It was the brainchild of Sras Rinpoche, the head lâmâ of the monastery. He was supposed to have been a Ladakhi prince in his previous birth.

Warm- up events: The festival proper lasts just two days. However, warm- up events start three days before. Prayers are offered to the Guru on the 7th and 8th days of the Bodhi calendar. The final rehearsal for the dance is held on the 9th day. It is no substitute for the real thing, because it is not a dress rehearsal.

The thangkâ: Once in twelve years, in the Year of the Monkey, the monastery's massive thâñgkâ is displayed. This is a richly embroidered cloth with religious icons. The images in this case are mostly of Guru Padma Sambhav).

The contents of the festival: There are mask dances of the Dugpa sect, at the end of which sacrificial offerings are destroyed. Made of barley flour, these offerings represent the devil that we call 'ego' in English, the one who makes us commit so much sin.

Some of these dances take you through the eight important phases of the master's life, in each of which he put on a different disguise. The gods and goddesses would dance for him and sing songs praising him.

The sequence of events: Events begin early in the morning. There is a lunch break, after which dances resume and continue till the evening.

DAY ONE (The 10th Day of the 5th Month): The day begins with a musical prelude. There is also a ritual veneration of the portraits of great teachers, especially Sras Rinpoche. It is followed by three dances before lunch and seven after lunch. In order, these are:

i)Thirteen dancers in black hats. Two of these represent parents, one of them is their son and the remaining ten are angry gods. ii)Sixteen dancers, who bless the land. iii)Eight aspects of the personality of the great Guru are enacted by as many players. Monks, lay persons and five goddesses precede him. Sixteen female deities and sixteen others follow him. [A lunch break.]

iv)The twelve protectors of the faith. v)Religious rituals. vi)The Four Guardians (or Sentinels or Kings) of the Four Quarters. vii)The Four

Keepers of the Cemetery. viii)Five fearsome manifestations of the Guru, in which he vanquished evil spirits. ix)Five angry goddesses who crush demons. x)Ten heroes and heroines who fight evil.

DAY TWO (The 11th Day of the 5th Month): There is a ritual veneration of the portrait of Sras Rinpoche. It is followed by seven dances. In order, these are:

i) Thirteen dancers in black hats. However, today they are angrier. ii)Prayers. iii)The eleven respected teachers. iv)A small procession of monks, 'black women', heroes and others, mostly in foursomes. v)Religious rituals. vi)The buffalo- mask. vii)The smiling Buddha with five deities.

Karshâ: The two- day Gustor (see above è) is held in January.

(Lâmâ) Yûrû Festival: A two- day festival of the Dringungpâ sect, held in July. (Phyâng, below, is the only other gompa of this sect. The two have the same head lâmâ.) Masked lâmâs dance and destroy sacrificial offerings. The dances, too, are similar to those at Phyâng.

Lâmâ Yûrû also has a two- day festival in December- the Kangish

Likir: See 'Dosmochey' above. This is two- day festival in February.

Losar: This is the Ladakhi Buddhist New Year. (Lo, pron. 'low'= year; sar, pron. 'sir'= new.) The Ladakhis, like the Tibetans, follow the same 12- year cycle as the Chinese (with similar names: Year of the Dragon etc.). Ladakh's New Year moved away from the Tibetan in the 17th century when King Jamyang Namgyâl needed to defend his kingdom against the Balti army during the winter. His astrologers told him that it wouldn't be good for his army if they went to war before the New Year. So, he simply changed the day when the New Year occurred: bringing it forward by two months. Losar is now celebrated during the eleventh month of the Buddhist calendar.

The celebrations begin with prayers during which offerings are made to god. The young similarly greet their elders with silk scarves (*khataks*). Everyone dresses in the festive best.

The Buddhists consider the ibex auspicious: they believe it brings prosperity and fertility. On Losar the Buddhists make images of the ibex (and other holy things) and place them on their doors and in the kitchen.

The *metho* ceremony: That evening the Buddhists march through the streets, torches in their hands. They chant holy words to drive out evil spirits as well as the effects of their own sinful karma (actions). The procession- as well as the old year- is over when the torches are thrown away outside the town. The new year now begins.

Children go from door to door to 'beg' for money. This is much like the American Halloween. They pool together all the money they collect thus and spend it on a children's party towards the end of the festival.

(New Year celebrations are an extended affair in Ladâkh- *really* extended. They begin, in December, with the Galdan Namchot [above è] and end with the Dosmochey [also above è], six to ten weeks later, in February. It is not a coincidence that these are the coldest months. In Ladakh one has to find things to do in the prolonged winters when any kind of labour outside the house is not possible.)

Matho gompa: The Nagrang festival: (Also spelt Nakrang.) This two- day festival of prophesy is organised by the Saskyapa order at Matho, its only monastery in Ladakh. For a month before the festival, two lâmâs of the Matho monastery go into seclusion to meditate. While there, they fast frequently, meditate and go through self- purification. All this is aimed at giving them spiritual strength- and to make them pure enough for the deity to possess them.

When they emerge before the public for the festival they have been so sensitized spiritually that they go into a trance and start calling holy spirits. Soon enough, the holy spirits possess them. Now they are blindfolded with several scarves, *after* which they start running up and tall rooftops and jumping from balcony to balcony, walking on narrow parapets, performing potentially dangerous gymnastics. They also perform awesome feats with swords and knives.

More importantly, these two monks are designated oracles who now make predictions about public events as well as what the future holds for the individuals who go to them.

The robes and masks worn by monks at this festival are on display at Matho's richly endowed museum.

Monasteries, festivals in: Each gompa (monastery) has a number of lâmâs (monks) and almost all lâmâs live in or around the monastery. The head of the gompâ is called the *rimpoche*. It is he who directs all festivals held in his gompa. (Except for Losar and Galdan Namchot, all festivals mentioned in this section are linked to one or more gompas.)

Almost all these festivals include lâmâ dances: more accurately *chhams* (see 'Chham' in a footnote later in this chapter è). As in much of South

Asia, these ballets are enacted outdoors (despite the cold, the only concession to which is that they are performed by day). The rimpoche, and other ranking lâmâs, alone sit in a designated section- the rimpoche on a throne. The rest of the audience sits- or stands- anywhere.

All these festivals are celebrated according to the Buddhist calendar, which does not correspond exactly with the Gregorian. The Tourism department of Jammu and Kashmir has been commissioning a Buddhist astrologer to determine dates five years in advance. I have appended below a chart based on his calculations.

During these annual festivals devotees visit the main hall as well as the smaller shrines in the same building. According to M.A. Pandit, 'They prostrate themselves before the statues of Buddha saying, "I bow before Buddha, Dharma and Sangha" or "I take refuge in Buddha, Dharma and Sangha". They burn lamps of butter and oil. They offer flowers and burn incense, they move round the Gonpâ uttering the sacred Mantra: "Om Mani Padme Hung", meaning, "O Budhisatva Chanras Ziks, give me the blessing of your body, speech and mind." Thus they offer prayers as Shantideva has said in his book *Bodhisatva Charya*:

'May there be inexhaustible wealth like the treasure and store of Gandharas; May all live in perfect freedom without any quarrels and violence.'

Mulbek Chambâ: The one- day 'Shubla' festival is celebrated in July.

Padam: (Zâñskâr) The two- day Skurim festival is in November.

Phugtâl: This takes place on the 18th and 19th days of the 12th month of the Tibetan calendar.

Phyâng gompa: The Tsedup festival. (Also spelt Tserook or Tseruk.) 17 km from Leh, this is one of the two gompas in Ladakh of the Dringungpa order, which was founded by Skyabje Jigten Gombo. The founder's *thâñgkâ* is displayed during the two- day festival. Devotees come from all over to see the thâñgkâ. Chhams, too are performed.

M.A. Pandit says that this is a March festival. July/ August, says our astrologer. The 'Ladakh Region Gazetteer' says February. Our astrologer has given precise dates for the years 2000 to 2014. Therefore, the astrologer has to be right.

Sani: (Also spelt 'Seni'; rhymes with 'Nanny'.) The Nasjal of Sani is perhaps the only festival in Zâñskâr that occurs in the summer (July). Its timing makes it, like the Hemis festival, a big tourist draw. In the Tibetan calendar it occurs between the 15th and 20th days of the 6th month.

Sha(c)kukul: (Also Shachukul and Shashukul) The two- day Dumchhot festival is held in June; the Gustor in August.

Shey: The two- day Shubla (or Srubla) festival is held in July at the Dresthang Gompa. There is also a two- day festival called the Rullo in March.

(S)pituk festival: (The 's' is silent in some parts.) The Spituk gompa is close to the Leh airport and this two- day festival is generally in December or January. (See also 'Gustor' above.)

Stok (Gurphuk monastery) festival: This Tse chu (lit.: the tenth day), too, is a two- day festival of prophesy, in February. (See 'Matho' above.) It is also called the Guru Chhe- shu and is held on the 9th and 10th days of the first month of the Tibetan calender. However, unlike Matho, the designated oracles at Stok are not monks. They are ordinary people whom the lâmâs of the Spituk monastery have purified spiritually and sensitized to be able to summon holy spirits.

Stongde: A two- day festival in January.

Thiksey festival: See 'Gustor' below. (M.A. Pandit says that 'the fair(s) of Thiksey and Deskit Gonpas also fall in the month of January together.' Might once have. In the first decade of the 21st century- this is an October- November festival.)

Toktak: This two- day festival, known as the Angchok, is held in February.

nYarma Gonbo: This is a monastery in Nubra. However, most categories of tourists are not allowed to enter the region in which it is located. Gonbo is the Tibeto- Ladakhi equivalent of the Shiv lingam.

Yûrû gompa: The Kabgyat: See '(Lâmâ) Yûrû' above.

Modern festivals

Baudh Mahotsav: This is a young festival, first held in 2001 at the initiative of the Government of India. I had the fortune of being associated with it from its inception. In 2001 the venue was Nubra and in 2002 Karsha (Zâñskâr). The aim is to make it a mid- season (July/ early August) festival at a non- traditional venue. There is an equal emphasis on an all- India seminar on national integration as well as folksongs and dances. It has been my endeavour to use this occasion to bring together seminarists from all over India, especially the Himâlayân Buddhist belt (Leh, Padar, Zâñskâr, Manali, Sikkim, Bhutan and Arunachal Pradesh).

Kargil Festival: I started this festival as part of the overall Ladâkh Festival in 1993. It did not catch on. The needs of the two districts are different. So, in 2000 we delinked it from the Ladâkh Festival. While both festivals are season- extenders, in Leh the festival prolongs the season when tourist arrivals start flagging. Tourism in Kargil is nowhere near as successful as in Leh. Therefore, the festival is held from the 15th to 25th June every year. This is when the tourist season has just begun but arrivals are weak.

Kargil Festival

In Leh, the Ladâkh Festival is held mainly in Leh town. The Kargil Festival, on the other hand, has no headquarters. It is peripatetic and spends a day or two each in Goshan (Drass), Trespon, Sankoo, Panikhar and Mulbek. It stays longer at Padam (Zâñskâr).

Activities during the festival are centered around polo and archery. At Mulbek and Padam- and even Sankoo- there is song and dance as well. The culture of Da- Hanu is highlighted at Mulbek.

Ladâkh Festival, Leh: Before I introduced the concept of a 'season extender' in 1993, tourists would start leaving by the third week of August.

Ladâkh Festival, Leh

Therefore, after studying the pattern of tourist arrivals in the previous decaded, I decided that the Tourism Department would host a festival from the 1st to 15th September every year. If I may say so myself, this festival is now a household word among travel- priented people all over India. It is known among travel circles in the target countries, as well.

A colourful two- hour procession marches from the Lamdon School, through the main bazar to the polo- ground. There is a contingent from every ethnic group of the district, and some from Kargil. The inaugural show, too, tries to showcase the songs and dances of every region of this huge district.

Since 2000 I have been trying to get performers from all over the Himâlayân Buddhist region, together at this festival.

Polo and archery form an important part of the festival.

Sindhu Darshan, Shey and Leh town: This is the brainchild of the then Home Minister of India, Mr. L.K. Advani. It was started in the mid-1990s. At my request, the Government of India very kindly allowed us to hold this festival on the 1st, 2nd and 3rd June every year. Normally, the tourist season would begin around the second or third week of June. As a result of this festival we have managed to extend the season at its start as well. Because of Mr. Advani's personal involvement, we get enormous

Sindhu Darshan

publicity in the press and on television in early June. This translates into greater tourist arrivals during the rest of the season.

Mr. Advani belongs to the Sind province of undivided India. River Sind/ Indus, which has given India its name, terminates in that province, where it meets the Arabian Sea. The river originates in Tibet- Ladâkh. Therefore, Mr. Advani decided to honour the source of the river. Thanks to him we received funds to construct a pavilion and *ghat* (landing) near the banks of the Indus. The inaugural function of the Sindhu Darshan festival is held here. Other events take place in Leh town as well.

Buddhist, Hindu, Muslim and Christian prayers are offered at this ghat, and in boats moored to the ghat, at the inauguration. Songs and dances, from Ladâkh as well as the rest of India, follow.

Because this is a generously funded festival, it has its own website, CD and other publicity materials.

The songs and dances of Leh and Zâñskâr

Chham (pron. somewhat like 'chum', the 'chh' being closer to 'sh') Chhams are loosely called 'lâmâ dances' because lâmâs (male Buddhist monks) perform them. In fact these are intricately crafted ballets in which sacred (or historical) stories are acted out by lâmâs in the courtyards of the gompas they live in, around the flagstaff. An ensemble of drums, twelve- foot horns, cymbals and the 'shawm' plays as they dance. There might be singing, too. Or, to be precise, the chanting of holy verses connected with what is being enacted.

The lâmâs wear expensive silk robes in vibrant colours and equally colourful masks. On the masks are painted (and sculpted) the faces of either the various deities of that monastery or historical/ legendary characters. In their hands might be ceremonial objects or even faux weapons. In India, television soap opera versions took the *Mahâbharat* (and some details from the *Ramâyan*) to the Hindu masses. Masked ballets serve the same purpose in Ladakh. They familiarise devotees with the deities 'they are to encounter during the 49- day, 'Bardo' (or transit) period between death and rebirth in one of the six forms of existence depending upon one's Karma (deeds).' (Quoted from a government handout.)

These slow moving ballets (accompanied by songs) are in three acts. The first, the *ser kyem* invites God and the deities to watch the dance. (Such invocations are part of many other Indian forms of classical dance as well.) Sacred water and sanctified food are offered to the deities. Now the main story is acted out. *Entre acts* offer comic relief: clowns dressed as skeletons jump about, often skillfully. In the last act, evil, represented by a doll made of dough, is destroyed, and literally, by the *jha nak*. (See also 'Gustor' above.)

All Ladakhis dances are slow. They take all day to do a 360° twirl. Or so it seems. Seriously, the dancers certainly take five or six minutes to do a pirouette. Elsewhere the same would take a few seconds. The standard explanation is the lack of oxygen in Ladakh. You can't afford to do anything very energetic at 12,000' above the sea.

Yet, there are three exceptions. The dances of Chang Thâñg (Leh) and Drâss (Kargil) are relatively fast. Drâss is a mere 3,230 feet above the msl. So that explains. Or does it? Chang Thâñg is between 13,000' and 15,000'. It thus is higher than most inhabited parts of Ladakh. On the other hand, Dâ- Hânu is a good two thousand feet lower but its dances are slower than those of most of Ladakh.

Chapter- 21

Islam in Kargil

Amrood Cho, also known as Mureed Khan was king of central Kargil (c.1450- 1475). This was when Islam first spread in Purîg, through the efforts of the saint Ameer Kabeer Syed Ali Hamdani and his disciple Syed Muhammad Noor Bakhsh. (According to some historians, Syed Muhammad was a disciple of Khwaja Ishhaq of Khatlan and that it was the Khwaja who was a *khalîfâ* or disciple of the Ameer Kabeer.)

That Amrood Cho had an alternate, Islamic, name seems to indicate that he, too, had converted to Islam, or followed two religions (as twelve per cent of India does even today). Khan, incidentally, is *not* an Islamic surname. (Genghis, to take a particularly celebrated example, was not a Muslim. The word is variously spelt and pronounced Qâ'an, Khân and Hân in various Central Asian languages. In the Mongolian language, the word means 'king.')

Khokhor Baghram (c.1535- 1555) inherited the throne from his father Ahmed. He made friends with Gyâpo Tsewang Namgyâl in order to buy peace for his eastern borders. His younger son Tsering Malik was the governor of Chiktan. The people of Chiktan believe that Tsering Malik was the first Muslim to rule that area.

A later king called Dooroo Cho died childless. He was succeeded by his younger brother Habib Cho (c. 1490 to 1510). During Habib's reign Mir Shams ud Din, propagated Islam in Purîg and Baltistân. Some historians say that the Mir advocated the Imamiya or Shia school in particular. The Mir was a saint from Iraq and a disciple of the son of the great Syed Muhammad Noor Bakhsh of Khurasan. Habib Cho accepted Shia (Shiite) doctrines. His father had already converted to Islam.

The Chaqchan Mosque is one of the earliest mosques in Baltistan (1504 AD), and is attributed to Syed Ali Hamdani

(Other missionaries from Kashmir and Baltistân carried the message of Islam from village to village. Their descendants are known as Aghas, or the exalted ones. Till, say, the 1950s, before elections began to be held in Kargil, the district was informally divided into turf controlled by two major and several minor Aghas. The Aghas were religious as well as temporal leaders. On festivals each family would present a small tribute to the Agha that it owed allegiance to. This would be in cash, a tithe to wit. The system still continues but the hold is quite informal now, and much weaker. Real power has shifted to the state, which pumps more money into the Ladakh region, per capita, than in any district of India.)

Chapter- 22

Islâm in Leh and Zâñskâr

Muslims live in Leh town and in twenty-five other villages of Leh district.[1] Before 1947, the Muslim population was greater. In the 1950s some Muslims[2] migrated to the areas occupied by Pâkistân. In Zâñskâr the Muslims live in Padum (the 'capital') and Pipiting.

The first Muslims—and mosques

The advent of Islâm: Hussain Mansûr Hallaj of Baghdad was among the first known Muslims to have travelled through Ladakh. This was in the 10th century. Historian Abdul Ghani Sheikhi asserts that 'the first Muslim set foot in the area as early as in the 7th or 8th century.'

By way of proof he mentions a group of boulders near Tangchey (Tângtsé?) on which a verse from the Holy Qurân and the names of some Arabs have been engraved in Arabic. These Arabs include Nâsir ibn Sâleh Abu Mansûr, Abul Âyat and Zakâriâ ibn Qâsim. On cross checking with Central Asian records, Sheikh found that these were Arab army commanders and administrators of the 7th//8th century. That, incidentally, was the first century of Islâm, internationally.

However, it was Amîr Kabîr Mîr Syed Ali Hamadâni who first propagated Islâm in Ladâkh. This great 14th century saint spent some time in Ladâkh while travelling between Kashmîr and Kâshghar (Chinese Turkestân).

1. The district has 112 villages in all.

2. The entire Muslim populations of Sespol, Khâltsé and Nemo, and many from Bazgo left for the occupied territory.

The first mosques: Amîr Kabîr Mîr Syed Ali Hamadâni built the first mosque in Ladakh. He did so in Shey, perhaps in 1381. The mosques at Tiyaqshi and Padum are among the many said to have been built by him in Leh and Zâñskâr.[3] He also got several mosques constructed in Baltistân.

Chhushat Yoqmâ has an extremely old mosque and an almost equally old Imâmbârâ (Shiite place of worship). No one knows when either was built.

The Jâmia Masjid, Leh: For some reason most histories put the construction of the first mosque in Ladakh at more than two—even three—centuries after 1381. An official publication of the state government puts the date of the first mosque as 'later' than the '15th century'. Many books seem to indicate that Leh's Jâmia Masjid, built in 1594 or 1666, was the first mosque in Leh district.

However, evidence of the Shah é Hamadân's 1381 visit to Shey is overwhelming. Equally certainly it was he who got the first mosque (perhaps, mosques) built in Leh district.

Trying to put a date on when the Jâmia Masjid of Leh town was built has been an interesting exercise for this author. A publication of the J&K Tourism Department says that 'built in 1594 by Senggé Namgyâl [as] a tribute to his Muslim mother, the Leh mosque, an exquisite work of Turko-Iranian architecture, stands majestically in the main bazar.'

This belief is based on a folksong, which tells us that Senggé had donated land for the mosque.

The grand mosque that we see today is mainly in the Indo-Islâmic style. There is a smaller and older mosque close to it.

Now we know that Prince Nawâñg Namgyâl, too, had a Muslim mother, Queen Tsering rGyâlmo. (See 'A History of Kargil'). The mother and son were definitely alive in 1594. Senggé probably wasn't even born then. So Nawâñg could have got the mosque built. He was one of the sons of King Jamyâñg. But he never got to be king. Nor is there a belief in Leh that it was Nawâñg who built the mosque for his mother.

---

3. According to most historians the first Muslims went to Zâñskâr with Day-tsok (some time between 1570 and 1642). Therefore, would the Shah é Hamadân have built a mosque there in 1381-82?

Ali Shér Khân Añchan, the emperor of Skardu, defeated Jamyâñg around 1600, imprisoned him and ransacked and briefly ruled over Leh. Jamyâñg married Ali's daughter, Gyâl Kâtûn. Jamyâñg died around 1616. His son Senggé was a minor then. Therefore, his Muslim mother Gyâl Kâtûn ruled as the regent for a while. According to many historians, all that she got built was one room in the Bazgo palace. (However, Sheikh says that she got mosques constructed at Hunder, Leh and Bazgo.)

Obviously the minor Senggé could not have built the mosque in 1594. On the other hand Ali Sher could, and there is some weak evidence that he might have. At one stage, his name, or that of his grandson, Shâh Murâd, had been inscribed on the mosque. But why would Ali Sher, a Shia, have got a Sunni mosque built? Even Nawâñg's mother was a Shiite.

However, Jamyâñg could have built the mosque for either or both of his Muslim wives. No one says that he did. Therefore, we have to accept the theory that the Jamia Masjid was built in 1666. This followed the 1663 agreement between the Sunni Mughal Emperor Aurangzeb and Gyâlpo Deldan Namgyâl of Leh. But then the question arises as to why the names of Ali Sher and/ or Shâh Murâd got to be written on a Sunni mosque.

Other sects: The Muslim world is not divided neatly into Shîâs and Sunnîs, as simplistic accounts would have us believe. As I have shown in the volume on Kashmîr, there are sects that have tried to bridge this divide. The Nûr Bakhshîs are one such sect. (There is a major Nûr Bakhshî population in Turtuk which, since 1971, has been on the Indian side of the Line of Control in Leh district. For almost two and a half decades before that it had been under Pâkistâni occupation.)

The Kelumcheh, a clan from Purîg (Kargil), which went over to Baltistân around 1730, were neither Shia nor Sunni. Like the Shîâs they did not accept the first three Righteous Caliphs of Islâm. However, they gave an extremely high place to Hazrat Abu Bâkar's daughter, Âyéshâ, and Hazrat Usmân's daughter, Hafzâ. (Both noble ladies were the wives of Hazrat Muhammad, peace be upon him, the prophet of Islâm.)

Apparently, there was a Muslim saint in Kashmîr who put his interpretation of Islâm down in a book. He probably migrated to Baltistân in the late seventeenth century. The Kelumcheh follow his principles.

Later mosques: In the 19th century, an Imâmiâ (Shiite) mosque was built in Leh.

Conversion and Migration

Conversions: The defeated Deldan, and his son, went through the motions of converting to Islâm. They went back to Buddhism immediately thereafter. No other conversions from Buddhism to Islâm took place in that era, certainly not in significant numbers. And yet almost 16% of the population of Leh (and 4.76% of Zâñskâr) is Muslim. How come?

Migrations: Since mediæval times Ladakh had extensive trading links with the neighbouring Muslim-majority Yârqañd. This came to an end in 1949. Over the centuries, some Yârqañdi traders settled in Leh and married local Buddhist women. Their descendants form a community that is now called the Argons. Most Argons are Sunnis and follow the Hanafiâ school.

Muslims from Yârqañd (and Tibet) continued to trickle into Leh (and Kashmir) even after 1949, like their Tibetan Buddhist counterparts. The head of one such Muslim family reached Leh through Darjeeling (where he married a Tibetan Buddhist). Another Yârqañdi family, including the women and children, did the difficult journey over the Kârâkorams on foot and horseback. Muslim or Buddhist, post-1949 immigrants have been very few.

Till the late 1970s there were almost two dozen Yârqañdi families in Leh. Many went over to Kashmir and settled there. One such family migrated to Kargil instead. Then the Government of Turkey invited all ethnic Turkestanis to return to Turkey. Almost all Yârqañdis living in Kashmir accepted the offer.

By the 21st century there were just two Yârqañdi families left in Leh.

However, the Argons as a whole make up only around a third of the Muslims of Leh district. The rest are Shia or, as in Turtuk, Nûr Bakhshî.

In 'A history of Leh' we saw how the pashmînâ trade of Ladâkh was controlled by Kashmîrî Muslims. This was commented upon by visiting Europeans as early as in 1715. That tells us why there is a small Kashmîrî population, dependent on the wool trade, in Leh district.

Today the Dogrâ contingent of the Sikh army that conquered Gilgit-Ladâkh for the Punjâb (and, thus, India) is sought to be painted as a Hiñdu (all right, Hiñdu-Sikh) force. However, it had a very substantial number of Muslim officers and soldiers. Some of them settled in Ladâkh.

Each of the Muslim queens mentioned earlier brought a small retinue of maids and musicians with her. These would be Muslims from her land.

A village of Balti Muslims was set up in Chushot, perhaps in the sixteenth century. Shiites from neighbouring Purig (Kargil), too, sometimes settled in Leh district: often to escape some natural calamity back home.

Migration by invitation: The Buddhist kings of Leh and Zâñskâr often invited talented Muslims to come and settle in their land. (King Ranjit Dev of Jammu would later follow their example. Some, like the Zargars of Kashmîr, were brought in to mint coins for the Government of Ladâkh.[4]

The Persian language skills of yet others, notably the elite Khowjas of Leh, were in great demand in Ladâkh. In the 17th and 18th centuries the Lo Pchak religious and trade missions to Tibet were managed by Ladakhi Muslims. The Khowjas were often the Muslim family that controlled these missions.

King Jamyâñg Namgyal's favourite traders were a group of seven Kashmîrî Muslims. He gave them land to settle on, in and around Leh town. Each of them went on to found an important clan.

All over India, except in Sikh and Christian areas, butchers almost always are Muslims. The majority of Buddhists in Leh and Zâñskâr eat meat but do not kill animals themselves. So, Muslim butchers were requested to come to Leh.

Emigration: Over the same centuries Kashmîrî and Ladâkhi Muslims too went to Yârqañd and Tibet to trade. To this day there is a small community of two thousand Kashmîrî-Ladâkhi Muslims in Tibet.

A growing population: On the whole the population of Muslims in Leh has been rising consistently. P.H. Francky'[ii] wrote in the early 20th century, 'The Arghon population of Ladâkh (Leh in particular) is increasing more rapidly than the Buddhist population.'

This was at a time when Ladâkh (and the state) was supposedly ruled by Dogrâ Hiñdus.

---

4. Ladâkh has a very old tradition of its kings inviting talented Kashmîrîs to settle in Ladâkh. Rinchen bZangpo, for instance, brought a hundred artists from Kashmîr to Ladâkh in the 11th century A.D. Of course, they were all Hiñdu-Buddhists.

The Argons

Most Argons are well educated. Some of them have risen to senior positions in the government and academics, though the odds are stacked against them.

Exclusion from affirmative action: In the 1980s the Government of India determined that all the people of Leh and Kargil, including the Gyâpo princes, the Lungpo nobility and the Kargil aristocracy, were tribals. All the people were tribals, except the Sunnis of Leh and Kargil. Tribals are entitled, by law, to several kinds of affirmative action, including a certain number of jobs at every level in the government.

The Argons have always distinguished themselves through hard work and high standards of honesty. They now have to redouble their efforts just to stay where they are.

The title: The Argons mainly live in and around Leh town. Till the 1980s 'Argon' was a very exalted title. Only the wealthiest Sunni Muslim businessmen, who traded goods in Lhâsa, Yârqañd and Kâshghar, were called Argons.

It's the politics of 'reservation' (affirmative action) that welded the Sunnis together. Till then they were known as Yârqañdis or Puriks (Purgis), depending on where their male ancestors had migrated from. Now that they alone had been excluded from the benefits of 'reservation,' they had a common goal, and identity. They needed a name to call themselves, and the word 'Argon' came in handy. The entire community started using a title thitherto confined to the elite.

The Shias

As in Kargil, the Shias account for the majority of Muslims in Leh district. They live in the villages where the two districts meet, as well as in Bogdang, Nubra, Pheyang, Thiksey and Chechot.

References

i Sheikh, Abdul Ghani, 'Muslims in Ladâkh and Sufi Traditions', *New Hope*, vol.4, no.1, January-February, 2003.

ii Quoted by Sheikh, op. cit., p. 36.

Chapter- 23

Monasteries, monks, icons and sacred Buddhist structures

Gompas, monks and nuns

The monasteries (*gompas*) of Ladakh are one of the two main attractions of the region: the other being its spectacular landscape. One reason why there are so many major *gompas* is that there are so many monks. And there are so many monks because, till the 1970s, when prosperity suddenly came to Ladakh, almost all families would oblige one of its sons, normally the second son, to join a monastery as a celibate monk. Many families still do, especially the poor and those in the villages. (*Lâmâ* is the Tibeto-Ladakhi word for 'monk'. Lâmâs of the Kargyutya sect are allowed to get married.)

Ladakh is a desert. Its few fertile tracts are not sufficient to support a large population. The practice of forcing the younger son to be a monk was started by King Tashi Namgyâl (c.1500-32), perhaps as a method to keep the population from growing. Tashi was a cruel man, and on his death this ceased to be enforced by law. However, soon it became a custom followed by most families, including the kings of small states like Zâñglâ (Zâñskâr). Around 1750, a council of wise men and elders met at Hanle and made this custom binding on royalty.

Some girls choose to become nuns (*chomo tsomo* or *ani*). However, this practice was never very common. That is why nunneries (*chomo gompa*) as not as numerous as monasteries.

Collectively, the clergy is known as the *gedun.*

In 1847, Cunningham, the British scholar, estimated that 7 per cent of the population of *Ladakh* (not Leh alone) became monks and nuns.

Over the centuries the gompas grew very rich. People, and kings, would gift land to them. Food grown on gompa lands would feed the monks. Hemis has the largest amount of land. Land ceiling laws passed by the government do not apply to gompas.

Gompa means 'solitary place' and most *gompas* (monasteries) are indeed built away from populated areas, according to the orders of the Sakya Muni. Some, like the Rangdum *gompa,* are located in the middle of nowhere. However, some gompas are close to important villages and cities. Such gompas are normally built atop a slope well above the main village, thus achieving the required solitude.

Inside a gompa

The main places of worship inside a gompa are the *Lhâ- khang* and the *Du-khang* (assembly hall). The head lâmâ (*kushok*) lives on the highest floor. He is normally given the title of *Rimpoche* (priceless jewel).

Architecture: Apart from the Leh palace, the gompas are the grandest buildings in Leh and Zâñskâr. Most gompas are built atop a hillock. Monks' houses (*labrangs*) are built on the slope leading to the peak. The outer (and, often, inner) walls of all these buildings are normally whitewashed. Broad strips of red break this whiteness: around windows and along parapets. Roofs are flat, as is the case with ordinary houses.

Most gompas have at least one large, open courtyard inside. Mask dances and festivals are held in these courtyards. Prayer flags on tall poles might be found inside the courtyard. These are long, vertical but slim strips of white cloth with prayers, texts and invocations *printed* on them. (The Chinese, the Tibetans and the Ladakhis printed books, using plates with immoveable typefaces, several centuries before the rest of the world. Gütenberg invented the moveable type, not printing itself.)

Prayer instruments: There are three main instruments used in rituals. These are the cylindrical prayer wheel, the bell and the thunderbolt sceptre.

The prayer wheel (*maaney chhos khor*) can be small and hand- held or taller than a human and fixed to the ground. Lâmâs normally carry hand- held prayer wheels almost everywhere, which they keep spinning as they chant their prayers. Thus prayer wheels serve much the same function as rosaries do for Christians, Muslims and Hindus. The prayer that is chanted is normally *Om Maaney Padmey Hum* (variously translated as 'O lotus jewel, amen' and 'Hail [to] the jewel in the lotus'). This prayer is engraved on prayer wheels, on the stones placed on '*maaney* walls,' almost everywhere. Janet Rizvi says that this is 'an invocation of secret tantric significance, particularly associated with the Bodhi-Sattv of Compassion, Avalokiteswara'.

When devotees come across a fixed prayer wheel, normally at the entrance of a gompa or by the roadside, they normally give the wheel a spin. It is considered auspicious to do so. All prayer wheels are cylindrical with a stem at the centre. The wheel rotates on this stem. Fixed prayer wheels are normally around 5 or 6 feet high. Some such wheels are built atop streams, the waters of which keep rotating the wheels.

The bell is used during the daily prayers.

The Lhâ Khang: Lhâ means 'God' and khang 'room'. Every gompa has a very large hall, normally next to the courtyard, which is the main prayer room or temple, and is called 'God's room'. Monks sit, in rows, on mats on the floor of this long, rectangular hall.

Most Lhâ khangs have elegant tankhas on their walls, or suspended from the ceiling. These are silk scrolls on which brilliantly coloured pictures related to Buddhist mythology have been painted and/ or embroidered. Many of these tankhas are invaluable, not only because of their antiquity but also because gold thread might have been used in the embroidery.

The room might also contain *musical instruments*: long trumpets, shawms, bells, horns, big drums and large cymbals. In Tibet it is common to find wind instruments made of the human thighbone in gompas. In Ladakh I have come across such a musical instrument only in the museum of the Rangdum gompa. Yes, some gompas have small museums, too, consisting of a few dozen exhibits.

Tsan (or Tsha or Tshogs) khang: At one end of the Lhâ khang hall is either an altar or a room that open into this hall. This room is the tsha (image) room. On these altars are placed images of the Buddha. The larger images are almost life size and painted with a golden colour. Banners and tankhas might hang from the ceiling in this room, too.

On the altar there would also be dozens of little images (often made of brass), some of them bejewelled and expensive, little oil- lamps made of brass, figures made of cheese, and bowls of butter. Some devotee would have placed the butter there. A cotton wick is inserted into the butter and lit when needed. Incense, too, is burnt at the altar. This room might also contain much grain (normally powdered barley).

On auspicious days these altars are decorated with symbolic figures. Devotees bring milk, butter, tea, flour and similar offerings. Animal sacrifices are strictly forbidden.

Prayers are offered in the Lhâ khang and tsha khang at the break of dawn, noon and sunset. On certain specified days, special day- long prayers are held. Prayers normally include the chanting of passages from the holy texts. Often they just chant 'Om mâney padmey hum'. Normally the musical instruments mentioned above are played during prayers. The monks are called for prayer by ringing a small bell. They then sit in rows in the order of their rank. During their rituals the lâmâs use rosaries, prayer wheels, prayer flags, holy relics, charms and talismans.

Tourists will not give offence if they enter the room while prayers are going on, so long as they do so unobtrusively.

Gon-khang: Every monastery has a guardian deity or two: and a tiny, red temple, the gon-khang, dedicated to them. Women are not allowed inside the gon- khang. There are very few icons in this room. These guardians are not only fierce- looking, they are libidinous, too. They are often shown copulating with female angels in what is known in tañtr as the *yab-yum* position.

Kahgyur khang: lit.: the room of the scriptures. These are libraries that could be either along one of the long sides of the Lhâ khang or in a separate room nearby. The books in these libraries have been printed in extremely limited editions from carved wooden blocks. The paper (*shugu*) used is made from a local grass. Two kinds of paper are made: fine paper for books and coarser paper for prayer rolls.

These books are long and narrow. Their covers are made of wooden boards and thus are extremely durable. Each library shelf looks like a series of 'pigeon holes' of the kind used at institutions to place snail mail in. Each pigeonhole can accommodate one such book.

Tibetan Buddhist scriptures consist of two major groups, namely sacred books and commentaries on these. The sacred books consist of the teachings of Lord Buddha, translated from Indian and Chinese texts.

There are more than a thousand such works. These are bound together in a hundred volumes of around 1000 pages each. The commentaries are not considered as sacred as the canon but even they add up to almost a hundred equally thick volumes.

Chortens: All through the Buddhist areas of Ladakh you will come across brick structures, normally one- or two- storey high, with whitewashed walls. They are called chortens and you will find them on the roadside, near gompas, almost everywhere. They have a square base and four walls at the bottom. Above these walls would be four large circular steps that lead to a dome on top. The dome is normally an inverted cone painted red. The grander chortens can be 30 feet (10 metres) high, with doorless passages on either side that you can even walk through.

These chortens (called stupas in much travel literature) are sometimes dedicated to Sakya Thubba or one of the incarnations of the Buddha. There are eight events ('stages') in the life of Lord Buddha that all Buddhists consider significant (e.g. Lord Buddha's enlightenment and death). Chortens normally commemorate these 'stages'.

The eight stages are: i) Buddha's birth, ii)his descent to earth after imparting the doctrine to his mother in heaven; iii)his enlightenment; iv)his performing miracles; v)his turning the wheel of *dharm* (the faith or doctrine); vi)his uniting the Bhikku Sangh (group of monks); vii)prayers for Lord Buddha's long life and viii)his *parinirvân* (salvation), i.e. his death.

There are, thus, eight kinds of chortens, one for each stage of the Lord's life. These types differ with respect to the size of the steeple, the pattern on the section below the steeple and the design and colour of the next (i.e. middle) section. The bottom section normally remains the same. Even the steeple doesn't vary much.

However, chortens often contain the ashes of an incarnate monk, king or, rarely, important citizen, in which case they are called *dungtens*. In such cases they probably correspond to the mounds that were built at various places atop the distributed ashes of Lord Buddha.

(There is a serious shortage of wood in Ladakh, which is a desert. Therefore, the Ladakhis do not cremate their dead on funeral- pyres. Instead they seat their dead on their haunches in a crouching position and cremate them inside a tiny, closed chamber. Such cremations are anaerobic: they use no air except that which is trapped inside the chamber. Thus they use very little wood, too. Incidentally, in distant Basohli [Jammu province] I found fossilised skeletons of humans who had been buried in the same crouching posture.)

Large chortens, with a path leading through them, are called *kaganis* and are to be found at the entrance of villages.

Inside many Lhâ khangs, on the altar, you might see richly detailed and ornamented miniature chortens, about a foot and a half (0.5 metres) high. They would be made of silver or similar coloured metal, with the ashes of some very important, top ranking, historically significant, incarnate monk.

Gompâ lands: Over the centuries each gompa tends to acquire several hundred acres of land. Some of these lands are cultivated to feed the monks. In addition, people donate money and goods to gompas to feed and clothe the lâmâs.

Iconography: Alchi: The paintings on the walls of the Alchi gompa (monastery) are much older than those of all the other gompas. They are also vastly different, in style as well as choice of themes and deities. That's because Buddhists who drew inspiration from Kashmir and central India founded the monastery. The painters were certainly Kashmiri. Kashmir's Shaivite influences are obvious. The same is true of Mulbek. (See also '*The murals*' below.)

The gompas: the pecking order

So many gompas, so little time. Which ones should you see? The more famous gompas and shrines are Alchi, Hemis, Phyâng, Shey, Spituk and Thiksey.

You can choose to see the most conveniently located gompas. Or you can visit the oldest ones. Or you can go to rich, touristy Hemis.

Or you can do what the local Buddhists themselves would do. The gompas that the Ladakhis rank the highest are:

By antiquity: The Ladakhis hold in great veneration the monasteries set up by or attributed to Lhotsava Rinchen, the great translator (see 'History'): partly because they are among Ladakh's oldest. Of these Alchi Choskor, Sumdah and Mangyu(r) are perhaps the highest ranked in all Ladakh. In the days before automobiles, it was considered particularly auspicious to offer prayers at all three monasteries within a 24 hour span. It still is, except that now it is no longer as difficult to do so.

The other old monasteries and idols held in reverence are Lâmâ Yûrû, Wânlâ, the ruins near Thiksey and the rock- cut sculptures at Mulbek and Kartse Khar (both in Kargil district).

Natural wonders: The Gongo Kargyat sites in Nubra are close to the top of the Ladakhi Buddhist pecking order.

Kanishka's chorten: Emperor Kanishka (aka Kanika) had got 108 chortens constructed in the first century AD. One of them is in Sani/ Seni, Zâñskâr (Kargil district). The holy site at Sani is called Turtot Gyat and is one of the eight holiest Buddhist sites in the world. That is why most of the luminaries of Himalâyan Buddhism- including Padma Sambhav, Nâropâ and Marpa- have visited Sani.

So where does that leave Hemis, the no. 1 favourite among tourists? Nowhere, I'm afraid. It is a 'royal monastery' because it was patronised by two of Ladakh's greatest kings, Jamyang Namgyâl and his son Sengge. As a result, it is the biggest and richest monastery in all Ladakh and owns the most land. It also has the most famous festival, partly because its festival (like Sani's) is one of the few to take place during the tourist season.

The murals: Over the centuries everything about the gompas evolved and changed: their architecture, the style of the artwork and the content of the murals. The artwork at Alchi, of course, is famously Kashmiri and philosophical. Gompas constructed in the eighteenth century, and later, were quite Tibetan. They are full of pictures of gods, goddesses and Bodhi-Sattvs.

The style at 16th century monasteries (e.g Basgo and Namgyâl Tsemo) was somewhere between these two extremes. The artists at the 16th and 17th century (e.g. Chemray, Hemis and Stakna) monasteries seemed to be full of fresh ideas. Their creativity was not weighed down or curbed by tradition, as was to be the case later. By the 20th century so many conventions had developed that the style was invariably classical, and never innovative. Themes, too, had begun to be restricted to those laid down by custom.

The gompas: Grouping them together by location

The gompas can also be grouped together by location. You can see all the major ones in just two days:

Day 1: Shey, Thiksey, Stakna, Matho, Chembray, Tak Tak and Hemis.

Day 2: Spituk, Phyâng, Likir, Alchi and, possibly, Rizong. If you include Lâmâ Yûrû, which is on this route, plan on spending the night there or at Alchi. Most tourists go to Lâmâ Yûrû before Alchi and spend the night at Alchi.

Sani is in Zâñskâr (Kargil). If you want to go there, you could leave Lâmâ Yûrû on Day 3 and spend the night at Kargil. Leave Kargil on the morning of Day 4. If you have a powerful vehicle you can reach Sani on the night of Day 4. Most vehicles take two days to do this trip. Therefore, in all likelihood you will reach Sani on the afternoon of Day 5. The return journey could take equally long. Kargil is halfway between Srinagar and Leh. So if you had come in through Leh you can return via Srinagar (or vice versa). Most small vehicles take 7- 8 hours from Kargil to Srinagar. Buses might take 10- 11 hours.

Maaney walls

In all the Buddhist areas of Ladakh you will find by the roadside long, waist- high 'walls' made of loose stones. Some of these walls are almost a kilometre long. Most others are one or two hundred metres long but only around two or three metres (six to nine feet) wide. The stones placed on these walls are slim, grey, oval tablets, about an inch or two (3-5 cm.) thick and about a foot (30 cm.) long. Their two main surfaces would have been flattened smooth.

On the upper surface the words 'Om Mâney Padmey Hum' would have been carved in very shallow relief in beautifully calligraphed in the local Bodhi script. Each tablet would have been placed there by a devotee who wanted to thank God for some prayer answered, some boon received.

Over the centuries thousands of such tablets accumulate in a maaney, giving it height and length. However, these 'walls' rarely go higher than 4 feet, because it is difficult to see the stones placed on a wall which is higher than that.

Etiquette

Whenever you pass a sacred Buddhist construction try to keep it on your right. This applies to gompas, chortens, mâney walls, prayer wheels etc. This might not always be possible, especially if you are in an automobile and there is no road to the left of the sacred building. However, do try. It is considered rude- almost sacrilegious- to do otherwise.

The worst offence you can commit is to catch or kill fish in a Buddhist area. It's like killing a cow in a Hindu area.

Never enter a monastery (or mosque or temple or Sikh gurudwara) with your shoes on. It would be good if your body is covered: bare legs and arms are not appreciated. Do not drink alcohol or smoke inside a monastery.

If the monks are praying, please do not disturb them.

Entry fee

Most gompas charge an entry fee. Among the prominent monasteries entry is free to the Rizong gompâ alone.

Chapter- 24

Buddhist deities: and their depiction in Ladakhi paintings

Interpreting the body language of the icons

As in Indian classical dance, the hands convey a lot in Buddhist icons.

The two hands: The right hand: The index finger and thumb represent wisdom. The remaining fingers are 'the three containers of the tenets of Buddhism.' The right hand often represents the conferment of blessings. The left hand: The three 'remaining' fingers (middle, ring and little) represent the people of the three worlds (the skies, the earth and the netherworld/ Hades) who practise Buddhism. This hand as a whole represents meditation.

The two hands convey these meanings in most postures, especially 'The Wheel (or *chakr*) of the Faith Posture' and 'The Benefactor (or Bestower) Posture.'

The tips of the thumbs touch each other: In much of Asia people prefer to sit cross- legged, whether on the floor or on a throne or seat. In Buddhist icons often both hands have been placed on the lap and the tips of thumbs meet. Ancient Indians (and, I suspect, Michelangelo) believed that enlightenment passed through nerves that were located in the thumbs. When the tips of the thumbs meet, the circuit, so to speak, is completed and enlightenment begins to flow. This, in turn, develops the mind for its ultimate enlightenment. This is 'The Meditation Posture.'

Touching the earth with the right hand, or attempting to do so: In such icons the left hand might be horizontal, the little finger raised and the thumb diagonally across the hand. The right hand is asking the earth to see for it itself that Lord Buddha has, through meditation, overcome all the problems that had come its way. The arrangement of the left hand indicates the enlightenment. This is 'The Touching- the- Earth Posture.'

Bringing the right hand close to the heart: The tips of the index finger and thumb of the right hand meet and make a circle, as in A-OK. This represents the wheel of *dharm(a)* (the faith). In such icons, too, the left hand might be horizontal, the little finger raised and the thumb diagonally across the hand. It represents meditation. This is 'The Wheel (or *chakr*) of the Faith Posture.'

The palm of the right hand faces the viewer, its fingers pointing upwards. The hand is at the same level as the shoulder. The deity seems to be blessing the devotee. It is. It is bestowing fearlessness (*abhay*) on the devotee. This is 'The Fearlessness Posture.'

Both hands 'folded' together: Both hands are vertical. Their palms face inwards and join each other. The hands are 'folded' together thus at roughly the same level as the heart. This is the way most Hindus, Buddhists, Jains and Sikhs greet each other with a 'namaste' or 'namaskar.' This is also the posture most people, around the world, assume when they pray to God. This is 'The Salutation (or Prayer or Devotional) Posture.'

The index finger raised upwards, normally of the right hand: The rest of the fist is clenched. The stern finger warns people of the wrath of God. This is 'The Index Finger Posture.'

The two hands crossed at the wrist and held close to the chest. We see the backs of the hands. Each hand holds an ornately crafted object, normally two- headed, slightly bigger than the hand itself.

The object in the right hand is the *vajr*, which literally means 'the thunderbolt.' Ancient Hindu warriors used to carry enormous clubs/ maces. These were made of metal (normally brass), were elegantly moulded and were of the same size as the clubs of cavemen. Hindu deities, especially Srî Hanumân jî, always carried them. Now, these, too, represented the *vajr*. The non-violent Lord Buddha is unlikely to have any use for a club. And yet his *vajr*, too, is made of some metal and is a symbolic thunderbolt, rather than a real thunderbolt. ('Vajr' has been discussed further in the entry on Alchi monastery.)

There is a bell, again finely decorated, in the left hand.

This posture represents wisdom and technique. It is called 'The Roar of the Thunderbolt Posture.'

The Giving Posture: The literal meaning of this posture is 'The Wealth Posture.' The right hand is on the right knee, but doesn't quite touch the ground. The left hand is just below the abdomen and rests on crossed-legs, the palm facing upwards.

The Buddha in the art of Ladâkh

DEPICTING THE BUDDHA: The lord is traditionally depicted in several forms. These include the forms of

i) A monk (Shâkyamuni); ii) An angry god (Mahâ Kâla or Vajr Bhairav); iii) A goddess (Târâ); iv) An apparently erotic goddess; and v) an animal (which depicts a certain stage in the evolution of the Bodhi-Sattv).

The Dhyâni-Buddhas: There are seven Dhyâni-Buddhas. Five of them are known as the Tathâgats. Western scholars call them The Five Buddhas.

THE FIVE BUDDHAS (or Tathâgats) are:

i) The fair **Vairochan** who rides a lion. The Buddhists believe that this Buddha created the first World Cycle(è). When he was born (incarnated) as a human he was known as Kaku Chandr(è). As a Dhyâni Bodhi-Sattv he is Sâmañt-Bhadr(è), the great and good king. In art he is seen sitting in The Wheel of the Faith Posture. He is, thus, preaching the doctrine or faith. He holds his hands before his chest and form a circle ('wheel').

The five Buddhas

ii) The red **Amitâbh** whose steed is the peacock. Amit= without boundaries; Aabhaa= light; thus the name means 'the one whose brilliance is everywhere.' The Buddhists believe that this Buddha created the fourth World Cycle, the one that we live in. His human manifestation is as Shâkya Muni(è). As a Dhyâni Bodhi-Sattv he is Avalokités(h)var. He is shown in The Meditation Posture.

iii) The green **Amogh Siddhi** who flies atop the sacred *garud* bird, the Dward Garud in particular. Amogh= successful, 'not gone in vain'. Siddhi= success, expertise, wholesomeness in the sense of being entire in itself. The name can mean 'the successful one.' This is the Buddha of the north. He is portrayed in The Fearlessness Posture.

iv) The blue **Akshobhay** who rides an elephant. Aksh== 'the eye'; ubhay= 'both.' Idiomatically, the name could mean 'the one who does not blink.' Snellgrove and Skorupski have translated it as the 'imperturbable one.' The Buddhists believe that this Buddha created the second World Cycle. In paintings he is shown in 'The Touching- the- Earth Posture.'

Akshobhay has two manifestations. As a human he is Kanak Muni(è). As a Dhyâni Bodhi-Sattv he is the Vajr-Pâni.

v) The yellow **Ratna Sambhav** whose steed is the horse. Ratna= jewel or gem; sambhav= '(made) possible (by).' The name means= 'the one born of a jewel.' The Buddhists believe that this Buddha created the third World Cycle. He has two manifestations. As a human he is Kas(h)yap(è). As a Dhyâni Bodhi-Sattv he is the Ratn-Pâni. This Buddha is painted in The Wealth Posture.

THE REMAINING DHYÂNI-BUDDHAS

Vajrâyan Buddhism includes two more Dhyâni Buddhas. Both wear ornaments that are regal and are those worn by a Bodhi-Sattv.

vi) the blue **Vajr Dhar** ('the one who holds the thunderbolt'). He is shown seated in The Roar of the Thunderbolt Posture. In his hands are either a thunderbolt and bell or a thunderbolt and bell- on- lotus.

vii) the white **Vajr Sattv** ('the one who is like the vajr'). In his right hand is a thunderbolt, held near the chest. His left hand rests on his left thigh and holds a bell.

SOME DHYÂNI BODHI-SATTVS

Four Dhyâni Bodhi-Sattvs, which correspond to four of the Five Tathâgats, are:

i) The blue **Sâmañt-bhadr**: Samant= king or great. Bhadr= good. The name thus means 'the great, good king.' This Buddha sits it the meditation posture (dhyân âsan). He does not wear any ornaments- or clothes. His hands are as in 'The Roar of the Thunderbolt Posture.'

ii) The white- skinned, four- armed **Avalokitéshwar** is the Bodhi-Sattv of Compassion. The main pair of arms hold a jewel and in The Salutation (or Prayer) Posture. There is a rosary in the rear right- arm. There is a lotus in the rear left- arm at the same level as the shoulder.

iii) The blue-black **Vajr-Pâni:** His name means 'he whose hands are like the thunderbolt.' It is the name of Lord Indr, the Rain God of the Hindus. So here, again, Lord Buddha becomes a god in the Hindu pantheon. This ferocious deity holds a thunderbolt in one of his hands. He is always depicted standing, often with a huge 'Afro' mop of hair. Vajr-Pâni wears a loin- cloth made of tiger-skin. He seems to be moving towards the right (our left).

iv) The yellow **Ratn-Pâni:** The name means 'the one whose hands are like gems.' His right hand is in The Benefactor (or Bestower) Posture. There is a gem, the *chinta mani*, in this hand. The left hand is in The Meditation Posture. In some pictures he is shown standing and, in others, seated.

SOME OTHER BODHI-SATTVS

Manju Shrî: This is the Lord of Wisdom. There is a sword (*khadga*) in his right-hand, and yet he is non- violent. The sword is meant to cut through ignorance. In his left hand are a lotus and the Book of Wisdom.

THE MÂNUSI-BUDDHAS:

There are five Mânusi-Buddhas. Mânusi means 'human.' The Dhyâni-Buddhas were born (incarnated) in these human forms so that they could preach the faith.

i) **Kaku Chañdr** sits on a lotus in The Meditation Posture.

ii) **Kanak Muni**, too, sits on a lotus. His right hand is in The Fearlessness Posture while his left hand is in The Meditation Posture.

iii) The yellow **Kas(h)yap** sits of a lion. His right hand is in The Benefactor (or Bestower) Posture. There is a rope in his left hand. Kashyap is a renowned Hindu saint, associated with the settlement of humans in Kashmir.

iv) The golden **Shâkya Muni** is the fourth Buddha, the one we know as Siddharth Gautam. He is the Buddha of our age. This saint-prince was born around 563 BC to the Shâkya royal dynasty. He is depicted in various postures, including The Touching- the- Earth Posture, The Meditation Posture and The Wheel of the Faith Posture. He is likely to hold a leaf/ plant with his right hand.

v) The yellow **Maitreya** is the human Buddha of the next (fifth) World Cycle. Like the Second Coming of the Messiah and the Shiite Mahdi, the Maitreya is the Buddha that the world waits for. He sits in The Wheel of the Faith Posture. In most Ladakhi sculpture (e.g. at Mulbek and Kartsé Khar) he is shown standing. He is likely to be shown holding lotuses (often with their stems). Atop these lotuses, near his shoulders, he might hold a little, sacred vessel (the *kalash*) and a wheel.

The other important icons:

THE DEITIES OF THE MURALS: What the deities portrayed in the murals signify is thus:

Dharm Paals, the: These are the guardians of the faith.

*Mahâ Kâl (*or *Gonbo):* 'Kaal' literally means 'time' and 'Mahâ' means 'the great'. However, 'kaal' also alludes to mortality and the circle of joy and sorrow. This dark blue- coloured deity is normally shown with six arms and legs. He has one or many heads. The Hindu deity Vinâyak (the elephant- headed Srî Ganésh) is under one of his feet. His steed is the mule and his symbol is the trident. He has a flower in one hand and a begging bowl (*kapâl*) in the other.

Shugdan: A guardian angel of the Ge Lugs Pâ. Normally seen riding a beast.

Vajr Bhairav: This is the fierce 'tutelary divinity' of the Ge Lugs Pâ sect. 'Reach Ladâkh' adds that this is 'another form of [Yamantak, and] has nine heads, thirty-four arms and sixteen legs. The [central] head is that of [a bull] and [the one above it] is of Magasaris… He is sometimes shown embracing [the *shaktîs*, who are female supernatural beings].'

Yamantak: The dark-skinned deity of death. His colour could be black, blue or even red. He corresponds to the Hindu Yam Raj. The difference is that a bull accompanies the Hindu deity, whereas here Yamantak himself has the face of a bull. He carries a begging bowl in one hand and a ritual cleaver in the other.

THE LORDS OF THE FOUR QUARTERS: A warrior-god, normally of Hindu origin, rules each of the four directions or quarters. They are painted on the walls of the corridors outside the du-khang and are portrayed as Mongols. These four deities are thus:

North: *Kubér* or *Vaisravan*, yellow skinned.'He rides a lion and is the Hindu-Buddhist god of wealth. He carries a flag and a mongoose (*nakul*).

South: *Vim Dhak* or *Viru Dhak*, blue-skinned. Has an elephant's head. He wears a loincloth made of tiger's skin and carries a long sword (*khadga*).

East: *Dhrit Rashtr*, fair (white) skinned. Plays a stringed instrument. He also protects religion.

West: *Viru Paksh*, red-skinned. Holds a chorten in his right hand. In his left hand is a snake.

THE WHEEL OF THE WORLD (SANSAAR CHAKR): As in Hinduism, this is the wheel of time, of sorrow and joy, of anger, desire and ignorance. An animal represents each of these. 'Sansaar' is translated more precisely as 'phenomenal existence'.

KÂL CHAKR: This is the name of a deity with four faces and thirteen arms and hands. Each of the four faces has a different expression:

Kâl Chakr

wrath, passion, contemplation and peace. In Hindu- Buddhist iconography we often see fierce deities standing atop the body of an evil person they have just killed. The Kâl Chakr is seenwith his left foot on the body of Mahéshwar and his right foot on Kâm. He hold Vishwamata in his embrace.

FOUR GODDESSES are linked with the Five Buddhas (è). These are:

i) the blue **Lochan**, whose name means 'eyes.' She is, appropriately, associated with Akshobhay.;

ii) the yellow **Maamaki** ('the one who is affectionate in a maternal way') who is associated with Ratn Sambhav,

iii) the red **Pândur Vâsini**. Her name, interestingly, means 'the one who lives in pale yellow (clothes?)' and who is associated with Amitâbh;

iv) the **Green Târâ** who is associated with Amogh Siddhi. Her name means 'the pupil of the eye.' Some have translated her name to mean 'the saviouress.' Târini, indeed, means 'the benefactress' and is the diminutive of Târâ. (There is also a White Tara.)

The Green Tara is a protecting deity and is the goddess of life. There are flowers in both her hands. Her right hand is in The Benefactor (or Bestower) Posture.

SAINTS: The depiction in art of the four most important saints of Ladakhi Buddhism has been discussed in the chapter on 'Buddhism' in the section entitled 'Sects within Tibeto-Ladakhi Buddhism.'

Chapter- 25

A Calendar of Buddhist Festivals

Christmas is one of the few festivals in any religion to occur on a fixed date. To find out when most other festivals will take place people either consult an almanac—or a chart like this one.

Venue/ Name of festival	**2010**	**2011**	**2012**	**2013**	**2014**
Spituk/Gustor	Jan 13, 14	Jan 31, Feb 01	Jan 21,22	Jan 9,10	Jan 28,29
Deskit, Leh, Likir/ Dosmochey	Feb 11,12	Mar 2,3	Feb 19,20	Feb 8,9	Feb 27,28
Stok/Guru Tse-Chu	Feb 23,24	Mar 14,15	Feb 2,3	Feb 19,20	Mar 10,11
Matho/Nagrang	Feb 27,28	Mar 18,19	Feb 7,8	Feb 24,25	Mar 15,16
All Ladakh/ Buddha Purnima	May 27	Jun 15	May 4	May 25	Jun 13
Hemis/Tse-Chu	Jun 21,22	Jul 10,11	Jun 29,30	Jun 18,19	Jul 7,8
Lama Yûrû/ Yuru Kabgyat	Jun 10,11	Jun 28,29	Jun 16,17	Jun 5,6	Jun 24,25
Karsha/Gustor	Jul 8,9	Jul 27,28	Jul 16,17	Jul 6,7	Jul 24,25
Phyâng/Tsedup	Jul 9,10	Jul 28,29	Jul 16,17	Jul 6,7	Jul 24, 25
Korzok/Gustor (Lake Tsomo Riri)	Jul 14,15	Aug 2,3	Jul 22,23	Jul 11,12	Jul 30,31

DakThok/ Tse-Chu	Jul 20,21	Aug 8,9	Jul 28,29	Jul 18,19	Aug 6,7
Sanî/Naro Nasjal (Zangskar)	Jul 24,25	Aug 12,13	Aug 1,2	Jul 21,22	Aug 9,10
Shachukul/Gustor	Jun 28,29	Jul 17,18	Jul 5,6	Jun 25,26	Jul 14,15
Thiksey/Gustor	Oct 25,26	Nov 13,14	Nov 1,2	Nov 20,21	Nov 9,10
Chamday/Angchok	Nov 4,5	Nov 23,24	Nov 11,12	Nov 30, Dec 01	Nov 20,21
All Ladakh/ Galdan Namchot	Nov 30	Dec 20	Dec 8	Dec. 27	Dec 16
All Ladakh/Losar	Dec 06	Dec 25	Dec 14	Jan 02	Dec 22

The schedule of the immediately preceding decade has been listed for reference.

Annual festival at the Hemis monastery

Monastery/ Festival	2000	2001	2002	2003	2004
Stongde (in Zâñskâr)/ Gustor	Jan 4-5	Jan 22-23	Jan 11-12	Jan 30-31	Jan 19-20
Spituk/ Gustor	Jan 4-5	Jan 22-23	Jan 11-12	Jan 30-31	Jan 19-20
Deskit/ Dosmochey	Feb 3-4	Feb 21-22	Feb 10-11	Feb 28, Mar 1	Feb 18-19
Leh/ Dosmochey	Feb 3-4	Feb 21-22	Feb 10-11	Feb 28, Mar 1	Feb 18-19
Likir/ Dosmochey	Feb 3-4	Feb 21-22	Feb 10-11	Feb 28, Mar 1	Feb 18-19
Yarma-Gonbo/ Ltung-Shaks		not		available	
Stok/Guru TseChu	Mar 14-15	Mar 4-5	Feb 21-22	Mar 12-13	Feb29Mr1
Matho/Nagrang	Mar 20-21	Mar 9-10	Feb 26-27	Mar 17-18	Mar 5-6
Buddha Purnima	June 16	June 6	May 26	June 14	June 3
Hemis/ Tse Chu	July 11-12	Jun30-Jul 1	June 20-21	July 9-10	June 27-28
LamaYuru/Kabgyat	July 18-19	July 7-8	June 26-27	July 15-16	July 4-5
Karshâ/Gustor	July 28-29	July 17-18	July 7-8	July 26-27	July 14-15
Phyâng/Tsedup	Aug 1-2	July 22-23	July 12-13	Jul 31-Aug 1	July 19-20
Korzok/Gustor	Aug 2-3	July 23-24	July 13-14	Aug 1-2	July 20-21
Dakthok/Tse Chu	Aug 9-10	July 29-30	July 19-20	Aug 7-8	July 27-28
Sani/ Naro Nasjal	Aug 14-15	Aug 3-4	July 23-24	Aug 11-12	July 30-31
Shachukul/ Gustor	Aug 20-21	Aug 16-17	Aug 5-6	Aug 24-25	Aug 12-13
Thiksey/ Gustor	Nov 14-15	Nov 4-5	Oct 24-25	Nov 12-13	Oct31-Nov1
Chamday/ Angchok	Nov 23-24	Nov 13-14	Nov 2-3	Nov 21-22	Nov 10-11
Galdan Namchot	Dec 20	Dec 9	Dec 29	Dec 18	Dec 7
Losar	Dec 26	Dec 15	Jan 3, 2003	Dec 24	Dec 12

Monastery/ Festival	2005	2006	2007	2008	2009
Stongde (in Zâñskâr)/ Spituk Gustor	Jan 8-9	Jan 27-28	Jan 17-18	Jan 6-7	Jan 23-24
Deskit/ Dosmochey	Feb 6-7	Feb 26-27	Feb 15-16	Feb 4-5	Feb 22-23
Leh/ Dosmochey	Feb 6-7	Feb 26-27	Feb 15-16	Feb 4-5	Feb 22-23
Likir/ Dosmochey	Feb 6-7	Feb 26-27	Feb 15-16	Feb 4-5	Feb 22-23
Yarma-Gonbo/ Ltung-Shaks	Feb 12	Mar 3	Feb 21	Feb 10	Feb 28
Stok/Guru TseChu	Feb 17-18	Mar 8-9	Feb 25-26	Feb 15-16	Mar 5-6
Matho/Nagrang	Feb 22-23	Mar 14-15	Mar 3-4	Feb 20-21	Mar 10-11
Buddha Purnima	May 23	June 11	May 31	June 18	June 6
Hemis/ Tse Chu	Jun 17-18	July 6-7	Jun 25-26	Jul 12-13	July 1-2
LamaYuru/Kabgyat	Jun 23-24	July 12-13	July 2-3	July 20-21	July 8-9
Karshâ/Gustor	July 3-4	July 22-23	July 11-12	July 29-30	July 18-19
Phyâng/Tsedup	Aug 7-8	July 27-28	July 16-17	Aug 3-4	July 22-23
Korzok/Gustor	Aug 8-9	July 28-29	July 17-18	Aug 4-5	July 23-24
Dakthok/Tse Chu	Aug 15-16	Aug 4-5	July 24-25	Aug 11-12	Jul 30-31
Sani/ Naro Nasjal	Aug 18-19	Aug 8-9	July 29-30	Aug 15-16	Aug 3-4
Shachukul/ Gustor	Aug 31 Sep 1	Aug 20-21	Aug 10-11	Aug 27-28	Aug 16-17
Thiksey/ Gustor	Nov 18-19	Nov 8-9	Oct 28-29	Nov 15-16	Nov 4-5
Chamday/ Angchok	Nov 29-30	Nov 18-19	Nov 7-8	Nov 25-26	Nov 13-14
Galdan Namchot	Dec 26	Dec 15	Dec 4	Dec 21	Dec 10
Losar	Jan 1, 2006	Dec 21	Dec 10	Dec 28	Dec 16

The Religions

Buddhist monument

Thiksey Monastery, 14mt golden statue of Maitreya Buddha, Ladakh

Chapter- 26

Buddhist monuments and monasteries in Jammu province and the Valley of Kashmir

Jammu province

The Buddhist population of Jammu province is almost entirely based in Pâdar (Kishtwar; old Doda district). In 2001 there were all of 1,866 Buddhists in the province and in 2011 an estimated 2,500. Within Pâdar, the two main (but not only) Buddhist enclaves are Upper Pâdar, where the Buddhists have been living for several centuries now, and Gulabgarh, to which they migrated in the early 1900s.

Historically the area around Jammu has been a major seat of Buddhism—with its headquarters at Sakala (now called Sialkot, which is in Pakistan and is the major city closest to Jammu). Therefore, it was only natural that there would be a major ancient Buddhist site within Jammu district—at Ambaran.

Jammu district

Ambârâñ: (28km. from Jammu town.) This is the most important archæological site in Jammu province. It is near Akhnoor town, on the right bank of River Chenâb.

A large number of Buddhist terracottas were excavated from Ambaran/ Pamberwan throughout the 20th century. Many of them were sent to the

Lahore Museum and other museums across the world (including the Dogra Art Gallery, Mubarak Mandi complex, near the Old Secretariat, Jammu). The terracottas include Buddha- heads, the 'heads' of sundry men and women and the torsos of human sculptures. Also found were shreds of drapery, the possessions of monks and laymen, and elaborately decorated women.

These heads are all of high quality and come in different sizes. The most celebrated of the lot is the Great Buddha. Charles Fabri, working at the Lahore Museum, felt that they belonged to around AD 700. The fourth century AD is now considered a more accurate date. Other artefacts found here date to the 4th, 5th and 8th centuries.

The people shown wear fancy headdresses. Interestingly, they all have matted hair. However, Charak and Billawaria assert that the Akhnoor School of terracotta is 'unique [and] free from Græco-Buddhist influence... They reveal the Gandhara influence, and though some specimens are devoid of spontaneity and freedom of the early Gandhara...[they are] the earliest examples of such an art in this region.'

In April 2001 archæologists made an extremely exciting, and important, set of discoveries here. They found a silver casket, gold and silver leaves, pearls, coral, carnelian, amethyst and three copper coins, all dating to between the 1st and 4th centuries AD. This author is not aware of a similar treasure trove, especially one that old, having been excavated from any other part of the state.

And the treasure wasn't even the best part. The place where it was found was. This was the 6m. x 6m. base of a Sarirka Stupa. A copper reliquary was found half a metre above the base. The aforementioned treasures were inside the reliquary, and inside the silver casket were a gold casket, some bones and ash. Ambaran was, clearly, an important Buddhist site in ancient India.

The exteriors of the stupa were made of moulded and plain bricks. Its core was filled with pebbles and earth. Dr. Mani writes, 'The stupa was constructed in the style of Stupas at Kalawan and Jaulian at [Takshashila]. Some votive stupas around it were also constructed during Kushan and late- Kushan period.'

Other artefacts found at this site are basins, beads, copper coins, bowls, lamps, lids, pots with handles and spouts, small sculptures made of stone, sprinklers, terracotta human figures and vases. Things made of iron and copper have also been found. Huvishka, Kanishka and Soter Megas had issued the coins excavated at Ambaran.

The Kushan period: Going by the richness of the art of the period, an advanced civilisation flourished here in the Kushan period (1st to 3rd centuries AD). Considerable building activity took place: especially the grand stupa mentioned above. Around the same time (1st-3rd centuries AD) a large building, prhaps a monastery, was constructed nearby. Floods damaged it. In the 4th- 5th centuries AD the building was rebuilt, only to be renovated and expanded several times thereafter.

The artists of Ambaran- Pamberwâñ were obviously in touch with- and influenced by- their better known Gândhâr counterparts. They mainly stuck to the Takshashila style. Red ware dating to the Kushan period has been found at Ambaran.

Kishtwar

As with the Buddhists of neighbouring Ladakh, with the collapse of polyandry and compulsory monkhood for one boy from every family, the Buddhist population of Padar is growing far more rapidly that the national (or world) average. By way of comparison, there had been only 1,113 Buddhists in 1981 in all of Jammu.

Ethnically the Buddhists of Padar are Mongoloid and akin to their cousins in Ladakh, especially Zanskar, with whom they intermarry and which borders Padar. The Buddhists of Padar (sometimes, wrongly, spelt Padder) normally have two names, a 'Hindu' name for school and other government records and a 'Buddhist' name at home. Thus my friend Ram Lal was also known as Nowang Tshering. This practice is followed in much of Buddhist HP as well, perhaps because of the huge Hindu population around them in both Padar and HP.

The Buddhists of Gulabgarh: In the year 2001 there were around a thousand people in Gulabgarh. Nasir Faridi estimates that the Hindus and Buddhists numbered around five hundred each. The obvious theory is that the Buddhists must have migrated here from Ladâkh. They belong to the same Mongoloid racial stock, have the same culture, wear the same clothes and speak, well, the same language. (Each part of Ladâkh speaks a different dialect of the Ladakhi language. A study of the variant spoken in Padar will indicate which part of Ladâkh—or HP—they migrated here from. Based on the matrimonial links of Gulabgarh's Buddhist elite I would suspect that they came from Zâñskâr.)

Monastery There is a fairly big Buddhist monastery in Gulabgarh village. The Sarai Gonpa is a branch of the Haloti Gonpa, which lies upstream, and has two monks. The monastery runs a private primary school by the local Buddhist monastery for 150 students.[1]

The Sanga Choling Gonpa in Haloti, in turn, was founded around A.D. 1910 or 1920 by Guru Choing Dorje Rinpoche who came here all the way from eastern Tibet, which is one or two months' trek away. The great scholar saint Naropa (c. A.D. 1015-1100) is said to have visited Padar.

The valley of Kashmir

Bârâmullâ-Bandipora

The Buddhist golden age of Bârâmullâ*:* Among the famous people received at the region's border outpost Drang was Hiuen Tsang. King Darlabdurana went there to personally welcome the Chinese scholar in AD 631. The watch-station continued to perform its functions at least till 1823, when Moorcroft, the British scholar, visited it.

In ancient times, there used to be a major Buddhist centre called Hashikoporâ, also known as Hushkipur. It was across the river from Bârâmullâ town, where **Ushkara** village now is. It was founded by the Indo- Scythian king Hashkha , also called Hushki and Huvishka. (He died AD 140.) Hashkha also constructed a Buddhist vihar (monastery) there.

With the addition of another two vihars, one each by Queen Dahhana and her brother Prince Jalauka, the place became a major centre of Buddhism. In fact, the baroque terracotta of Hashikoporâ has a prominent place in Indian art. (Some credit King Hashkha with the founding of Bârâmullâ itself and claim that Hashikoporâ is the oldest—and seminal—part of the town.) King Lalitaditya got a Buddhist stupa constructed at Ushkara much later. Only some ruins remain of that.

Then the renowned King Kanishka built the city of Kanishkaporâ close to Bârâmullâ town, where the present day village of **Kanis(h)porâ** is. This further increased the limits and size of Bârâmullâ town. It was in this village that the 4th Buddhist conference was held, under the chairmanship of Nâgarjun.

Historian Kalhan says that three Kushân kings founded as many cities in Kashmîr: in the expanse between Bârâmullâ and Srinagar. The kings were (H)ushka, Jushka and Kansihka. There is evidence that these cities

[1] My own datesfor the Kushan era, based on well-reasoned sources, are from the beginning of the Chistian era to AD 178.

had a regular trade with central Asia. The trade route ran through Drass and Khaltse in Ladâkh.

Excavations at Kanisporâ have yielded several artefacts from Kanishka's period.

Guréz: The Guréz valley was on the segment of the ancient Silk Route that went from the plains of Kashmîr to Gilgit and then Kâshgar. Hundreds of stone inscriptions in Kharoshthi, Brahmi, Hebrew and Tibetan have been found in the valleys north of Guréz, along the Silk Route, especially in Chilas (Pakistan occupied Kashmir).

These inscriptions contain priceless information about the history of Buddhism in ancient Kashmîr. They add to our knowledge about the various Buddhist Councils that were held between the 1st and 2nd centuries AD and how in the 6th century missionaries took Buddhism from Kashmir to Tibet. The last Buddhist Council was probably held at Kanzilwan.

Parihâsporâ: (21km. from Srinagar, 3km. off the Srinagar-Bârâmullâ road.) There are two major groups of ruins. Each set is on top a low hillock and each hillock can be seen from the other. The view from both is panoramic. (Stalin did something similar in Moscow: he built his grandest monuments atop hillocks.)

These hillocks, three in all in this area, are what in Kashmir would be called karéwâs.[2]

The main ruins consist of the grand foundations and bases of three stone temples and lots of rubble. A couple of steps, as wide as the foundations and of dimensions similar to Mayan ruins, rise up towards to what must have been the sanctum. The grand steps and the base are still intact. The walls and superstructure are not.

Minor ruins atop a third mound are the base of a stone temple. Just the foundation is visible, and that barely. I discovered a stone Shiv ling amidst the rubble. Obviously, this was a Shiv temple. Proves my thesis that the Buddhists worshipped Hindu deities as well.

The grand, main stone structure is on the large kâné shehr [city of stones] mound or karéwâ. The other mounds are called the Govardhan and Buddh

---

2 'The word karéwâ in Kashmiri dialect means, "elevated table-land." This term was first used by Godwin-Austin (1859) and later by Lydekker (1878) for an unconsolidated to semi–consolidated sand-clay-conglomerate sequence,' writes India's Directorate General for Hydrocarbons. In plain English this means that lake sediments were deposited on ancient rocks. 'These sediments [became] terraces, [plateaux] and mounds,' the Directorate adds.

karewas. There are ruins at Dewar Yekhmanpur and Teirgam as well. Apart from temples, some of these buildings were palaces and forts. History records that King Lalitâditya had got major buildings called Govardhan, Mukta Keshav, Parhas Keshav, Mahavrah and Raj Vihar built here.

King Lalitâditya-Mukt'pida (AD 725- 753 or 724-761) shifted the capital of Kashmir to Parihaspora. Ruins of a Buddhist stupa built by his Turkish minister Chinkan or Chuknan can still be seen here. However, nothing remains of the fort made of iron bricks that Lalitâditya is said to have fashioned. The iron must have been vandalised.

According to a Kashmir government source,[II] 'The devastation of this monumental city has been due to several wars between kings. The last destruction of the city has been ascribed to Sultan Sikander [1389- 1413] though till the era of Sangram Raj (1003-28 AD)...the palaces and temples [were still largely intact]. Some historians say that during the Kushan era (79-15 BC)[4] a royal Bodh Vihar was constructed here and 3rd [Buddhist] Conference of Kashmir is believed to have been held here (79 BC) as evident from the inscriptions of certain stones discovered.'

During Parihâsporâ's heyday the area was served by a network of waterways. As a result Kashmir could do without major roads till as late as the1700s. The rivers Jhelum and Sindh met at Naîd Khâi, and later joined Nigli Nallah to flow into the massive Lake Wular.

Till the 1800s the area was called the parganâ [district] of Paraspur.[III]

Srinagar city

Hârwan excavations/ Buddhist Ruins: Sir Aurel Stein was of the opinion that the present village of Harwan is the Shadar-hadvana (the grove of the six saints) referred to by the mediæval Kashmîri historian Kalhan in his *Rajatarangini*.

It was in the first years of the 20th century that some moulded brick tiles were unearthed at Harwan, when the Dogrâ government started constructing the conduit of the Harwan water-supply scheme. However, it was only in the 1930s that the state's Archaeological Department began to excavate the place. A flat, square patch covered with grass, which stood amidst a rich cornfield, intrigued them. Nothing grew on it except a stunted tree.

Excavations revealed a small township. Its buildings had been constructed in two distinct styles: a relatively primitive one, which archaeologists date to AD 300 and call the "pebble" style, and a more advanced one, which they call the "diaper pebble" style and date to the sixth century and later.

The discovery of a copper coin of the White Hun ruler Toramana (c. fifth century AD) under the foundations of the stupa helped date it to at least the sixth century, if not the fifth.

There are two major buildings in the diaper-rubble style: a "medium sized" stupa, of which the three-terraced base survives, and a set of rooms, which scholars like Kak assume must have served as chapels (or even dormitories). Some of the structures have been built in steps.

Regarding the artworks at Harwan, archæologist Dr. B.R. Mani says, 'The [Takshashila] model remained the prototype which was followed by the artists of [Ushkara, Bârâmullâ] and Harwan.' Some tiles bear images of people who could be from Yarqand or Kashgar, going by their general appearance. A few of them have been shown in Turkish caps and leggings. (Stitched garments came to India only after A.D. 900.) These artefacts are on display at the Ramnagar Palace Museum (Udhampur).

Explaining why the Harwan excavations are such an exciting and important discovery, R.C. Kak wrote, "Among the antiquities that this area yielded, were a large number of broken fingers and toes… belonging to images of the Buddha, …and a few clay votive tablets bearing in relief miniature stupas. These last are extremely interesting, inasmuch as they give an idea of the kind of stupas that were built in Kashmîr in the early centuries of the Christian era."

Harwan remains a major source of water supply to Srinagar. That was obviously a major reason for the ancients to have chosen it for their city. There are two springs nearby with drinking water of good quality.

Shâh é Hamadân, the Khânqâh of : *The compound:* There is a small graveyard in the shrine's compound. It houses two Buddhist stone sculptures, each about three feet high and rooted to the ground. According to Maulvi Abdul Aziz of the Research Library, Srinagar, 'Look eastward, i.e. to the left. One of these sculptures is a stone pagoda of the Buddhists. This was the Chinkan Vihar. Chinkan was a vizier of Lalitaditya. He built one vihar each here and in Parihâsporâ. Khânqâh e Mu'alla was built on the site of the serai of King Qutubuddin. There are no old stones left in the Khânqâh e Mu'alla. The Pandits used all those stones to construct the bund (embankmant).'

References

I The Padder Valley Trek: An Introduction, http://www.travelpod.com/travel-blog-entries/lraleigh/youarehere./1185775020/tpod.html#ixzz1IqjSjGyZ

II Department of Tourism, Government of Jammu & Kashmir, http://www.jktourism.org/inside.aspx?id=76

III http://www.jktourism.org/inside.aspx?id=76

Holy Family Catholic Church, Srinagar

St. Mary's Church, Gulmarg

Chapter- 27

Christian houses of worship and missions in Jammu, Kashmir and Ladakh

Jammu province

Doda, Kishtwar, Ramban

Doda and Kishtwar districts: none.

Batote: Gospel for Asia; Gospel for Kashmir

Ramban: Kashmir Evangelical Fellowship

Jammu, Samba

Jammu's oldest **church** is the 19th century Protestant Church on Wazarat Road. There is a Catholic Church near Jewel Chowk, and St. Mary's Church on the national highway near Gandhi Nagar. The Pentecostals have their own church. St. Paul's is among the better known.

Akhnoor: Independent church; Friends Missionary Prayer Band

Badyal: North India Pentecostal Fellowship

Bari Brahmana: Indian Evangelical Team

Bishnah Arnia: Masihi Rajdoot Sabha

Chakrohi: North India Pentecostal Fellowship

Gandhinagar: Independent; Indian Evangelical Team; Gospel for Asia

Gangyal: Bethel Gospel Mission, Masihi Rajdoot Sabha; Assemblies of God; Gospel for Asia

Janipura: Masihi Rajdoot Sabha

Jammu Cantt: Indian Evangelical Team

Jammu Tawi: Evangelical Church of India, Church of North India, Indian Evangelical Team, Independent, Evangelical Mission, Indian Pentecostal Church

Jammu Tawi: St. Paul's Church, Wazarat Road

Jammu Tawi: St. Peter's Church, Christian Colony

Kandoli Nagrota: Indian Evangelical Team

Miran Sahib: North India Pentecostal Fellowship

Muthi: Indian Evangelical Team

Qilla Bahu: Gospel for Asia

Ranbir Singh Pora: North India Pentecostal Fellowship

Reharhi: Independent

Samba: Indian Pentecostal Church of God

Simbal Camp: North India Pentecostal Fellowship

Kathua

Bhaddu: Kashmir Evangelical Fellowship

Billawar: Masihi Rajdoot Sabha

Janglot: Masihi Rajdoot Sabha

Kathua: Independent, Indian Evangelical Team

Poonch

Mandi: Church of North India

Poonch: Indian Pentecostal Church of God (for the Gujjar community)

Rajouri

Nowshera: Independent; Gospel for Asia

Rajouri: Indian Pentecostal Church of God (for the Gujjar community)

Udhampur, Reasi

Arnas: Indian Evangelical Team

Chenaini: Kashmir Evangelical Fellowship

Garhi: Kashmir Evangelical Fellowship; Independent; Indian Pentecostal Church

Jaganoo: Kashmir Evangelical Fellowship

Katra: Independent; Indian Evangelical Team

Krimchi: Kashmir Evangelical Fellowship

Kud: Independent

PTS (Police Training School): Kashmir Evangelical Fellowship

Ram Nagar: Moravian Church

Reasi: Indian Pentecostal Church of God

Training Centre: Kashmir Evangelical Fellowship

Udhampur Kashmir Missions Inst

Udhampur: Independent

Udhampur: Kashmir Evangelical Fellowship; Masihi Rajdoot Sabha

The valley of Kashmir

Anantnag

Anantnag: Church of North India

Anantnag: Cooperative Outreach of India

Bandipora

None

Baramulla

Bârâmullâ: St. Joseph's Church, India Gospel Outreach

Gulmarg: Church of North India, St. Mary's

Ganderbal

None

Kulgam

None

Kupwara

None

Pulwama

Pulwama: Full Faith Mission

Shopian

None

Srinagar city

All Saints' Church: This a small but pretty Protestant/ Anglican church near Srinagar Club. It was built in 1896 under the supervision of M. Nethersole, a retired Chief Engineer. Till 1947 the British Resident in Kashmîr would be the President of the church. The Srinagar Club and Nedou's Hotel had a close relationship with the church and would post service timings on their notice boards. In 1979 Pâkistân executed its former Prime Minister, Mr.Zulfiqar Ali Bhutto. The hangman was a Christian. This provoked mobs in Srinagar, who set the All Saints' Church on fire. It has been reconstructed since.

Holy Family Catholic Church: A Catholic Mission was established in Srinagar 1891. The Revs. Cunningham and Donsen, both of St. Joseph's FM Society, Mill Hill, London, were its founders. Franklin Wrinkley built the present church a few years later, perhaps in 1900, on what was then known as the Hotel Road. The road has since been renamed Maulana Azad (or MA) Road. The church was expanded in 1928 and 1932. Arora notes that 'valuable donations' by local Christians as well as visitors 'helped to build a Presbytery in 1931.'

Munshi Bâgh: Protestant Church, Maulana Azad Road: Roman Catholic Church

Assemblies of God: Batwara

Various locations: All Saints Parish; Full Faith Mission; Intern Social Services; Pentecostal; Independent; Church of North India

Ladakh region

Kargil

Mulbekh: Cooperative Outreach of India

Padam: Cooperative Outreach of India

Sankoo: Cooperative Outreach of India

Leh

Khaltse: Moravian Church

Leh: Moravian Mission Karzu; Moravian Church

Shey: Moravian Church

Chapter- 28

The Dards of Dâ-Hânu: Religion and Customs

The Dards have settled in two broad areas under the Indian flag, Drâss in Kargil (where they are entirely Muslim) and Dâ- Hânu on the Leh-Kargil border. The people of Dâ- Hânu are mostly Buddhist by religion. They retain a way of life and culture that is totally different from that of the Buddhists of Leh or even the Muslim Dards of Drâss. Their language is similar to that of the Muslim Dards of Drâss and Gilgit (Pakistan-occupied Kashmir), though. Their Buddhism, on the other hand, is nothing like that of the Buddhists of the rest of Ladakh. In fact many local people say that they are neither Buddhist nor Muslim.

In any case, they converted to Buddhism only around the 1820s or '30s, because of the efforts of Lâmâ Samphel of nearby Lâmâ Yûrû. Before that the Drokpâs belonged to a religion called Bon-chos and worshipped animals, nature and ancestors. They still retain many Bon-chos rituals, including the great harvest festival , Bono-na or Chopo Srupla. Their shamanism, their songs and their cosmic system, too, are Bon-chos. ('Chos' means 'religion.' 'Bon' means 'animism' and includes the worship of fire and nature.)

Islam and the Drokpâs: The Brokpas of Chuli Chan and Da Da Do have converted to Islam. However, they live outside the areas covered in this chapter (i.e. the Leh-Kargil border). They do not practice the customs described here. However, they speak the same language and often come over to watch the festivals of their Buddhist and animist cousins. The Dards of Drâss can not be called Drokpâ or Brokpa. However, even they sometimes participate as spectators.

Eggs and dairy products are taboo: The Drokpâs abhor the cow as well as all dairy and other products obtained from it. This, as J&K

Tourism's web site notes, is 'most baffling for a people believed to be of Aryan descent.' On the other hand, they consider the ibex sacred and sing songs about ibex hunts. They worship the goat and consider it a symbol of fertility and prosperity.

The web site adds that the goat is the Drokpâs' cult animal and is the 'preferred animal for offering as sacrifice [at the altar of Shringman Lhâmo, the Goddess of Wealth on important occasions such as] Bono-na, held alternately in Garkun and [Da] villages, with a one- year break in between.' The sacrifice is conducted by the Lhâbdag-pa, 'who is the traditional officiant for this deity'. Indeed, the number of goats and sheep a family has is a measure of its wealth. Many families have hundreds of each.

Regarding the cow, the web site explans is that it is only the Indian and Iranian Aryans who worship the cow. German Aryans, for instance, don't. E. Joldan has a better theory. Cattle are clumsy animals. The narrow and precipitous terrain of Dâ- Hânu is much too dangerous for them, for they routinely slip off and die. Besides, feeding them in winter is expensive and difficult. Goats, on the other hand, are sure-footed.

Eggs and fowls, too, are taboo. But men, being men, are bound to ignore taboos when away from the watchful eyes of the womenfolk and elders. When in Kargil or Skardu they would eat eggs as well as dairy products. However, even they would maintain the sanctity of their land. There is an auspicious Kagaaney Maaney three kilometres west of Da. The men would eat up all the egg and dairy products they had bought in Kargil at this point, so that the area beyond was undefiled by eggs, milk or butter.

The Zo (or dZo) is what is born when a cow mates with a yâk. It is the only cattle the Drokpâs put up with, though quite unwillingly. They need this tough animal to plough their fields. As soon as ploughing is over, they drive the dZos away, to the mountains above. They don't even use dZo dung as manure in their fields. (The dZo is male. The female is called Zomo or dZomo. The dZo is sterile, but the dZomo is not. In this respect they differ from that other crossbreed, the mule, both genders of which are sterile.)

Things are changing, at least in Hanu, where some families took to rearing cows in the 1980s.

Astronomy: The Drokpâs have a rudimentary knowledge of astronomy. But they are fairly accurate at whatever little use they make of it. From the movements of the sun they can predict when the solstices and equinoxes will take place, dates that the rest of us take as a given.

Disputes: Like many other tribals (especially the Gujjars), the Drokpâs try to settle their disputes themselves, rather than in courts of law. (For that matter the same is true of most of Zâñskâr and much of rural Leh.) If neither party in a dispute can prove its case conclusively, both parties are taken to the monastery (gompa). There both are asked to swear that they are telling the truth. Such is the fear of God that the liar rarely agrees to swear. He looks for excuses to wriggle out. The party that swears wins.

The two are then kept away from each other on festive occasions, so that they don't start fighting again. A year later, by when the dispute would have been forgotten, the two are made to sit together and patch up.

Are the Drokpâs insular? In theory, yes. For centuries they tried to keep away from the other people of Leh and Kargil. And yet there is so much of Leh in their lives. In turn they have influenced the culture of Leh. Most importantly, they became Buddhists, even if their practices are quite distinctive. Like other Buddhists they call their gods and goddesses Lhâ and Lhâmo, even if their main Lhâmo is entirely their own, as are several other deities. Their new year, too, is called Losar, even if it's on a different day. They have a gompa, even if tiny with just two or three lâmâs. They, too, have maaneys.

On the other hand, other LadakhiBuddhists have adopted Drokpâ customs like throwing lit torches on a designated spot during Losar celebrations. Joldan argues that perhaps 'the Ladakhi custom[s] of making wild sheep from dough and decorating their kitchen walls with crescent and other designs, at Losar, have their origins in Brokpâ traditions. Tibetans don't do such things.' He adds that the bass drum (Dang Dang) of the Drokpâs was once part of Ladakh's royal orchestras. The Namgyâl Tsemo in Leh has a wall painting in which musicians play on such a drum for the king. Joldan also points out that 'the fashion among [other] Ladakhi ladies of wearing goat skin having long white hair, to cover their back comes from Brok-land [Dâ- Hânu].'

The people of Dâ- Hânu must surely have had some contacts with the Kashmiris, too. Several Drokpâ families possess elegant brass pitchers and other handicrafts of Kashmiri origin.

Funerals: The Drokpâs cremate their dead on pyres, on the banks of a river. This is very Hindu, and quite different from the anaerobic cremation of other LadakhiBuddhists.

The Great Harvest Festival- Chopo Srupla

Shringman Lhâmo is the Drokpâs' Goddess of Wealth and Fertility. (Lhâ is exactly the same as the Hindu 'devata' or deity. Lhâmo in turn is the precise translation of 'Devi' or goddess.) The Lhâbdag-pâ or Lapdraks is variously defined as 'the caretaker of the gods' and 'the traditional officiant for [the Lhâmo alone]'. Da and Garkun have one Lapdrak each.

The Drokpâs' Great Harvest Festival is called Chopo Srupla as well as Bono-na. It is held at Da and Garkun in alternate years. There is no festival in the third year. In the fourth year, the three- year cycle begins all over again. The festival lasts four to five days. It is normally held in October, in the first or second week. Apart from the religious rites performed at this festival, what strikes most outsiders (including people from the rest of Ladakh) is the ritual public kissing that takes place.

The dancing ground at Da is much bigger than the one at Garkun. Two large walnut trees, and some willows, grow over it. In both villages this is a largeish, circular patch of land in the open, and has been designated specially for this purpose. (The details given below are mainly about the festival when held at Da. The one at Garkun is almost identical.)

Warming up for the festival: At most Buddhist, and some Hindu, festivals stories taken from religious lore are acted out in the form of a play or an opera. The actors as well as the audience take these plays most seriously. At Basohli (Kathua district, Jammu province), for instance, actors who are supposed to play the Gods lead a life of abstinence and purity for several weeks before the actual show.

A little boy is chosen to play the Lhâ. He is between eight and ten years old. There is a rock near Da. It has a designated section on which the boy lives for many days before the festival.

The evening before the festival 'warming up' exercises begin. The sweet smelling pencil cedar wood is burnt, a bass drum is played near the Da fort and a young goat is sacrificed, all to please the gods. Men gather in a room near the gompa and silently drink *chhang* as they listen to the music. (The chhang is sometimes served in elegant Kashmiri pitchers made of brass in the Central Asian style.)

The procession: In the early afternoon of the first day, some meat from the sacrificed goats is given to all the families assembled near the designated rock. The top people of the village, including the Lapdrak, then dance up to the rock, where the boy who plays the Lhâ (god) awaits them in 'divine clothes'. They bring him down, after which he leads a slow procession. They first go to a field, where they dance. The procession ends at the village square. After that the Lapdrak takes over.

On that and subsequent evenings, the Lapdrak sings the famous epic songs mentioned above. The men, and later the women, start dancing.

The dancing: Ladakhidances must surely be the slowest in the world. My theory is that they take half an hour to do a pirouette, though on occasion it's known to have been done in as few as twenty- nine minutes. No, seriously, they take forever. Their own explanation is that because oxygen is in short supply at those incredibly high altitudes they have to move very slowly. I suppose they are right. But the fact also is that before the advent of electricity they used to have so much time on their hands in winter that they had to look for things to do. (For that reason, Ladakhi mothers work all summer and don't tell their children fairy-, folk- or religious stories till after the first snowfall.)

And yet other Ladakhis consider the Drokpâs' dances much too slow even by their standards. Dâ- Hânu is almost two thousand feet lower than the areas around Leh town, with far more oxygen all around. Therefore, they should have been dancing faster if the altitude/ oxygen theory was the only explanation. The other difference is that in the rest of Leh the sexes intermingle while dancing: every other dancer would, for instance, be a woman. (Most Ladakhis, including the Drokpâs, enter the dance floor in a single file. After that they generally form a wide circle. The circle goes around the dance- ground several times.) The Drokpâs, too, enter in a single file. However, the men come first and then the women. Thirdly, most Ladakhidances have three sections. The Drokpâs' dances have only two. Finally, unlike other Ladakhis, Drokpâ dancers cut an anti- clockwise circle when they go around the ground.

Mentog Stanmo- the flower dance: This joyous dance is popular in Darchiks (Dartsiks) and Garkun (both villages are in the Dâ- Hânu region). However, it is also the main dance of other places in Kargil and Leh, which as far apart as Mulbek, Wâkhâ, Puring and the Nubra valley.

Men and women hold bunches of flowers as they dance. Flowers cheer up people everywhere. They do the same here, to the audience as well as dancers.

The musicians: In most of Buddhist Ladakh (i.e. Leh and Zâñskâr) musicians form two specific castes, the Mons and the Bedas, which are considered socially inferior. In Dâ- Hânu any talented person can perform professionally in public on festive occasions, something that doesn't happen in most of rural, feudal South Asia. (Classical music is the preserve of the Brahmins and Khans of India, and traditionally they did not perform before the masses. Folk- artistes are given a low status among the Hindus as well as Muslims.)

E. Joldan says that the respect that is accorded to musicians is unique to the Buddhist Dards: even the Dards of Gilgit (PAKISTAN-OCCUPIED

KASHMIR) have a separate, and inferior, caste of musicians, the Doms. My theory is that there's so few of them that the Buddhist Dards can't afford the luxury of having a separate caste of musicians.

But then having specialised castes of musicians has its advantages. The Mons and Bedas know as many as 350 different tunes. The music of Dâ- Hânu is quite basic in comparison.

Ritual public kissing: After it gets dark, the dancing picks up. The men are quite high by now. They start kissing their lady friends/ wives. Joldan calls this 'mass kissing.' However, it is no orgy. The men normally kiss only their own beaux. Maybe I am making it sound a bit antiseptic. Oh, no. They all get their kicks, as in the rest of the world. They then go home for dinner, after which they come back for another round of dancing. (And yet they complain that the Lhâs were overly fond of dancing.)

Other festivals

The Drokpâs have the same word for the New Year as other Buddhists-Losar. However, the date is not the same. The Drokpâs celebrate it shortly after the winter solstice. From Gilgit they brought the custom of lighting many wooden torches and throwing them all together at a designated place in the village. The custom was later adopted in Zâñskâr and the rest of Leh. ('Lo' means 'year'.)

The Drokpâs' calendar, like that of the Chinese, Tibetans and other Ladakhis, follows a twelve- year cycle. Each year is named after an animal. Lo-dron is the festival of completing a twelve- year cycle. Instead of celebrating birthdays every year, people do so after every twelve years. A feast is laid out on the occasion of Lo-dron. (The Lo-dron is often celebrated on the occasion of the Great Harvest Festival, and not on the precise date of birth.)

When girls complete their first cycle (i.e. turn thirteen), they normally attain puberty. During Losar all girls who celebrate their first Lo-dron that year have to perform a group dance.

Like the baker's dozen, the Drokpâs are deliberately inexact about the completion of the sixth Lo-dron cycle, except that they err on the other side. People are deemed to have completed six Lo-drons a year in advance, i.e. when they complete 71 years. This, too, calls for a major celebration.

Chapter- 29

The Hindu Shrines of Jammu, Kashmir and Ladakh

Jammu Province

Doda, Kishtwar, Ramban

Festivals and fairs

Like the neighbouring Banni valley, but on a slightly grander scale, the people of Bhaderwah love their fairs, at which co-ed pairings (officially called *mitri* or 'friendship') are made and formally accepted by society. These fairs consist of folksongs, dances, kitsch trinkets and, maybe, a religious ceremony.

The snow- covered winters are somewhat subdued. However, spring brings with it these colourful fairs. The first is a three- day April fair at the famous *Subarnag* temple dedicated to Lord Shiva. From there the merrymaking shifts to the Reushira peak nearby, where festivity lasts a week.

The Baisakhi [13th April] Kud (pron. 'could') lasts almost a month. During the rest of the year there are other festivals, also called 'kud' (e.g. the Pateru Kud). Kud is also the name of an energetic local dance.

The most famous fair of Bhaderwah tehsil is variously called the Mela Patt and the Pateru Kud. The other well known fairs of the area are held at Subardhar and Vasak (Bâsak) Dehra, Khangal, Gatha and Nolthi, Nandna, Malothi, Gugsu, Trown, Chagsu, Jora, Renkha, Gwalo, Bheja, Cheka, Manthla and Alabani.

Mela Patt is a three - day fair. It is held in the centre of Bhaderwah town, in ***and*** around the Vasuki Nag temple. The palace of the kings of

Bhaderwah once existed in this neighbourhood. The fair takes place in late August or early September on the Nag Panchami day, fifteen days after the Kailash Yâtrâ. Not just the town, the entire Bhaderwah tehsil comes alive during this colourful fair. Girls dress in their Sunday best. Love is in the air and there is co-ed pairing. Hindus as well as Muslims of all classes take part. Festivity starts in the afternoon and ends with sunset.

Akbar, the Mughal Emperor (AD 1556-1605), is said to have bestowed silken robes of honour on King Nag Pal of Bhaderwah. During this fair a *chela* brings the *patt* out in procession. It is a wooden cone, covered with colourful pieces of silk. It symbolises the robes that Akbar had given to Nag Pal.

Chela literally means disciple. In the hills of Jammu a *chela* is a devotee, and thus a 'disciple', of a deity, normally the Mother Goddess. During the days before the fair he lives in the house of the Raj Gurus (tutors and spiritual advisers to the kings). There he subjects himself to extreme austerities and hardship. He also meditates intensely till, at least by the night before the fair, he is possessed by the deity which, in this case, is Bâsak Nâg.

An ensemble of flutes, horns and drums begins to play. People start dancing. Some of them bring the chela from the house that he is in. The musicians form the vanguard of the procession. They go to the open ground where the dance is to be held. The chela dances there for a while, the patt still above him. The frenzied crowdshouts religious slogans like 'Nagraj Bâsak ki jai!' (Glory to Bâsak, the king of the snake gods!) The people, all wearing colourful clothes, sing hymns in praise of the deity and throw flowers on the icon.

The whole thing must be quite exhausting for the chela, because he takes a break from time to time. Since he is in a trance he indicates that he is tired by casting the patt aside. Others hold the patt while the chela rests.

When the dance is over, the patt is taken back to the house that it had been stored in. Once again this is done in procession.

Kings, its own as well as those of Chamba and Jammu, ruled Bhaderwah till 1947. They would pay for the organisation of the fair. In these democratic times the organisers collect donations from the local people, especially from the rich.

Pilgrimages

The **Kailash Yâtrâ**, normally held in August, is the best known pilgrimage of Bhaderwah. It consists of a trek to the holy Kailash peak. Also around the same time of the year are pilgrimages to the Gupt Ganga and Bâsak (Vasak) Nag. The Pândavs (who else?) built the temple at the Gupt Ganga. (*The Mahabharat* says that during their *agyat vas* the Pândavs passed through the land of snakes. This was the period when the five brothers were supposed to hide themselves so that no one would know where they were-. The people of Bhaderwah believe that their land was the place indicated by the epic. In fact a giant footprint on a rock near the temple is supposed to be that of Bhim Sen, the second of the Pândavs.)

The idol of Bâsak Nag at the temple of the same name probably dates to the 11th century and is made of a single stone. The temple is also called the Mandalekh Shrine.

Machail is famous for its sapphire mines, which are not open to the public. Its biggest tourist attraction is the shrine of Chandi Mâtâ. This is also the place where the equally famous Machail Yâtrâ pilgrim- trek comes to an end. (The pilgrimage starts in Bhaderwah.) It takes two days to trek from Atholi (Padar) to Machail, through Gulabgarh. You have to spend the night at Chashoti.

If you trek from here to Zanskar, you should plan on spending the night at Rujwass.

The Machail Yâtrâ: This celebrated, 7- day pilgrimage (*yâtrâ*) takes place in the second week on August. In 2001, for instance, it commenced on the 12th August.

DAY ONE: Thousands of pilgrims gather at Chinote (Bhaderwah) on, or on the night before, the first day of the yatra. They follow the holy mace, which is carried by the designated cleric. The mace is decorated with colourful festoons. Every year devotees try to make the mace look more attractive and colourful than in previous years.

When the procession begins its journey (and several times en route), devotees cry out, 'Jai Chandi Gosh!' ('Glory to goddess Chandi!') The holy mace and the procession pass through several villages and towns, where the mace is worshipped. On the first day these halting points include Bhala, Pranu, Pul Dodâ, Premnagar, Thâthri and Kandni. At each stop the local people greet the pilgrims and offer them sweetened water, halwa (a sweet), channa (cooked grams) and puri (a bread). And at each stop some local people join the procession.

The biggest free kitchens and congregational prayers are organised at Pul Dodâ, Thâthri and Kandni. The people pray for peace for and the prosperity of all humanity. These prayers are chanted in as many languages as the regions from where the pilgrims have come: Hindi, Urdu, Punjabi, Dogri, Bhaderwahi and Pâdri.

Before it became possible to travel by bus, pilgrims would follow the mace on foot. However, by the end of the 20th century the pilgrims were all travelling by bus, jeep and car. At every stop a couple of buses get added to the caravan.

The pilgrims camp in Kishtwar town for their first night halt. In 2001 there were fifty buses in the caravan by the time it reached Kishtwar. The people of Kishtwar gather in large numbers to receive the holy mace and the pilgrims.

The camp is normally set up in the Government Girls' Higher Secondary School. Kitchens are set up in the premises to feed the pilgrims, who sleep in and around the school.

In the evening thousands of people, pilgrims as well as local folk, gather in the school's compound to join a religious congregation. Invited speakers deliver lectures on various aspects of the Hindu religion. Their interpretation of Hinduism is normally liberal. The speakers normally emphasise a brotherhood of man that cuts across religious lines.

DAY TWO: The pilgrims have to wake up very early. They go over to the Shiv Temple, Vassar, Kishtwar, to offer early- morning prayers. After an early breakfast they leave for Atholi (Pâdar), where they camp on the second night.

DAY THREE: The third day's journey begins at Massu (Padar). In 2001 the number of pilgrims had swelled to 12,000 by the third morning.

The trek is extremely picturesque. A substantial part of the track runs along the banks of the Bot Nallah stream. The pilgrim is now in the valley where sapphires are mined.

Chishoti is the village where the mace halts on the third night. It is housed in the Kalka ji temple, where it is worshipped at night. There are forests all around the village. Chishoti is known for the hospitality of its people and the extreme cold of its winters. The people of Chishoti invite the pilgrims, total strangers all of them, into their houses for the night. They fetch water from the spring for their guests amd also serve them tea.

Around dusk the pilgrims and their hosts start singing religious songs. Most of these songs are devoted to Machail Mata, the goddess of the pilgrimage. This goes on till late in the night.

DAY FOUR: Once again the pilgrims leave the camp very early in the day. They reach Machail, or, more precisely, the Chandi Dhâm Machail (Padar) by around two in the afternoon. Most of the journey is on foot, because buses can't ply on the rough hilly track. Many devotees, including women, walk barefoot. This is a sign of humility before the goddess. Devotees also seek to please the goddess by putting themselves to discomfort.

Including the return journey, the whole pilgrimage takes 7 days.

Sarthal: 18 km. from Kishtwar, Sarthal is best known for the cave temple of the eighteen- armed Devi Athara Bhuja. The deity is also known as Srî Ashtadash Bhuji Devi.

The legend: The Mother Goddess (Devi) is said to have come to this cave from Hari Parbat (Srinagar).[i] Like most comers from Kashmir, she entered through the Singhpora pass.

The story of the temple: In ancient times, Kishtwar had a king called Agardev. He ordered for a road to be constructed. While digging the earth his road-gang discovered an idol of Jagadambâ Mahâ Mâyâ. The king got a temple constructed at Agral to enshrine the idol in. Later, some people destroyed the temple. The idol disappeared.

Many years later, a farmer from Agral took his cow to a forest (where Sarthal now is) to graze. The cow would sometimes lick a large rock in that forest. Whenever it did so, it would produce enormous quantities of milk. One day a very good- looking little girl appeared before him. She asked him to remove that rock, because the missing idol of the goddess lay buried beneath it. He did so.

Word reached King Maha Singh who got a temple built where the idol was found. He also encouraged people to settle near the temple. It was thus that Sarthal village was founded. (According to a variant, someone called Rajesh Kirti Singh built the temple.)

There is a legend in Kishtwar about the time when the Mughals attacked Kishtwar (AD 1620). Apparently the blessings of the goddess ensured that the Mughals were miraculously repulsed, and that Koki Devi single-handedly pushed the Mughal army back. The History of Kishtwar, of cource, has a different tale to tell about the events of 1620. (The people of Bhaderwah similarly believe that their guardian deity helped defeat Emperor Akbar. In Anantnag there is a similar belief that the blessings of a [Muslim] saint ensured the Kashmiris' initial victories over the Mughals.)

The fair: Every year in July/ August a very famous fair is held here to celebrate the birth anniversary of the goddess. The exact date is the Har Shudhai Ashtmi of the Hindu calendar. One of its highlights is that devotees, possessed by the Devi, walk on fire. The fair is so important that the government gives employees posted in the area a day off to attend the fair.

The procession of pilgrims forms at the Srî Gauri Shanker temple, Sarkoot, around noon. It arrives at Sarthal in the late afternoon.

Jammu city

If **Bahu Mâtâ** is the presiding deity of Jammu, the dargah of Peer Budhan Ali Shah Saheb (**"Peer Baba"**: see the chapter on Islamic Shrines) is the other shrine that protects Jammuites.

Bahu Temple and Fort: The temple of Maha Kali is considered second only to Sri Mâtâ Vaishno Devi ji in terms of spiritual power. It is better known as Bahu or **Bâwey Wali Mâtâ** and is located in the **Bahu Fort**. The present temple building was completed shortly after the coronation of Raja Gulab Singh, in 1822. The fort, as well as the Mansabdar's Palace inside it, was constructed in 1820.

However, the sanctum of the shrine, especially the black stone image of the goddess, is said to be as old as Jammu city itself (anywhere between 1400 and 2500 BC). Dr. DC Sharma says that rulers of the Bahu dynasty (which came to an end around AD 1675) constructed both the fort and the shrine. It is possible that they did, but not the buildings that you see today. The township of Bahu is slightly older than Jammu, which used to be its twin town. Today both are part of the same town, Jammu. A river separates the two.

Tuesday is the main day of worship at the temple. Sunday is a close second. The temple has two fairs every year, during the spring and autumn *navaratras*. The one held in April is the more important of the two. The government observes a public holiday on that occasion so that all Jammuites can attend.

At several temples in the Jammu hills animals (mostly sheep and goats) used to be sacrificed on particular occasions. This is still done in Nepal and Assam, and at the Jaurhian Mâtâ temple of Kathua district. It was so even at the temple of the Bâwey Wali Mâtâ till the reign of Maharaja Pratap Singh (1885- 1925). A saint used to meditate in the nearby temple of Lord Narsimha. He was so offended by the slaughter of animals in the temple of Maha Kali that he tossed the idol into River Tawi. The goddess then appeared before the Maharaja in a dream. She told him that the saint was right. Animal sacrifice had to stop. The Maharaja agreed to ban this practice. The saint brought the idol out of the river and installed it once again in the sanctum.

The dream part could be a legend, but the rest is recorded history- and very recent history at that. Till well into the 20th century, and much after the ban, animals continued to be brought to the temple. They would still be kept in the enclosure meant for sacrificial animals. However, instead of killing them, some sacred water would be sprinkled on them, as a symbolic slaughter. The animals would leave the temple alive. Since then all offerings made at the temple have been vegetarian.

Jammu City is around 36 km. from the nearest Pakistan border. During the 1965 war Pakistani bomber aeroplanes entered Indian airspace and hovered over the town at night. However, they did not drop their bombs on the city. (So far we are with recorded facts.) The story in Jammu is that years later when the Pakistanis were asked why they did not bomb Jammu, though they easily could have, they said that they could not see the city. Instead they saw a small sea, with a young girl in red standing above it. Jammuites believe that it was the Mâtâ who was in red and who thus protected them.

(Some Jammu Muslims have told me the same story, but with a small twist. They, too, said that Pakistani bombers had hovered over Jammu in 1965. In fact they said that this had happened during the 1971 war as well. However, they said that Pakistan did not bomb Jammu because its pilots had found no military installations worth bombing in the town. But the question arises, in that case why did Pakistan send its bombers to Jammu city at all? Surely bombers don't set out on missions without deciding on the target in advance.)

According to Dr. DC Sharma, Raja Sarang Dev constructed the mosque right outside the Bahu Fort, in order to 'win favours from Mughal ruler Aurangzeb.'

Also near the fort is the samâdhi of Bâbâ Amboo. He is the presiding deity of the Khajuria clan of Brahmins. They visit his shrine throughout the year, but once every year they gather there in large numbers for mass prayers- and festivity.

Mela Bahu Fort (fair)

Also called the Ramanavami fair, the Mela Bahu Fort is held twice a year during the Navrat ras of Baisakh and Assuj (April and September). Tens of thousands of people attend.

The ancient Mahamaya temple is perched on a hilltop overlooking the Tawi. It is located within –or, to be precise, at the riverside extremity of the **Mahamaya City Forest**, which is accessed from the bypass. Devotees have to walk or drive through acres of a very pleasant forest to reach the temple, which has the best views of the city across the river. It is named after Mahamaya, a Dogra Queen, who was killed during a battle with foreign invaders around A.D. 700.

The Peer Kho cave temple, close to River Tawi river, and the Panj Vakhtar temple are the other important Shiv temples.

The fifteenth century Shiv mandir at **Panj Vakhtar** (just off Residency Road) is the oldest surviving temple in town. Its sanctity derives from its svayambhuv (self-created) Shiv ling. Some claim that it existed during the Shankaracharya's ninth century A.D. visit to Jammu.

The **Peer Kho** is said to have been consecrated by Raja Ajaib Dev in the 15th century for the saint Siddha Ghareeb Nath. The temple consists of two caves which are some twenty or thirty feet below. It is around 2 km. from Residency Road, on the outer 'circular' road that leads to the radio station and Raj Bhawan. The main icon is a *svayambhu* (naturally formed) Shiv ling, certainly at least six hundred years old—many say that it was always there. Stories abound about the existence of underground tunnels that lead to other cave shrines.

Raghunath Temple, Purani Mandi: While researching for this book I learnt that Raja Mal Dev had constructed Jammu's first public buildings in the 14th century in what now is the Purani Mandi. The present Raghunath temple, however, dates only to AD 1888. Rani Bandral, the wife of Maharaja Ranbir Singh, built it. As its name suggests, it is a Ram temple. It has paintings depicting the lives of Sri Ram and Sri Krishna.

Raghunath Mandir, Raghunath Bazar: Maharaja Gulab Singh commenced work on this 17- temple complex, in the crowded downtown "bazâr" named after it, in 1851. It was left to his son, Ranbir Singh, to inaugurate it six years later. (According to another version, Gulab Singh commenced work on the temple in 1835 and Maharaja Ranbir completed it in 1860.)

This is the biggest temple complex in Jammu and, arguably, the most popular temple north of Benares. There are hundreds of thousands of *saligrams* in the complex. These are little stones, each of which represents a deity from the Hindu pantheon. Thus the temple claims that it has representations of almost all Hindu deities, whose number is countless. The emphasis, though, is on the various incarnations of Lord Vishnu. (As mentioned before, the Dogra kings claimed to be Suraj Vanshi, and thus descendants of Sri Ram, an incarnation of Lord Vishnu.)

The complex houses a rich collection of ancient texts and manuscripts. Sheets of gold cover the three walls of the inner sanctum. The smaller temples around the main temple belong to the various gods and goddesses of the Ramayan. There also are temples dedicated to Lord Shiva and Lord Ganesh.

The **Ranbireshwar** temple, built in 1883 by Maharaja Ranbir Singh (1857-85), is the biggest Shiv temple in north India. The biggest lingam in the temple is more than 7-feet high. (A lingam, called ling in much of north India, looks like an inverted thimble and is a phallic symbol.) The temple also has twelve Shiv Lingams of crystal, between 15 and 38 cm. high. In addition, there are 1,25,000 tiny bona (dwarf) lingams, brought from the central Indian River Narmada, and embedded on two raised platforms.

Jammu rural and Samba

On the Jammu- Akhnoor route

Most of the Jammu- Akhnoor route runs along a cold- water canal. After you leave Jammu town in the direction of Akhnoor you will first pass through Barnai. Immediately thereafter is **Nâgbani**, which has an old temple of Nag Devta, the snake god. Devotees make offerings of milk, cereals and other uncooked foodstuffs at the temple. Maharaja Hari Singh's armoury used to be at Nagbani. Nagbani is 11 km. from the heart of Jammu and now almost a part of the city. the temple is on a side road, less than a kilometre from the main road.

The Jhiri fair: This 'mela' is held on the Puran Mashi (full moon) day of November. The date is known all over India as the Kârtik Pûrnîmâ. It began as a peasants' fair to commemorate the martyrdom of Baba Jitto. The Baba is now seen as a revolutionary peasant leader who died fighting for the rights of peasants. He was a contemporary of Guru Nanak Dev ji, the founder of Sikhism. As the descendants of those peasants grew prosperous, so did the fair.

Bawa Jitto: Jitto belonged to Ghâr, a village near Katrâ (Udhampur). He went to Kalyanpur to work as a farmhand on the estate of Bîr Singh, a *jâgîrdâr.* The landlord refused to give Jitto his legal share of the harvested crop. The Bawa tried to reason. When Bir failed to see reason, Bawa Jitto committed suicide.

When other farmers heard the news, they rose in revolt. This snowballed into an uprising against the feudal system in general.

The Jhîrî area begins close to the main road, though the main temples and *sarais* are a few kilometres down a side road on the left.

A few kilometres ahead of Jhîrî, also on the side road, there are two temples, at **Sui** (see 'Details' below) and **Burj**. In turn they are almost a kilometre away from each other. (Details at the end of this chapter.)

Akhnoor town is picturesquely located on the banks of River Chenâb. It has an ancient cave temple said to date to the age of the Mahabharat. It also has an old fort. The Chenâb is mostly fit for river- rafting. Some enterprising youths from Jammu occasionally bring over rubber rafts.

On (and off) the Sâmbâ- Jammu highway

Purmandal is 39 km. from Jammu, in the southeast. (To get there, travel from Jammu on the highway towards Sâmbâ/ Pathankot/ Delhi. Shortly after the town comes to an end, and well before Bari Brahmana, there is a side road on the left. This road branches off just before a major bridge, at a place called Kalu Chak. You will see many army buildings in Kalu Chak.)

Purmandal is an ancient pilgrimage.

Its twin pilgrimage is called Utter Behni. Between the two is a Sanskrit school, run in the old Indian tradition. (See also the section 'Between Jammu and Sâmbâ' in the chapter 'Jammu: the temple circuit'.)

Chi Chi Mâtâ: This is a large, prominent temple atop a low hillock on the Pathankot- Jammu national highway, two kilometres from Sâmbâ. Those who go to the shrine of Sri Mâtâ Vaishno Devi ji entirely by road normally stop here first to seek the blessings of Chi Chi Mâtâ.

It is believed that the body of the Devi Mâtâ once blew into pieces, which were scattered all over the Dogra hills. Her little (*chi-chi*) finger fell near Sâmbâ (Jammu). The Chi Chi Mâtâ temple is part of a chain of temples in Jammu and HP which commemorate places where parts of the Mâtâ's body fell. (See also 'Jammu- the temple circuit.')

If you are travelling from Jammu to Sâmbâ, then the prosperous temple of Chi Chi Mâtâ will be on the left, and before Sâmbâ. A few hundred metres further ahead there will be a major side road on the left that leads to the Mansar and Surinsar lakes. (Mansar is in Udhampur. For Surinsar, see below.)

On the major road that leads from Chi Chi Mâtâ to Lake Mansar there's a village called Nud. An unmetalled side road from here will take you to the Mahorgarh- Dhergarh- Bapnergarh complex (see in 'Details' below).

Details

Akhnoor: *The Jeo Pota* (or Jia Pota) *temple*, in Akhnoor proper, on the banks of River Chenâb, has a huge sedimentary rock that has been used as a royal throne. It was on this rock that Maharaja Ranjit Singh of Punjab gave the *raj tilak* (anointment as king) to 21 year old Gulab Singh on the 16th June 1822. Gulab thus became the Raja of Jammu and later the Maharaja of Jammu, Kashmir and Ladakh.

The magnanimous Ranjit left nothing to chance. He summoned all the top chieftains of Jammu province to witness, and thus endorse, this 'coronation.' Mian Nihâl Singh was the pre-eminent Rajput leader of the time. He pierced his finger and with his blood applied the *tilak* on Gulab's forehead: thus signalling that he, and othe other hill chiefs, accepted Gulab as their king.

The Kâmeshwar temple is extremely significant for scholars and national-integrationists. Its courtyard has yielded 6th or 7th century inscriptions- pilgrim records- in a Dravidian script. These are shell inscriptions on rough pebbles.

Nâgbani: (Also spelt Nâgvani.) *The legend:* Bâsak (Vâsuki) Nâg, the king of the snakes, is the presiding deity of Bhaderwah. (See 'Dodâ, Kishtwar, Ramban' districts.) Lord Shiv gave him a boon, because of which he had four sons. The Hindus of Jammu province regard each of the sons as a deity. They believe that these snake gods protect them and soak up all poisons that might happen to be in the neighbourhood. The arid areas of Jammu are infested with poisonous snakes. Rural Jammuites often die of snake- bites. However, according to Purshotam Bargotra, 'There have been no snake bite cases in the area around [the temple], among the devotees…' (*Daily Excelsior,* April 15, 2001.)

Bhairh Devta was the oldest of the four sons. Surgal came next and is worshipped at domestic altars. Raja Kai was the youngest. His temple is near Ambaran (tehsil Akhnoor). The temple at Nâgbani is dedicated to the third son, Nâg Râj of Tallan.

History: This temple (not the present building) is said to have been established in the 15th century AD.

The forest: Nagbani means 'the forest (*bani* or *van*) of the great snake (*nâg*)'. Like all old temples of importance, Nagbani is set inside a substantial- in this case, 25 acre- forest. Because it is right next to the winter capital of the State, this is prime land. It is said that a local king decided to clear the forest and grow crops on the land. As soon as his men started felling the trees thousands of snakes emerged from the ground and started moving about on the land that was to be cleared. The local people- and the king- felt that this meant that the Snake God had been offended. In atonement the king decreed that the 25 acres around the main Devasthan (temple) would henceforth formally belong to the temple.[1]

Purshotam Bargotra says that around 1984 'it was decided to construct buildings by reclaiming some forest land around the Temple. A bulldozer was put to use for levelling the ground. But the machine often developed mechanical defects and refused to work.' The bulldozer then sank into marshy land from which it was pulled out with great difficulty and after propitiating the deity. Bargotra says that as a result the project 'had to be abandoned.' (*Nâgvani, the Abode of Tallan Serpent God*, Daily Excelsior, 15 April, 2001.)

Therefore, the forest has mostly been left alone. Consequently many of the trees in the compound are several centuries old. Some of these trees belong to species that are now considered rare.

The temple: The temple- and its forest- have been designed to provided peace and calm. Therefore, they are considered ideal for meditation. The complex includes a small pond. Devotees often rinse themselves in the pond before entering the temple. The holy waters of the pond are said to cure diseases of the body and the mind.

1 At Shahdra Sharief (è) the legend is reversed. There it is the king who tries to prevent deforestation. At the shrine of the Peer Baba of Satwari (see 'Jammu City'in 'Islamic shrines') the story is that all officers who planned to shift the shrine died. All three stories have the same message: Don't mess with the land around our shrine or you will come to grief.

The 'bâmbi' ant- hill: There is an ant- hill inside the Nâg Devatâ temple in the west. Atop the ant- hill are images of the Snake God, etched on stone of made of silver or brass. Many of these images date to mediæval times. They were placed here by devotees whose prayers offered at the temple were answered.

Offerings made at the temple: Most farmers offer a portion of their harvest to the deity. Others offer the snake gods a drink called 'dalassi,' a sweet *chapati* (wheat bread) called 'rote' and fruit. The rest follow the North Indian tradition of offering sweets.

Fairs and festivals: The temple's own festival is held on the day after Baisakhi, i.e. on the 14th April in most years. Punjabi- style Bhangrâ dances are held and sweets (especially the *jalebi*) are cooked. Being a Nâg temple, Shiv Râtri (February) and Nâg Pañchmi are also celebrated.

Auspicious days: As at other Hindu temples, all days are good, but certain days are considered more auspicious than the rest. In the case of this temple these days are Sundays, Mondays and Tuesdays.

The Bengal connection: On the authority of a local priest, Bargotra mentions a Bengal- connection that is several centuries old. The priest says that learned Brahmins from Bengal would come over to Nagbani and spend a month at a time there. During their stay they would meditate and serve the serpent gods. Brahmin priests often have *jajmâns* (clients), the way family doctors do. Such *jajmân-* priest relationships are handed down over the generations and can be one or two thousand years old. Apparently the snake- gods of Nagbani are the *jajmans* of Bengali priests, before whom they appear in their divine form and whom they shower with gifts, as *jajmâns* normally do.

Sui is roughly 35 km. from Jammu, in the Kahna Chak area, in the direction of Akhnoor. One way to get there is to turn from the main Akhnoor road towards Jhîrî, and then continue on a rough country road for two or three kilometres.

Sui and the temple at **Burj** a kilometre away grow their own food and are on some kind of an all- India *sadhu-* trail. Sadhus (mendicant saints) travelling (normally on foot) from, say, the holy cities of UP (Benares, Haridwar etc.) know that in Jammu district there are these two temples where they will get free food and accommodation. Sui's more than ten acres of farmland, gifted by Maharaja Gulab Singh, yield enough grains and lentils to feed them all.

One such saint was the early 19th century spiritual master Baba Prem Das. The baba had gone to Kashmir for the Amarnath Yâtrâ. He passed through this leafy grove on his way back to Rajasthan. He noticed that the shaded grove at Sui was an ideal place to meditate. Around then he met Gulab Singh, and prophesied that this army officer would one day become a king. Gulab Singh went on to become the Maharaja of the state. Around the middle of the 19th century he got a Raghunath Temple, dedicated to Sri Ram, built at Sui at the Baba's behest. The baba's octave samadhi (burial place), with a marble palanquin in the middle, is located next to the main temple. The impressions of two feet have been carved in stone and kept inside the palanquin. These represent the feet of the master.

Sui is renowned for its fine wall paintings. Most of the artists were brought from Rajasthan and were assisted by local artists. The temple has two storeys. Each floor is used for exactly six months, during which period the priests are not allowed to enter the other floor. Considering that the area is quite hot in summer, it makes sense to be in the lower floor then.

Architecture: The walls around the temple are around twenty feet high and are made of large stones. The complex, thus, looks a bit like a fortress. Its entrance, too, is quite big and reinforces this impression. Dr. Ashok Jerath is of the opinion that 'this temple was constructed prior to the construction of the old palaces at Jammu. Hence, the design of this [temple] was used for the construction of the main palaces at Mubarak Mandi.' (Quoted from *Fascinating wall paintings of Raghunath temple Sui* by Dr. Jerath, Daily Excelsior, 14 February, 1999.)

The paintings: If you want to see an excellent array of Rajput miniature paintings in their natural surroundings (i.e. not in a museum), then this is the best place in the state and one of the best in North India. Of course, these are wall paintings and not on paper. The style is not pure Paharhi or Dogra, but then what is? The colours are still almost as bright as when they were first painted around AD 1850. There are images of Hindu deities and floral motifs all over. In those days Sikhism was not a faith outside Hinduism. Therefore, portraits of Guru Gobind Singh ji and Guru Nanak Dev ji (and their disciples Bala and Mardana) are given pride of place. The syncretism doesn't stop there. The weaver saint, Kabir, who was part Muslim, is seen weaving yarn.

Lord Vishnu and scenes from the Ramayan, naturally, dominate. Paras Ram and Shravan Kumar, too, are depicted: because sub-plots in the

Ramayan are dedicated to them. Dharam Raj is shown administering justice to sinners by sending them to hell. However, ordinary mortals like Bhartri Hari, the scholar- king from Rajasthan who perfected Sanskrit grammar, are also portrayed. After all, this is a shrine of a Rajasthani saint and the master craftsmen had come from that state.

Kathua

Shrines and temples

When I first went to the Banni valley I would ask the people why it was that their region (which includes the neighbouring hills of Udhampur) was so full of shamans, exorcists, ghosts (good as well as bad) and shrines and temples with magical powers. The reply I would invariably get was that ghosts and spirits were attracted to the beauty- and the quietness- of the mountains. The same holds good for the profusion of shrines in Kashmir. There one is told that rishis [saints] - Hindu as well as Muslim- have always flocked to the mountains of Kashmir because of the peace they would find in the mountains. Good point. And factually correct, too.

Billawar is 2 km. off the Dhar- Udhampur road, on a side- road that emerges at the Bhaddu crossing. While crossing the river to enter the town, on the left you will notice a large rock with an image of Sri Hanuman carved on it in relief.

Apart from the shrines and temples mentioned in the entries about individual towns in this chapter, the more important ones are:

Temples of the mother goddess

The Mother Goddess (Mâ or Mâtâ) has a different name at each temple. However, throughout Jammu and Himachal she is always shown riding a tiger, wearing a red sari and even looks the same. Essentially what we are looking at are different incarnations of Durga Mâtâ.

Chamunda Devi: This temple is in Basohli proper, in the town square. The idol is in the form of a natural rock.

Dhoula Wali Mâtâ: This mountain- top temple at 6,500 feet is a 10 km. trek from Jourhiâñ Wali Mâtâ è. It can also be reached directly, again on foot, from Bhoond. A shepherd built this temple. The Mâtâ advised him through a dream to go to a nearby mountain peak called Mandhi Dhâr (10,000'). At the Dhâr she appeared before him in the form of a little girl. It snows heavily at the Dhâr in winter. The Mâtâ noticed the hardship devotees were being put to because of the snow. So, again on her advice, the temple was shifted to its present location. Attendances at the temple are highest during the spring and autumn navaratras.

Jasrota Wali Mâtâ: This shrine of the Maha Kali goddess, where too pilgrim arrivals peak during the navaratras, was rebuilt in the 1980s atop a hillock near the old Jasrota village.

Mâtâ Bâlâ Sundari: A fairly old, perhaps mediæval, temple near village Parole, 13 km from Kathua town. Built by a Brahmin farmer whose sickle accidentally struck a stone, which began to bleed. Apparently, the stone was an incarnation of the Mother Goddess, who came to the Brahmin in a dream and asked him to install the stone under a banyan tree. It is a Hindu tradition to place sacred stones under banyan trees where they serve as symbolic idols and are worshipped. Such clusters of stones, if they attract enough devotees and offerings, later get placed in temples specially built near that tree. That's obviously what happened with this stone which is now in a temple in a mango grove. A fair is held at the temple during the navaratras.

Mâtâ Sundari Kote: This temple is a 5 km., trek (illuminated at night) through the woods from the Bhini Nallah bridge on the Dhar- Udhampur. Alternatively it is nearly 20 km. (much of this on foot) from Kathua town on the other side of the hill. The temple has been built atop a hillock with a grand view. One has to climb 107 steps to get to the temple. The idol of the Mâtâ is said to have been found under the berry tree that still grows near the temple, which was built later for the idol.

Nukwali Mâtâ: Another name for 'Dhoula Wali Mâtâ'è.

Shakti Mâtâ: Located in Banni proper. Apparently there once was a shepherd whose sheep and goats would die on touching one particular stone in the Sirah hamlet of Banni. To make sure his sheep did not come in contact with that stone again, the shepherd decided to throw it into the Sewa river. However, when he tried to lift the stone, it swelled miraculously and became too heavy to lift. That night the goddess came to him in a dream and asked him to build a temple around the stone, which was a representation of her.

Every year a fair is held here in the month of Shrâvan (July- August) on the occasion of the Sankranti, when all the people of the villager lunch together.

Sukrâlâ Mâtâ/ Devi: This shrine of the Mother Goddess Mal Devi attracts more pilgrims than any other shrine in the district. They come mainly from the neighbouring Punjab and Himachal Pradesh.

A large number of devotees of Sri Mâtâ Vaishno Devi ji from other parts of India like to combine their pilgrimage to the Bhawan and Katrâ (è) with a trip to this little village. A 9.6 km. motorable road from Billawar winds its way uphill to a low hill (3,500 feet above the msl) where this white, limestone- coated, temple has been built.

The legend of Trilochan, the saint: It is said that around AD 1500, Trilochan, a resident of Sukrala village, went to Kashmir to study Hinduism. When he completed his education, his guru gave him some money for the expenses of his return journey. Trilochan used the money to buy materials (*samagri;* mainly dried herbs and butter) for a *hawan* instead. (A hawan is a formal prayer, conducted near a low fire.) He performed the hawan at Baramulla.

At regular intervals, Trilochan would throw some of the sacred herbs and butter into the fire, as is the custom. After a while he ran out of these inflammable materials. However, Trilochan wanted to keep the sacred fire going. So, he chopped off one of his limbs and threw it into the fire. (Throwing human or animal flesh into sacred fires has always been taboo in Hinduism.) When the fire had consumed the limb, he cut another part of his body, and then another, followed by a fourth, to keep the flame alive. At last he took the meat chopper to his head, to offer it to the sacred fire.

Mal Devi, who had been watching, could take no more. She appeared before her devotee in person. This is what he was subjecting himself to so much torture for. She asked him not to sever his head. Trilochan said that he would do so only if the goddess agreed to settle in his village. Mal Devi had no choice but to agree.

The goddess restored her devotee's body. She also decreed that his grandson would be her devotee. (*'Story of Sukrala Mata'* by Shiv Ram Malguria, Daily Excelsior, Jammu, 19 August, 2001.)

Mal Devi is an incarnation of Sharda Mâtâ/ Devi. She appeared at this place in the form of a *shila*, a slab of stone. She sits astride a lion whose trunk is made of brass and its head of silver. The goddess has four arms and a sword in one of her hands. Behind her is the image of Mahishasur Murdini, an incarnation of Mahalakshmi, standing atop the slain demon king Mahishasur.

The goddess is said to be the younger sister of Srî Mâtâ Vaishno Devî jî.

A history of the temple: This temple was built by Prince Madho Singh of Chamba (HP), during his exile. (Malguria says that the prince was called Mehad Singh.) Madho/ Mehad had to leave Chamba because, on the death of their father, the king, his younger brother had seized the throne. He was related to the king of Billawar. So he chose to settle here.

The local people say that the temple was built in the sixteenth century. Because of the shrine's popularity several *sarais* (rest houses for pilgrims) have been built by the government and by the temple's management. Stylistically, the architecture of the temple belongs to the same group as the ancient temples of Krimchi ('Udhampur-Reasi districts') and Billawar.

The legend of the temple: Trilochan's grandson, Shiv-Nandan, was a scholar. Mal Devi visited him in a dream. She told him how to find her idol, which she had placed in the woods under a creeper with white flowers.

Shortly thereafter Prince Madho Singh went on a hunt and killed 120 wild ewes. Immediately afterwards he fell terribly ill. The physicians had no cure.

So they contacted Nandan. He called over a Thakur from a hilltop village, because the Thakur, too, was a devotee of Sukrala Mata. The two meditated on the goddess. Nandan then pounded Madho's back with his hands. As soon as he did so the Thakur found himself saying, 'Prince Madho can be cured only if he builds a temple dedicated to Sukrala Mata.'

Madho said that he would be glad to do so. However, he did not have that kind of money because he was no longer a king. At this the Thakur, who had been possessed by a spirit, perhaps by the goddess herself, said, 'You will soon regain the kingdom of Chamba.'

Madho replied, 'As soon as I become the King of Chamba I will build a temple here.' When he said these words Madho was cured. Three days later he was told that his brother, who had usurped his kingdom, had died and that the people of Chamba wanted him back as their king.

Once Madho became the king he forgot all about the promise he had made. So, two years later the King of Nûrpur conquered Chamba and imprisoned Madho. Then Sukrala Mata appeared in the dreams of both Madho and his captor. Madho begged forgiveness and promised to build the temple. On her part the goddess advised the King of Nûrpur to restore Chamba to Madho, which he did.

As soon as Madho got back his kingdom, his family and he went to Sukrala village on foot. They carried stones and other things needed to build the temple on their heads, as labourers do. That the temple has been built entirely of construction materials brought from Chamba is a fact, and not a legend.

The Lusara tree: There is a green lusara tree and a green rock near the remple. The fruit of this tree is not eaten raw. Instead it is either cooked or pickled. It is said that Madho once dared the goddess to turn the then dry tree and the then grey rock green overnight. She did both. He was trying to test her divinity.

Malguria says that the word Sukrala is a contraction of Sûkha (dry) Lusara.

Best time: As with most shrines of the Mother Goddess, attendance peaks during the spring and autumn navaratras. (In autumn, normally in October, these are the nine days preceding Dussehra.) On such occasions, special buses are pressed into service from Jammu, Billawar, Kathua and Udhampur to the shrine. Since 1998 small buses have started plying between Katrâ and Sukrala Devi, on demand, if there are enough passengers, throughout the year.

During the navaratras, especially in autumn, devotees combine their pilgrimage to Sukrala Mata with a visit to the shrine of Mata Bala Sundari, also in Kathua district.

Temples of Lord Shiva

Airwan, the Shiva temple of: 15 km. from Kathua proper, and near village Parole, this 4th century temple is said to have been built by the legendary Indian king Vikramaditya. The village derives its name from the ancient river Irawati, now called the Ravi, which flows not far from the village. Devotees bathe in one of the many wells near the temple before offering prayers. As in some other parts of Jammu province, a 'Gupt Ganga' (lit.: the secret or hidden Ganga) exists here, a substitute for the real Ganges of Uttar Pradesh, where the ashes of the dead can be immersed. Two fairs are held here every year, on Shiva Ratri (roughly mid- February) and Baisakhi (13th or 14 April).

Basohli, the Neelkanth Mahâdev temple at: King Bhupat Pal of Basohli conquered Kishtwar. Thereafter he married the princess of Kishtwar, perhaps in 1627. The princess brought with her a Shiva idol, to house which Bhupat got this temple constructed near his palace.

Billawar and the Mahabilvakeshwar temple: The majestic and ancient *Mahabilvakeshwar* temple of Billawar, which is made of bricks of stone, has a curious tradition attached to it. Over the centuries, when Billawar was a kingdom, one of the stone- bricks would pry loose and fall off just before a king was about to die. When Billawar was merged with Jammu a stone would fall off just before one of the Jammu Maharajas was to die. This happened again in May 1963, just before the death of Pandit Nehru, Prime Minister of India. (However, I don't think the temple presaged the death of the other two serving Prime Ministers, Mr. Shastri and Mrs. Gandhi.)

This Shiva temple was once known as the Hari Hara temple. Its present name (which means 'the great bilva God') is derived from the bilva trees which grow near the temple and which are believed to be dear to Lord Shiva. In addition to an idol of a five- headed Shiva (rare in India, though I've seen a many- headed Shiva at Angkor Vat), the temple also has idols of the Lords Brahma and Vishnu, Sri Ganesh and Bhairon ji.

The temple has a square sanctum and a pillared *mandap* in front. At the top is a *shikhar*.

How old is the temple? No prizes for guessing. The Pândavs are said to have visited Billawar during the last year of their 12- year exile, liked the grove of 'bill' trees and offered prayers at the spot where the temple now is.

Stylistically, the architecture of the temple is much like the 9th- 11th century Krimchi and Babor temples (see 'Udhampur-Reasi districts') and probably belongs to the same age as well.

Incidentally, could the 'bill' in *Bill*awar, too, refer to the bill/ bilva trees of the area?

Mahanal: A kilometre away from Jakhole, on a bank of river Ujh, this is a famous shrine inside a cave, with almost a dozen natural Shiv lings. Water drips from the ceiling and falls on the Shiv lings, something that is otherwise done artificially in Shiv temples.

It is believed that once upon a time milk (a substance used during Hindu prayers and poured on Shiv lings) used to fall on these ling(am)s till a milkmaid started collecting and selling it for money. Because of this blasphemous act the milk disappeared, leaving only water behind. The 'milk' must have been a mixture of limestone and water while the ling(am)s clearly are stalagmites.

In addition, in Kathua there are several lesser- known shrines of Lord Shiva, of the serpent deity Nag Devta and of the mother goddess. The ones mentioned are those that attract pilgrims from more than just the neighbourhood.

Narasimha temple. Ghagwal: (35 km. from Kathua town, on the National Highway in the direction of Jammu town.) This is one of the few temples of its kind in the district. It has a large pond and its annual fairs are on the occasions of Janam Ashthami (late August/ the first week of September) and Makar Sankranti (14th January). Local handicrafts, especially blankets, are sold during these fairs. (Lord Narasimha is the incarnation in which Lord Vishnu descended on earth in the form of a creature that was half man and half lion, in order to destroy evil.) This is the most popular of the five such temples in the province. The other four include the Raghunath Temple (Jammu town), and at Utterbehni (Jammu-Samba) and Mansar (Udhampur).

Kough: (c.2,000'; 12 km. from Mandli on the Dhar- Udhampur road.) This Narasimh(a) temple is unique in that its priest belongs to a 'scheduled' caste. This is revolutionary because the scheduled castes were not even allowed to enter temples ***in*** most parts of India till, in the early 20th century, an enlightened Dogra maharaja gave them the right to do so in Jammu and Kashmîr.

The Kough temple, however, has an infinitely older association with the 'scheduled' castes'

Lord Narasimh is the half man *(nar)*- half lion (*simh*) incarnation of Lord Vishnu.

Panjtirthi: Panj means 'five' and a tir(a)th is a 'pilgrimage'. The idea is that by going to this one place you can, in effect, perform the equivalent of five pilgrimages. Located 2.5 km. from Bhaddu è, five rivers converge at this place, viz. Ujh, Bhini (pron. bhee-nee), Talain, Nâj and Khad. A mediæval Shiva temple still exists on a low rock at the point where the five rivers meet. Also since mediæval times, a fair is held here every year on the occasion of the Chaitra Chaudas (the day before the navaratras of March/ April).

Shamans

There is this very likeable *chela* (lit.: disciple) in Banni proper. Every year, just before the monsoons, he performs a day- long religious ceremony to invite the weather gods in.

He used to hint that but for his prayers the monsoons wouldn't come to the Banni valley at all. No one ever bothered to call his bluff.

But you know how things are. With education, science and all that we tend to dismiss such talk as superstition. Well, I, the callow young Sub-Divisional Magistrate (SDM) of Basohli, freshly out of a particularly cynical college, with all my public school 'modernity', certainly did.

So did the educated folks of Banni who, in 1980, neglected to ask the chela to perform his annual, all- day *havan* ceremony. (A havan is a Hindu prayer around a holy fire. These chelas are shamans who modestly call themselves 'disciples'. The guru, or teacher, of all these Himalayan chelas is the Mâtâ, the mother goddess who rides a tiger, herself.)

So what do you think happened? Well, it might have been a coincidence, but the rains skipped Banni on the appointed day. The farmers were, naturally, in a bad shape. They rushed to the chela and begged his forgiveness, as did the aforementioned educated youth.

The chela smiled, forgave them and agreed to perform the havan. And later that evening, call it another coincidence (in 1980 I did, now I don't), it started raining.

Banni is a fairly big valley (popn.: 20,000) in the Basohli sub- division of Jammu and Kashmir, where the state's borders meet Himachal Pradesh. It is not far from the state's border with the Punjab either.

The nearest railway stations are Kathua (Gobind Sar) and Pathankot. From Pathankot there is a direct bus to Basohli every morning. Banni is a few hours' bus ride from Basohli. Including the wait at bus stops, you will get to Banni by sunset. There are government rest houses at several places in the Banni valley. Trekkers normally bring their own tents. Local dhabas are the other alternative.

So when did I stop being a cynic and a, what do you call it, rationalist, and start believing? Well, obviously when I started seeing. I decided to (One thing I must clarify is that there is nothing specifically Hindu about these chelas, even though most of them are disciples of the Mâtâ. Some of Banni's mystics are Muslim.)

During the course of my research I noticed that the chelas tended to specialise. Thus the chela of Banni- proper made it rain and the Jourhiâñ Mâtâ è chela drank the blood of freshly- slaughtered animals. The chela near Raolka and Daolka would have what New Age- types call out of body experiences. He could get you herbs from hundreds of miles away within minutes. He would simply disintegrate at Raolka, reassemble at the other place, pick up the herbs and come back to Raolka. I dismissed eyewitness accounts of this as hypnotism.

At Banni proper there are chelas devoted to the Hindu deity Sri Hanuman, as well as Muslim mystics, who can identify thieves and recover stolen property. Again possible through mass hypnotism- which would show up on video film. So, was any chela willing to perform his magic on videotape?

The chela at Lowang, a Kashmiri Muslim- dominated village, was. I had gone there to investigate the damage caused by a fairly bad earthquake. It was a wet and chilly night a few days before the first snowfall of the season.

All the village notables, including the chela, came to call on me. By now word had gone around Banni that I was working on a book about Banni. One of the persons helping with my investigations told the chela that I had heard much about his annual ritual. So, could he perform it for my benefit?

The chela goes through his ritual only on what the people of Banni call the rakkharh punnya (Pûrnîmâ)- the full moon night of early August. The rest of India knows this occasion as Raksha Bandhan. On this day the chela walks on red-hot coals and pierces his tongue, ears and nose with tiny *trishul* tridents. So the others, I included, chided the person who made the suggestion because it was wrong to interfere with a centuries-old tradition.

However, the chela thought for a while and announced that he would do it, even though it was November. While live coals would be difficult to arrange at a short notice (not to mention the rain outside, and the considerable expense) he would do the trishul bit. And he did.

Dussehra at Jourhiâñ Mâtâ

(Jourhian rhymes with the French Evian; the 'n' is nasalised.)

The chela of Jourhiâñ Mâtâ, near Bâñjal starts performing his prayers on the arid side of the pass early on Dussehra morning. A couple of his assistants surround him. Soon the village people start bringing sacrificial goats and sheep to the chela. By now the chela is in a mystic trance. The animals are slaughtered by chopping off their heads.

The chela puts his mouth on the torso, at the place where the neck was, and drinks up all the blood of each slaughtered animal. And he does this to every one of the 150 or 175 sheep and goats brought to him in the first few hours of that day.

I had read about such things happening in pre- Islamic Arabia, but this was the first time I ever saw such a thing myself.

If I've got you interested, here's how you can plan your trip: On the eighth and ninth day of the autumn Navaratris you can catch Basohli's famous Ram Lila. Spend the morning of the tenth day, i.e. Dussehra, at Jourhiâñ Mâtâ. And after the ceremony at Jourhiâñ Mâtâ is over, which should be by the noon, you can trek down to Banni.

You need to trek for 4 to 6 km. (depending on whether you take short cuts) uphill from Banjal Galla to get to this small mountain- top (7,250 feet) temple, which has a resident *chela* (shaman). It's an easy trek even for those who are not fitness buffs.

The place really comes alive on Dussehra morning (and the nine days before) when its annual fair (*mela*) is held. A lot of merrymaking (and matchmaking: and not merely for matrimonial purposes) takes place. The women turn up in all those loud, colourful clothes and garish make- up that the Dogra hills are famous for.

Non- mainstream Hindu, ceremony: A rather overpowering (I spent several minutes looking for a non- judgemental adjective) ceremony commences around seven or eight that morning. (Muslim and Christian fundamentalists would have used a much stronger adjective.) People from the neighbouring villages, as well as some distant ones, bring over goats for sacrifice, either to thank Jourhian Mâtâ (the Mother Goddess) for some wish granted, or to ask her for a boon. Typically, more than a hundred goats are lined up.

The chela goes into a trance. ('He has been possessed by the Mother Goddess,' is what the local people say.) Then one by one someone other than the chela chops off the heads of all the sheep. So far the ceremony is much like what used to take place at Jammu City's Bahu Fort till the early 1900s and what still happens at temples of the Mother Goddess in Nepal and Guwahati [Assam].

Where our chela differs is that he puts his mouth on the bleeding torso of each goat and sucks up all the blood of as many sheep as are brought to him while he is in the trance. I have witnessed this ceremony on more than one occasion. In 1993 alone did the chela say that he wasn't in a mood to drink the blood. Normally these chelas are in a fairly foul mood when in a trance. In 1981 he was angry about the way the world had gone to seed and about rising corruption and sin.

In 1993 I got completed and inaugurated a rest house near the temple. It has large rooms where, for a token fee, you get to sleep on blankets on the ground. (You are not allowed to sleep on beds in the vicinity of most hill temples dedicated to the Mother Goddess.) The place is cold throughout the year, more so on an October (Dussehra) night. The view from this peak, of less exalted mountains all around, is grand and 360, even if many of the mountains are treeless. You can see Himachal Pradesh even on a slightly cloudy day.

Poonch

Budhâ Amarnâth: (Budha is pronounced 'buddâ' as in 'old man', and not as in Lord Buddha.) This is this very old Shiva temple. The lingam is made of 'white stone' (flint or quartz). It is the most popular pilgrimage in the district and the most frequented Hindu pilgrimage in the Poonch-Rajouri belt. Even including Muslim shrines, it is next in popularity only to Shahdra Sharief.

Location: The temple is 25 km. north east of Poonch town, on the left bank of the Loran stream. This is the point where the Gagri Nallah and Pulast Nandi streams meet. It is 244km. from Jammu. The shrine is two kilometres above Mandi village, in a region known as Rajpura Mandi.

In the 19th and early 20th centuries Rajpura would briefly be the summer seat of Poonch royalty and nobility. During that period every year the place would really come alive. Apparently, one of the things that make this shrine unique is that it is not atop a hill, but in the foothills instead. The range in question is the Pir Panjal.

The sanctity of the place: Lord Shiv is believed to have started telling his consort, Goddess Parvati, the Amar Kathâ ('immortal story') at this scared spot. (He completed the story at the other Amarnâth, the one in Kashmîr.)

Devotees believe that to this day Lord Shiv comes down to this temple on Raksha Bandhan day every year. As a result, the prayers of everyone who visits the temple on that day are answered.

K.D. Maini writes, 'This temple is considered older than the Swami Amarnâth jî of Kashmîr. That is why [this] shrine is known as Swami Budha Amarnâth. It is believed that one must visit this sacred place before performing the yatra of Amarnâth, Kashmîr.' (*The shrine of Swami Budha Amarnâth,* by K.D. Maini, Daily Excelsior, 5 August, 2001.) 'Budha,' of course, means 'the old man.'

Could this claim to Budha Amarnâth's antiquity be a recent invention? Maini quotes from the ancient *Nîlmat Purân*, which reads thus, 'By seeing the Goddess erected by Pulast, one is freed from all one's sins and obtains the highest knowledge.' This is like absolution for sins. Even if the *Nilmat Puran* is wrong about the authorship of- or even the benefits of a visit to- this temple, this passage does indicate how old the idol here is.

The legend: It is believed that Pulast rishi meditated here. (If true, this would have been several thousand years before Christ.) He was a great saint and sculptor. However, he is better known as the grandfather of the demon king Râvan. Pulast performed *tapasya* here, which is a prayer that goes on for months or even years, during the course of which the devotee deprives his body of all comfort- often even food.

Such was Pulast's devotion that Lord Shiv appeared before him at the spot where the temple now is. To show how grateful he was to the Lord for the visitation, the saintly sculptor carved a lingam out of quartz. After he died the local people built a temple around it.

Maini adds, 'Even today a number of [ancient] idols… are available in this area. it is possible that these idols may have been chiselled by Pulast Rishi.'

The Loran stream is known as the Pulast stream in this area, after the rishi (saint).

The temple: The present temple is 60' (roughly 20m.) high. It was built in the late 1990s. The older temple that stood here had been carved out of a single large rock. The temple has four doors, each pointing to one of the four cardinal points (directions). This signifies that the temple welcomes devotees from all four *varns* (castes).

It was repaired and expanded during the eras of Raja Moti Singh (AD 1850-92) and Raja Baldev Singh (1892- 1918). Apparently the temple was a summer retreat of sorts for the 19th century Poonch royalty. Other citizens, including the Poonch aristocracy, would follow them to Rajpur where, for a few weeks, there would be enormous social activity. (To this day, every summer countless affluent Indians get away from the scorching plains and head for temples in the cooler mountains.)

The icons: The main icon is a natural Shiv ling made of quartz. Ancient idols found in neighbouring villages have been gathered and established here.

The main pilgrimage lasts ten days and on the same day—Shrâvan Pûrnmâshi—as the more famous Amarnath yâtrâ of Kashmir. This is the day of the full moon on which Hindus elsewhere celebrate Raksha Bandhan (early August). The festival is known simply as the Mela Swami Budha Amarnath.

The rituals of this festival are similar to those at its namesake in Kashmîr. They revolve around a holy mace (*chharhi mubârak*), which is carried from a 'base temple' (called the Dashnâmî Akhârhâ in both cases) to the main Amarnâth temple. Devotees follow the mace in a procession. In this case the Dashnâmî Akhârhâ is now located in Poonch town.

There is a major congregational prayer at the Akhârhâ in Poonch three days before the Mela/ Raksha Bandhan. The *chharhi mubârak* is consecrated afresh and worshipped at a *havan*. The head priest (swami ji) with the mace sits in a palanquin, which devotees carry on their shoulders. There is a guard of honour from the police outside the Akharha. The holy mace, which is in the palanquin with the priest, is then taken out in a procession. People, who number a few thousand, sing devotional songs and shout (non- political, inoffensive) religious slogans during the procession. More than a hundred *sadhus* are part of the group.

Elsewhere in the State such processions now travel towards the final destination in buses and cars till they reach the 'roadhead.' At Machail and Shrî Amarnâth jî of Kashmîr devotees start walking only after the roadhead. The trip to Budha Amarnâth can be done entirely by vehicle because the road is 'motorable' all the way. And yet devotees in Poonch choose to walk all the way, because it is more pious to do so and because it is such a short (and not difficult) walk anyway.

Chandak is the only place en route where the procession halts. The Muslims of Chandak greet the *yatris* with soft drinks, which they serve free of charge to almost all pilgrims. The *yâtrîs* go to the temple of Chandakâ Devi, where they are given a free lunch. The people of Chandak set up colourful stalls to welcome the holy mace and the pilgrims.

The procession arrives at Rajpura Mandi the same afternoon, where an equally colourful reception awaits them. Once again, food is free.

History: Both here and in Kashmîr the headquarters of the Dashnâmî Akhârhâ has shifted several times over the centuries. The procession of the *chharhi mubarak* first began in the late 19th century, several decades after (and clearly inspired by) its Kashmîrî counterpart. Dashnâmî Akhârhâ was first located in Tetrinote (which is now in 'Azad Jammu and Kashmîr'). It then shifted to the Shivalay Khakhanaban.

Then towards the end of the 19th century or the beginning of the 20th, the Raja of Poonch got the Dashnâmî Akhârhâ renovated. The royal priest (Rajguru) made the Akhara his headquarter. Ever since, the procession has commenced every year at the present Dashnâmî Akhârhâ.

Holy springs: There used to be four springs in the temple. Now the waters of all four have been channelled into the spring to the south of the temple. All pilgrims are expected to bathe with this holy water before entering the temple.

Accommodation: The charitable trust that manages the temple built a Yatri Sarai (free dormitory for pilgrims) in the 1990s. All pilgrims can eat three meals a day for three days, free of charge, at this sarai. The sarai can accommodate six hundred pilgrims at a time without any difficulty. At times a thousand pilgrims manage to squeeze in.

Ram Kund: 68 km. from Poonch and 11 km. from Mendhar. Mendhar, incidentally, is supposed to have been named after Menander: yet another Greek connection.

The legend is that Sri Ram, who stopped at Ram Kund en route Kashmir, personally got this temple constructed and that King Lalitaditya of Kashmir merely got it renovated. Others say that the temple dates to Lalitaditya's time and was built at his instance. 'Kund', naturally, refers to water bodies, in this case to the three springs near the temple, in which it is considered auspicious to bathe before offering prayers.

Sakhi Maidan (Mendhar): The ruins of an ancient, Kashmir- style 'Pândav temple' are to be found here.

Rajouri

Mañglâ Devi/ Mata: This is an ancient cave shrine on a hillock in Bhawan (Nowshera). The shrine is 5km. from Jhangar and close to the 'line of control.' It is almost half way between Jammu and Rajouri, being 70 km. south of Rajouri.

The main cave is much like the more famous cave shrine of Srî Mâtâ Vaishno Devî jî. There are two other caves nearby. However, getting to those caves it quite difficult.

Like almost every ancient shrine in the state, the cave of Mangla Devi ji is said to date to the era of the Mahabharat. Prayers offered here are said to be answered miraculously. This has made the shrine very popular with soldiers of the Indian Army.

Monday is the day and Dussehra the festival associated with the goddess. A sarai (dormitory) has been built to accommodate devotees from out of town, who gather in large numbers on these days in particular. There is a major *bhandâra* (prayer) at the shrine on the eve of Dussehra. Even non-believers climb the hillock because of the splendid view it affords.

Udhampur-Reasi

Agâr Jitto: Just ahead of Katrâ town when you travel towards Reasi, this is where Baba Jitto, the revolutionary peasant leader, was born. The spring that emerges from the hill here is said to curative properties, including some miraculous ones. Childless women bathe in it to augment their fertility. Because of the popularity of this shrine, the SMVD Shrine Board has created some facilities for devotees.

Babore/ Babour/ Babor/ Babbaur: (30km. north-east of Jammu.Roughly 50 km. from Udhampur town. Can also be approached from the Mansar lake.) This is a group of six ruined stone temples, spread over an area of one kilometre. It is located on the Dhar- Udhampur road, in a village now called Manwâl. The five main temples are Dera, Devi Bhagwati, Kala Dera I, Kala Dera II and Nand Babor.

Along with Krimchi, this complex is one of the two most important surviving ancient monuments of Jammu province. Its style resembles that of Nara Nag (Ganderbal district). Three of the temples- dedicated to the Mother Goddess and to Lord Shiva- are still in use. The whole complex was probably in use till around the 16th century.

There are some fine sculptures. The Nataraj, for instance, is very North Indian and quite unlike its stylised Chola counterparts. There were idols of the Hindu gods Vishnu, Shiv, Surya and Ganesh in the complex. Originally there were thirteen temples.

The temples were probably built in the Pratihâr style, modified somewhat by the time the style reached Jammu. Without doubt, they are the finest specimens of ancient Jammu architecture.

What distinguishes them is the grand scale they have been built on. The temples are big. Each of them is made of large pillars and beams: and each pillar or beam has been hewn out of one, single, huge rock. To top it all, the pillars have been carved deep.

F. Drew wrote in 1875, '(T)he buildings were of great solidity and considerable beauty, the chief feature of one of them was a hall, whose roof was held up by eight fluted columns supporting beams of stone 10 feet in length; on these beams were laid flatter stones chequerwise so as to fill up the corners of the square as far as the centre of the beams, and to make a new square corner-ways to the other, on this was laid a new set of stones cornerwise to this, and so on till the whole space was covered; this square mass of stone was ornamented with carving. The material of these buildings is a slightly calcareous sandstone, which is found among the strata near. It has well stood against weathering, and its toughness may be known from one of the beams of it, used in the construction, being as much as 14 feet in length. No mortar was used in the building: this must have been a predisposing cause of the lateral shifting of some of the stones, one upon the other, the moving cause being, I take it, earthquakes. The other neighbouring ruins have a great resemblance to the first, but they are not all equally ornamented.'

Babor(e) probably was the capital of the Jammu state around the tenth or eleventh century, when it was attacked by invaders from the west. These temples could well date to that era. The earliest they might have been built could be the 7th century AD. The best estimate is that the complex was built around the 8th century AD.

The Dera temple: This is the biggest temple in the complex. It has been built on a high platform. Therefore, one has to use the steps on the west to climb up. There is an *ardh-* (half) *mandap* before the main *mandap* and four *garbha grihas* around it.

The Devi Bhagwati temple: The outer walls of this temple, as well as its jambs, have splendid carvings. The temple has a *garbha griha* (sanctum) and *antarala*. The *mandap* is square and there are eight niches in its walls. The roof collapsed a long time ago.

The Kala Dera temple I: This temple, too, has been built on an elevated platform. Some fine reliefs have been carved on the jambs of the sanctum. There are two Natarajs of the aforementioned kind among the ruined panels of the *mandap.s*

The Kala Dera temple II: The Nandi bull outside this temple shows that it was a Shiva temple. On the northern wall of the mandap is an inscription, now mutilated, in the Sharda (Kashmiri) script.

The Nand Babor temple: This is an elaborate temple. Dr. Mani writes, 'The ceiling of the *mandapa* rested on fluted columns decorated with pot and foliage decoration.' He adds, '[The temple] has three *garbhagrihas,* each preceded by an *antarala* attached to a common *mandapa.*'

Deva Mayi Mâ: This is a pine forest on either side of the main road a few kilometres before Katrâ when you drive up to Katrâ from Jammu.

All pilgrims to the shrine of Sri Mâtâ Vaishno Devi ji pass through this forest but most just rush through it. A path leads uphill to the temple of Deva Mayi Mâ.

Gauri Kund: See 'Jammu: the temple circuit/ Between Jammu Katra and Patni Top.'

Kali Mata Mandir, Manthal (on the National Highway 40 km from Jammu): This temple has been built close to a waterfall.

Krimchi: (Also spelt and pronounced Kiramchi.) (2,500') While travelling on the National Highway from Jammu towards Kashmir or Patni Top, well after the fork that leads to Katrâ, you will enter the leafy army area of Udhampur town much before the town itself. You will pass a fairly big cinema hall (the Chinar) on the right. Shortly after that there will be a major, if at times rough, road on the left. This will take you to Krimchi and, after that to Pancheri.

There are five temples in all in this quadrangular complex. Three spiral stone temples are on one platform and the other two on another. The local people date these temples to, yes, the Mahâbhârat era. More realistically, they were built between the 9th and 11th centuries AD. Some scholars feel that a Kushan ruler who was on his way to Srinagar got them built. That would date them to around the 2nd century AD. Dr. Mani assigns the temples to the 8th/ 9th centuries AD and credits them to the Dev dynasty of Jammu.

Stylistically these temples resemble the Baij Nath and Linga Raja temples of Bhubaneshwar (Orissa). Thus, the exterior is in the *tri-rath* (three-chariot) style and the sanctum is square. The spiral *shikhar* (top; roughly: steeple) is characteristic of the Nagar style, once popular in north India.

The architecture of the temples belongs to the same school as that of the temples at Sudh Mahadev (Udhampur), Sukrala Mata and Billawar (both in Kathua district), and Bhimbar, Rajouri, Panjnara and Saidabad (all four in Rajouri district). These temples use a local variant of the Indo- Aryan style of architecture, with considerable Kashmiri, and some local, influences.

The group includes four east- facing temples, one of them completely ruined. The ASI has done some splendid restoration work in the 1990s. Dr. Mani observes that these 'four temples comprise a *garbhagriha* with [a] curvilinear *sikhara* and an *antarala* with *sukanasika*.' The fifth, smaller, temple faces west.

The sculptures and carved motifs resemble those in the ancient temples of Kashmir. The deities worshipped here were the Trimurti of Lord Vishnu, Lord Shiva and Sri Ganesh.

There is a fort atop a nearby hill almost 60 metres above the plain. Even in the 19th century it was in ruins though the Dogra maharaja and his family would stay here in a specially done up section while travelling towards Kashmir. Krimchi village was then on the route to Banihal and, thence, Kashmir.

In the 18th and early 19th centuries Krimchi was the capital of a small state ruled by a Mian (Rajput Hindu feudal chief or small- time raja) of the Patheyâl clan. He would give the king of Jammu an annual tribute of Rs.2,000 in cash plus the services of ten horsemen. In 1834 Raja Gulab Singh of Jammu sent a contingent of his army to capture the Krimchi fort. After that the state was ruled directly by Jammu.

Mântalâî: See 'Jammu: the temple circuit/ Between Jammu Katra and Patni Top.' Visitors can take a pleasant, low-gradient 5-km. trek from here through the forests of Naina Devi, for the scenic beauty during the trek and at the highest point.

Nau-Piñdiâñ: A pindi is a natural formation of stone or mineral and represents a deity. Nau Pindian has nine pindies that symbolise the nine incarnations (avtars) of Mahâ Shakti. This shrine, three kilometres off the Katra-Reasi Road, has been built on the banks of a picturesque stream.

Pinglâ Mâtâ: You can drive or take a bus from Udhampur towards Ramnagar. En route get off at a place called Kaua. From there you will have to trek 6 km. uphill, through a pretty pine forest, to the hillock in village Pinger where this shrine is. Because of its popularity, a sarai has been built to provide shelter to pilgrims

The legend: It is said that the Mother Goddess used to appear as a little girl before a group of shepherds from Pinger. She would give them food to eat when they'd come to graze their sheep on the meadow where the shrine now is. As a result they stopped bringing lunch along from home. This alarmed their parents who thought that their children had started skipping lunch.

The shepherds could not reassure their parents by telling them that this was not so, because the girl had asked them not to tell anyone about her. So, the curious parents decided to spy on their children, the shepherds. At the pasture they saw a girl serve food to their children. When the girl realised that her secret had been revealed, she rushed into a cave from which she never emerged again.

The shrine: That cave is now the shrine of Mother Goddess Pingla Mâtâ. Inside, there is a clearance large enough to accommodate 500 pilgrims together. A stone cauldron, the *dudhnu*, and a large ladle, the *karhshee*, displayed at the shrine are supposed to be the very utensils the Mâtâ had used to serve food to the shepherds. The dudhnu has now been placed in a manner to collect the water that drips from the ceiling of the cave. Devotees drink this water as the *charnamrit* (nectar) of the goddess.

There is a hole in the cave through which a glow can be seen. It is said that some hunters once saw a lion emerge from the cave, through the rocks, Casper- style, at the point where this hole now is. They entered the cave and beheld the Mother Goddess herself.

The fair: During the autumn navaratras in particular there is a major festival at the shrine. Pilgrims travel in a long procession (*shobha yâtrâ*) from the foothills to the shrine, carrying the *akhand jyoti* (eternal flame). They chants devotional songs as they climb up. This is normally on the first navaratra. Free meals are served during the festival.

Shiv Khori: Going by the trends of the turn of the century, the hotel owners of Jammu and Katrâ consider this pilgrimage to be the Great New Investment Destination of the first decade of the 21st century. This shrine is inside a huge cave that is certainly half a kilometre long, if not more. There are stalactites and stalagmites inside.

A very popular three- day fair is held on the occasion of Shiv Ratri (mid- February/ early March). Devotees come from Maharashtra, Gujarat, the Punjab and most states in between. Some of them set up stalls at which food is served free to every one of the thirty or forty thousand pilgrims who visit the shrine on those two days. Since 1999, at my instance, the Tourism department has been sponsoring the fair, especially the rural wrestling matches held on the occasion.

History: This cave was 'discovered' perhaps in the 1890s by shepherds whose flock had strayed into the cave. They found saints meditating inside. So, obviously, the cave was not unknown before that. It's just that the common man did not know about it. (Kho and khori mean 'cave'.)

The story of the cave: An ancient scripture, the *Bhagwat Shiv Puran*, says that Bhasmâsur, a demon, prayed to Lord Shiv for several years. This pleased the deity, who granted him a boon. Bhasmâsur asked for the power to destroy anything that he touched. Lord Shiv agreed. 'So be it *(tathâ astu)*,' he said.

Being a demon, Bhasmâsur could not restrain the evil within. He decided to make Lord Shiv his first target. The deity could not take back the boon he had granted. So he fled to an obscure cave in the mountains, to protect himself from the demon. It is believed that this cave was Shiv Khori. (The Lord later killed Bhasmâsur with his bare hands.)

Inside the cave: The first roughly 100 feet are through a wide tunnel that has a high- ceiling. There is no need to bend or crouch. This is a comfortable waiting room of sorts before the descent. Naked and semi-naked sadhus normally sit with their backs to the two walls of this corridor, often near a low fire (*dhooni*).

After that you crawl or slither along a narrow slope for another 100'. Then there will be a 20' descent into a well. This will be followed by another crawl, this time for 50'. Now you will enter a grand hall, where even a gathering of 500 can sit.

Images on the ceiling are believed to represent the Shesh Nag. A hollow in the middle of the ceiling is said to be the coiled bun of hair (*jatâ* or top- knot*)* atop Lord Shiva's head. There is also one major 4' tall, natural *lingam,* made of stone, which is surrounded by countless *shaligrams* (little stones, each of which represents a different Hindu deity). At Shiv temples across India milk is made to drip one or two drops at a time from a vessel above the Shiv ling. At Shiv Khori, milk-like limestone water drips from a small stalactite protruding downwards from the ceiling and falls exactly on the lingam. This coincidence strengthens the faith of the devotees.

Besides, the cave itself is shaped like Lord Shiva's double-headed drum (damroo)—wide at both ends and narrow in the middle.

Miracles: Ved Kesar writes, '[In 1996, the child of a devotee] was suffering from polio. He was unable to walk normally. He suddenly started walking after having a darshan [glimpse] of the Shiv Lingam in the cave shrine.' Apparently this incident was the turning point in the shrine's popularity. (*Shiv Khori pilgrimage, a unique experience*, by Ved Kesar, Daily Excelsior, 6 March, 1997.)

The pilgrim boom: J&K Tourism, headed by me, and the Shiv Mandli started promoting and developing this destination in 1998. That year around sixty thousand pilgrims had come visiting. By November 2001, when I left the Tourism Department, the number had swelled by seven and a half times to 4.5 lakh (0.45 million). In 2009 as many as 8.6 lakh (0.86 million) paid homage. The next year, in 2010, the number pilgrims increased by almost another half—to 12.75 lakh (1.27 million). In 2011 ninety thousand pilgrims attended the Maha Shivratri fair (mela) during its first two days March alone. This kind of a sustained and multifold increase must surely be a world record—and has been possible only because of divine intervention.

Within the state, Shiv Khori thus ranks behind only Sri Mata Vaishno Devi ji and Shahdara Sharief in terms of the number of pilgrims who come to pay homage.

On our part, the Tourism Department got one bridge constructed or sanctioned during each of the three years that I was there—and three was the number needed to help pilgrims cross the stream even when it was in spate. (When I first went to pay homage and supervise arrangements I had to walk through ankle-deep water on a riverbed of rough stones in March.) We also improved the path, installed lights along the path for night pilgrimage, built a dormitory for budget tourists, promoted the shrine at Katra, advertised it in the national press and sanctioned a Tourist Reception Centre at Ransu. This has made it an all-day, year-round pilgrimage. I also encouraged the setting up of a privately owned 3-star hotel in Ransu.

Above all, the national media—print as well as television—helped us enormously by accepting my invitation to trek with me over the then-rocky path to the annual mela. (Nowadays it is a pleasant stroll up a very gentle gradient.) *The Statesman*, then the biggest selling paper in eastern India, did a half-page article, leading to many pilgrims from Bengal.

How to get there: You can begin your journey from either Jammu or Katrâ. You can travel by bus, car or jeep only up to Ransu. After that it is a 35- 40 minute walk up an easy slope to the shrine.

From Katrâ: Drive to Reasi and thence to Ransu. Ransu is 79 km. from Katrâ. (Jammu- Katrâ- Ransu is 127 km.)

From Jammu: You can drive from Jammu to historic Akhnoor on a plain road. Then drive up the pleasant, pine- clad Kâli Dhâr range in the direction of Sunderbani. Just before Sunderbani you will come to crossroads at a place called Pâmblâ. From here you should take the rickety road on the right to go to Pouni and thence to Ransu.

Ransu is 105 km. from Jammu on this route. This route is slightly shorter than the one through Katrâ. But then most visitors want to combine this pilgrimage with that to Sri Mâtâ Vaishno Devi ji. The people of Jammu city prefer this route. Visitors can go to Ransu through Katrâ and come back through Akhnoor.

Pouni to Ransu= 16 km. For Ransu and onwards: Essentially, it takes a little less than an hour on foot to reach the cave. Part of the trek goes along a rivulet that swells whenever there are heavy rains. In 2000 and 2001 I got two bridges built to help pilgrims cross the rivulet when it is swollen. My department also sanctioned a third bridge for 2002.

Where to stay: There are 'paying guest houses,' inexpensive and rather basic, at Ransu itself. Almost half- way through the trek you will notice a fairly grand building on the right, below the road level, across the stream. This is a *sarâi* (dormitory) built by the Tourism Department for pilgrims. Charges are nominal and there are plans to charge nothing at all.

Sudh Mahâdev: (88 km./ **120km.** from Jammu; roughly 50km. north of Udhampur. Around 1225 m./ c.5,000' above the msl.) This, perhaps, is the only place in the State with an iron pillar on which there are ancient (6th or 7th century AD) Brahmi inscriptions. It has a mace that is said to have belonged to Bhim of the Mahabharat fame. There are 'sculpted statues' of Lord Shiv and the goddess Pârvati in the temple.

Architecturally, the temple belongs to the same school as the temples at Krimchi, Billawar and Sukrâlâ Mâtâ. (The latter two are in Kathua districtè.)

There is a major, three- day fair in mid- June, on Ashad Pûrnîmâ (full moon night). Buses are available to (and from) Jammu, Udhampur and Chenaini on the national highway. If you don't get a direct bus from Jammu, take the bus to Udhampur and change buses there. (See 'Jammu: the temple circuit/ Between Jammu Katra and Patni Top.')

Bâwâ Tarmîn: (11km. from Ramnagar; 144km. from Jammu.) This is a religious- cum- picnic spot on the Ramnagar- Dudu Basantgarh road. 'Tarmin' means 'where roads from three villages meet.' The local people consider such tri- junctions auspicious. Therefore, they perform the *mundan* (head- shaving) ceremony of their children here. Besides, people choose to meditate at Bawa Tarmin because of its peace and solitude. The place owes its beauty to its pine forests and the hills around it.

The valley of Kashmir

Anantnag-Kulgam

The holy cave of **Amarnâth jî** is the best known shrine of South Kashmir- and the one that attracts the largest number of pilgrims from outside the Valley. The annual pilgrimage reaches its high point on the first full moon night of August (rarely in late July): on the day when much of India celebrates Raksha Bandhan. (See the chapter on 'The Amarnâth Yâtrâ'.)

Devsar: An old and important temple in Devsar is dedicated to the goddess Shri Tripura Sundari, called Khanabarani by the Kashmîrî Pandits on the village. On the 4th day of Magh (roughly the 19th January) a fair is held in honour of the deity.

Kother (also Kothair)**:** 5 km. from the Achabal gardens. According to a legend there was a king in South India who sprouted horns on his head. The horns fell off only after the king had had a bath in a pond at Kother. In gratitude he built a reservoir around the pond and a temple next to it. The ruins of both are still extant. However, their architecture is much like that of other ancient ruins in the Valley.

There are iron mines near the village, possibly rich in ore.

Mârtañd: (5,817 feet above the sea level) The temple is 64 km. from Srinagar and around 7 km. from Ânañtnâg town. It is a brief diversion from the road to Pahalgâm; and 3 km. from the Mârtañd pilgrimage at Mattan. Easily the grandest of Kashmîr's ancient ruins, this temple complex is supposed to belong to 'the era of the Pandus and Kauravs'. But so are all the other ancient monuments of Kashmîr and Jammu. (Many historians feel that the tendency among the general public to date every ancient monument to the Mahabharat era is due to the fact that precise dates are not available. Besides, 'the era of the Pandus and Kauravs' is really the North Indian expression for the two thousand years or so before the Christian era- and perhaps a few centuries afterwards as well.)

In this particular case, Hindu priests call the temple 'the house of the Pandus'. The common man calls it the Mârtañd, or sun, temple. The temple was probably dedicated to the sun. However, that is not certain. Some historians claim that it was a Shiv temple. Bakaya points out, 'The four figures represent Lokesvara, Barov, Nataraja and Trimurti with a female figure in swimming attire, symbolically representing Gañgâ.'

British colonial historians were of the opinion that the foundations of the temple were laid between AD 370 and 500. The Rajatarangini says that King Ranaditya (5th century AD) built the temple, his queen Amrita Prabha built the smaller chapels on the side and Lalitaditya the colonnade. Many modern historians, however, dispute both these versions and credit King Lalitaditya Muktapida (AD 725-753 or 669- 739) with the authorship of the temple. Jonaraja says that King Sikander caused damage to the temple.

The temple has been built atop a *karewa*. Younghusband raved about the 'sublime site' of the temple. He said that it was 'finer than the site of the Parthenon or of the Taj, or of the St. Peter's or of the Escurial. We might take it as the representative or rather the culmination of all the rest and by it we may judge Kashmîr people at their best.'

The temple itself is on flat land. There are tall mountains behind, a lawn all around and sloping ground in front.

Its architecture consists of what *The Gazetteer* calls bold strokes and outlines, solid walls and an absence of 'petty confused details'. The pillars of the colonnade around the temple are fluted. It is not certain if it was built as a 'sun temple' or was later converted into one by a different sub-sect of Hindus. Younghusband says, '(The) temple (is) second only to Egyptians in massiveness and strength and to the Greeks in elegance and grace. It is built of immense rectilinear blocks of limestone, betraying strength and durability… The ruins (220' x 142') consist of a lofty central edifice, which are [sic] calculated to have been not less than 75 ft. with a small detached shrine on either side of the entrance, and of a quadrangular courtyard of imposing dimensions surrounded by colonnades of 84 columns, being the multiple of number of days in a week with the number of signs in the Zodiac. Water was brought to it by a canal from the Lidr [sic].'

There certainly are some Greek features in the architecture of Mârtañd, Nârâ Nâg and Awantiporâ: especially the pillars and the triangular pediment atop the pillars in the façade. However, their layout, conception and general framework is almost identical to that of temples like Angkor Vat (Cambodia).

The Mârtañd Cave Festival: According to a Government document, a festival is held at the Mârtañd cave 'during Malamâs and Bânamâs… [Kashmîrî Pandits] from all over south Kashmir assemble at the cave on these days and perform religious rites. The date for Banamas is determined according to the solar system and Malamas on the basis of lunar months.

'The temple at Bhawan [nearby Mattan] also attracts pilgrims during Banamas and Malamas. These celebrations are known as 'Vijay Saptami'.'

Mattan (or B(h)awan): 61 km. from Srinagar or 6 km. east of Ânañtnâg. This pilgrim village is just off the road that leads to Pahalgâm. It has traditionally been a major Hindu pilgrimage. Since ancient times, Lord Vishnû Surya hâs been worshipped here in his Mârtañd manifestation. The word 'Mattan' is an abbreviation of 'Mârtañd.'

The waters of a sacred spring collect in a large tank in which fish abound. There are temples- and a Gurûdwara- around this tank. It is said that Surya, the Sun god, was born to Aditi from a lifeless egg called Mârtañd. Aditi was the wife of Kashyap, the saint from whom Kashmîr probably takes its name. Surya was her thirteenth child. The spring at Mattan is connected with this legend.

As at Hrishikesh or Benares (both in Central India), Mattan used to have *pandas*- Brâhmins who record family- trees and genealogical tables for their clients. Most of these *pandas* migrated to Jammu in 1990. Dormitory- type accommodation is available at Mattan.

Arora notes, 'A few furlongs ahead of Mattan on [the] Pahalgâm road is a cave situated on a hill spur a little distance up to the right from the road. This is said to be 200 feet long and to contain the remains of a recluse.'

Other important Hindu shrines in the area include the temples at Bijbehara, Akingam, Lukbavan (Luk Bhavani), Deviangan and Goswami Gund.

Bijbehara: *The Waheed Bâbâ Wudar* is to the west of Bijbehara. On this wudar grows a tree sacred to the followers of Lord Shiva, i.e. to all Kashmîri Hindus, who offer prayers here. (A wudar is a table- land.)

Kulgâm: *Durgi Shuri* is a festival of the Kashmîrî Pandits of Kulgâm town and tehsil. It is held on the 8th day of the lunar month that falls in July.

Luk Bhavani: Travel 8km. from Ânañtnâg/ Islâmabad town on the Vérînâg road till you come to Larkipora. Take a side road from here. The shrine is around one kilometre ahead.

Baramulla, Bandipora

The Hindu temples of the area include

Asthapan Nund Kishur at Sumbal, Sonawari

Boniyar is 64 km. from Srinagar, on the road to Urî. The temple there is one of the oldest in Kashmîr, but in good condition. Little is known about its history, or even its original name. So it is automatically credited to the Pandavs. The consensus is that it was built around 5th cntunv AD.

There is a tall central building, at the centre of a large quadrangle. Around it is a colonnade of pillars, with trefoil- headed recesses in between. Bakaya adds, 'Its cella is of large dimensions 13 sq. ft. (interior). Its walls are supported on a basement 4 ft. sq. It retains a cloistered quadrangle measuring 145' x 120'.'

Earthquakes and other natural calamities have played havoc with the other ancient temples of Bârâmullâ in particular and the Valley in general. Besides, the process of weathering is inevitable in a place as cold as Kashmîr. The temple at Boniyar is among the few of its vintage in the region to have survived nature. It had restoration efforts to contend with instead.

In the 1960s one Mr. Khajuria, a senior forest officer, noticed that that there was no idol in the temple. Therefore, he installed an idol of Lord Shiv. Units of the Indian Army did the rest. They put 'chips' at the entrance, a marble Nandi bull a little further inside and, in the sanctum, disco lights that blink. They obviously didn't approve of the ancient Indian (and South East Asian) tradition of creating temples out of slabs of rock. They felt that the rocks looked bare. So, they painted much of the temple a deep saffron, plastering over the elegant carvings of the pediment. They added regimental yellow and white stripes on the lower steps. Mr. Khajuria and the army unit have also embedded marble slabs in the structure, proclaiming their contributions to the temple.

Maybe they should go over to Angkor Vat with cans of paint and teach UNESCO how to spruce up those dull, grey stone temples.

Festival: The Boniyar Temple Jâtrâ

Pilgrims throng the temple in big numbers during all major festivals. Those who live within commuting distance come every morning.

Chhota Amarnâth ***at Arin, Bâñdîpora***

Delta Mandir: This is an ancient temple much like the one at Boniyar, and of similar vintage

Devi temple at Khanporâ, Bârâmullâ

Gosâmi temple at Gosâmi Teing, Bârâmullâ

Nârâyan Thal temple, the: The 6th century AD scripture, the *Nilmat Puran*, mentions this temple, though only casually. Therefore, the temple dates to at least before then. It has been built some 2km. from Bârâmullâ town, in the hollow of a hill that towers above it. The temple is on the right bank of the Jehlum.

There is a spring in the hill. Its waters form a spring and flow down towards the temple. There these waters stay for a while in a tank that has been built around the temple. Several temples of the Kashmîrî Pandits have been built in a similar fashion.

The temple is not very big. It measures 13' x 13'. There used to be a well- attended annual festival at the temple.

Pandav temples (ancient) at Boniyar, Urî (see 'Boniyar' above)

Kupwara

The **Badri Kali** Asthapan is a temple dedicated to Goddess Kali and has been built atop a hillock surrounded by a forest, 14 km. from Hañdwârâ town on the Hañdwârâ- Wadiporâ road. Its annual fair is held in September.

The shrine of Parkash Akhoon is in **Gurhi**, 3 km. from Kupwara proper. Also known as Parkash Pandit, this akhoon (teacher) earned the respect and affection of his fellow men because of his inspired teaching of Islâmic texts. Apart from Arabic and Persian, he was proficient in Sanskrit as well. (As for the name 'Pandit,' the formula is best summed up in the words of my senior colleague, Mr. Mehmood ur Rehman, 'In Kashmîr if you find someone with the surname Pandit, he is bound to be a Muslim, and if a person has the surname Mulla [or, for that matter, Wali- PD] he will invariably be a Hindu.')

The **Kheer Bhawânî** Asthapan: Though not as well known as its namesake in Tulamula, this temple, just a kilometre away from Kupwara town, in a village called Tikker, on the Chowkibal road, has a well attended annual fair in April- May.

Pulwama, Shopian

Awantiporâ-The Awanti Swami temple: (28 km. south of Srinagar) This is the temple the ruins of which everyone gets to see on the National Highway, while going from Srinagar to Jammu or Pahalgâm. Close to the banks of the Jehlum, it was built between AD 852 and 854. Awanti Varman founded this temple *before* becoming the king. It is also known as the Pandav Lari. 18th century accounts refer to the place as Bhyteepur.

There is dispute as to which deity the temple is dedicated to. Some say that the presiding deity is Lord Vishnû. Others insist that it is Lord Shiva. However, at least one scholar has stated that this was a Buddhist temple. The balance of evidence points to this being a Shiva temple. In the twelfth century, Raja Jai Singh's commander Bhasan is said to have used the temple as a fortress in the course of a civil war.

The style is generally the same as that of the Mârtañd quadrangle. However, as the *Gazetteer* notes, 'the semi- attached pillars of the arched recesses are enriched with elaborate carving of very varied character, while the large detached columns are somewhat less elegantly proportional.'

So, what caused these two temples to get silted up? The war Bhasan fought inside one of them? A more likely explanation is the artificial lakes these temples- like most other Hindu temples of Kashmîr- were surrounded by.

Some excavations began in the late 19th century, but it was mainly in 1914- 16 that this temple was excavated.

Degam: (South of Shopiâñ.) Shrâddh ceremonies of those who die as children are performed during the Kapal Mochan festival of Degam village People donate clothes and utensils in the memory of these children.

Jawbrari- The Awantishwar temple: The ruins of this temple, in all probability dedicated to Lord Shiva, were excavated in 1914- 16. Awanti Varman built it in the 9th century AD, *after* he became the king, for the use of commoners. This temple, too, is on the national highway, a kilometre north of the Awantiporâ ruins, in a village now known as Jawbara.

Khrew: *The temple and the fair:* On the fourteenth day of Sawan/ Har (July/ August) a fair (mela) is held at a Hindu temple atop a hillock in Khrew, 22 km. from Srinagar. It is about 5km. from Woyin. Nearly 200 steps lead from the plain to the temple. The hillock is believed to once having been a volcano and the fair is called the Fair of the Volcano (Mela Jwala Mukhi). The deity of the temple is Sahoala Bhagwati, the goddess of fire. There is a sulphur spring at the bottom of the hillock in which the pilgrims bathe before climbing the stone steps that lead to the temple. there is a dharmshâlâ with the temple, for pilgrims. (There is a sulphur spring at Woyin as well.)

Substantial offerings are made at the temple, which are collected by its managers, the Dharmarth Trust. Several Muslims take part in the fair.

More than three hundred stalls are set up during the fair, most of them run by Muslims. However, the Hindus own the stalls which sell earthen lamps with *ghee* (clarified butter) and cotton wicks, to be lit during religious ceremonies, especially during the rituals of the fair.

Ludov: 25 km. south-east of Srinagar. This is one of the oldest temples, indeed one of the oldest extant structures, in Kashmîr. It is a Rudresh temple. Bakaya, who rightly uses the word 'primitive' to describe this 'plain and simple walled structure', writes, 'Its early character receives confirmation from the fact that it resembles in several respects one of the buildings of Gândhâra, the Vihara of Guniyar in the Swat valley…'. By comparing it with the 5th century Vihara in what is now Pâkistân, Bakaya surmises that the Ludov temple might have been built around the 7th century AD.

Narasthan: Around 50 km. from Srinagar. These temple ruins are located where the Trâl valley begins. There are tall mountains behind the temple. In front of it is a small valley. Percy Brown, quoted by Bakaya, wrote, 'The pediment and arch motif appears in a further process of development… the flat offsets have been elaborated into moulded niches with triangular canopies and sunk trefoil arch introduced. Around the shrine is also thrown an enclosure wall forming a courtyard entered by a prominent gateway. Here the style is seen approaching its final form.'

The **Payer** temple: (Also referred to by historians as the **Pa Yech** temple): It is not clear who constructed this temple. However, stylistically it is similar to the Pandrethan temple. One theory is that the 9th century King Narindraditya built it.

There is debate even about the deity or deities this temple is dedicated to. Some feel that the sculptures above the doorway represent the Hindu trinity (the Lords Brahma, Vishnû and Mahesh/ Shiv) and the goddess Durgâ. Others say that all four figures represent Lord Shiv, albeit in different manifestations: Barov, Lokeshwar, Nataraj etc. In any case, the bull shown is Nandi, which indicates that this is at least partly a Shiv temple.

The *Gazetteer* says that 'surrounded by a few walnut and willow trees… [the] temple… in intrinsic beauty and elegance of outline is superior to all the existing remains in Kashmîr of similar dimensions. Its excellent preservation may probably be explained by the retired situation at the foot of the high table- land which separates it by an interval of 5 or 6 miles from the bank of the Jhelum [sic], and by the marvellous solidity of its construction.'

Its roof consists of ten stones.

Srinagar city

The important temples in town include:

The Durgâ Nâg Temple, Durgâ Nâg (between Jan Bakers and the UN observers' office)

The Hanuman Temple, Amira Kadal

The Raghunath Temple

The hilltop Shankarâchârya Temple that you see from everywhere: climb up from behind Jan Bakers or drive right up to the temple from the Boulevard (from opposite the Nehru Park island)

The Shârikâ temple on the Hari Parbat

Durgâ Nâg temple: This is a large temple complex located close to the Dal Gate. It is between the so-called UN (United Nations) office (UNMOGIP, actually) and Dal Rock/ Jan Bakers. It is one of the first landmarks that the visitor goes past on entering Srinagar by road from Jammu/ Pahalgâm while going towards the Dal Lake. Several categories of pilgrims stay in the temple's guest house.

Kâlî Asthâpan: The oldest wing of this ancient temple was constructed in AD 79 by King Pravarsen II. The temple has been built on the right bank of the Jehlum below the 3rd bridge, which is close to the shrine of the Shâh e Hamadan.

Raghu Nath (or Rugh Nath) temple: Arora, writing in 1940, called this 'the biggest temple of Hindus in Srinagar.' It is located between the 2nd and 3rd bridges on the left bank of the Jehlum. Four small temples surround the main temple.

The **Rishi Pir Fair** is organised in a modest temple near the Fifth Bridge (Kadal). It is in honour of Pîr Pandit Pâdshâh, a leading saint of the Kashmîrî Pandits. He was a disciple of Krishna Kar. He performed several miracles and was respected by both Muslims and Hindus. His was a message of tolerance and mutual cooperation.

The fair occurs in the Bikrami month of Baisakh: to be precise, in the third week of the corresponding lunar month.

Shankarâchârya: Most laymen believe that this hilltop temple got its present name from the great Hindu saint and reviver Adi Shankarâchârya (788-820). There is little evidence to support this view. The name probably derived from Shankará and Chachra, two kings who ruled in Kashmîr in AD 954-6. The original name of the temple (or, as is more likely, another temple that had stood where the present structure does) was Jyéshthéshvar.

Cunningham (1854) and Cole, writing separately in the 19th century, subscribed to the local belief that the temple was built in the age of Jalauká (said to have lived around 22 BC). "This theory has been rejected, firstly on architectural grounds, and secondly because of the doubtful character of the tradition", writes Kak.

There are Persian inscriptions still extant on the side walls, on the south west column. These indicate the dates AD 1644 and AD 1659 respectively. At least the concerned columns/ walls were completed during the tolerant reign of Shâh Jehan. They were, perhaps, commenced by his father Jehangir, as the British historian James Fergusson [1910] believes. Another two inscriptions are no longer in existence, though they were probably there even in the early 20th century.

Sober examination of the architectural evidence (comparing it with the Mârtañd temples, for instance) tends to indicate that the temple was built around the seventh century AD. Kak concurs with this view.

Kashmîr was once known as Bâghe Suleiman. The hill atop which this temple is located has, since the 14th century, been called the Takht é Suleimân (the throne of Solomon). The Shâh é Hamadân named it thus. It is likely that the Solomon in question was a noble, perhaps of Persian origin, who held high office in the royal court of Kashmîr, and not the Biblical Solomon.

Shârikâ Shrine: See the chapter 'The Kashmîrî Pandits' favourite shrines' in the section on 'Religion.'

Srinagar rural, Ganderbal

Meru Vardhan is just outside Srinagar city, off the highway, in the Badami Bâghcantonment.

This is a tenth century Shiv temple, named after the minister who built it. It is made of stone and is in good condition. The tenth century represents the last stage of ancient Kashmîri architecture. New features had been added by then. Percy Brown notes, '(T)he horziontal moulding cutting across the upper angle of the high pitched pediment is omitted... The ceiling is also unusually attractive, as it consists of diagonally placed beams, with brackets, like dentils, supporting its outer framework, all very wooden in treatment, but on the other hand the general principles applied in this design are much the same as those in coffered ceilings of many Hindu temples.'

Ladakh region

Kargil

Matâyan is 20 km. before Drâss/ 78 km. before Kargil town. It is the first village you will come upon after the pass. Good rock climbing is possible on the hills between Matâyan and Drâss. The areas to the south (right) of the National Highway are a vast green expanse.

1.6 kilometres after Matâyan, right next to the highway, is the so-called **Draupadi Kund** (10,840'). It is now being said that Queen Draupadi of the *Mahâbharat* fame had bathed there. I suspect that the belief dates to after the 1830s, when the first Hindu soldiers arrived in Ladakh. What is certain is that the belief was quite well established in the late 19th and early twentieth centuries. The local Muslims of that era had heard that an ancient Hindu queen called Draupadi used to bathe and wash her clothes in that spring. Indeed, they would point to a fortress- like structure on a peak no one had been able to climb. That is where Draupadi's family lived, they were told. The Muslims of Drâss would even celebrate the legend at a festival which would be held every year near the Kund, after the crop had been harvested, i.e. around October. There would be much singing and sport, mainly polo.

When was the festival discontinued, I asked.

After the highway from Drâss to Srinagar was built, in the 1960s.

And why?

'After the road was built no one had the time for festivals in October,' I was told.

Leh

Wangchuk Chhenmo: 'The Amarnath of Ladâkh': (This is a slight detour from the main 'Padam- Hemis' trekking route.) Between Markha and Hankar is a little- known holy cave. I am confident that it will become a national phenomenon as soon as this discovery is made public. I have been trying to promote it since the turn of the century.

Inside the cave is a stone that looks like a Shiv Ling. Few Ladakhis have even heard of it. Fewer still have actually been there. Most of those who have are childless Buddhist women. Over the centuries such women have been visiting this cave to lick the stone, in the hope that they will then be able to bear children. Apparently it works. This cave is in a valley before Stok.

Wangchuk is the Ladakhi name of Lord Shiv. Chhenmo means 'the great.' Together, the name means 'the great Shiv.' Thus even in Ladakh the cave is associated with Lord Shiv and the lingam with fertility. This association and religious sanctity has been there for centuries. And yet neither Shaivites nor Western scholars are aware of the cave's existence. It has the potential of becoming another Amarnath or Mansarovar in terms of pilgrim traffic.

The cave is on the Junglam route. It is a steep 25 feet above the road. Therefore, the traveller is likely to miss the cave unless he is looking for it. It can be reached from the Hemis/ Markha (Leh) side as well as from the Zâñgla (Zâñskâr) side. People prefer the latter, because the climb is easier- and the walking portion shorter. From the Hemis/ Martselang side we have to cross two passes, which can be tiring. On the other hand, the journey by jeep from Leh (or Srinagar) to Zâñskâr takes at least two (but typically three) days.

Travelling from Zâñgla, there is a very narrow gorge after the Chhar Char La. It is colourfully called the Stâ Chhung Gâmî Chhung: 'a horse can go through it [the gorge] but not the horse's saddle.' It is also called the dZo Chhung Rûmî Chhung: 'a dZo (cattle) can pass through it, but not the dZo's horns.' Indeed, one cannot stretch one's arms while passing through this gorge.

Tsrar e Sharief, Kashmir

Urs-e-Mubarak (saint's day) decorations at the shrine of Peer Roshan Shah Wali Sahib, Jammu

Chapter- 30

The Islamic Shrines of Jammu, Kashmir and Ladakh

Jammu Province

Doda, Kishtwar, Ramban

Hazrat Farid ud Din and Hazrat Asrâr ud Din

The saints: Hazrat Farid ud Din's links, on the other hand, are with Baghdad. Hazrat Farid reputedly had the power to stop earthquakes and give sight to the blind. (Kishtwar—indeed, the whole state—is part of a seismically active zone.)

He is said to have prayed for the early death of his own son Hazrat Asrâr ud Din, because the son had developed a spirituality that disturbed the father. A number of Islmic books have mentioned this. Some go on to say that Farid ud Din Saheb gave his son a bowl of water to drink. Asrâr ud Din Saheb died on drinking the water.

Mian Basheer, the eminent Gujjar leader, scholar and spiritualist, explained this to me differently. He said that Hazrat Farid was a conservative in religious matters. He believed that if a pious Muslim were to receive a divine visitation or a mystical vision in his dreams, he should keep the experience to himself. He should not talk about it. Hazrat Asrâr, on the other hand, believed in talking about the experience and sharing it with others. The father felt that such behaviour was outside the *shariat*, the Islamic law. Therefore, through his spiritual powers, Hz. Farid caused his son to die prematurely. (There are similar legends about Baba Reshi of Gulmarg and Sheikh Noor ud Din Noorani of Tsrar e Sharief.)

Historian Aseer Kishtwari disputes the veracity of these anecdotes. He says that Hazrat **Asrâr ud Din** died a natural death at the age of 18. He adds that the 'offer [of the bowl of water] and [its] acceptance amounted to the perfection of transfer of spiritual power and not unhappiness' [with the son]. Aseer then writes that 'one day Shah Asrâr ud Din Sahib (R.A.) was delivering a lecture on Islam which got interrupted by a voice "Oh! My friend come back' and Asrâr Sahib (R.A.)[1] disclosed about his death. He took a white sheet over his head and left this mortal world.'

When he was just a teenager, Hazrat Asrâr ud Din brought a dead Hindu child back to life. This child used to play with the young saint. Asrâr ud Din Saheb saw his friend's corpse being taken for cremation to the north- western end of the chaugan. He prodded the corpse with his stick and said, 'Arise. You had promised to play with me.' The dead boy did just that. It is said that Hazrat Farid ud Din was disturbed that his son was going about performing miracles like this one.

The shrines of the two saints are at a slight distance from each other. They are among the finest in the state.

Urs: The urs of Asrar ud Din Saheb is observed on the 25th Kartik (October/ November.) This is a major event for the state. It is one of the few state festivals that the government marks with an official holiday. The saints have a following throughout the state.

Jammu city

The 16th century shrine of **Peer Baba** at Satwari was renovated in 1985 and is just ahead of the airport. A roof and walls were built around it in 1998. Till then the shrine was roofless, as is the tradition in the Punjab and Jammu. Shah Saheb, a bachelor and a vegetarian who mainly lived on milk. He was born in Talwandi (Punjab) in the 15th century and was a contemporary of Guru Nanak Dev ji.

Peer Baba is one of the generic names for respected Muslim saints. The saint of this shrine was popularly known as Hazrat Baba Buddhan Shah. His formal name was Shams ud Din Fard i Wahid Imad ul Mulk. Baba Buddhan Shah was born at Talwandi (Punjab). There is said to be another shrine dedicated to him at Anandpur Saheb (also Punjab).

The shrine is right next to the Jammu airport. The airstrip has, at least since the 1960s, needed to be expanded, so that the kind of aircraft that came in after the 1950s could land there. The obvious place to expand the airport is into the premises of the holy shrine. It is said that plans were drawn up on two separate occasions to either shift the entire shrine or at least to extend the runway in its direction. According to the modern legend, the officers who drew up those plans died in two separate air crashes. That the crashes took place is beyond doubt. Did the senior officers who died in those air accidents plan to expand the runway at the expense of the holy shrine? This needs to be probed.

Peer Mittha was a contemporary of Ghareeb Nath. Both saints were famous for their prophesies and miracles. An imambara and a Shia (Shiite) mosque are located near the Peer's tomb. (An imambara, or the abode of the imam, is a Shiite house of worship.)

The Peer Mittha neighbourhood takes its name after the shrine of the same name. The shrine, in turn, got its name from the sweet (*mittha*) tempered saint (*peer*), Qutab e Alam, better known as Peer Mittha (died 1467). [According to another version, he was thus known because the only offerings he would accept- in life as centuries after his death- would be a pinch of sugar.] The shrine is in the heart of Jammu, being about two kilometres from the City Chowk, up a slope.

The saint, who was probably born in Iran, migrated to nearby Lahore. From there he made a brief journey to Jammu, a city he so fell in love with that he ignored his brother Syed Fateh Ali's pleas to return to Lahore. Instead, he offered to play a game of chess with Fateh on the condition that the winner would decide whether to go or stay. The *peer* won and his entire family agreed to settle in Jammu. (The other graves in the shrine are of Fateh and family.) The shrine is the starting point of the annual Muharram procession. As with other Muslim shrines of Jammu (and the plains of much of South Asia) devotees throng to the shrine on Thursdays in particular.

The *peer* shot to prominence- throughout Jammu and the neighbouring Lahore/ Punjab- when water he had sanctified with his mere touch cured the wife of Jammu's Raja Ajaib Singh of a thitherto incurable disease. The Maharaja of Lahore sent a (Hindu) saint called Ghareeb Nath (a siddh yogi called Gorakhnath, according to other versions) to check the *peer* out. The *yogi* set up camp at the nearby Peer Kho (cave), where a riverside Hindu cave- shrine exists to this day. The peer and the yogi each conceded that the other was genuine and possessed enormous spiritual powers.

According to Rehmat Ullah Râd[2] the two brothers came from Bukhârâ (Uzbèkistân). The architecture of the shrine is 'Afghân, being devoid of beauty.' The urs of the saint is held every year 'in the month of Katak [Kârtik]...[Before 1947] most of the devotees [were] low caste Âghâ Khânîs from Siâlkot.'

A fortnight before the festival, drummers would start announcing its advent, early every morning. Devotees would arrive several days before the urs, on which day a colourful fair was held. Clay lamps would be lit, as on Diwali. Some of the devotees were accomplished singers and would sing nâ'ats [songs in praise of Prophet Muhammad, peace be upon him] and kâfîs [a genre from Multân, now in Pâkistân] set to classical tunes.

Baba Roshan Shah Wali, the shrine of: This unusually long grave built atop the Gumat hillock in the heart of the city is of the mediæval Arab saint Jalal ud Din Jamal Noorani Nakki Modani aka Roshan Shah. He is best known as Peer Baba Nau Ghâzîa) because he is believed to have been 'nau gaz' (nine yards or 27 feet) tall. His grave isn't that long either, but that's the way legends are.[3] (The people of Jammu aren't really short. However, when a six feet plus Arab came to their land, legends of his being nine yards tall naturally took root.) This Muslim shrine and the adjacent mosque were constructed during the reign of the (Dogra Hindu) Maharaja Ranbir Singh (1857-85) around a much older grave. Here, too, Hindus dominate the congregation on Thursdays.

The three major mosques in town are the impressive **Jama Masjid** (in Talab Khatikân), the tastefully rebuilt white Vazirni Mosque (on the Palace Road) and the Shahi Masjid (Mastgarh). The Ibrahim Masjid is among the more popular mosques. The Shia Karbala is on the Wazarat Road, close to the Chief Minister' official residence.

For 'Pânch Peer' please see the chapter 'Shared shrines.'

The important **mosques** of Jammu Tawi are

- Jamia Masjid, Talab Khatîkâñ
- Masjid, Ustad Mohalla
- Masjid, Gole Market
- Ibrahim Masjid, Ahâtâ Shér Shâh, Rajinder Bazar

Jammu rural and Samba

For 'Chamliyâl' please see the chapter 'Shared shrines.'

Kathua

Peer Chhatter Shah: People suffering from skin diseases visit this shrine near Parole, 13 km. from Kathua proper. They bathe with the waters of the nearby spring in the hope that the waters would cure them.

Peer Fazal Shah: The annual fair at this Muslim shrine near Parli Vand is celebrated- as is not uncommon in India- according to the Hindu calendar, on the 24th Kartick (mid- to late- November).

Poonch

Chhotay Shah, the ziarat of: 58 km. from Poonch and 4 km. from Mendhar, this is a popular shrine in a village called Sakhi Maidan.

Sâîñ Ilâhi Baksh, the shrine of: This popular, though recent (1976), ziarat (shrine) is 39km. north of Poonch and 4km. from Loran. It is located in a picturesque village called Battalkote (è), which is in the Mandi 'block.'

The saint: Sâîñ Ilâhi Baksh was a Sufi saint and a bachelor. He belonged to Pathanateer village in Mendhar block. His father migrated to Poonch because he was appointed a water carrier (*mashki*) in the government of the Raja of Poonch. Ilâhi joined the British Indian Army and served in Basra during the Second World War. While at Basra he had a mystical experience because of which he decided to resign from the army and take to spirituality.

He came to Battalkote in 1948 to teach Muslims, Hindus and Sikhs alike the Sufi philosophy of peace and universal brotherhood. He would often meditate and pray all night, chanting 'Tû hî, tû hî' ('Only you, only you,' meaning 'You are the only one, the only God.')

The Sain died in May 1976. Since 1997 a three- day annual *urs* is held in his honour, from the 3rd to 5th Jaith (May).

The shrine: A local Muslim politician initiated work on the shrine. A Hindu forest ranger got the woodwork done in the Roza Sharief. A Hindu army officer got the guest house made.

Sâîñ Mîrâñ Saheb, the ziarat of: (pron.: sâ-ee*n* mee-râ*n* sâ-hib) Located in village Guntrian, 10 km. from Poonch town. The most frequented Muslim shrine in the district, and the second most popular in the region (after Shahdra Sharief).

Rajouri

There is a separate chapter on Rajouri's biggest and Jammu's second biggest tourist draw, Shahdra Sharief.

Chingus: (Rhymes with 'bus.' Also spelt Chingas.) Chingus means 'intestine' in Persian. If the intestines of an animal, including a human, are removed on its death, the body takes much longer to decompose.

In AD 1627, the Mughal Emperor Jehangir was travelling from Srinagar to Agra. He died in the royal howdah when his caravan passed through a village called Khanpur. His queen, Noor Jehan, wanted to influence the selection of the next emperor. She knew that if news of Jehangir's death reached Agra before she did, his sons (and their supporters) would try to kill each other for the throne. Therefore, Noor Jehan tried to keep Jehangir's death a secret.

So she got a trusted surgeon to remove Jehangir's intestines, which were buried in Khanpur (c.2,000' above the sea). Jehangir's body was propped up in the howdah. However, a fly came and perched itself on Jehangir's nose. Jehangir was obviously in no position to swat the fly. Those in the caravan who saw this knew that he was dead. Poor Noor Jehan's scheme did not work.

A major Mughal monument, a caravan sarai, was later built around the 'grave' where the intestines were buried. The village came to be known as Chingus after its most famous possession. Its location on the main road that leads from Jammu to Rajouri- Poonch has added to its popularity with tourists. There is a small rivulet nearby. A well inside the premises provides fresh water.

The old mosque was expanded beyond recognition in 1997. There is a mediæval tree in the vicinity under which there is a small shrine, also much revered.

However, it is the tomb of the intestines that draws the largest number of devotees. R.C. Kak wrote about it thus, 'This hallowed spot has since assumed [the] status of a shrine for Hindus and Muslims alike. Prayers at the Tomb are considered very effective, the sick come here for recovery of health, the poor for riches, the weary for divine comfort.'

Nao Ghazi Ziarat: This popular shrine of Qutab Shah Wali is in Dhanidhar, near Rajouri town. Nao means 'nine' and a 'ghaz' is a yard (a little less than a metre). Nine- yard long graves of sufi saints hold a particular fascination for the north Indian and Pakistani mind. There is a similar '9- yard' grave in Jammu city, that of Roshan Shah Wali Saheb, who belonged to the same clan as Peer Qutab Shah Wali Saheb.

Panj Peer: The other sufi tradition that fascinates north Indians and Pakistanis- of all religions- is that of groups of five (pânch in Hindi and panj in Punjabi) saints (peer). Panj rhymes with 'grunge'. This shrine is on the main road leading to Rajouri town, and just a few kilometres from the town. The five saints who are buried here came from the Punjab. They were brothers. The sixth grave here is of their sister. On Thursday evenings Hindu- Sikh devotees, especially officers and soldiers of the Indian Army, outnumber the Muslims.

The valley of Kashmir

Anantnag-Kulgam

The shrines of the eminent Réshî saints Bab Zain ud Din Wali (at Aish Muqâm) and Bâbâ Hyder Réshî (in Ânañtnâg town) are the most famous Islâmic shrines of Ânañtnâg-Kulgam. Sheikh Noor ud Din Wali, the Alamdar of Kashmîr, had himself foretold where the resting-places of these two major sai nts, among the last of the great reshis, would be.

Ânañtnâg town *Baba Hardi Rishi: Shrine and Urs* One of the several mosques in town has been built in honour of Rishi Malu. It is believed that Emperor Akbar's first defeat at the hands of the Kashmîri army, when his forces tried to annex Kashmîr, was because of the Rishi's prayers.

The Jâmâ Masjid is located near the tomb of Rishi Malu, also known as Bâbâ Haidar and Hardi Rishi.

The annual *urs* of Baba Hardi Rishi (aka *Rishi-moul*) are celebrated on the 1st Poh (roughly 15th December). Like most Rishis, the Baba was a bachelor and a strict vegetarian who did not eat onions or garlic either. Out of respect for the Bâbâ almost all the people of Anantanag, and many other Kashmîris, stop eating meat for a whole week at the time of his annual *urs*. Even during the rest of the year it is taboo to visit his shrine after eating any kind of meat or havind consumed an intoxicant. It is believed that tragedies befall those who violate this taboo.

Baba Hardi Rishi was a disciple of Makhdoom Sâheb, the leading Kashmîri sufi of his day ('Srinagar City'). Ironically, Makhdoom Sâheb's disciples had invited Akbar to annex Kashmîr. The Baba died in 986 Hijri at the age of 77, as indicated by the chronograms Abid and Sheikh Din Bud.

Other important shrines in the Anantnag-Kulgam districts are those of Bâbâ Dawood Ghani (at Vailoo), Hazrat Noor Shâh Baghdadi (at Kund), Hazrat Sheikh Syed Samnani (at Kulgâm) and Bâbâ Naseer ud Din Ghâzî (at Bijbehara). The shrines at Kaba Marg and Khiram Sirhâmâ posses holy relics of Prophet Muhammad, peace be on him.

And then there is the difficult- to- slot shrine of Harut and Marut.

Aish Muqâm (6,070', 76 km. from Srinagar; 20 km. from Pahalgâm.) *The shrine:* This powerful shrine is perched atop a hillock right a hundred metres above the main road that leads from Ânañtnâg to Pahalgâm. Therefore, it is clearly visible in all its majesty from the main road. A side road branches off to the right from the Pahalgâm road and climbs gently uphill to the shrine. After you drive for a few hundred metres you will reach the bottom of a row of steps that lead to the shrine.

The shrine is located inside a deep (and often very narrow) cave. Several relics associated with the Bab are kept in a room just outside the cave. They will be and brought out and shown to you through a window for a small fee. Do you remember the rod, the staff, that Moses parted the waters with? It is supposed to be one of the relics on display.

The saint: Sheikh Zain ud Din Wali belonged to the (Hindu) royal family of Kishtwar (Doda). His name was Zia Singh and he lived in the 15th century AD. He came to Kashmîr for spiritual guidance and became a disciple of Sheikh Noor ud Din Wali (Nund Rishi). (See 'Budgâm.')

According to another version, Sheikh Noor ud Din Wali had gone to Kishtwâr to proselytise. Zia Singh suffered from a disease that the doctors were not able to treat. The Sheikh cured him miraculously. Zia became the Sheikh's disciple and accepted Islâm. Though his formal name was Zain ud Din, his followers knew him as the Bab.

In those days Aish Muqâm was said to be a place where the devil lived. In any case, it was full of snakes, which would terrorise the local people.

When the Bab went to Aishmuqâm the snakes all ran away and the demon, too, vanished. Instead, a fresh- water spring emerged from the ground. A wave of joy ran through the countryside, and people began to settle at Aish Muqâm. The village became a place of pilgrimage. To this day the *Urs* of the Bab is celebrated as the victory of good over evil.

THE 'ZOOL' FESTIVAL: This is a one- week festival held at Aishmuqâm (near Pahalgâm), on the annual *urs* of Sheikh (Bab) Zain ud Din Wali. It takes place in April, to celebrate the end of the winter and the beginning of the sowing season. This is the most picturesque local festival of Kashmîr, and also one of the most popular. It takes place in the evening when it is still quite cold and the days are still short. Because it normally rains on this auspicious occasion it is likely to be colder and darker still. In 2001 I got the Tourism Department to sponsor part of this unique festival.

The several relics housed in the shrine are displayed before the public. This signals the beginning of the festival.

Torchlight procession: The highlight of the festival is a torchlight procession in the evening. By six in the evening children start lighting *léshî* torches. These are made of a local wood. Strips of leshi, about six to eight inches long and an inch wide, are tied around the top end of a straight wooden staff. It is slightly longer than an Olympic torch, but much thicker than a walking stick. Besides, it is tubular, like a thick rod, and not conical. Children's torches are thick, but rarely longer than 15".

As soon as a lit match is applied to these leshi strips, they catch fire. 'Like petrol does,' someone remarked. Once lit, even rain can't douse this flame. Indeed, rain is considered a good omen on the evening of the zool. It rains heavily, though only for a few minutes, in most years. This brings the temperature down considerably: and Kashmîr can be quite cold in early April.

The other quality this flame is said to have is that it does not burn clothes. I don't see how, because a flame is a flame. But highly educated people vouched for this.

237 steps and some seventy landings (most of them redone in expensive devri stone by the Tourism Department during my tenure) lead from the car park to the shrine. Around dusk people start climbing up these steps, normally single file, in small processions. Each procession consists of one group of friends and/ or relatives. The intervals between processions are irregular. Sometimes, when attendance is at its peak, there are so many processions that they merge into one, long row of torches.

Entranced youths: The processions end at the uppermost landing. There you might find a dozen or so youths, all in a mystic trance (*hâl*), jumping up and down, shouting Islâmic- and shrine- specific slogans. The slogans are wholesome and offend no sect. After a while these youths run towards the not- very- large courtyard outside the shrine. A few thousand people, all charged with devotion, some of them also jumping about in a trance, would already be assembled there.

Ten or fifteen minutes later, another group of similarly entranced youths might rush into the courtyard, alsojumping up and down, leaping about and running fast at the same time. They all jump a few feet above the ground.

By now one of the previous groups, equally frenzied, would have left. After a while yet another group comes up, running. The chain continues for more than an hour.

This spiritually- charged atmosphere is called *phrow* (rhymes with 'flow'). This is a Kashmîrî word used exclusively for Aish Muqaam.

The progression of the evening: After a while, *bhânds*, the traditional minstrels of Kashmîr, walk in, wearing elegant green clothes and green caps.

By 6:30pm. smoke from torches placed of the middle- level begins to rise. There would be around twenty unlit torches in the courtyard. Around 7pm, just before the *namaz* of the *maghrib*, these are straightened and lit.

By 7:30 the courtyard empties out. People extinguish their torches and leave. But before they do they create a bonfire. After a while, the *namaz* having been performed, other people start coming in.

The multitudes: There are a number of buildings around the shrine. A few thousand more people watch the festivity in the courtyard from the windows and from atop the roofs of these buildings. In all there were more than ten thousand such devotees on the evening of the zool of 2001.

Around 60,000 people are said to visit the shrine during the course of the day of the zool. The biggest crowds come the next day. The elders sing hymns on the night before *zool*. In most Islâmic lands this is known as *shab khwâni*. This whole series of religion and festivity lasts around five or six days.

As in all lands and with all religious groups, children see it more as a festival, with lights everywhere, as in the Hindus' *Diwali*.

Layout: The architecture and layout of the Aish Muqâm shrine and the surrounding houses is closer to that of a *gompa* (monastery)- complex in Ladâkh than any other group of buildings in Kashmîr. There are fascinating eavesboards made of logs sliced into two.

The surrounding valleys: Gujjar tribals live in the hills and valleys around the shrine. Those who can't make it to the *zool* place lit torches outside their doors. At night this can be a nice sight, except that the torches are much too thinly scattered. There'll be one torch one one hillock, and the next torch might be half a kilometre away. Wood is getting expensive- and difficult to obtain. Therefore, every year the number of torches is a little less than the year before.

THE ROD/ STAFF OF MOSES/ JESUS

Several histories of Kashmîr claim that Lord Jesus' Rod or Staff was once stored in Srinagar's Khânqâh i Mo'ulla. Some believe that the rod was later taken by disciples of the Shâh é Hamadân to Hazara (now in Pâkistân). Aziz Kashmîri, an expert on the 'Christ in Kashmîr' theory, says that it was taken to Aish Muqâm instead.

The keepers of the shrine told Mr. Kashmîri that what they had was the Rod of *Moses* and that it had indeed been brought there from Srinagar's Khânqâh i Mu'allâ. They said that Mîr Syed Ali Hamadâni had gifted the rod to Sheikh Noor ud Din Wali, who gave it to his disciple, the Bab.

Who knows, perhaps at some stage the rod had been with Lord Jesus, too, because Christ is believed to have visited the cave at Aish Muqâm. In fact, some scholars argue that the 'Aish' in the name of the shrine is derived from 'Isa,' the Eastern name for Jesus. ('Isa,' also spelt and prnounced 'Eesa,' sounds eerily like 'Eesh', the Hindu word for God.) Muqâm means 'place'. So the whole name could mean 'the place of Jesus'.

Kashmîri quotes the mediæval *Rishi Nama* as saying that 'during the time of Prophet Isa' a demon used to live in the cave. A wrestler called Buma Sen killed the demon. The name Buma Sen indicates that this must have been in the first millenium after Christ.

The rod is almost 8 feet long and is covered with a green cloth. Aziz Kashmîri writes, 'It is a sacred rod, which should be honoured and touched by the eyes'. Whenever an epidemic or natural disaster strikes the people of the area, they take the Rod to the Idgah. It is said that the calamity then disappears.

Architecture: This an exceptionally picturesque shrine, especially because of the way it sits atop a low hillock just above the road to Pahalgâm. As at Srinagar's Khânqâh i Mu'allâ, there are features in the woodwork of this shrine that remind you strongly of Ladâkhi gompâs.

Islâmic monuments built or renovated in Kashmîr after the 1970s have mostly been made of brick and cement, Till the year 2000, Aish Muqâm was one of the few shrines left the architecture of which was purely Kashmîri. Some renovations made inside the cave in 2001 have used non-Kashmîri building materials.

There is some fine latticework *(pinjra-kâri)* at the shrine, as well as colourful panels. Right opposite the entrance to the shrine there is a longish verandah with a roof but no walls. (This is also the pattern at some other shrines, notably Makhdoom Sâheb in Srinagar.) You can see the Lidder river and the surrounding countryside from this open verandah. Families bring along cauldrons full of food. They picnic on this verandah before or after paying homage inside the cave shrine.

There are two other well-known shrines on the road to Pahalgâm, Bam Zoo and Seer Hamadân.

Bam Zoo (bam rhymes with 'gum'): In Urdu it is spelt and pronounced Bom Zoo, the 'Bom' rhyming with 'home'. (It is also spelt Bum Zu, Bhum Ju, Bumazuv and Bhaumajo.) This, the shrine of Hazrat Bâm ud Din, is on the main road itself, also on the right as we drive up from Ânañtnâg to Pahalgâm. You just have to climb a few steps from the main road to enter this very old building.

Hindu sadhus going to Srî Amarnâth jî would often camp here during the Amarnâth Yâtrâ. Bakaya writes, '[The Bumazuv] temple, [was] known in ancient times as Bhimkesava, [and was] erected by Bhima Shahi, during the time of Khsemagupta [sic; Kshemagupta is meant] (950-58 A.D.). It is now converted into a Mohammadan [sic] 'Ziyârat' and covered inside and outside with a thick coat of mud plaster. It is supposed to be the resting place of Bâbâ Bamudin and is a place of pilgrimage for Muslims. Local tradition records that the saint, before his conversion, was a Hindu ascetic. Close to this temple there is a small cave in a cliff, containing a well preserved stone temple. There is another small cella closeby which also has been converted into a tomb.'

Bam Zoo, too, is a cellar of sorts, a kind of an artificial cave, its ceiling not high enough for tall people at places, and just high enough at others.

Several historians rate Bam Zoo among the four oldest monuments in Kashmîr. The *Gazetteer* notes, 'The cave- temple stands at the far end of a natural but artificially enlarged fissure in the limestone cliff. The entrance to the cavern… is carved into an architectural doorway, and a gloomy passage, 50 feet in length, leads from it to the door of the temple.'

Bîjbehârâ Apart from its physical charms, this small town is home to several temples, around a dozen mosques and almost as many *ziyârats* (Muslim shrines). The most famous ziyârat is that of Bâbâ Nasîb ud Din Ghâzî, built on a bank of the Jehlum, near the Jâmâ Masjid. Both are in the heart of the town. (Lal Ded is said to have died just outside the courtyard of the Jâmâ Masjid, where there is a grave that is said to be hers.)

The shrine and urs of Bâbâ Nasîb ud Din Ghâzî:

The saint: Baba Nasib ud Din was a followerof the Shâh i Hamadân. He was what, in Islâmic lore, is called a *mast qalander*: a saint oblivious to the world around him, and lost in a mystic trance, in communion with God.

The Baba was known for his self- denial. He was a strict vegetarian and did not ever eat any animal flesh. He got 1200 mosques constructed in different parts of Kashmîr, in addition to bathrooms and sarais. Also wrote fourteen books on religion. The Baba spent all his life serving the poor. Therefore, the people would call him Abul Fuqrâ ('the father of the needy').

He would gather a group of disciples and go to a village. There he would preach the message of Islâm. His style was simple and appealed to the heart. The people would go into a state of mystic frenzy (*hâl*). The Ghâzî would then persuade them to construct a mosque. The charged crowd would, in that state, start building a mosque. By the evening the basic structure would be ready. The fundamentalists consider such methods unIslâmic.

The Baba died on the 13th Muharram 1047 Hijri (AD 1637).

Dhambâlî: There is a famous festival at this important shrine in June. The festival is held when the paddy crop is transplanted and is often called the dhamâl (or dhambâlî) festival. The word is drawn from an archaic Persian word for 'mystic trance' or 'to run after.' Bhâñds (folk singers and actors) go from house to house enacting satires and beating drums. According to the local calendar, the festival is celebrated on the 13th of Har. It is Bîjbehârâ's most important festival. In 2001 I got the Tourism Department to adopt and promote the festival.

The singers and actors (*ma'it*) do not perform for money alone. Their goals are spiritual. They chant a *duâ* (blessing/ prayer), 'O God, please protect the people of this village/ house. Keep them free of disease.' At this stage the others present chant 'Âmeen' ('may it be so'). The performers then rub their hands on a large drum. After that they rub their hands on the faces of children. It is said that God would accept their prayer.

Officially, *dhambâlî* is a two- day 'festival.' In practice, till the 1960s and '70s it would last for fifteen days. Modern people are pressed for time and can't afford long festivals. Some of them don't even believe in mysticism. Mr. Justice Mir says that those who find bliss during *dhambâlî* tell the unbelievers, 'The dhambâlî recharges my batteries for fifteen days. What's your problem?'

Ka'abamarg: A medium- sized shrine here plays host to the *moo é pâk* (the holy hair). This is one of three hairs from the beard of Prophet Muhammad, peace be on him, enshrined in Kashmîr. The other two are in Srinagar and Shopiâñ. The present shrine was built in 2001 in the unfortunate Gothic tradition mistaken in post 1970 Kashmîr as Islâmic.

Travel 8km. from Ânañtnâg/ Islâmabad town on the Vérînâg road till you come to Larkipora. Turn right here. The shrine is a kilometre ahead, close to the main road.

Kulgâm: This picturesque town is on the southern side of a table- land. There are two major ziyârats, the bigger and older one being that of Syed Hussain Samnani and the smaller one dedicated to the Shâh é Hamadân.

Syed Hussain was one of the first three Syeds who migrated from Iraq to Kashmîr because of the persecution of the Syeds by Amir Timur, 'the Lame.' He was an eminent scholar and saint. The Syed died on the 11th day of Shaban in 792 Hijri (AD 1389) His *urs* is held on the 13th day of Katik near his shrine. A major fair is organised on the occasion. Thousands of people come from the neighbouring areas.

Seer Hamadân: The shrine is on the left while going to Pahalgâm. You take the side road on the left and drive around a kilometre into the village till you come to this very colourful shrine in a large open area deep inside the village.

Baramulla, Bandipora

Bâbâ Réshî, near Gulmarg: *The shrine:* An 1890 description of this famous and powerful shrine reads thus: 'Bapumreshi [is] the name vulgarly applied to the shrine of Bâbâ Paiyam ud din…[which] is prettily situated on a grassy slope, surrounded by a forest… Around the shrine is a cluster of buildings, built of timber, the lintels and door- posts of which are embellished with some elegant carvings.'

Timber? Elegant carvings? The author of the above passage (taken from the *Gazetteer*) would be hard put to recognise the place today, for he had gone on to add: 'Slips of papercontaining prayers, vows, and notifications of pilgrimages made to the shrine by important persoanges, are pasted on the entrance, and an inscription affixed to the carved doorway states that it was added (in the year 1849 A.D.) by Subbur Réshî, the [then] khalifa or superior of brotherhood… Among the pilgrims are many Hindus…There is a small wooden pavilion for the accommodation of European visitors.'

The cluster of buildings has grown, at the expense of the said grassy slope. These include hostels, some of them built by the Tourism department during my tenure. I do not accept responsibility for the cement architecture, though. All pilgrims are given free board and lodging.

There hasn't been a pavilion for Europeans (or, indeed, for any foreign devotees) in several decades. The only thing that hasn't changed is the number of Hindu (Kashmîri Pandit, as well as Punjâbi) and Sikh pilgrims. The shrine itself, and thus the carved doorway and inscriptions, has got burnt (accidentally) several times. The most recent martyrdom of the shrine was in 1989. A serious and respected Srinagar newspaper had then interpreted this as a sign that several years of misery would follow, as had happened each time this much loved shrine was gutted.

A fairly acceptable wooden building came up shortly after the 1989 burning and I even persuaded myself to like it. However, in the mid-1990s the wooden structure was pulled down and a 'modern' brick- and-plaster structure came up in its place.

The order: By tradition, forty reshis (saints), committed to a life of celibacy, have been attached to the Bâbâ Réshî shrine. They join as novices at a very young age and they first serve as shepherds or in menial jobs. (In the Indo- Persian tradition children are trained in specialised fields like music, painting, wrestling and mysticism not at schools but by personal tutors, known as Gurûs or ustads. For the first year or two all that the children are allowed to do are menial tasks such as carrying the master's shoes- and soaking in the atmosphere.) There is a formal hierarchy of ranks among the reshis. As and when a vacancy occurs in their ranks it is filled by selecting from among the novices. If any of the brotherhood deviates from the binding of celibacy, he is expelled from the community, which is guided by visions and dreams.

Till the early twentieth century, revenues from the neighbouring villages of Tsont Patthar, Al Patthar and Nambal Nar would be earmarked for the maintenance of the shrine. On its part, the reshis of the shrine would look after the food and other essential needs of all poor travellers.

The answering of prayers: Offerings made at this and other shrines normally consist of money, jewellery or other valuables. However, devotees who go to Bâbâ Réshî to ask for particular boons are required by tradition to sacrifice a sheep and give the priest its right leg, head and skin, keeping the rest for themselves.

The Baba used to cook on an earthen stove, which is still intact. Childless women smear a layer of fresh mud on the stove in the hope that a child will then be born to them. The keepers of the shrine gift some of this extra mud to devotees who, they feel, need special blessings. That way the stove, too, retains its original size.

The saint: Bâbâ Payam ud din (d. AD 1475) was a disciple of Bab Zain ud din Wali aka Zaina Shâh (of Aish Muqâm fame).

The Baba belonged to a village called Chhañd-nau (Tshondan), which is near Zakûra (a suburb of Srinagar, just outside the town on the way to Sonamarg- Ladâkh). He was born to a wealthy family. Before he took to religion, the Bâbâ was a leading noble, a vizier of the rank of Governor of a province.

One day, during a hunt he saw a long row of ants, each with a grain in its mouth. He got off his horse and kept staring at the ants till the sun set. The Baba then said, 'These ants are working so hard to stock up for the winter. On the other hand we do not stock up for the next world.' Saying this he renounced the material world. For a while he became a disciple of Hazrat Sheikh Zain ud Dîn.

The Baba soon became famous for his spirituality. He then sought permission to meditate on the Ranboh (Ranbuah) hill (in parganâ Bâñgal), hidden from the rest of the world. Khwaja Âzam Dedmari wrote (around AD 1747) that this was where the Dévs[4] used to live. The Baba went to the hill and in a loud voice read the call (*âzân*) for prayers (*namâz*). Dedmari says that the Dévs could not 'compete with' this call. They accepted defeat and converted to Islâm.

Hassan, the 19th century historian, says that ghosts used to live in Ranboh. They told the Baba that they would not leave Ranboh unless Allah ordered them to do so. So, Baba Payâm ud Din prayed to God. A strange sheet of paper then descended from the skies. The ghosts read what was written on that sheet and, without further ado, left Ranboh.

Mian Basheer, the eminent Gujjar leader and religious scholar, told me that Bâbâ Réshî had married and even had a young son. Once a man came up to the saint and said that the Bâbâ's son had misbehaved with his, the complainant's, daughter. The saint knew that this was true. So, the Bâbâ prayed to God that if the allegation was true, his son should die. And that is what happened. (Hazrat Fariduddin of Kishtwar had a similar fate.) Dedmari does not mention this incident or even say whether the Baba had ever married.

Bâbâ Réshî spent the rest of his life on that isolated hill, where, in 889 Hijri (AD 1475), he died.

The annual urs: These are celebrated in Poh (December). Attendances are very large. On this occasion people ask for special boons. They vow to make particular offerings if their prayers are answered.

Bâbâ Shakur ud din Sâheb at Watlab: This is a picturesque village to the north of the Wular lake and south of the Shakur ud din hill, which can be climbed from the village. The hill takes its name from the famous saint Bâbâ Shakur ud din Sâheb, whose tomb is located close to its top. From the shrine you will get an excellent view of the Wular Lake and the Haramukh range.

Bârâmullâ town: *Shrine of Syed Jâñbâz Wali:* Syed Muhammad Rifayc alias Syed Yousuf, a great saint and scholar, migrated to Kashmîr from the Middle East, probably Ispahân. Jâñbâz means 'dare- devil' or, literally, 'a person who plays with his own life.' Wali, of course, means saint. The Syed came to be called Jâñbâz Wali because his spiritual practices involved enormous hardship and self- denial. This won him the respect of the people.

The saint was buried at this shrine, which has been built close to the left bank of the Jhelum. Every year, on the death anniversary of the Saint, people from the neighbouring areas gather at the shrine to seek the blessings of the Saint. A community kitchen is established for the occasion. Some of the rice is cooked in a large copper cauldron, which is as old as the shrine itself. It can hold two maunds of rice at a time.

The entrance of the shrine is brightly coloured in the style that prevailed till the 1950s. The courtyard has graves, many of them covered with slabs of slate, known throughout Kashmîr as 'Bârâmullâ stone.' The shrine itself is green and in the traditional style. One of its highlights is a rectangular 'yoni' made of devri stone (expensive granite). This is an integral part of all Shiv temples. Its presence in the shrine of a Central Asian Muslim saint speaks volumes about those syncretic times and this great shrine.

The Khânqâh of **Sopore**: Sultan Sikander, King of Kashmîr (15th century AD) built this shrine/ mosque. In this he was inspired by Mir Syed Muhammad Hamadani. In AD 1,884 there was a major earthquake in north Kashmir, because of which theshrine was destroyed. However, it was built again and augmented over the years. There are congregational prayers every Friday and on Muslim festivals. However, on the sixth day of the Hijri month of Zilhaj there is a major gathering to observe the death anniversary of Shâh i Hamadan, who was the father of the Mir and one of the greatest Muslim saints to have visited Kashmîr.

Sumbal: (Roughly 30km. north of Srinagar; 5km. from Shadipore.) The shrine of *Syed Hilal Naqshbandi* is in Sumbal, close to Manasbal lake. Syed Hilal was a mystic of the Naqshbandi order. He was not an ethnic- Kashmîrî. However, it is not clear where he came here from. The Syed is entombed here. His piety and scholarshp won him a large following. The urs of the Saint falls on the 15th day of the second lunar month (Safar). It is a major event in the Sumbal- Manasbal area.

The tomb of Ahmed Sâheb on the left bank of the Jehlum is one of the town's main attractions. A narrow channel links Lake Manasbal and the Jehlum here.

The other well-known Muslim shrines of Baramulla-Bandipora are:

Aasâr Sharief at Khwaja Sâheb, Bârâmullâ

Bâbâ Jangi at Shilwat, Sonawari

Bâbâ Usman Ghani's ziyârat at Jahama, Bârâmullâ

Dastgîr Sâheb at Plan, Bâñdîpore

Dastgîr Sâheb at Qazi Hamam, Bârâmullâ

Hazrat Mîr Syed Ali Hamadâni, Khankah e Moula, Sopore

Hazrat Sultan ul Arifeen's ziyârat at Aham Sharief, Bâñdîpore

Hazrat Sultan ul Arifeen's ziyârat at Ramporâ, Bâñdîpore

Hazrat Sultan ul Arifeen's ziyârat at Tujar, Sopore

Hazrat Syed Ahmed ud Din Sâheb at Bulgam, Bârâmullâ

Hazrat Syed Sâheb at Kreeri

Imam Bara at Mohalla Sona Buran, Inderkote, Sonawari

Karim Shâh Sâheb at the Qadeem Idgah, Bârâmullâ

Khwaja Hilal Naqshband Sâheb at Nsasbal, Sonawari

Khwaja Rahim Sâheb at Chewa, Sonawari

Sofi Satar Sâheb's ziyârat at Chakla, Rafiabad

Syed Ghareeb Sâheb at Gund Nowgam, Sonawari

Syed Hazrat Sultan's ziyârat at Kanisporâ

Syed Jâñbâz Wali at Khanporâ, Bârâmullâ

Syed Kirmani in Bârâmullâ

Syed Malik Bukhari Sâheb at Nadihal, Bârâmullâ

Syed Muhammad Dâniyâl at Talarzoo, Sonawari

Syed Sâheb at Naid Khai, Sonawari

Budgam

Chrâr é Sharief (Correctly Tsrâr é Sharief. 28 km. south- west of Srinagar on the road to Yusmarg.) The tomb of *Sheikh Noor ud Din Rishi* at Tsrar e Sharief is, without doubt, the most popular, the most revered Kashmîri Muslim shrine in the Valley. Hindus and Muslims alike accept him as the patron saint of Kashmîr.

There is a mosque next to the shrine. It was built by Sangram Dar, a disciple of the Sheikh. Sangram was the owner of the land on which both the shrine and the mosque now stand. Every Friday afternoon the Sheikh, also known as the Alamdâr (flag- bearer) of Kashmîr, would offer prayers at this mosque.

There are many legends about the Sheikh ul Âlam's out of body experiences, powers that are said to have continued after his death as well. The Sheikh died, in 1438, at some distance from the mosque. So his body, wrapped in a shroud, flew to an open space next to the mosque, where he was subsequently buried. (The other graves in the shrine are those of the Sheikh's disciples, including the renowned Bâbâ Nasr ud Din.)

King Zain ul Abedin (1420- 70), better known as Budshah, came over from Srinagar to attend the Sheikh's funeral. He got a shrine built over the grave. Being made of wood, the Chrar e Sharief shrine, like almost all major Kashmîri Muslim shrines, got burnt several times over the centuries. Its oldest recorded gutting was in the 1580s, following which Yaqoob Chak, the last independent king of Kashmîr, got it repaired. That a king who happened to be Shia got repaired a shrine dedicated to a Sunni saint is further proof that sectarian histories are wrong.

Then in the early 19th century almost the entire town got burnt. Ata Muhammad Khân, the Afghân governor of Kashmîr, got the shrine reconstructed. (He probably added the adjoining mosque.) The Prime Minister of Jammu and Kashmîr, Bakshi Ghulam Mohammad, got several cosmetic changes effected around the shrine in the 1950s.

In the winter of 1994- 95 some Pâkistâni mercenaries, led by one Mast Gul, a Pâkistâni national, came over to Kashmîr to terrorise the local people and wreak havoc in the state. They set up camp inside the holy shrine of Chrar e Sharief, confident that the Government of India would not be so insensitive as to send the Army or even the police inside a house of worship. They were right in their assessment.

The Indian Army surrounded the shrine instead. The siege lasted several weeks in the summer of 1995, at the end of which Mast Gul and party simply set the wooden shrine on fire. The government sent in fire tenders. Mast Gul climbed into the empty tank of one of these fire- engines after all its water had been squirted out, and escaped.

Work on the construction of the present shrine building began in 1997. It is quite different from its precursor which 'was a large oblong building with a wing at either end. The plinth [was] of brick masonry and the upper structure [was] of hewn logs placed traversely, log on log. The roof [rose] in tiers and [was] supported on pillars.' (Bakaya)

Sheikh Noor ud Din Rishi/ Wali

Also known as Nund Rishi, the Sheikh ul Âlam is arguably the most respected Muslim saint of Kashmîri origin. He was born on the occasion of Eid ul Zuha in AD 1377 in Kaimoh (once known as Katimusha), near Bijbehara, in the Kulgâm area. His parents were Sheikh Salar ud Din and Sadra Moji. (The tombs of his mother Sadra, son Haidar, daughter Zoon Ded and wife Zai Ded are all at Kaimoh, where his father's turban is still on display. Sadra Moji was born a Hindu Rajput and was a widow with two children at the time of her marriage with Sheikh Salar. Yasman Rishi had converted her to Islâm.)

This 14th century seer is also considered the founder of the 'rishî' order. (See also the section on 'The Rishis' in the chapter on 'Islâm in Kashmîr'è') The Sheikh was a second generation Muslim. His father, who was from the royal family of Kishtwar, converted to Islâm under the influence of either the eminent seer Syed Hussain Simnani or Yasman Rishi.

Sheikh Noor ud Din was inspired by the teachings of Lal Dedè (aka Lallâ Ârifâ), on whose milk he is said to have been reared. (He refused to drink his own mother's milk as a baby.) The Sheikh took to religion at a very early age, observing the austerities of Islâm and going from one end of Kashmîr to the other to disseminate its teachings. He entered a still extant, 10- foot deep, cave near Kaimoh and meditated there for twelve years. Such acts won him an enormous following during his own lifetime.

This following was (and remains) totally non- partisan. It consisted of Muslims as well as Hindus, royalty as well as the poor, Sunnis as well as Shias. All Kashmîri kings vied to be a part of the Sheikh's legacy. Even rulers from outside, like the Afghân Governor Ata Muhammad Khân, were not immune. Almost five centuries after the Sheikh's death Ata struck coins in his name.

Sheikh Hamzâ Makhdoom would always walk barefoot to the shrine at Chrar e Sharief: the ultimate mark of humility in a devotee and of respect for the master. (The shrine of Makhdoom Sâheb, the 16th century divine, has almost the same status in Srinagar City as Sheikh Noor ud Din's does in rural Kashmîr.)

The Sheikh was a prolific poet and one of the three major pillars of the first phase of Kashmîri poetry. (Shiti Kantha and Lal Ded were the other two.) His sayings are didactic in nature and were collected, two centuries after his death, by Bâbâ Naseeb ud Din Ghâzî in the *Nur Nama*.

According to a publication of the Govt. of J&K, the 'Sheikh's poetry, commonly believed to be the Quran in Kashmîri verse, is popular among the locals. His poetry revolves round [sic] the oneness of God, [the] temporâry status of the world and underscor[es] the importance of good deeds.'

Annual urs: The Sheikh died on the 26th day of Ramzân. According to the Kashmîri calender this was the month of Poh (December). Therefore, his *urs* is observed in Poh and is one of the most popular urses in Kashmîr.

Other shrines

The **Budgâm Imâmbârâ :** Aga Syed Mehdi was, as mentioned above, a major spiritual leader of the Shias (Shiites) around the middle of the 19th century. He used to pray under a chinar. On his death another famous

Shia guide, Aga Syed Mohammad, got the present imambara constructed, in 1857, near the chinar. Its interiors were designed by Asghar Ali of nearby Mirgund. The exteriors are Indo- Iranian. The imambara was enlarged in 1924 on the orders of Aga Syed Sâheb and panels of *papier mache*, a French craft that has struck roots among the Shias of Iran and Budgâm, were added. In 1955 Aga Syed Yusuf Al Mousavi Al Safvi got the imambara augmented further through the Anjuman e Shari Shian organisation. He also got a mosque constructed next door.

Today the imambara is octagonal and has five grand doors, each twelve feet wide. Of these, one door is earmarked exclusively for women.

Hamchaporâ- the Alamdar e Kashmîr ziyârat: The Alamdar of Kashmîr, Sheikh Noor ud Din Wali/ Rishi, travelled extensively trough the land, to meditate but also to spread his message. On entering the Khag region he chose a rock to meditate on, and left his footprints on it. The rock came to be called Shâh Kean (the king of stones). A lady spiritualist, Sham Ded sought the Sheikh out at Poshkar for religious instruction, which she received and which helped her become one of the major saints of Kashmîr. The present ziyârat (shrine) marks the place where the Sheikh ul Âlam lived during his longish stay in Hamchaporâ.

Kanihama- Hazrat Syed Zia ud Din Bukhari's tomb: One of the major events in the history of Kashmîr is the migration of 360 Syeds from Bukhara (Central Asia), following their persecution there. Syed Zia ud Din chose Kanihama for his mission. Of the many miracles associated with him the best known is about a blind girl whom he asked to bring a *kangri* . (A kangri is a pot made of clay, enclosed in a cane basket, in which embers are kept smouldering. The kangri is kept close to the body in the winters, much like a hot water bottle.) The girl told him that she could not do so because she was blind. So, the Syed put his hand on her eyes and she began to see. The Syed died in Kanihama. His annual *urs* is on the 26th of Rajab of the Hijri calender.

Khân Sâheb- Hazrat Saleh's shrine: This shrine is located in the administrative 'block' called Khân Sâheb, after the shrine. Hazrat Syed Saleh Khân, the saint of the shrine, was born in Pakhla (in present day Pâkistân) in the 16th century. There were omens and signs at the time which told those who could interpret such things that a major saint had been born. As many as 99 saints went to the house of Khân Sâheb's father, Ismail Sâheb, to see Saleh the day he was born.

An uncle wanted to adopt Saleh when he was five. When his requests failed to move Ismail Sâheb, he started resorting to pressure. Things were getting unpleasant, so Ismail Sâheb packed his bags and migrated to Kashmîr, along with his son. En route they met the renowned Central Asian saint, Bu Ali.

In Kashmîr they sought out Bâbâ Naseer ud Din Ghâzî (è), the leading seer of the age, who let them stay with him. Ismail left after a year, but Saleh Sâheb remained with the Bâbâ for the next twelve years as well. Then for another twelve years Saleh Sâheb meditated in a cave, which is still associated with him and is called Khân Sâheb. It was during this phase that legends of his spiritual powers began to spread. He acquired a huge following, which would flock to his cave. For a while he shifted to Srinagar, before moving to the woods to pray and meditate.

Khân Sâheb was an outstanding calligrapher. A copy of the Holy Quran copied by him is still extant and is in the Watal Kadal area of Srinagar. The Syed died on the 17th day of the month of Zeeqad, in the 1019th year of the Islâmic calendar. The annual *urs* of Khân Sâheb is, therefore, held in the month of Zeeqad at his tomb.

Lassaporâ- Syed Mohammad Samri's shrine: The Syed belonged to Shopiâñ, and lived perhaps in the 17th or 18th century. He went to meditate in the forests of Lassaporâ, seven kilometres from Habir, a village in Khag. After some years of such meditation, he died and was buried there. His annual *urs* is celebrated on the 12th day of Phagun (roughly, the 3rd March).

Palaporâ (Poshkar)- Hazrat Gañgâ Bâbâ Rishi's shrine: The rishî migrated from Mârâz to Palaporâ (3 km. from Khag). During his lifetime he got 360 mosques built. He also got an equal number of culverts constructed over streams in the Khag area. In the tradition of that great environmentalist, Sheikh Noor ud Din Rishi, Gañgâ Bâbâ too got thousands of trees planted. At least one of these trees, a poplar, went on to acquire a diameter of 12 metres (40 feet).

Poshkar- Bâbâ Latif ud Din Qazi's tomb: Born Ludo Rainâ in Kishtwar, the Bâbâ came over to Kashmîr looking for a job, a spiritual guide and a cure for some disease that he was suffering from. In the Sheikh ul Âlam he found all three, during the Alamdar's stay in Poshkar. The Sheikh agreed to take Ludo Rainâ as his disciple and Rainâ became Hazrat Bâbâ Latif ud Din Qazi. He followed his mentor's method of meditating on the one hand and serving his fellow men (i.e.. performing what we now call 'social service') on the other.

The Sheikh also taught the Bâbâ how to meditate in a cave. So, the Qazi left Poshkar, never to return. He spent many years, and died, in a cave quite far from Poshkar. The cave and the meadow around it have since been known as Bâbâ Marg (the meadow of the Bâbâ).

The Bâbâ's distraught disciples were unable to reach the then inaccessible cave to collect his body for burial. In death as in life the Bâbâ followed his guide. The Bâbâ's body, wrapped in a shroud, flew from the cave to Poshkar to land where the tomb now is. The Bâbâ's annual *urs* is celebrated not according to the Hijri calendar but according to the local calendar, on the 7th of Phagun (roughly, the 26th February) every year. On the occasion the Bâbâ's sword and some other relics associated with him are displayed.

Poshkar- Sham Ded's tomb in: Sham Ded died and was buried in her own village, where her father had been a blacksmith. 'Ded' (pron.: d-yed) means 'sister' (as in the Hindi 'didi'). 'Sham' means 'the evening'. The saint got her moniker because when her spiritual guide, the Sheikh ul Âlam, died, it was she who carried the news to Bâbâ Latif ud Din Qazi and it was evening when she did so. The Qazi, too, had been a disciple of the Sheikh.

Sikandarporâ, the tombs of the Syeds Taj ud Din and Alla ud Din: Syed Taj ud Din first went to Sukh Nâg to pursue his spiritual mission. After a longish stay there he went from village to village with the goal of reaching Sikandarporâ. Legend has it that the Mala Kol stream followed him silently as he travelled from Sukh Nâg to Sikandarporâ, where he settled down and, later, died. His son Syed Alla ud Din proved a worthy successor. The tombs of both are in Sikandarporâ.

Kupwara

Among Kupwara's better known shrines are:

The Muqâm e Shâh Wali Mazâr e Sharief of **Zati Shâh** in **Muqâm** (also Mugam) village near Drugmullâ. This shrine is 4 km. to the south-east of Kupwara proper. The three- day annual *urs* is observed in May.

Bâbâ Abdullah Ghâzî, who was a disciple of Bâbâ Naseer ud din Ghâzî. His ziyârat is in **Kralporâ Guzrail**, which is some 20 km. north west of Kupwara town.

The ziyârat of Mîr Muhammad Ibrahim is in the Lolâb valley in a village called **Kanthporâ**.

Pulwama, Shopian

Awantipur- Mantaqi Sâheb's ziyârat: Diagonally across the road from the Awantiporâ ruins is the grand ziyârat of Syed Hussain Mantaqi, better known as 'Mantaqi Sâheb.' Most truck, bus and taxi drivers, regardless of religion, bow before the shrine as they drive by. Most of them place some money in the collection box kept on the roadside. Mantaqi Sâheb is believed to be the protector of drivers at the Kashmîr end of the drive, to or from Jammu. Apart from his spiritual qualities, the saint is famous for having married a daughter of Kashmîr's most important and popular king, Zain ul Abedin @ Budshah. Mantaqi Sâheb lived and died in this village. The saint's father had migrated from Central Asia to Kashmîr during the reign of Sultan Sikander (AD 1389- 1413).

Dâdasar: (Dadasar is about 5km. from Trâl.) The shrine of Akber Deen Sâheb at Dadasar is considered one of the better instances of *pinjra-kâri* on wood. This is a medium- sized, rural shine. It has been constructed atop an octagon, a style that was often used in Buddhist shrines. The main structure is in the Iranian style common in Kashmîr. The roof has three sloping tiers, often mistakenly to as the pagoda- style. The octagonal 'steeple' is a very fine example of the Rûm- style spires used in Kashmîr. (Rûm, pron. 'room,' refers to Ottoman Turkey. It literally means 'Roman Turkey.') Tall windows, made in the *pinjra* style of lattice, surround it. Each window has a unique design, different from the other windows. The architect's intention was to showcase in a single monument as many examples of contemporary pinjra kâri as possible.

What fascinates me about the architecture of shrines like this (and Srinagar's Khânqâh e Mu'allâ, and the shrine that got burnt at nearby Tral) is the architraves. These are elaborate doorframes. The doorframes at my house (and perhaps at yours, too) are flat. The architraves of some Kashmiri shrines at are four or five levels, and each level has a different pattern. You might find the colours very bright, but that is part of their charm. The wooden exteriors of this shrine (and the one in neighbouring Drumbal) have been painted green. I prefer the wooden being left unpainted, as at Khânqâh e Mu'allâ. However, this green, too, is what makes this kind of architecture unique.

Akber Deen Sâheb was the father of Zay Ded. In turn, Zay Ded was the wife of Sheikh ul Aalam Sheikh Nur ud Din Réshî.

Drumbal: This village is sometimes called Amîrâbâd, after Hazrat Ameer Kabeer Shâh e Hamadân. It is on the Trâl- Dadasar road and is roughly 3 km. from both. To reach the shrine you have to get off the main road and take a side- road that slopes downwards. Your car will take you to the beginning of this charming village, through which a stream runs. From there you will have to walk around 600 metres to get to the small but pretty shrine dedicated to the Shâh.

It is said that this shrine is a scaled- down version of the much bigger Khânqâh e Faiz Panâh at neighbouring Tral, which burned down in 1997. Even in its own right it is a very fine example of Kashmîri woodwork.

Sheikh Bairzid Shimnagi's ziyârat is located above Payer village, towards the wudar.

Pinjoora- Asar Sharief: 12 km. from Pulwâmâ town, in the director of Shopiâñ. This is easily the most venerable Muslim shrine of Pulwama-Shopian because it houses some relics of Prophet Muhammad, peace be on him, which are displayed on special occasions. It is the only shrine in all South Asia to have relics (in this case, hair) of three of Islâm's most venerable figures. The other two are Hazrat Abû Baqar Siddîq and Dastgîr Sâheb. There is a rectangular pond nearby, the waters of which were considered sacred enough to take home in bottles. It has got polluted considerably since.

Shopiâñ- Jâmâ Masjid: 48 km. from Srinagar, Shopiâñ is an important town in its own right. Its importance increased because of its position as a halt on the Mughal Road. The picturesque Jâmâ Masjid here is believed to have been built during the Mughal period (1586- 1752). The architecture, especially the arches, cornices, windows and doors, is very Saracenic, though.

Trâl- Shâh é Hamadân's shrine: The Khânqâh e Faiz Panâh was originally built by Mîr Syed Muhammad Hamadâni as an ornate wooden shrine, in the centre of a sunny courtyard. It was gutted in a fire in 1997. Dr. Farooq Abdullah gave me the honour of head the reconstruction, even though it was not part of my official work, because he knew of my commitment to the shrines of Kashmir. I was not able to convince the people of Trâl to rebuild the shrine in wood.

Dr. Abdullah's government gave me a carte blanche for the reconstruction—and a very handsome sum of money—when I was the Tourism Commissioner of the state. When I was made Divisional Commissioner of Kashmir the money and powers were shifted to that office. So, clearly I had been involved because of the faith the government had in me as an individual.

I could have forced my views on the people of Tral—that the shrine be constructed in wood, stone and papiér mâchè, the way Kashmir's stunning Islamic monuments had always been fashioned. My view was, and remains, that just because buildings made of wood tend to get burnt periodically we should not substitute that beautiful material with ugly bricks and cement. After every fire we should do what our ancestors have been doing—build the shrine all over again, in wood.

However, the people gently argued against materials that could catch fire again.

As a compromise we went in for grand dimensions: but a stone façade.

If you want to see what the original might have looked like, go over to neighbouring Drumbal, where a smaller version exists.

The original *khânqâh* was also known as the Khânqâh e Âlâ. This alternate name is also a chronogram, which tells us that the shrine had been constructed in 868 Hijri (AD 1469).

Festivals: This shrine has two well- attended annual *urses*. That of Mîr Syed Ali Hamadâni is held on the 6th day of the Hijri month of Zilhaj. His son's *urs* is on the 17th day of Rabi ul Awwal.

Nearby, in **Trâl Pain**, is the ziyârat of **Hazrat Mîr Syed Muhammad Hamadâni,** the renowned son of the Shâh é Hamadân, Mîr Syed Ali Hamadâni. Among the prized possessions of the shrine is a relic of Hazrat Abu Bâqar Siddiq, one of the four righteous Caliphs of Islâm and one of the closest companions of Prophet Muhammad, peace be on him.

Srinagar city

Akhoon Mulla Shâh's Mosque: Now in ruins, the mosque of Akhoon Mulla Shâh, is one of the most beautiful mosques in Kashmîr. It is one of the three stone mosques of the Mughals (the Patther Masjid and the Hassanabad mosque being the other two). Baron Hugel, the 19th century explorer, said that this mosque deserved notice on account of the finely wrought black marble and stone lavished upon it. Its gates were carved out of a single stone "and polished like a mirror; but the wanton love of destruction has torn some out of their places, and others lie perishing on the earth."

It was built by the Mughal crown prince Dara Shikoh for his tutor Akhoon Mulla Shâh in AH 1059 (AD 1649).

Aishan Sâheb: The shrine of Sheikh Yaqub Sarfi, an eminent scholar, poet and sufi saint is on the left bank of River Jehlum, close to the 4th bridge. Sarfi belonged to the Kubrawia sub-sect of sufism, in which he was trained at Khwarizm (Uzbekistan). It is believed that one day Prophet Muhammad, peace be on him, visited the Sheikh in a dream and gave him the title 'Aishan Sâheb' because of his godliness. The Sheikh's annual *urs* is celebrated on the 12th day of the Hijri month of Ziqab. A few thousand people, mainly from the neighbouring localities, attend. They start praying in the evening and continue till midnight. The name of the saint is also pronounced **Asian Sâheb** (or Eshiyan Sâheb). His ziyârat has a niche following, and is known mainly to its devotees.

Aali Masjid: Mîr Syed Muhammad Hamdâni bought a large chunk of land in the north of Srinagar City to create an Idgah (an open ground where Eid prayers are offered and a fair organised). Ali Shâh, the Sultan of Kashmîr, built the Aali Masjid (mosque) on the Idgah in AD 1398. In the 1990s a small part of the Idgah became a martyrs' graveyard. However, in normal times officially this historic Idgah is still used for Eid festivity twice a year. Hundreds of shops and foodstalls spring up on those occasions. On Baqr Eid (Eid ul Zuha/ Azha) thousands of sheep are sold here, for the ritual scarifice.

Historically, these grounds have also been used as pologrounds: Sultan Ali Shâh Chak (16th century) died while playing polo here. Armies have camped here in peacetime, and battles have been fought here during wars.

Batamâloo Sâheb: (Near the Civil Secretariat and Police Headquarters.) 'Bat' means 'rice' (and, at a remove, 'food') in Kashmîri. Sheikh Dawood, the saint after whom the shrine and the locality take their name, is better known as Batamaloo Sâheb. He had something to do with rice. Mâloo means father.

'Batt(a)' is the Kashmîri word for 'Kashmîri Pandit.' This community was much attached to the saint, who had a very large number of Kashmîri Pandit followers. It is possible that Batamaloo means 'the father of the Batt(a)s.' The 't' in 'bat' (rice) is soft. That in 'Batamaloo' and 'Batt(a)' is hard. Therefore, the latter meaning is more likely.

The Sheikh was disciple of Sheikh Hamzâ Makhdoom.

The son of a poor farmer, he was a strict vegetarian, as his followers are required to be on certain days of the year. Legends of his piety and kind heartedness abound. He would wash the hooves of his cattle as also the earth sticking to his ploughshares before either left the fields. This was done to ensure that 'dust from one place was not transferred to another.'

The Sheikh tilled his own lands. Every day he would take a large vessel filled with boiled rice to his fields. There he would serve the rice to everyone who happened to pass by. It is because of this that he is known as Batniaioo or 'father who feeds others with cookeri rice'.

The urs:

This is celebrated in the month of Chet (Chaitra). Attendances are very large. People come from the city as well as the suburbs.

The **Bat Mazâr**, (bat, pron. butt= rice/ food; mazâr= tomb, shrine) is located where the canal enters the Astawhol division of the Dal Lake. It is known as the shrine where rice is eaten. "The boatmen going to, and coming from, the lake often stop there and cook their dinners. It is remarkable in the distance from its single chunar (sic) tree, and commands a good general view of the lake and the mountains around it." (*The Gazetteer.*)

The Bulbul Lankar, is a small and decayed wooden building on the right bank of the Jehlum, about 200 metres below the Ali Kadal. It is said to be the first mosque built in Kashmîr. It contains the ashes of Bulbul Shâh, a saint, who is said to have introduced Islâm to Kashmîr in AD 1320.The fact is that Muslims- and mosques- had existed in Kashmîr for at least five hundred years before Bulbul Shâh. The Lankar is the oldest *extant* Islâmic building in Kashmîr, not the first. (See 'Islâm in Kashmîr'è.) The building we see today is a 20th century reconstruction, effected with little regard for tradition, antiquity or the immense historical and religious importance of the place.

Dastgîr Sâheb: *The saint:* Pîr Dastgîr and Kahnoav are among the many titles that the people gave Sheikh Abdul Qadir Jîlânî. 'Dast' means 'hand.' 'Dastgîr' means 'he who extends his hand [to help people].' 'Kahnoav' means 'he who has many names.' Jîlân is close to Baghdâd in Iraq.

Prophet Muhammad, peace be on him, once ascended to heaven for a brief visit. He rode on a divine horse called Burâq during the journey. This ascension is known as the Merâj Sharief and is as important to Muslims as Moses' vision of the Burning Bush is to Jews. Some Kashmîris believe that during the final lap of this ascension the Holy Prophet rode on the soul of Dastgîr Sâheb- and not on Burâq. The bit about the 'final lap' can not be true because Dastgîr Sâheb was born much after Prophet Muhammad, peace be on him. However, votaries of the belief argue that

Dastgîr Sâheb's soul had always existed in heaven. (Note: The 'final lap' legend has no Qur'ânic sanction.)

The shrine: If you have never seen a Kashmîri mosque or shrine before, you might be intrigued by their Indo- Saracenic architecture. This style typifies many of the older mosques and Muslim- shrines of Srinagar in particular, and Kashmîr in general. The dome, so characteristic of central Indian, Pâkistâni and Persian mosques, is a post- 1950 import into Kashmîr. Before that only the three stone- mosques of the Mughals had domes.

Among the important shrines of Kashmîr, the Khânqâh e Meer Syed Abdul Qadir Jeelani, popularly known as Dastgîr Sâheb, is the most accessible and closest to the tourist circuit. It is located in the Khanyar neighbourhood, which is just over a mile from the Dal Gate.

In the evenings the large windows of Dastgîr Sâheb are opened and one can look inside even from the road. The beautiful khatamband ceilings, the elaborate wood carvings, the grand chandeliers, and other finery are typical of the more affluent shrines of Kashmîr. Many tourists don't even get out of their cars to take in the grandeur of the shrine's interiors.

The relics: The sacred relics of some of the most important figures of international Islâm are kept in this shrine. Its importance owes considerably to these relics.

Dastgîr Sâheb never visited Kashmîr (or, indeed, South Asia). A traveller from Kabul brought one of his hairs to Kashmîr in AD 1802. Sardar Abdullah Khân, the then Governor of Kashmîr, acquired it from him. The Sardar, in turn, gave this relic to a Kashmîrî saint so that it could be periodically shown to devotees.

The urs is observed on the 11th day of of Rabi-ul-Sani, the 4th lunar month of the Hijri calendar. The hair of the saint, enclosed in an elegant vial- and- casket, is taken to the balcony of the shrine. A cleric then holds the relic aloft and shown to the almost one lakh (one hundred thousand) people assembled. This display takes place on the main day of the urs as well as on the first Friday after the urs.

Festivity lasts for a fortnight, beginning on the 1st day of Rabi-ul-Sani. Every morning and evening during this period devotees gather at the shrine and chant religious verses and seek the blessings of Dastgîr Sâheb. Shops and stalls are set up on the entire road between Nowhatta and the Rainâswari crossing.

Because the shrine is right next to the main road, the presence of tens of thousands of devotees at any given moment throws traffic out of gear.

Therefore, vehicles are not allowed to ply on that road for several days and are diverted to an alternative route instead.

Qawwalis (religious songs) are not sung at the shrine. However, it is a recorded fact that the founder of the Qâdiri order of Sufism heard qawwalis being sung and witnessed dervish dances being danced during his lifetime.

Khwaja **Habib Ullah Attar's shrine:** The Khwâjâ was a 17th century mysi ic of the Kubrawia order. He was an ethnic Kashmîrî and belonged to the Gani clan. He came from a wealthy family of traders. He performed several miracles and had a substantial following. Mirza Kâmil Beigh was the most notable of his followers.

Urs: The Khwâjâ's urs is observed at his shrine on the 2nd and 3rd days of Rajab, a Hijri month. Devotees offer prayers on the occasion.

Hasanabad: The Hasanabad Imam Bara, located on the lake, is a Shia mosque, said to have been built during Emperor Akbar's reign. The Gazetteer says,"[It] is one of the three mosques of hewn and polished stone which were erected at Srinagar in the time of the [Mughal -PD] emperors... An interesting cemetery is attached to it, and near it, on the south, is a pretty little wooden mosque recently [late 19th century- PD] built by the Sunis [sic])."

In terms of antiquity the Imâmbârâ of Hassanabad ranks next only to Jadîbal. The tombstones in the cemetery have some of the finest calligraphy in Kashmir—indeed, the Islamic world. Beautifully crafted letters, many in high relief, adorn the graves of the Bâbâ Mazâr cemetery where rest some great poets, litterateurs and other eminent Kashmiris—including Baba Ali, Syed Mirza Shah , Mullah Abdul Ghani and Hab Saheb Mullah.

Hazratbal, is one of the most venerable shrines for the Muslims of Kashmîr. In it is preserved a hair from the beard of Muhammad, the Holy Prophet, often respectfully called 'Hazrat' Muhammad, peace be on him. The shrine has been built on the western bank of Dal lake, about 6 km to the north-east of the centre of Srinagar. It is close to the University campus and the Naseem gardens. It can be reached by boat as well.

The Moo- e- Muqaddas (Holy Hair) was brought from Lahore to Kashmîr by Khwaja Noor- ud- Din 'of Ishber', in 1700, during the reign of Aurangzeb. He had purchased it from one Syed Abdullah of the Deccan. The Syed's ancestors had been the custodians of the shrine of Muhammad, peace be on him, at Medina, till they were forced to flee to

India. (Ishber is a suburb of Srinagar. However, the place the Khwaja belonged to was called *Ishâwar* and is in Central Asia.)

Because of its massive following, and political stature, the Hazratbal shrine is now housed in one of the most impressive twentieth century mosques anywhere in the world –a modern, Indo- Islâmic (rather than Indo- Saracenic) building, constructed in 1967. It is the only shrine of importance in all of Kashmîr that has been built in this modern, pan-Indian style.

The shrine that existed here till 1967 had the four- tiered roof typical of Kashmîri shrines. A particular kind of grass grew on the sloping roofs. The garden around it was named after its first owner, Sadiq Khân.

Festivals: "Five or six fairs are held at the Hazrat Bal in the course of the year; the principal one is on the Mairaj [the Shab e Meraj-PD]...Another great fair, held about the 1st of August, is called the Watul Myla, or fair of the Watuls [char- people; "sweepers"- PD], because that tribe intermarry on that day." (*The Gazetteer.*)

The Moo- e- Muqaddas is exhibited (in the casket in which it has been preserved) on several important occasions every year. These include the Eid ul Milad (Milad un Nabi), the Friday after this Eid, the Shab e Meraj and the anniversaries of the four Righteous Caliphs. This adds up to eight festivals in a year.

As can be imagined, almost all the adults of rural Kashmîr, certainly five or six lakh people (more than half a million), visit Hazratbal to see the holy hair on such occasions. Huge fairs are organised. At the other shrines and temples all the stalls set up for a fair are temporary. However, there is also a permanent market near Hazratbal because the shrine draws huge crowds (of male worshippers) every Friday afternoon as well.

The **Imâmbârâ of Jadîbal**[5] was the first Shiite house of worship to be constructed in the valley of Kashmir. Sultan Mohammad Shah (AD 1517-25) had a Shia minister called Kâji Chak who got this holy but ill-fated shrine built around 1518. It was set on fire and destroyed exactly thirty years later, in 1548, during the administration of Mirza Hyder Dughlat, the then viceroy of Kashmir. Daulat Chak got it built again in 1551. However, just two years had elapsed when, in 1553, it was set alight again, this time allegedly at the behest of one Zafar Kupwari. Its next versions lasted a little longer. The holy place was burnt again in 1635 (when Shah Jahan was the emperor of India), in 1682 (when Aurangzeb Alamgir ruled the country), in 1719 (during the Mukhtawi Khan clash), in

1748, in 1763, on the 24th June 1801 (a day before the Ashura procession, during an era when Kashmir was ruled by Afghan governors), on the 29th July 1830 (when Kashmir was under the Lahore-based empire of Emperor Ranjit Singh), and in September 1872 (when the Dogra Maharaja Ranbir Singh ruled the state).[6]

Hakim Mehdi Ali Khan Kashmiri, a minister in the court of Nasr ud din, the king of Oudh, financed the 1830s reconstruction. Maharaja Ranbir Singh sanctioned Rs. 3,00,000 for the 1870s reconstruction—at a time when a noble's palatial home on a half-acre plot cost less than a tenth of that amount.

The double-storeyed Imamabara was constructed with slim mahârâji bricks.[7] The floor in the centre is at ground level (pokhr), with the floor on the sides raised (ghulam gardish). There is a gallery above. The ground floor has an area of 75 square metres. [8]

Shia histories contain heart-wrenching details of each of the ten or eleven martyrdoms (as they are known in Islam) of the Jadîbal Imâmbârâ. I would only request my Shia brothers to look at how many times the Jama Masjid of Srinagar, Baba Reshi near Gulmarg and Khânqâh e Faiz Panâh at Tral have been burnt and martyred. And often these fires have been accompanied by dark rumours. At Tral, for instance, there were whispers about sects that believe that shrines have no place in pristine Islam.

I last visited the holy Imâmbârâ in 2004 when it was being readied for reconstruction. In a personal capacity I offered the All Jammu & Kashmir Shia Association my services for the architectural design. However, that was when I was transferred out of the state and, therefore, could not associate myself with the reconstruction.

The **Jâmâ Masjid** of Srinagar was first built by Sikander, king of Kashmîr, who spent four years (AD 1398- 1402) constructing it. It was founded at the behest of Mir Syed Muhammad Hamadâni, son of Syed Ali Hamadâni. The father and son dedicated their lives to the propagation of Islâm. Sultan Sikander's son, Kashmîr's most popular king, Zain- ul-Abedin (a.k.a. Budshah) enlarged it. He also added a generously endowed Islâmic school to it.

Most of the present structure was built in 1674-7, as many as three previous incarnations of the mosque having been burnt down by fire. Over the gate is an inscription which says that the mosque was built by the Mughal Emperor Shâh Jehan. However, the mosque has undergone several modifications even since then.

The 1674 fire must not have caused much damage, for this time the repairs (ordered by Shâh Jehan's son, the Emperor Aurangzeb) took only three years, and Shâh Jehan's inscription on stone survived. Aurangzeb, to his credit, ensured that the mosque was restored to Sikandar's original. Hence the mosque we see today strictly adheres to the 14th century plan.

The last king to rebuild some of the mosque was the Dogrâ Mahârâjâ Pratap Singh.

Except the roof, that is. It is now made of tin and not the *burza* bark (bhoj patra) that had adorned it for centuries. To make things worse, the tin has been painted an unIslâmic and unKashmîri red.

The mosque measures around 120 yards by 120 yards. It is thus the 'largest mosque in the Statc. 372 octagonal pillars made of deodar support the roof. All the pillars are seamless and each has been made from the trunk of a single tree. 32 of them are 90' tall and 12' wide.

*Major congregation:*The biggest congregational prayer is on the last Friday of the holy month of Ramzan. There are huge congregations on the two annual Eids as well. There is a colourful, permanent market in front of the mosque that sells clothes, handicrafts and other items of daily use.

The Jâmâ Masjid is in 'downtown' Srinagar, just ahead of Naqshband Sâheb.

Madeen Sâheb: Syed Muhammad Madeen was the Persian Ambassador to Kashmîr during the reign of Sultan Sikander. His tomb in Hawal (north of the mosque) was constructed during Budshah's reign. It once was one of the finest monuments in all Kashmîr. The basic architecture survives. However, the brightly coloured glazed tiles that adorned its interiors are now gone. Such tiles are a Central Asian tradition that I am trying to revive in Kashmîr, so far without success. Today you can find them in very few places in India. however, they can be seen on the exterior of a mosque on Curzon Road, Delhi and on the dome of a tomb near Hazrat Nizamuddin, also Delhi. I believe that the dome of Budshah's mother's tomb had glazed tiles on it.

Iqbal Ahmed writes that the colours used at Madeen Sâheb were mainly yellow, orange, blue, green, red and brown. He adds that the motifs used included 'graceful skulls glowing with floral patterns, sometimes interwoven with heads of animals, human representation and other neutral scenes.'

So how do we know that there were tiles in Madeen Sâheb's tomb? In the second half of the 20th century debris was removed from the tomb's outer chamber. Fragments of some such tiles were found there. They were taken to Srinagar's SPS Museum at Lâl Mandi. As Ahmed notes, there are floral designs on most of these tiles. He adds, 'I was told by the in charge of the gallery that there are [a] few such fragmentary pieces in [the] reserved collection, which when put in order make a picture of [a] turban headed horse rider.'

Madeen Sâheb used to wear a Persian turban of that kind.

(Iqbal Ahmed, 'Lost evidences of glazed tiles,' *Greater Kashmîr,* 26 August, 2001.)

Madni Sâheb: The mosque of Syed Muhammad Madni Sâheb was constructed during the reign of Sultan Zain ul Abedin. Glazed tiles were affixed on all its walls. Fine latticework on stone can still be found in the recesses of some of its walls.

Till the 1940s and '50s, the roofs of most middle- and upper- class homes would be covered with a bark known to Kashmîr as *burza* and to the rest of India as *bhoj patra.* So would the roofs of many mosques, shrines and important public buildings be. Madni Sâheb was one such mosque. Roofs (*pash*) constructed with bark would be called *burza pash.* (The roofs of the pavilions in the Mughal gardens and of some posh shrines are made of wooden shingle, painted an Islâmic green.)

Then in the 1980s and '90s the tin- roof epidemic swept through Kashmîr: town and country, rich and poor. Tin (or CGI- for corrugated iron) is easy to maintain- and inexpensive in the long run. Now, tin reflects light- and heat. It blinds migratory birds, which prefer to bypass places with tin roofs, which now means all of Kashmîr. The Valley is thus depriving itself of bird- droppings and other advantages that birds bring to agriculture and the ecological balance.

In the late 1960s, the Archaeology department of the state undertook a major project to reinforce the roof of this mediæval mosque. They struck a balance between the convenience of tin and the traditional charm of *burza.* They removed the old *burza pash,* replaced it with a tin roof, covered the tin with wooden boards and placed *burza* on the boards. To all appearances it seemed that Madni Sâheb still had a burza too.

Makhdoom Sâheb: The shrine of Sheikh Hamzâ , half- way up the Hari Parbat hillock, is one of the most venerable in Srinagar city. The inner sanctum has exquisite woodwork, embroidered cloth coverings and marble work. The chandeliers are of a mixed quality, though. There are two graves inside, that of Makhdoom Sâheb himself and of Bâbâ Dawood Khaqi.

After dusk, its lights can be seen for miles. They bestow a certain peace and serenity on those who, like this author, believe in such things. Unbelievers will find the same lights charming from a distance, and majestic if they are close to the shrine.

Whenever there is a drought in Kashmîr, devotees take vessels filled with water to the shrine and pray for rainfall. The act is called *muffal.*

The saint: Sheikh Hamzâ Makhdoom (AD 1394- 1476) was a leading mystic of the Soharwardi order. His family were Chandra Vanshi Rajputs before their conversion to Islâm. He met with considerable ideological opposition from the then ruling Chak dynasty. The Chaks exiled him to a village called Beru, some 30km. fuon Srinagar. He spent several years meditating at the Koli e Maran/ Hari Parbat hill.

The shrine: Nawab Inayat Ullali Khân, the Governor of Kashmîr, built the shrine in AD 1713, close to where the saint would meditate. The shrine is half way up a tall hill. Therefore, there are two sets of steps, both made of expensive, chiselled stone, that lead from the Kâthî and Bâchhî Darwâzâ ends, both at the road level, to the shrine.

Festival/ urs: The *urs* of Makhdoom Sâheb is a major event in Srinagar. Shops and stalls spring up everywhere between Khanyar and the shrine. It is a good marketing opportunity for shopkeepers. For rural folk it is a good time to purchase utensils, pottery, and other household goods.

Mirza Kâmil Sâheb's shrine is at the bottom of the Koh é mârâñ/ Hari Parbat hill. His grandfather, Malik Muhammad Khân, was the Mughal Emperor Jehangir's Governor of Kashmîr. As a child Kamil Sâheb was very close to the Mughal Emperors. He was born in the palace of Jehangir's son and successor, Shâh Jehan, who gave him his name. However, his spiritual guide gave him the title Mirza Akmal ud Din. Kâmil Sâheb proved to be an eminent poet, writer and saint.

The urs of the Mirza is observed on the 29th and 30th days of the Hijri month of Zilhaj. The gathering is medium- sized by Kashmîrî standards. It is drawn mainly from the downtown. They recite verses from the Quran Sharief and poems in honour of Prophet Muhammad, peace be on him, and Kamil Sâheb. Some shops are erected for the occasion.

Naqshband Sâheb: The Khânqâh e Muhammad Baha ud din Naqshbandi is an important shrine, located amidst a large garden. It is on the road between Dastgîr Sâheb and the Jama Masjid. The shrine is, thus, very close to all the important tourist attractions of the City. Part of its compound was converted into the Martyrs' Graveyard in 1931.

This mainly wooden shrine has some fine panels done in the pinjra-kâri style. Other parts are good example of Kashmîrî woodwork.

The saint: Syed Baha ud Din Naqshband was a leading mystic of Bukhara (Uzbekistan). He founded the order of sufi mystics that bears his name. There are only four such orders in the world. In this respect he was one of the half- dozen most influential sufis of all times.

Kashmîr and Afghânistan are the two major fortresses of this order. Adherents of the order are, to a lesser extent, also to be found in Iran, Pâkistân and other parts of India.

Naqshband Sâheb never visited Kashmîr. However, one of his descendants Khwaja Moin ud Din did, and is buried close to the main shrine.

Festival: The *urs* of the Naqshband Sâheb is observed on the 3rd day of the Hijri month of Rabi ul Awwal. This was the date on which he died.

People gather in large numbers at the main shrine and in the tomb of Khwaja Moin ud Din on the afternoon of the *urs*. They perform religious rituals and seek the blessings of Naqshband Sâheb.

Naushehra: This is a locality towards the northern end of the city. The shrine of Khwaja Habibullah Naushehri is one of its most important landmarks. The Khwaja was a leading saint, poet and musician of Kashmîr. He was one of the best- known disciples Sheikh Yaqub Sarfi. He belonged to and propagated the Kubrawia mystic order. *Fair:* His death anniversay, on the first third of the Hijri month of Zilbaj, is the occasion for a major fair.

Patther Masjid, the: (pron.: "pat- ther") Also called the No (=new) Masjid. This stone (=patther) mosque (=masjid) has a particularly hoary history. The mosque was built in 1623 by the Mughal Queen Noor Jehân. It was conceived in a manner that gave the impression that it was carved out of a single stone. However, a careless remark by the Queen angered the clergy. Pointing to the jewels on her slippers she is said to have told people that the mosque had cost her treasury "As much as these." The clergy then forbade the use of the mosque as a place of worship.

According to some scholars, the fact that the mosque had been constructed at a woman's behest had been enough to pique the clergy. My theory is that stone is too cold (and alien) a material to be used in a Kashmîri mosque. Therefore this house of worship was doomed from the start. (Muslim shrines in Kashmîr and Baltistan were, till the middle of the twentieth century, almost invariably made of wood. Wood gives a feeling of cosiness in winter, late autumn and early spring.)

While the (Muslim) Afghâns ruled over Kashmîr (1753- 1819) the mosque was mostly used to store grains. This did not offend the local Muslims at all. Briefly (in 1792- 93) during this period an attempt was made by the Afghân Governor Mîr Hazar Khân to get people to pray at the mosque. A famine struck Kashmîr soon after that and the people attributed it to the fact that they had worshipped in an unconsecrated mosque. The building reverted back to being a granary.

The Gazetteer calls it "perhaps the most massive and substantial building in the city" and notes the "total absence of decoration".

Since the late- twentieth century some people have been offering prayers at the mosque. Also called Shahi Masjid is next to Mujahid Manzil near Fateh Kadal.

Shâh é Hamadân, the Khânqâh of : This exquisite shrine on the right bank of River Jehlum, close to the Fateh Kadal bridge, was first built around 1395. It was rebuilt several times thereafter. The present building dates to 1732. It is the oldest extant wooden structure in Srinagar and was once used as a symbol for the city.

Architecture: The Khânqâh [shrine] of the Mu'alla' is the most breathtaking Islâmic shrine in Kashmîr: perhaps in the whole sub- continent. The brightly coloured papier mache, the intricate stone carvings, the coloured khatamband ceilings (khatamband ceilings elsewhere are normally wood-brown or white), the elegant devri (granite) stone base, the minute woodwork and the array of chandeliers distinguish this shrine from all others.

The saint: Mîr Syed Ali belonged to Hamadân, a town in Persia. He visited Kashmîr three times. However, he is not buried in Srinagar. He died in Kafîristân in AD 1384 (which happens to be a particularly auspicious year in the Muslim calender: 786 Hijri). According to one source, he died in Pakhli, in the Hazârâ district of Pâkistân.The shrine in Srinagar was built by the then Sultan around the room where the Shâh's chilla khânâ (place of meditation) used to be. The Sultan was, in all probability, Sikander, though some say it was Sikander's father, Qutb ud din.

I once mentioned that while the other orders of sufi mysticism were well-represented in Jammu and Kashmir, the Chishti order (which dominates India, Pakistan and, to a lesser extent, Bangladesh) has a very tiny presence. Two of the highest ranking Chishti-Nizami saints in South Asia cut me short and insisted that the greatest of all saints who influenced Islam in Kashmir, Shâh é Hamadân, was a Chishti. (He is normally seen as a Kubrawi.)

The Hijra Khâs: The room where the saint would meditate is now called the Hijra Khâs. It is in the north-western corner of the shrine. This room has a very special place in the hearts of most Kashmîrî Muslims. This is partly so because the Shâh is perhaps the most important Muslim saint to have come to Kashmîr from another land.

Some very important Islâmic relics are also on display in this room. The Shâh brought them over to Kashmîr. These include the banner of Propher Muhammad, peace be on him, as well as a thick wooden pole from the Holy Prophet's tent. It is said that whenever the Prophet sat in that tent, he would rest his back on this pole.

Whenever Kashmîr faces a major natural disaster these two relics are taken to the Idgah, which is around three miles away. Thousands of devotees follow the relics. Prayers are then offered at the Idgah. This goes on till dusk. Then the relics are taken back to the Khânqâh, again followed by a large number of devotees.

The compound: See the chapter 'Buddhist monuments and monasteries in Jammu, Kashmir and Ladakh'

Restrictions: Women are not allowed in the graveyard. Neither women nor non- Muslims are allowed into the shrine.

Urs e Khatlân: The Shâh was not the first Muslim saint of Kashmîr. Nor even was he the first to proselytise. However, it was because of his efforts that mass conversions to Islâm took place in Kashmîr. The first *urs* of a Muslim saint to be observed in the Valley was his.

The *urs* of the Shâh occurs on the 6th day of Zilhaj. However, festivities begin on the first day of that month. During the *dhambâli* people go into trances. Attendances are large.

Other major festive occasions at the shrine are the two Eids (Zuha and Fitr) and the Shab e Qadr. Apart from prayers these are also days of great festivity.

Srinagar rural, Ganderbal

Salora (tehsil Ganderbal) (26km. from Srinagar City): *The saint:* Qamar Sâheb, an eminent saint and scholar, was a Syed from Iraq. He migrated to Kashmîr with Mir Muhammad Hamadani. He spent his last days and was buried in Salora (tehsil Ganderbal).

Urs: His *urs* is observed as a major festival in the month of Bhadon (roughly the second Thursday and Friday of August). People travel all the way from Srinagar City, many of them in doongas (traditional houseboats).

This colourful tradition is slowly giving way to more mundane ways. Most people now travel to Salora by bus or car.

Though the festival is held in a village, cityfolk have traditionally attended in very large numbers. Rural people come from all over the Ganderbal and perform at various places near the shrine. Over a hundred thousand people attend the Sonawari tehsils.

On Thursday evening trained singers collective prayers of Friday afternoon. This is also an occasion for feasting. Celebrated cooks, too, hire doongas, where they set up shop. They serve those travelling to and from Salora by boat, as well those camping near the holy shrine.

The festival comes to an end after the Friday prayers.

Wutta, Lâr: This is a village in Ganderbal tehsil. It is famous for the tomb of Shâh Sadiq Qalander. Shâh Sadiq was an eminent Naqshbandi scholar and saint. Qalanders are mystics who walk about and live in a semi- conscious state. They can not respond to the people or the world around them the way that others can. Shâh Sadiq reached this state after several years of meditation. In that altered condition he would do things forbidden in Islâm: he would drink alcohol, smoke opiates and shave off his beard.

In between Shâh Sâheb would go through lucid intervals. During them he would live the Islâmic life. He would take part in Friday prayers, fast during Ramzan and recite the Holy Quran.

Urs: This is a major occasion is celebrated for the villages of Ganderbal tehsil. It takes place on the last day of Ziqad.

Zakûrâ: This is a suburb of Srinagar, just beyond Hazratbal and the University campus, on the road to Sonamarg- Leh. The shrine of Lâl Bâb Shâh, a Muslim mystic, is its main attraction. Once a year an all- night dhambâlî festival is held.

Ladakh region

Kargil

Yogmâ Kharbu: *Muslim shrine:* This is the tomb of Mîr Syed Hussain Shah (16th century AD). He propagated Islam in Kargil a generation or two after Hazrat Mîr Shams ud Dîn Irâqî. The original tomb is still intact- more or less. Every year the people of the surrounding areas recite the

Fâtehâ (a chapter from the Holy Quran) at the tomb. Devotees ask god for special boons. People give money and gifts in charity.

Kartse Khar: *The tomb of Queen Rgyâl Bibi:* Rgyâl was the wife of Thi Sultan. She is buried in a small forest, amidst rose bushes. It is said that her horse, her clothes and some of her other valuables were buried with her. The tomb is close to the palace and across the river.

Syed Mir Hashim: Thî Namgyâl, a Buddhist, was the king of the Suru area in the 16th century. His palace was at Karpo Khar. Thî converted to Islam. So he invited the Syed to come from Kashmir to teach him Islam. The Syed's shrine is nearby, on one of the routes to Drass.

Trespon: Its *Imambara* (Shiite place of worship), built atop a hillock, is an 'awesome fusion of Saracenic and Tibetan influences' in architecture and interior decoration, 'a real treat.' (The quotes are from *The Indian Express*.) Childless couples come here to pray for children in general and sons in particular. It is believed that their prayers are mostly answered. According to *The Times of India*, the Imam Bara was built in the 11th century. (I would put it at around the 16th century.)

Leh

Shey: *Mosque:* Mir Syed Ali Hamadani is said to have built this small mosque in Shey. That would have been around AD 1381. He was a Sunni. And yet most of the Muslims of Shey are Shias. Kachu Sikander Khan's theory is that the mosque was built by the sultans of Kashmir in the fifteenth century around the time that they invaded Ladâkh. He adds that according to a local tradition the Shah of Hamadan had offered prayers in this mosque. The dates of the Shah's travels have been recorded quite accurately. Therefore, either the legend about his having performed the *namaz* here is wrong, or the mosque was built at least in the 14th century.

Leh: *Jamia Masjid:* This large mosque was probably built in AD 1666, following the 1663 agreement between the Mughal Emperor Aurangzeb and Gyâlpo Deldan Namgyâl of Leh. What you see today is a much renovated and changed version, with 'modern' masonry, and little of the original. It is located in what is now the main market of the town. (See also the chapter 'Islam in Leh and Zâñskâr.')

Kachu Sikander Khan's theory is that the construction of the mosque was started during Sengge's reign and completed during Deldan's 'on orders from Emperor Aurangzeb. The emperor had sent over the architectural drawings and design for the msoque.' If Aurangzeb had sent the design then how could Sengge have started construction?

Dera Baba Banda Bahadur

Gurudwara Mata Sundar Kaur Ji

Chapter- 31

The Sikh Shrines of Jammu, Kashmir and Ladakh

Jammu province

Jammu

Bibi Chand Kour was the wife of Kharak Singh, the eldest son of Maharaja Ranjit Singh of Lahore. On the death of her husband and infant child she was first forced to flee to Jammu and then killed by her maid- servant at the behest of Sher Singh, who had staked claim to the Lahore throne. Her late-19th century samadhi is the city's best known Sikh monument.

Important Sikh **gurudwaras** (temples) in the city include the **Sunder Singh** Gurudwara on Gurudwara Road; the Gurudwara Singh Sabha at Nanak Nagar; the Kalgidhar Gurudwara in Rehari; the Singh Sabha Gurudwara at Raghunath Bazaar; the Tali Sahib Gurudwara in Talab Tillo; the Maharani Chand Kaur Gurudwara below the Gumat; and the Digiana gurudwara.

Udhampur-Reasi

Dera Baba Banda Bahadur: This gurudwara is 25 kilometres from Katrâ, off the main road.

Baba Banda Bairâgi is said to have been the most beloved saint-soldier of the Sikh Guru, Gobind Singh ji. During his last days Baba ji came here to meditate by the banks of the Chenâb river. He would say his prayers under a berry tree, near which this grand gurudwara was later built. It is famous for the paintings on its walls. Hindus and Sikhs come from all over North India to worship at this temple. Many combine it with their pilgrimage to Katrâ.

The shrine: It is a fairly grand structure located amidst noiseless woods near the banks of River Chenab. The Baba's spiritual heirs probably built it. Its walls have fine miniature paintings of the Sikh Gurus and Shri Krishn's celebrated Leela (acts). The shrine also has the Baba's 48' tall Nishân Sâhib, crafted out of deodar wood.

There is an old berry tree in the compound. People believe that this is the precise spot where the Baba would meditate. Therefore, the tree is held in reverence.

Festival: The main festival is held on Baisakhi day (normally the 13th April). People come from all over Jammu province and the Punjab to attend.

The saint: Lakshman Das was born in Rajouri around AD 1670. He turned out to be an ace marksman and good with swords, too. His arrows once killed a pregnant doe. He noticed that had she not died, the doe would have given birth to triplets. This started weighing on his conscience. The event changed the course of Lakshman's life. He gave up hunting and decided to seek spitual knowledge instead.

Lakshman's wanderings finally took him to Nanded (Maharashtra). He spent eighteen years there, meditating near the banks of River Godavari. Gobind Singh ji, the Sikh Guru, was moved by Lakshman's piety. He noticed that the saint was a good warrior, too. The Guru took Lakshman under his wings. At some stage Lakshman became a Sikh with the name Baba Banda 'Bairagi.'

A few years later the Guru was killed in Delhi. Many of his followers decided to make the Baba their leader in the fight against the rulers of Delhi. Together they captured Sirhind (Punjab) and most territories between the Yamuna and the Chenab. The Baba's title thus changed from Bairagi (the ascetic) to Bahadur (the brave).

However, the imperial army soon reclaimed the territories that they hand lost. The Baba sought refuge in Thannaur, which is now better known as Dera (the camp of) Baba Banda. Two hundred of his followers and he were later captured and taken to Delhi, where they were executed.

Treks: From here you can trek southwards to Nagrota or northwest to Katra.

The valley of Kashmir

Baramulla, Bandipora

The important Sikh Gurûdwaras are

Chhattî Pâdshâhî Gurûdwârâ at Rajghat, Bârâmullâ; and

Chhattî Pâdshâhî Gurûdwârâ a kilometre short of Urî.

Pulwama, Shopian

There is a Sikh population in Tral and, hence, a gurudwara.

Srinagar city

Chhatti Padshahi

The **Chhatti Padshahi Gurûdwara** of the Gurûdwara Singh Sabha is right next to the Kathi Darwaza, on the way to the University Campus. This Gurûdwara (Sikh temple), the most important in all of Kashmîr, has an imposing modern marble exterior. It is located on the main road that goes to Hazratbal (and Ladâkh). It is also at the bottom of the Hari Parbat/ Koh é mârâñ hill on which Makhdoom Sâheb and the fort are. Entry is from just before the Kathi Darwaza.

On the left of the main hall is the room where the Sixth Gurû of Sikhism, Gurû Hargobind Singh jî, received a cloak from an old Pandit woman who had worn her eyes out weaving the white cloak for him. The Gurû shot an arrow in the ground and water gushed out. He took the water and sprinkled it on her eyes. Her eyesight was miraculously restored. Today there is a well at the spot where the arrow had struck. Its water is sweet and is considered holy.

Annual celebrations: The birth anniversaries of Gurû Nânak Dev jî and Gurû Hargobiñd jî are celebrated on the 28th November and 4th June respectively. Major fairs are organised on these occasions. Scores of shops and foodstalls are set up for the occasion. Thousands of people attend the special prayers held on these two days. All of them are given *karhâ prashâd* (a pudding), as is the Sikh custom. The Granth Sahib is recited for several hours on both occasions. (For '*The story of the Gurûdwara*' see the chapter 'The Sikh Gurûs and Kashmîr.')

Ladakh region

Leh

Patther Sâheb (24.5km from the Leh city centre; 23.3km. from the SNM Hospital.) Guru Nânak Dév ji founded Sikhism. He then started travelling all over South and Central Asia on a series of now- celebrated missionary tours.

During the 2nd Missionary Tour he visited and meditated in Nepal, Tibet, Yarqand and Ladakh. In AD 1517 he set up camp in Nimmu, on the bank of the river. He would meditate at the spot now known as the Taposthân (on the right side on the highway).

A demon used to live on the hill across the road. He would terrorise the local people. When he saw the Guru meditate near the river he decided to kill him. So, he rolled a substantial boulder down the hill, towards the Guru.

The demon saw the boulder hit Guru Nânak Dév ji. He came running down the hill, hoping to find the Guru dead. When he saw that the Guru was alive, the demon knew that he had erred. He begged the Guru to forgive him. The demon then gave up his evil ways, reformed and dedicated the rest of his life to serving humanity.

When the boulder hit the Guru, not only did it come to a halt, the Guru's powerful body left a permanent imprint on the boulder at the place where it had touched him. The boulder with the imprint is now preserved inside the gurudwara, which is maintained by the 3rd Sikh Regiment of the Indian Army. There is a non-stop *kîrtan* (singing of Sikh devotional songs) at the Gurudwara from dawn to dusk, conducted by priests from the said regiment. There is also a Yatri Niwas (free guest house) inside the gurudwara complex.

The Nanak Hill is to the left of the highway.

Chapter- 32

Jainism in Jammu and Kashmir

The Jains are the least populous religious group of the state. Most of the present Jains of Jammu and Kashmir belong to the Bhabra community. The Bhabras, in turn, are part of the Bhavadar or Bhavada Gachchha group associated with the legendary Jain saint Acharya Kalakacharya. It is possible that their ancestral home was in Bhabra town, now in Pakistan. There are inscriptions which show that the Bhavada Gachchha community was active till at least the 1600s.

However, it is wrong to assume that Jainism came to Jammu and Kashmir only with the Bhabra community.

Ancient Kashmir: Jainism has been present in the state, especially in the Valley of Kashmir, since ancient times. It is part of recorded history that the great Sankaracharya (AD 788- 820) engaged in debates with Jain, Buddhist and native Hindu scholars at the Shârdâ Peeth (now in the so-called Azad Jammu and Kashmir), which was at the time the greatest university and centre for religious research in the region.

India being India, religion meant religion and not any particular creed or faction. Though today the Shârdâ Peeth is seen as an old Hindu seminary, it was patronised equally by Buddhists and Jains. The *Prabhâvâkacharit*, a Jain historical work (1277–78) records that Hémachandr, the great Shvétâmbar Jain scholar, had consulted grammatical texts kept in the Peeth's library, to provide a basis for his own grammar, the *Siddhahéma*.

One of the most eminent Kashmiri scholars of that era was Somadév, a Jain. He authored the *Nitivâkyâmritâ*, which was a contemporary retelling of Kautilya's 3rd century BC political science classic the *Arthashâstr*.

Successful businessmen: The Jains, especially those in Jammu city, are mostly businessmen—each in the top rungs of his field. Till the advent of the Industrial Age, history books rarely found the need to mention the names of businessmen. However, Diwan Kirpa Ram (1827-31), who proved to be one of the kindest and best governors of the Sikhs, recorded in his epic *Gulâbnâmâ* that Bhawâni Shah Bhâbrâ had loaned money to Diwan Amir Chand.[1]

Information about the history of this talented and self-disciplined community is hard to come by. Syed Jahangir Hashmi informs us that "Jains in J&K are concentrated mostly in Jammu city (Jain Bazar and Jain Nagar near Tallab Tillo). There are 3 Jain families in Doda town and 2-3 families in Udhampur. Perhaps, there are around 20-30 families in Srinagar as well. I know 1-2 families living in Gogji Bagh Srinagar."[2] Jahangir's is perhaps the only detailed account. Jain elders say that there are 525 Jain households in Jammu province, and four that live in Kashmir around the year (the others migrate to Jammu for the winter).

Temporary modern temple in Kashmir: Visitors from Gujarat and Maharashtra are the mainstay of tourism in Kashmir. A very large number of them are Jains. In 2008 Mrs. Doshi, whose children run a travel agency in Mumbai, got her family to build a small Jain prayer area within a hotel in Srinagar so that Jain guests of the hotel and other Jain visitors could start their day with proper prayers. A priest, who belonged to a village near Lucknow, was appointed. Three idols, which were made of panchdhâtu (an alloy of 'five elements,' i.e. gold, silver, copper, iron and zinc), were installed. In 2010, when the travel agent's contract with the hotel expired, the idols were shifted to the Chintamani Parshwanath derasar (congregation) in Sabarmati, Gujarat.

Temples in Jammu: Jahangir adds, 'There are two Jain temples in Jammu, one in Jain Nagar and another in Jain Bazar. One temple is coming up near Jehlum Resorts at Trikuta Nagar [in the 21st century Jain colony].' Jain sources agree that the Jain Temple at Patel Chowk in the heart of the old city is their most beautiful and best known. It has marble icons of Lord Mahavira and other Tirthankaras. There is also a small Jain temple near the Jain School on Rani Park/ Rani Talâb road in the city, which many Jains go to.

1 A History of Maharaja Gulab Singh of Jammu, by Kirpa Ram, Sukh Dev Singh Charak, 1977.

2 Syed Jahangir Hashmi, personal communication, 01/04/2011

Chapter- 33

Shared Shrines

All Sikh gurudwaras and Buddhist monasteries can be said to be shared shrines because the Hindus offer prayers at both. Many Hindus combine obeisance at Dera Baba Banda Bahadur with their pilgrimage to Katrâ. Besides, this grand gurudwara is famous for the paintings on its walls, these being fine miniatures of the Sikh Gurus and Shri Krishn's celebrated Leela (acts).

Similarly, most of the icons in the murals of Buddhist monasteries, beginning with Lord Buddha himself, are worshipped by the Hindus as well.

As far as shared Hindu-Muslim shrines are concerned, almost all of them are built around graves. Hindu adults are not buried, Muslims are. Therefore, it does seem that at some stage of their lives the saints of these shrines had converted to Islam—either by giving up Hinduism (which is not likely because then the Hindus would stop claiming that saint as their own) or by practising both religions at the same time.

Jammu province

Jammu city

Pânch Peer

The identity of the five saints of this shrine is shrouded in mystery. In fact, the Hindus claim that the five Pândavs used to live here. In any case, what we get to see at the spot is the tomb of one Muslim saint, built by the (Hindu) Maharaja Gulab Singh. Apparently, the saint visited Gulab

Singh in a dream, which inspired the king to get the place excavated. A walking stick, a *hookah* and five drums were unearthed. Historian T.N.Moza says that the said saint was one of five brothers, all of them *peers*. The other four died at Basohli, Rajouri, Purmandal and Calcutta respectively. The annual *urs* is in July, naturally on a Thursday

Jammu rural and Samba

Chamliyâl: *How to get there:* This very important, though unprepossessing, shrine is smack on the India- Pakistan border, west of Sâmbâ. The road to Chamliyâl branches off from the National Highway near the Sâmbâ bus stand. Travelling from Jammu this is the road on the right. Coming up from Pathankot- Kathua it's on the left. Mini- buses from Sâmbâ go fairly close to Chamliyâl. The road is quite bad in the last few kilometres before the shrine. Therefore, if you plan to drive up on your own, try to use a jeep- type vehicle. On the day of the urs there is plenty of public transport to the shrine: including trucks and tractors with trailors. The shrine is just a few metres away from the border and is on the Indian side. The Pakistani village across the border is called Saîdâñwali.

Skin diseases: It is believed that the mud and water of Chamliyâl, if smeared on the body for seven days, cures skin diseases like eczema. (Cham is Hindi- Dogri for 'skin'.)

The legend: At Chamliyal there is an Islamic grave covered with a green, Islamic chadar (sheet). The Hindus of Jammu say that the sufi saint buried there was a Rajput called Bâbâ Dalîp Singh Manhâs. The Muslims claim him as their own.

The saint lived in the late 17th or early 18th century. Some say that an enemy beheaded him. Other accounts are even more gruesome. Apparently, the saint's body was chopped into pieces at Saidanwali. His disciples brought the remains to Chamliyal, and buried them there. The soil of Chamliyal is said to have acquired medicinal properties after that.

The annual urs is held on the fourth Thursday of June/ first Thursday of the Indian month of Âshâd. The Pakistani authorities set up an enormous fair some two hundred metres away from the shrine inside their territory. Pakistani Muslims come not just from West Punjab but all the way from Karachi as well. Crowds on the Indian side of the border are not as numerous: just a few hundred devotees, plus scores of government officials and engineers.

Indian engineers get their workers to scoop out Chamliyâl soil from near the shrine. It is filled into barrels to be given to the Pakistanis, who cart the soil away in tractor- trolleys. This soil is called *shakkar*, a word that normally means 'sugar'. The Pakistanis send over empty water tankers. Indian engineers get them, as well as Indian water tankers, filled with Chamliyâl water, all for the devotees waiting on the Pakistani side of the border. This water is called *sharbat* (sherbet), which is normally the word for an Indo- Turkish soft drink.

At the appointed hour a Pakistani Deputy Superintendent of Police drives over to the border in a huge Toyota, often with a 'Billboard' sticker on it. (As the District Magistrate of Jammu, and three rungs his senior, I would go over in a rickety old, non- air conditioned Ambassador.) The Pakistani authorities collect the *sharbat* and *shakkar* and distribute them among the devotees massed on the other side. Sometimes the Pakistanis bring over a green sheet (*châdar*) and some roses to be placed on the saint's grave.

In gratitude the Pakistanis give the Indians a few baskets full of exotic mangoes, which are distributed among the BSF jawans stationed there. In turn the BSF gives them Jammu's famous sweets. (BSF is India's Border Security Force.) This exchange starts around 11 in the morning and is over an hour and a quarter later.

Fluctuating fortunes: Till 1965 Pakistanis could simply walk up to the shrine, pay their respects to the saint and collect some water and soil to take home. Their annual fair was held on Indian soil, right next to the shrine. The war of September 1965 changed all that. Borders hardened after that war. The fair was shifted a few metres away, into Pakistani territory. However, India would ensure that the Pakistanis received plenty of *shakkar* and *sharbat*. The present system has been in operation since 1966.

In the 1990s the Pakistani army started pushing murderous saboteurs into India through border posts like Chamliyal. Despite that the Indian authorities ensured that the Pakistanis celebrated the annual *urs* with all the co-operation they had come to expect from India. Twenty to fifty thousand Pakistanis would attend the *urs*.

The 1999 *urs* marked an all- time low. A few months before, the Pakistanis had sneakily occupied unguarded Indian territory in Kargil. The 1999 *urs* were held at a time when Indian soldiers were bravely trying to get that land back. All Indians felt cheated. Most Pakistanis knew that they had done something terribly wrong.

However, the mood was extremely upbeat when the *urs* of June 2001 were held. India and Pakistan were about to begin peace talks. So, as many as 80,000 Pakistanis turned up for the fair. A Colonel of the Pakistan Rangers and a Deputy Inspector General (Brigadier) of the BSF led their respective teams. This was a change from the Captain-level Pakistani officer who would come over in the past.

Rajouri

Baba Khori: (20km, from Nowshera town.) This is one of the most popular shrines in all of Rajouri. Though dedicated to a Muslim saint, Hindus and Sikhs, too, visit it in big numbers. The shrine is located in a leafy mango grove. It consists of two structures, both built like Hindu temples. The outer walls of the shrine are Indo- Islamic. The main gate proclaims in large Devanagari (Hindi) letters: 'Jai Khori Baba' (Glory to the saint of the cave shrine). All this could be because of the influence of the Indian Army, which maintains the shrine.

The Hindus consider the cave (*khori*) shrine a *samâdhî* of the Baba. The head priest of the shrine is invariably a soldier of the Indian Army. Every army unit that is posted there places a new, richly embroidered, green silk- sheet (*châdar*) on the grave of the Baba, in the Islamic tradition. The unit also presents the shrine with a new flag, to be flown from its spires. (This looks like a Hindu tradition.)

History: The Baba was born to a Muslim Gujjar family of Mirpur (now in POK) in the early decades of the twentieth century. He got married and started living atop a hill near Kalsian in the Jhangar area.

There the Baba came to be known as a respected mystic. He performed some miracles and made a couple of accurate predictions. This won him followers from all communities.

In October 1947 Pakistan sent tribals controlled by its army to invade the area. Some of the invaders went to the Baba's house. They asked him to obtain information that would have helped them in their murderous mission. The Baba refused. So the Pakistanis shot dead his wife, three sons and a daughter. (The five were later buried where the Baba Khori shrine now is.)

The Pakistanis then began to torture the Baba to compel him to help them. The Baba rushed into the cave, never to return. (The cave, too, is within the present shrine.) The Pakistanis followed him into the cave and looked everywhere. However, they could not find the Baba. (It is not clear as to how the Baba's body was found, because his grave is between those of his wife and eldest son.)

Restrictions: The shrine is just a hundred metres from the 'line of control' between India and Pakistan Occupied Kashmîr. Therefore, for much of the year only army officials and their families can visit the shrine. However, on special occasions, civilians, too, are allowed.

The valley of Kashmir

Anantnag-Kulgam

Bîjbehârâ *The tomb and pond of Lal Ded:* There is a small grave in the south-eastern corner of the Jâmâ Masjid of Bîjbehârâ. It is supposed to be the tomb of Lal Ded. The Lâl Trâg pond (see 'Pulwâmâ, Shopian') is located close to the Jâmâ Masjid of Bijbehara and near the National Highway. To this day both Hindus and Muslims visit the pond. They pay homage by pouring the first milk of their cows into the pond. This ceremony and the miracle of the water which retained the shape of the pitcher are a recurrent theme in the miniature paintings of Kashmîr. In the past newly married Kashmîri Pandit couples would often go to the Lâl Trâg on the day after the wedding to obtain Lal Ded's blessings.

Harut and Marut: (pron.: hâ-root, mâ-root) This shrine is in Ranbir Pura village, which is on the Mattan karewa, a few hundred metres before the Mârtañd temple. There is a shaded picnic spot near the point where water gushes out of a well inside the shrine. It is not a Hindu shrine. Its adherents are entirely Muslim. The illiterate accept it uncritically as one of the many Muslim ziyârats (shrines) of Kashmîr. They pray for all kinds of boons at the shrine.

Yet the concept behind the shrine is unIslâmic, or at least pre- Islâmic Babylonian. The pre- Islâmic, mainly Jewish, belief is that Harut and Marut were angels who fell in love with Jupiter and were therefore hung upside down above a well. Almost all Kashmîris who pray at the shrine accept this version.

The Islâmic position is thus, 'Among the Jewish traditions in the Midrash [Jewish commentaries] was a story of two angels who asked Allah's permission to come down to earth but succumbed to temptation, and were hung up by their feet at Babylon for punishment. Such stories about sinning angels who were cast down to punishment were believed by the early Christians also… Being good men, Harut and Marut of course dabbled in nothing evil…. [They] did not withhold knowledge, yet never taught anyone [magic and 'such things'] without plainly warning them of the trial and temptation of knowledge in the hands of evil men.' (Commentary on sura 2, verse 102 of *The Holy Quran*, published by the Custodian of the Two Holy Mosques, i.e. the King of Saudi Arabia.)

Thus Islâm accepts that Harut and Marut had existed and were angels. It differs with the Jews on whether the two had sinned and therefore deserved punishment. Islâm holds that they were sinless.

Several Kashmîris believe the pre- Islâmic version. This indicates that the legend of Harut and Marut had reached Kashmîr well before Islâm did. Some scholars cite this as yet another proof that the people of Kashmîr had migrated from Israel and are one of the lost Jewish tribes.

Pulwama, Shopian

Lal Ded: Like her successor, Habba Khatoon, Lal Ded, too, had mother in law problems, was a female poet who wrote in Kashmîri (as opposed to the more elitist Sanskrit or Persian) and tended to break earthen pitchers. In much of India (and Persia) poets insert their name in the last verse of their songs.

That is the only proof we have that Lal (pron. 'lull') Ded ('d-yed,' with soft *d*s) –or Habba Khatoon- ever existed. Both were talented- and troubled-women. Their songs and verses have been passed on orally across the generations. And yet histories, contemporary as well those written several centuries later, are silent about them.

Lal Ded's *vâkhs* (verses) were compiled and reduced to writing as recently as in 1920 by the British scholars George A. Grierson and Lionel D.Barnett based on the oral renditions of Pandit Dharm Das Darvesh of Gush (Hañdwârâ).

Lal Ded was born 'maybe earlier but very likely not later than 1320 AD' (Jayalal Kaul) to a Brahmin family near Pandrethan (just outside present day Srinagar). Even as a child she would meditate in seclusion. Her career is believed to have been contemporaneous with the reign of Sultan Alauddin(1344-55). Her marriage, to a fellow Brahmin from Pâmpore, then known as Padmanporâ, seems to have been a disaster: painful scenes from her unhappy married life are the stuff of Kashmîri folklore. One theory is that she would generally be lost in meditation and her husband's family found this irritating.

Lal Ded took to meditating at the Zinpura ghat (river bank) near Pâmpore. Her husband wanted to find out where she went every morning.

So, one day the suspicious man hid himself and when he saw Lal Ded returning home carrying a clay pot filled with water, the suspicious man struck the pot with a stick and broke it.

Now a miracle took place. The water did not fall on the ground and spread. Instead, it retained the shape it had had inside the pot. So Lal Ded picked it up with her bare hands, and poured it into one of the pitchers inside the house. There was plenty left even after that vessel had been filled. So she used the water to fill up all the other vessels in the house and threw the rest outside the house where a pond was thus born.

This pond later came to be known as the Lâl Trâg. (See also 'Bîjbehârâ' in the section on 'Ânañtnâg-Kulgam' in the chapter on Islamic shrines.)

Lal Ded was a disciple of Sed Bayu, an eminent Shaivite and a direct descendant of Vasugupt, who founded modern Shaivism in Kashmîr.

Ultimately, Lal Ded renounced all worldly bonds, gave up her marital home and became a mendicant. She wandered from place to place singing of the unity of God. The Muslims believe that Lal Ded converted to Islâm. A grave in Bîjbehârâ is supposed to be hers. Some Hindus deny that such a conversion had ever taken place.

Srinagar city

Rozabal: The signboard outside this modest shrine reads "Ziyârati Hazrati Youza Asouph and Syed Nasirudin". This is supposed to be the Astân (shrine) of Lord Jesus Christ, if we are to believe a whole body of 19th and 20th century scholarship. Even if the identification of Hazrat e Youza with Lord Jesus is far fetched, the fact is that all Kashmîris believe that this is the shrine (and grave) not of a mere saint or sufi but an important *prophet*. (See 'Christ in Kashmîr and Ladâkh': especially the section 'What do we know about H. Yuz Aasaf?')

Instead of seeking to cash in on the current interest in the subject, the keepers of the shrine have put up large notices (in English) denying that the shrine has anything to do with Lord Jesus.

Inside the shrine you will find, in the centre, the graves of Hazrat Youza Asouph and Syed Naseeruddin. By their side, carved in intaglio on grey rock tablets, are large stylized images of human feet. These are supposed to be Hazrat Youza's footprints. Not only do the 'footprints' look too contrived to be real, they are much too large. But then, so is the grave of the person who is supposed to have been Jesus.

Index